USING THE RADIO SHACK
TRS-80 IN YOUR HOME

USING THE RADIO SHACK TRS-80 IN YOUR HOME

Kenniston W. Lord, Jr., CDP

 VAN NOSTRAND REINHOLD COMPANY
NEW YORK   CINCINNATI   ATLANTA   DALLAS   SAN FRANCISCO
LONDON   TORONTO   MELBOURNE

Van Nostrand Reinhold Company Regional Offices:
New York   Cincinnati   Atlanta   Dallas   San Francisco

Van Nostrand Reinhold Company International Offices:
London   Toronto   Melbourne

Copyright © 1981 by Litton Educational Publishing, Inc.

Library of Congress Catalog Card Number: 80-19389
ISBN: 0-442-25707-4

Manufactured in the United States of America

Published by Van Nostrand Reinhold Company
135 West 50th Street, New York, N.Y. 10020

Published simultaneously in Canada by Van Nostrand Reinhold Ltd.

15   14   13   12   11   10   9   8   7   6   5   4   3   2   1

Library of Congress Cataloging in Publication Data

Lord, Kenniston W. Jr.
Using the Radio Shack TRS-80 in your home.

Includes index.
1. TRS-80 (Computer)   I. Title.
QA76.8.T18L67   001.64   80-19389
ISBN 0-442-25707-4

Preface

There it is—Radio Shack's TRS-80 computer. Looks interesting, doesn't it? And perhaps strange too. Perhaps you've asked someone who owns one how to use it. Maybe he demonstrated by writing a small program on the computer. Perhaps you've watched someone play a game with the TRS-80. There's lots more you can do with it too. But $500—that's a lot of money.

If you're looking for me to sell you the computer, forget it. Only you can decide what's important to you. My interest lies in telling you how you can use the computer and how I use mine. Most important, I'll show you how the TRS-80, properly used, will not only pay for itself, but will also provide fun for you and your friends.

As I said, I have a computer of my own. A TRS-80. Am I rich? No. Am I a superbrain? No. A snob? I hope not. Why then did I buy a computer when I really need a new television set and I don't even *own* a stereo? Because it offers benefits that a television and stereo can't provide—and it pays for itself in the process. And, I like to have unique things. Perhaps you do too.

I've only had my TRS-80 for a little while, but I've already found many, many ways to use it. For instance, over the years, I paid countless late fees on my charge accounts because I could never keep track of when my payments were due. Now, my computer keeps tabs both on my checkbook and on the bills I have to pay each month. Yes, I could do it myself with a $5 calculator—but my computer not only takes care of my checking account, it automatically balances the bank statement, which saves me several hours of frustration every month.

Are you as absentminded as I am? Do you always forget things you need to remember? In the past, whenever I got home from the supermarket, I had usually forgotten to get detergent—or some other vital item. So, although I had other things to do, I had to go back to the store—about 10 miles roundtrip. Now, however, whenever I think of something I need, I merely record it on my computer. When the time comes to go shopping, my list is ready. Yes, I know pencils and paper are cheap—but the computer gives me my list organized according to the layout of the supermarket! And it tells me how much I'm going to spend—before I've even left the house! I figure I've already saved a hundred dollars or so on my grocery bills.

I have an old car that burns (and burns and burns) premium gas. Unfortunately, I also have 10 thumbs, and so I would no more mess with my car's

v

engine than climb Mount Everest. As a result, before I got my computer, the engine generally got tuned up only after the car wouldn't start and I had to call for road service. But now, I just tell the computer my mileage and how much I've spent for gas, and it not only tells me when I need a tune-up, but it keeps a running performance check on my mileage as well. It also lets me know what I'm spending for gas and keeps track of the fuel taxes I've paid for income-tax purposes. Next, I intend to add some features to keep track of tire wear. Adding up all these benefits, I've saved several hundred dollars.

My wife and I gave a dinner party one night for thirteen of our friends. When planning the feast, she merely went to our computer and entered what she planned to serve. In a very short time, the computer told her how much of each ingredient would be needed, how long each dish should be cooked, and even the calorie count. In addition, it gave her a schedule for preparing the meal. The dinner was perfect. The computer didn't do the whole job, of course. But having the computer's help meant she could concentrate on what she does best—cook!

That's what the TRS-80 computer is all about—helping. So far, I've mentioned a few of the ways I use the computer to help me at home. It can help in many other ways. In fact, as each day goes by, I think of another way to use it. Or *I* read of how somebody else has put it to work. If I want to use my computer in the same way, I can sometimes purchase the program. Most of the time, however, I take the idea and write the program myself.

No matter what activity you do, it usually has a language. Citizens-band radio users are familiar with *smoky, flip-flop,* and *10-36.* If you ski, you know what *tracks, slats, downhill,* and *moguls* are. Computers have their own language too. Don't let that scare you. Why? Because the computer is a stupid machine. It does only what you tell it to do—and you don't have to be a whiz to tell it what to do. You don't have to know algebra, electronics engineering, or even a foreign language. You need no special science or math skills. If you can read and write, you can make the computer work for you. The TRS-80 computer has its own language called BASIC. And it is. *Very* basic. Simple, in fact.

This book won't tell you everything you'll want to know about the TRS-80 or about computers in general. But it will tell you enough to get you started. And it will answer many of the questions you may have right now. It will show you how to have your cake and eat it too—how to have the computer pay for itself.

And now, if you'll pardon me, I've just learned a way to predict how much fuel oil I'm going to burn this winter. That's going to be worth a bunch of bucks.

KENNISTON W. LORD, JR., CDP

Acknowledgments

The following people are recognized for their contributions:

- *Debbie Gibbons,* who did yeoman work on the manuscript, reducing the hen scratching, matrix printouts, and rough drafting of about five type styles to a single intelligible mass. She spent hundreds of hours at the word processor.
- *Pat McCarthy,* who provided proofreading services. No doubt her index finger is considerably shorter today than when she began.
- *Robb Ware,* who was *supposed* to proofread, but instead kept asking, "What do you mean by this?" Actually, Robb is to "blame" for this book. Next time, he'll know what is about to happen when he calls up and says, "If I buy you a computer, will you write a book about it?" That phone call is what launched this effort. Robb's money purchased the original system, but my own investment, to enhance the machine, ran finally to a figure about six times larger.
- *Kip Taylor,* manager of the Radio Shack store in Southington, Connecticut, who answered innumerable questions, provided knowledgeable guidance, and a considerable amount of direct motivation.
- *Dave Gunzel,* manager of technical publications for Radio Shack, who provided insight to the system, technical guidance, and several of the pictures in the book.
- *Jack McHugh,* who photographed the various screens from the programs presented in the book.
- *Radio Shack managers* in three states, with whom I bartered demonstration programs for C-30 tapes.

To them all, I give my thanks.

The lovable li'l feller, whose picture appears below, is Clyde CLOAD. Clyde is the mascot of *CLOAD Magazine,* Goleta, California, and is reproduced here with permission of the publisher.

Some of the pictures were provided courtesy of Radio Shack Division of

Tandy Corporation. The graphics form used was reproduced from the *User's Manual For Level I,* with the permission of Radio Shack.

The balance of the pictures used were shot using extremely fast film and exposure timings. Even that speed, however, was not sufficient to remove the electronic "trace" lines that are visible to the camera but not to the naked eye.

With the exception of one program that is quoted, with credit, from *CLOAD Magazine,* all programming contained herein is of the author's own design. Any similarity of purpose, structure, or details to other programming sold on the software market, published in magazines, or gained in program exchanges is purely coincidental.

1978 **CLOAD MAGAZINE**

Contents

USING THE RADIO SHACK TRS-80 IN YOUR HOME

1
The Computer—A Space-Age Home Appliance

In 1930, American scientist Vannevar Bush built the first general-purpose analog computer. During World War II, computer scientists continued to design and develop early computers—they first set out to build a machine capable of rapid calculation of artillery shell trajectories. The first information processing digital computer was designed and built by Howard Aiken in 1944. These developments formed the basis for an entirely new industry. Though even in the mid-fifties some scientists were convinced that 50 computers would be sufficient to serve the needs of the whole world for ever!

The basic precepts of the computer had existed for at least 200 years. It began with the work of the 18th century scientist Joseph Jacquard, who designed the first loom to weave patterns, i.e., a very early and very simple "thinking machine." Another 18th century scientist, Charles Babbage, worked on a mechanical calculator which was an ancestor of today's machines. These were the forerunners of the concepts of computing *hardware*—the physical parts of a machine, the nuts and bolts. But simultaneously, there were those who were developing techniques which would ultimately be implemented upon the computer, either in the form of applications *software*, the programs that enable the system to function, i.e. programs that solve problems in one way or another, or as improvements to the workings of the hardware.

We have been building computers and improving on both hardware and software for over 30 years now. With each technological change, new and interesting devices emerge. We often develop a device, before finding it profitable and before finding useful ways in which to use it. The question of whether we *should* use a device becomes of equal importance with the question of whether we *can* use it. And there is the ever-present question of whether or not we could get along without it.

Radio Shack has made the microcomputer available at an affordable price. And it has provided the distribution and service facilities necessary to bring the microcomputer into the home as a consumer item. On the surface,

1

the home computer seems like a luxury, a sophisticated toy. And of course, it can be used as a toy, because there are countless games that can be played on the TRS-80 and other microcomputers. But the TRS-80 has many more important uses. Some of them can be accomplished now. Others, such as the use of the computer in electronic mail networks, must await the passage of time.

Figure 1. TRS-80 Level I.

A GLIMPSE AT THE FUTURE

Towards the end of the 20th century, or early in the 21st century, we will be sending our correspondence by electronic mail. The U.S. Postal Service has already begun to investigate ways to establish an electronic mail system (EMS). To use the EMS, you'll write a letter on your home computer, transmit it, and have the letter itself appear on the computer of the recipient at some distant point, having traveled through the telephone or satellite network. The response can appear on your computer within minutes. It is possible that the charge for such a service will be small in comparison to postal or long-distance telephone rates. One advantage amongst many might relate to guaranteed delivery at very competitive prices in comparison to other forms of guaranteed delivery.

People without home computers would be able to receive messages through a service similar to the current Mailgram. Junk mail could be screened out, by blocking it with codes given to the computer's program. While advertisers might have a fit, such a feature would allow the individual to exercise some control over incoming mail, thus managing his/her time more wisely. A person might decide to have the computer produce a list of his/her correspondents to determine which mail to read first. In fact, it may be possible for the home computer to read the correspondence, and present only the most important items for the person's viewing. The logical next step would be to have the computer automatically reply at least to routine correspondence, based upon guidelines prepared by the individual.

A home computer would make it possible to prepare a single invitation and have the home computer distribute it to potential guests via their own home computers. They in turn, would be able to reply in a matter of minutes. That's for the future, of course, but it is a realistic view of the future. Even now, the home computer can be programmed to remind you of birthdays and anniversaries, and it can send the greetings. Think how great that could be for Christmas letters, too.

Using the home computer, you'll be able to order a new outfit direct from Sears or a special tool from Black & Decker. You'll be able to use the computer to order your groceries, and coupled to a standard television set, your computer will enable you to view your purchases before you buy them. Think of the possibilities the computer offers to those people who are housebound.

The electronics funds transfer system (EFTS), which presently exists, will find its full implementation with the home computer. Using EFTS, you'll be able to complete both your purchase and all the financial work at the same time. The sequence of events will work like this: you will make your purchase, which will result in the purchased product being sent to your home; the act of the purchase will cause funds to be transferred from your bank account directly into the bank account of the firm from which you purchase the product. At that point, the firm's computer will take over, keeping its books, accounting for its inventory, etc. Some of this is beginning to happen now, as several "call and pay" services have sprung up around the country. The home computer will allow you to have more control over the process, providing reports of your purchases, and alerting you to the availability of bargains, etc. If you're looking for an appliance, your computer could do the shopping for you, locating the product for the most reasonable price.

Whole libraries will be placed "on-line" to your home computer. You'll be able to determine what books are available and to place them on reservation. Researchers will be able to find out which books mention a given topic and where they are located, or, they'll be able to do the research directly, via the computer's television display unit. Devices already exist that will convert printed type into computer-readable media. Such works as the *Encyclopaedia Britannica* will be scanned by these devices and will be made accessible to the home computer.

For a number of years, computers have been the basis of "word processing systems" used extensively in business applications. Currently, such applications are possible using some of the home computers, including the TRS-80. In the future, the home computer will go beyond current uses for word processing and will become a most useful tool for the student who must develop assignments, providing the written word in its correct and properly spelled form. It is not impossible, in a future context, for the computer to be used to perform research and write the paper which must be submitted. Educators may have problems accepting that capability.

However, some of the current capabilities of the home computer will please educators. Currently, applications exist for the use of the TRS-80 and other home computers to assist in the education process. Study and drill modules are available for math, spelling, chemistry—and in the coming years, as more home computers are purchased, we will witness greater use of the device in the educational process. It won't happen overnight, but the time will come when you will be able to walk into a bookstore and take home a book in the form of a cassette tape, readable on your home computer. Students who are having trouble in school will be able to obtain tutorials for home use. Such cassettes are currently in use in many school systems today. Much remedial education will take place in the home itself. Moreover, you can prepare tutorials for your children right now—and those tutorials can be implemented on the TRS-80. With this capability in the home, students will be able to progress at their own pace. It is not inconceivable that schools as we know them will be substantially different in the 21st century.

The computer will be an integral part of the design of the home of the future and will provide a variety of services for management of the home itself. They will be installed in the home itself, much as heating or plumbing systems are installed today. The home computer will take over the kitchen functions of food storage, preparation, and cooking. It will provide security functions, from screening visitors to locking doors at predetermined times. It will be used for energy conservation, drawing upon various forms of energy used within the home, based upon such factors as cost and comfort. And it will become a useful tool for entertainment.

What about today? If you've purchased the TRS-80, many worthwhile applications are available to you, and this book will provide some of them. But if you're still contemplating your purchase, the following are some ways you'll be able to use the device profitably, and may in the process be able to recoup your investment:

MANAGING YOUR MONEY

To begin with, there are many financial applications, and among the most important is the checking account.

Logging checks.   Of course, every time you write a check it will not automatically appear on the computer. You'll have to enter the information as it occurs. But the computer *will* keep an accurate balance of your account. Yes, you could do that in your head or with an inexpensive calculator. But consider how much time and expense you could save if, at the end of the year, your computer told you precisely how much sales tax you had paid and how much you had spent for medical expenses, auto repairs, etc? You would have the details necessary to itemize expenditures on your tax report, leading to diminished taxes. It is possible that this savings alone could justify the purchase of the computer.

Balancing the checkbook.   Using the computer, you can post the returned checks and then have the balance computed automatically. We have been moving for a few years now toward what has been termed the "checkless society," and in time the uses of checks to effect transactions will disappear altogether. The home computer, as previously described, will assist in that move. The checkless society will not be with us for some time, however, and in the meantime, it would be nice to have the home computer take over the balancing headaches we face every month.

Investments.   If you have an interest in stocks or bonds, the home computer provides you with the capability to manage your own portfolio. Using the home computer to compare investments, returns on investments, and potential areas of investment could not only save the brokerage fees, but also allow you to plan your investment programs more thoroughly. If your investments are in the form of property, the home computer can provide your necessary procedures for tracking rents, scheduling repairs, planning escrow accounts, comparing interest rates on available money sources, etc. Computer programs for the TRS-80 are already available to assist you with planning your investments.

Cash Management.   The computer can advise you when bill payments are due. It can also specify the optimum time for making those payments.

Many firms offer terms for early payment, such as a 2% discount if the invoice is paid within 10 days. Since running a home is no different from running a business, money can be saved by keeping track of when those discounts are available—but always keeping in mind the fact that the money you have can draw interest up until the final day of the discount availability. Thus, you can pay your bills promptly and still obtain all the available interest. Frequently, charge accounts have cut-off days before the interest is added to the account. This is particularly true of credit cards, including Master Card, Visa, and American Express. You can use your computer to schedule your payment to arrive immediately prior to the addition of the interest. The savings in managing your cash in this manner could be substantial.

Miscellaneous Expenses. You can use the computer to keep track of miscellaneous expenses that you pay in cash. Entering such purchases as the extra loaf of bread bought at the corner grocery, for instance, would give you a true picture of what you are spending for groceries. How about the lunch and bus money your children need each day? It adds up to a significant sum. No, the computer won't save that money for you but it will allow you to analyze the impact of such expenditures on your budget, allowing you to plan your expenditures more wisely.

Budgeting. A budget is a projection of the funds you will receive and the manner in which you plan to spend those funds. Using the computer, you can plan your expenditures and contingencies for specified times and then plan your known income to meet them.

THE COMPUTER AND YOUR CAR

Automobile maintenance and operation is one of the most effective areas in which to use a home computer.

You can keep track of your car's mileage, and plot its increase and decrease. If your car should have a given mileage rating, it would be helpful to know when it falls below that rating, especially in view of the rising cost of gasoline. If your car is designed to perform at 20 miles per gallon, it would be useful to know that its performance has dropped to 15 miles per gallon. The car's performance can be monitored by using the computer, giving an indication of when a tune-up is needed and wear-oriented parts require attention.

You'll be able to determine what your mileage is as well as your cost per mile. As that varies, you will be able to make certain key decisions about route selection, place of purchase, etc. Perhaps even more important, since a large part of the price of a gallon of gasoline is spent for taxes, you will be able to keep an accurate record of your tax expenditures, which is certain to save you a considerable amount of money at income-tax time.

The computer can assist you in planning a trip by presenting optimum routes, availability of services, etc. This cannot be done without some thought, but if you travel extensively, you might find that it will result in savings.

MAKING PLANS

Shopping can be made easier, especially for groceries. To use the computer in grocery shopping will require a little preparation and a carefully selected store, as well as some knowledge of current prices. But if you know those things, the computer can be used to prepare your shopping list, organized according to the store's layout, and can further use it to obtain an estimate of your grocery costs for any given shopping expedition.

Not only is the computer valuable for a shopping list, it can be used for any kind of list, from simple reminders to sophisticated checklists for the operation of equipment located in the home, such as a microwave oven.

Programming packages exist for the TRS-80 right now to assist you in the calculation of recipes. Suppose you have a recipe which gives quantities and directions for two servings and you wish to serve four people, the changes in quantities, cooking time, etc., can be easily determined. But further suppose that you have a recipe for four and you wish to serve it at a dinner party where 27 guests are expected. The computer can be used to calculate the precise amount of each ingredient necessary to serve the larger group. To use a computer simply as a card index for filing the recipes would be foolish and expensive. The real power of the home computer is its ability to schedule the preparation of the meal, keep a count on calories, if necessary, and compute the type of recipe calculations we have just mentioned.

The home computer can be used to plan power consumption, an increasingly important task with the rising costs of energy. Each item of equipment in a home is rated for its energy consumption. The cost of cooking a meal, for example, can be calculated, as can the cost of heating the home. Since these rates are known, cost comparisons of the various operating options could prove to be very important. Ultimately, the computer will be used to regulate home-oriented electro-mechanical systems, becoming the servant it is intended to be. In short, you can plan anything with the assistance of the computer. And in the process, you'll be able to save considerable sums of money.

EDUCATION

Let's not overlook the tremendous value of the home computer for education. As educators become accustomed to the uses of microcomputers, entire learning modules similar to those now in use in many school systems, will be developed in a variety of subject areas for home use. In time, these modules may be available for loan from libraries. The computer has tremendous capabilities for subject exploration, particularly in those areas where drill and exercise are important. The computer, being inanimate, can have infinite patience.

Almost any subject that can be supported by a textbook is a candidate for presentation via the home computer. The learning modules can be constructed so that any student can be taught almost any subject and can progress via his responses and at his own pace. As you look at ways for using the home computer, this application may seem beyond you, although in some instances, you may well be able to prepare the learning modules yourself. If not, you might have to purchase the programming itself or copy the programs others have published in the extensive literature available for the microcomputer. But as time progresses, experts in a variety of subject areas will begin to produce a greater variety of programming and learning modules for home use, and they will be available, in many instances, for very reasonable prices.

We are on the threshhold of some very startling and exciting advances in education using the home computer. Computers which are used for education are not new, of course. They have been in use in certain school systems for some time, and the reports have been favorable. The advent of the microcomputer puts the educational capabilities at our fingertips for very reasonable costs, however.

There will be some topics which can never be computerized, however. One cannot learn to appreciate music from a computer, although it would be possible to teach the basic mechanics, the staves names and appearance of the notes, etc., by this method. No one can gain a knowledge and understanding of painting or sculpture by computer, but its historical aspects can be taught in this way. And it would be a little difficult to learn auto mechanics or wine and cheese tasting with the home computer. But in those areas where the computer will be most useful, we will experience tremendous educational advances. The following are some of the ways in which we now know we can use the computer:

Mathematics. The home computer can provide guidance, geared to the student's grade level, in a variety of mathematical disciplines. If the student is having difficulty with multiplication tables, the computer can be used to exercise and reinforce that knowledge. In this instance, the computer can be used at home to reinforce learning which has taken place at school.

Reading and language. The home computer is the perfect device to assist students in reading, vocabulary, and composition. It can provide speed-reading exercises, spelling and grammar practice, etc.

Testing. The computer is great for testing, ranging from simple quizzes to complex tests. Used in the home, it is good practice for schoolwork. Used in the school, there is automatic recording of grades and sufficient analysis to allow a human teacher to guide the student in the areas where more work is required.

Career planning could be accomplished using the home computer. Given certain skills, programs could be developed that would guide the student into specific career areas and work assignments.

And, finally, the home computer allows the student to satisfy his/her curiosity by pursuing an avenue of interest at the speed determined by the individual. Thus, the home computer can become an extension of the individual's own intellects.

THE HOME BUSINESS

Do you run a business from your home? Perhaps you are a distributor for a line of cosmetics, jewelry, or household items. The home computer gives you the ability to operate that business with the same precision as General Motors. Included in this are:

- Lists of people who owe you money (accounts receivable).
- Lists of people or companies to whom you owe money (accounts payable).
- Lists of orders you've received. The computer can be used to produce bills (invoices) for your customers, orders (purchase orders) to your suppliers, and can keep track of the amount of each item you have down in the basement (inventory). Using the computer, you can determine the best time to buy and keep track of the profit margin on each item, discounts, and the like.
- Records of your business activities, useful to your accountant or the tax preparer. Checkbooks and ledgers fall within this category. Also, the ability to calculate your profits (or losses) in relation to your long-term plans may be extremely important to you.

2
How Computers Work

If you looked inside the TRS-80, you might be discouraged and become convinced that since you couldn't understand what you saw, it might be somewhat beyond you. Nothing could be further from the truth. We need not be experts on the internal combustion engine to use the family car, we need not be refrigeration experts to use a refrigerator or air conditioner. There are many devices we use daily whose inner workings are *technically* beyond our understanding, but which we know we can use for our benefit. The same is true of the home computer.

What *is* important to us is that we understand how the computer *operates* and how we can cause it to perform functions for us. It's something like the control exercise by pressing on the accelerator, which causes the car to speed up. Our action is to press a lever, which in turn causes certain changes to take place in the car's engine. With the computer, our control takes two forms. There are the *external* controls which cause certain things to happen on the inside and the *internal* controls, which cause things to happen automatically.

The external controls will take the form of switches and keys on the computer's keyboard. The internal controls are customarily called a *program*. The program is a sequence of steps which are defined to the computer for automatic performance. While there are many ways to program a computer, the programming is generally a function of a computer *language*. The language for the TRS-80 computer is called BASIC, which is short for *Beginner's All-purpose Symbolic Instruction Code*.

In simple terms, every computer has a means to enter data to the computer. It is known as *input,* and the input available to your TRS-80 is available in two forms: the keyboard, where you'll type what you wish to enter into the computer; and the tape (cassette) player, where programs may be entered directly from the tape on which they have been stored. Every computer has a place where information is stored, called *memory*. The memory which is available to the TRS-80 has 4096 positions, commonly referred to as 4K, and it is also available in 16K, 32K, and 64K versions. The memory positions are used to hold programs and *variables,* which are positions of memory designed to hold either numeric or alphabetic data.

Enclosed in the keyboard of the TRS-80, in addition to the memory, are the electronics which control the *logic,* that is the sequence of events which take place within the computer.

Finally, every computer has some form of *output.* In the case of the TRS-80, that output takes the form of a video (TV) display and the ability to record upon the cassette tape.

As mentioned, the basic TRS-80 has 4096 positions of memory, or 4K. Each individual position of memory is called a *byte.* Each byte can be used to store either a single alphabetic character (letter A to letter Z) or a single numeric value. The majority of these bytes will contain the program, but some will contain the data upon which the program will operate. These data, again, are called *variables,* and in the Level I TRS-80, there are 26 variables used for numeric data (identified as A through Z) and two variables that are used to contain alphabetic data (identified as A$ and B$). It is important to note that while these variables can occupy 1 byte, in some cases, they can occupy more, but there are limitations. The largest alphabetic variable is 16 bytes. The largest number which can be stored in a numeric variable is 32,676. The specific size of the variable is not important to us unless we exceed its design.

Let's concentrate first upon the numeric variable, and let's suppose, for instance, that instead of something which we know can hold or store a number, the numeric variables A to Z are addresses of houses on the street. Your name is Jones, and you live in house "J." Mrs. Smith customarily lives at house "S," but is currently in the hospital. You have decided to collect money from the neighbors for a get-well present. Other people who live on the street are: Mr. Brown, who lives at house "B"; Mrs. Greene, who lives at house "G"; Mrs. Martin, who lives at house "M"; and Mrs. Rogers, who lives at house "R." Get the picture? Thus, we have labeled each house with a letter, which is a symbol for its occupants and its address, and we'll treat each address as a repository of funds. For purposes of this illustration, your house, and the total dollars you collect, will both be given the numeric variable "J." You decide to kick the fund off with a contribution of $8. At this moment,

$$J = 8$$

In the computer, we would have placed the number 8, meaning $8, in the numeric variable J.

Mr. Brown chips in 10 lovely crisp dollar bills. Up to this point, those 10 dollars were located at B, that is, $B = 10$. But now, since Mr. Brown has given them over to you, $B = 0$. (Note that we have made a change in how the zero appears. In this text, and on the computer it will appear with a slash, like this: Ø.)

Up to this point, all that was located at J was 8, but now there is $18 at your house. In other words,

```
J = J + 1Ø
```

That might seem to be a little confusing. How can J be equal to itself plus ten? The first J is known as the result, or sum. Thus, we take the original value of J, 8, and add to it the 10 which represents Mr. Brown's contribution, providing a *new* J, or result, of 18. If we knew for sure that all the money Mr. Brown had was $10, then it could have been expressed as J = J + B. But we do not know that for certain. In our illustrations, we will continue to compound the dollars at the single address J.

Technically, your fund originally contained nothing—Ø. Thus, initially,

```
J = Ø
```

To that you added $8, like this:

```
J = J + 8
```

And then, Mr. Brown's $10:

```
J = J + 1Ø
```

J now holds the number 18, which is the representation of the $18 you have now acquired for the fund for Mrs. Smith.

Next, Mrs. White appears, and she offers to double the amount you have collected for Mrs. Smith at this point—two times $18 is $36. But how is that expressed on the computer? Like this:

```
J = J * 2
```

In the computer language, BASIC, the asterisk (✳) means to multiply. In this case, we took the value of J, 18, multiplied it by 2, and stored it again at J. J now has a new value of 36, representing $36 for the Smith Fund. The use of the asterisk is required by computer convention, to distinguish it from the "X" we use when calculating by hand. Don't forget that X is one of the 26 numeric variables.

Mrs. Smith calls from the hospital, and she's just heard about the fund. While she's appreciative of your efforts, she tells you that she's quite comfortable and doesn't really need the money. She asks you instead to distribute the money to her three favorite charities, the Heart Fund, the Cancer Fund, and the Home for Little Wanderers. Furthermore, she advises, Mrs. Greene (house G), Mrs. Martin (house M), and Mrs. Rogers (house R) are collecting, respectively, for those funds. How do we do that on the computer? Well, we know that Mrs. Greene is going to get one-third for the Cancer Fund and we know that Mrs. Greene is at house G. So, let's divide our pile of dollars by three, like this:

```
G = J / 3
```

In this instance, we took the value of the dollars at J (36), divided it by three (the ''/'' is the computer's division symbol), and stored 12 at G. In other words, we said that G was equal to one-third of J. But just because we said that G was equal to a third of J does not mean that we have taken the 12 away from J to give it to G. We must now tell the fund (J) that it is now minus $12. That's done like this:

```
J = J - G
```

Why didn't we just say that J was equal to J minus $12? We could have done that in this instance, because we know the value of J. But suppose there had been other contributors. We needed to take merely a third, and now that third is located at G. Thus, if the dollars at G are removed from the dollars at J, our totals will now be accurate.

Now there's $24 left at J, half of which is to go to Mrs. Martin for the Heart Fund and half to Mrs. Rogers for the Home For Little Wanderers. The following will place the funds in the proper place:

```
M = J / 2
R = J / 2
```

Of course, now there is nothing left in your fund, so:

```
J = Ø
```

There are, of course, many ways to obtain the desired result. We could have repeated the steps taken above, where we subtracted the variable from J (J = J − M and J = J − R), but the result would be just the same.

On first examination, you'll note that we have created a series of very simple formulas. Programming the TRS-80 need be no more complicated than this.

If you have bought this book *after* acquiring your TRS-80, you will already be familiar with the instructions which Radio Shack packed with the computer, and perhaps you have even tried some of the sample programs. What we've attempted to do up to this point is to explain some of the thinking which goes into developing a program, which, for the want of a better explanation, is known as *problem solving*. So bear with us while we review some of the fundamentals.

The keyboard of the TRS-80 looks very much like the keyboard of a standard typewriter. But some keys have been added which are designed to perform specific functions. One of these is the ENTER key. The ENTER key enables you to communicate with the computer, and it is used for a variety of purposes, which we'll explore. In this text, as in the Radio Shack literature, the ENTER key will be shown like this:

ENTER

It's the white key at the lower right hand of the keyboard. Go ahead and push it. When you push it, you'll see this on the TV screen:

> READY

For the second, we'll now refer to the TV screen as a CRT, which is the abbreviation for "cathode ray tube." (If you happen to make a mistake when entering a statement on the keyboard, just press the **BREAK** key and start over.)

Let's now walk through the program we've just discussed, seeing what the computer will do with it. Type in the following:

J = 8   **ENTER**

What happened? What you typed is visible on the CRT, but otherwise nothing much seems to have happened. Try this:

PRINT J   **ENTER**

Well, that's different. In addition to the things you had typed, there now appears the number 8. What happened was this: with J = 8 you set the variable J equal to 8. With PRINT J, you instructed the computer to display the value of variable J on the screen, which it did. Type this:

J = J + 1Ø   **ENTER**

Other than what you typed, nothing more seems to have happened. So type this:

PRINT J   **ENTER**

18 comes back. So far it seems to be working just like the example. Type this:

```
J = J * 2  ENTER
PRINT J    ENTER
```

If you did everything correctly, the answer 36 should have been displayed on the CRT.

Before proceeding, let's talk a little about form. One of the nice things about the BASIC language is that you can enter the input to the computer in its most readable form. For this reason, in the examples so far, we have included spaces (b̸) between units, like this:

$$J b̸ = b̸ 8$$

The character b̸ is customarily used to denote a space, an area of memory which contains nothing. It doesn't appear as a character on the keyboard, you need only press the large horizontal space bar at the bottom of the keyboard. In developing programs, it helps to include spaces, because it will assist your reading of the information from the screen. However, the space is *not* absolutely necessary. J = 8 will work perfectly well. You should be aware that the space does occupy one position of memory, and later on, when you have used nearly all the positions of memory, you may need to remove some of the spaces in order to fit the program into the 4096 available positions. However, for purposes of this book, we will present the information with spaces to permit ease of reading. Occasionally, when it is important to account for a position, we will use the notation b̸ to permit you to see that a space has been intentionally used. Let's proceed. Type this:

```
G = J / 3   ENTER
PRINT G, J  ENTER
```

Here we've done something slightly different. We've set G equal to a third of the value of J and then have displayed the values of G and J. As you can see, G certainly equals 12, but J still contains 36. In other words J is unchanged. That's why you should type the next instruction:

```
J = J - G   ENTER
PRINT G, J  ENTER
```

That should now show that the numbers are in their proper values. When you PRINT more than one variable, separated by a comma, the values of the variables will be printed (displayed on the CRT) in *zones*. There are four zones on the screen. To print them close together, substitute a semicolon (;) for the comma, like this:

PRINT G; J **ENTER**

See the difference? Now it's time to divide up the remainder between Mrs. Martin and Mrs. Rogers:

M = J / 2 **ENTER**

R = J / 2 **ENTER**

PRINT G, J, M, R **ENTER**

If you did that correctly, the screen should show, left to right, the numbers 12, 24, 12, and 12, one to each zone. Now, to "empty" J·

J = Ø **ENTER**

PRINT G, J, M, R **ENTER**

The screen should show 12, Ø, 12, and 12. Does it?
Now, let's dress it up a bit. Let's identify who gets what:

PRINT "MRS. GREENE", G **ENTER**

What happened? Did Mrs. Greene's name and the value 12 appear on the screen? It should have, because any time you PRINT something that is enclosed in quotation marks, it will appear on the screen. Be very careful about where you type the quote in relation to the comma. "MRS. GREENE," will produce an error. The comma, in this instance, is used to separate *operands* of the PRINT instruction. Because you used the comma, Mrs. Greene's name appears in zone 1, while the amount (variable G) appears in zone 2. (Operands are the list of variables upon which the instruction will perform its function.)

Up to this point, we have been operating in what is termed *calculator mode,* that is, we have used the TRS-80 in much the same manner as we possibly use an inexpensive hand-held electronic calculator. In the calculator mode, things happen more or less immediately. However, the strength of the computer is that you can cause things to happen automatically, wherein a program can be developed to handle data, even though the specific data is unknown until the program is operated. More on that later.

Before we leave the calculator mode, however, let's try something else:

J = ((G * 2) + M) / R **ENTER**

PRINT J **ENTER**

If you copied that into the computer and pressed ENTER at the appro-priate place, the computer would tell you how many people contributed to the fund. As you can see the formula used is different from the earlier ones. But in fact, you did nothing different from what you've been doing all along. The inserted parentheses group the actions to be taken in a specified sequence. In the computer's order of things, you have to multiply G by 2 *before* you can add M to it, and you would have to add M before dividing the total by R. The parentheses specify the order of operation of the instruc-tion within the computer. The inside parentheses are always "cleared" first, followed by the next set. Try it this way:

PRINT ((G * 2) + M) / R **ENTER**

It works just the same way. To illustrate the value of the parentheses, try the same formula without them, like this:

PRINT G * 2 + M / R **ENTER**

In the first instance, you came up with 3. In the second, you came up with 25. Do you know why? Here's how to find out:

PRINT G * 2 **ENTER** You should get back 24

PRINT M / R **ENTER** You should get back 1

And the sum of them, of course, is 25.

You could continue to operate in the calculator mode and cause the com-puter to produce answers for you. But suppose that you want to display all the answers at once, rather than singly as they occur. Furthermore, suppose that you want a method whereby *any* contributor could contribute to *any* fund, which would then be redistributed to *any* charity. In other words, the concept of a program is that it can be operated automatically, so long as you provide data for it, presenting the information you choose. And, you want *one* computer to provide all those services.

A *program* is to a computer what a road map is to a traveler. It's a way to get from here to there, making the necessary stops along the way and making the necessary alterations in route occasioned by changes which can only be determined en route. To the computer, a program is the prespecification (thinking through) of a process you wish it to undertake. Like a note left for a friend, you detail the steps you'd like him to accomplish, advising him of alternatives, and instructing him in methods. And just like the note, you number the steps. Using BASIC, here is the little program for the funds:

```
1Ø   J = 8
2Ø   J = J + 1Ø
3Ø   J = J * 2
4Ø   G = J / 3
5Ø   J = J - G
6Ø   M = J / 2
7Ø   R = J / 2
8Ø   J = Ø
```

On the TRS-80, type NEW **ENTER** , and then type in the above instructions, following each with **ENTER** . When you have completed, type RUN **ENTER** What happened? It looks as if nothing has happened, but many things actually have happened. All the answers which were determined by the program reside in the computer, but the computer just hasn't told anyone about it. You didn't tell it to. By the way, typing NEW **ENTER** erases anything else that is in the computer and prepares the computer to receive new instructions. Typing RUN **ENTER** causes the computer to begin *execution* of the program at the first instruction, continuing instruction by instruction. At the end, you'll get > READY.

As you typed the instructions into the TRS-80, you may have wondered why you didn't number the steps 1, 2, 3, etc. You did, only you did it in multiples of 10. You could have used any number, as long as the next number was higher than its predecessor. A spacing of 10 between instructions is usual; it allows you to later insert instructions between the ones you've written. For example, type the following instructions:

```
15 PRINT J
25 PRINT J
35 PRINT J
45 PRINT G, J
```

```
55 PRINT G, J
65 PRINT M, J
75 PRINT R, J
85 PRINT J
```

Again, after each statement, press **ENTER** .

When you have completed entry of these instructions, type LIST **ENTER**. You should now see the entire program arranged in sequence. Now type RUN **ENTER** . Your display should look like this:

```
8
18
36
12      36
12      24
12      24
Ø
```

Well, you got the answers, but there are other items of information on the screen. And you don't really know, from looking at them, what those numbers represent. To get rid of the extra information on the screen, insert the following instructions:

```
5 CLS
```

CLS stands for *clear screen,* 5 is the statement number.

RUN the program again. Doesn't that look better? Still, you don't really know what the numbers mean, so it's time to modify those instructions to tell something meaningful. Type the following, followed by **ENTER** . Then type LIST **ENTER** .

```
15 PRINT "MRS. SMITH'S FUND:b";J
25 PRINT "MRS. SMITH'S FUND:b";J
35 PRINT "MRS. SMITH'S FUND:b";J
45 PRINT "MRS. GREENE'S FUND:b";G,"MRS. SMITH'S FUND:b";J
55 PRINT "MRS. GREENE'S FUND:b";G,"MRS. SMITH'S FUND:b";J
65 PRINT "MRS. MARTIN'S FUND:b";M,"MRS. SMITH'S FUND:b";J
75 PRINT "MRS. ROGERS' FUND:b";R,"MRS. SMITH'S FUND:b";J
85 PRINT "MRS. SMITH'S FUND:b";J
```

You'll note that these statement numbers have been used before. When you retype them, they replace the old ones. This is useful as long as you're improving upon an instruction, as in the above example. Be careful not to rewrite an instruction you don't intend to rewrite. Note also that the ƀ was used to indicate a position held as a space and that the number is printed close to the message (because of the semicolon). If the mandatory space had not been placed there, the message and number would have been printed with no space between them. OK, now RUN **ENTER** . Doesn't that look better?

What you've done is to trace the progress of the Smith fund, the Cancer Fund, the Heart Fund, and the fund for runaways. Generally, we're only interested in the final results and not in the process and contents as we go along. So, let's get out the eraser. In the TRS-80, material is erased merely by typing the statement number followed by **ENTER** . Erase lines 5, 15, 25, 35, 45, 55, 65, 75, and 85. Was all that work wasted? Not really, because you did get to see what was happening when it was happening, and you will find that you must often take that approach when *debugging* a program (removing any errors).

With that done, add the following instructions:

```
 9Ø PRINT "MRS. SMITH'S FUND:ƀ";J
1ØØ PRINT "MRS. GREEN'S FUND:ƀ";G
11Ø PRINT "MRS. MARTIN'S FUND:ƀ";M
12Ø PRINT "MRS. ROGERS' FUND:ƀ";R
```

and RUN it. There should be four lines in the upper left-hand corner of the screen, containing the name and amount of each fund. There's also a READY message. Here's how to get rid of that:

```
13Ø GOTO 13Ø
```

RUN it again. You have now written and successfully run a computer program. (The GOTO is what is customarily called an *unconditional branch,* a means to change sequence without having to meet conditions. In this instance, the GOTO references the same instruction. This keeps the computer operative, but in a "locked" mode. If it were not programmed in this manner, the computer would display other messages such as READY, on the screen.

Let's recap what we've done so far.

We talked about the *calculator* mode and saw what it would do. We also talked about the *command* mode, although we didn't identify it as such. Recall that the calculator mode functioned precisely as a hand-held electronic calculator. The command mode included those actions at the keyboard which caused amongst other things LIST (which listed the program on the CRT), RUN (which caused the program to execute), **ENTER** (which was our way to signal to the computer that we had completed an entry on the keyboard), and **BREAK** (which was our means to interrupt the program in progress). The latter two are keys on the keyboard.

Another very useful command mode item is the statement PRINT MEM, which can also be entered as P.M. You should do a PRINT MEM immediately after turning the computer on. If you have the 4K system, PRINT MEM followed by **ENTER** should return the number 3583. If you do not have 3583, something is wrong. Turn the computer off and then back on.

We have learned that the Level I BASIC language (like most computer languages) is very picky about punctuation. Commas, semicolons, and quotation marks are used for specific purposes in BASIC. If you use them incorrectly, you may get results, but they will be unpredictable. The same is true for the colon (:), which we'll discuss later.

You won't have to worry about upper- and lower-case letters. All the letters on the display screen are upper-case (capital) letters, so the **SHIFT** key is used to type only the special characters printed on the top of the keys.

We've learned that we can use letters to represent numbers or, more specifically, the *value* of numbers. The letters used (J, G, M, R) are called *numeric variables;* as we have already mentioned there are 26 of them used in the Level I TRS-80.

Actually, the setting of the numeric variable to a value is an abbreviated form of another BASIC instruction—LET. Statement 10 could have been written like this:

```
10 LET J = 8
```

The designers, in their wisdom, however, decided to let us express the instruction without coding the LET.

We've learned that information can be displayed on the screen using the PRINT instruction, and that those things enclosed in quotation marks appear on the screen just as they are typed. We've learned that semicolons in the PRINT instruction cause numbers to be displayed in positions adjacent to other information which has been displayed, and if a comma is used, the information is presented in zones.

And, we've learned that if we want to "short-circuit" the instruction sequence, we have only to instruct the computer to GOTO some statement number. In the example, we had the computer instruction 130 GOTO itself, thereby causing the computer to seem to stop. In reality, it continues to operate, but the operation is not obvious because it takes place inside not on the CRT.

From this point, I'll trust you know when to use **ENTER** , **BREAK** , LIST, and RUN.

There are a couple of other important features. The symbol $>$ is called a *prompt*. The position where you will type on the screen, or rather where the data will be presented on the screen, will be underscored, and that underscore is called a *cursor*. If you make a mistake in an instruction, hit the **BREAK** key and retype the instruction. However, if you make a mistake and have not hit the **ENTER** key, hit the backspace key ($\leftarrow$) the proper number of times to return to the position you wish to correct; then correct it, and finish typing the line.

Occasionally, hitting the **BREAK** key does not work. If that occurs, press the RESET button under the little trapdoor at the left rear of the keyboard. Also press it before you turn the computer off. The RESET button does what you want it to do, without destroying what you have already typed in, which may happen if you turn the computer off.

Finally, if you'd like to erase the entire program from the computer at one time, there is one more command mode instruction. As previously mentioned, type NEW **ENTER** .

If you make a really bad mistake so that the machine just can't understand your command, it will answer with WHAT?, HOW?, or SORRY. There's no point right now in describing the difference between these answers, but if you get any one of them, examine the program you're working on; chances are you've violated a "rule."

If you want to document your program as you go along, there's a handy little statement called REM, for REMarks. Using the REM statement, you can type any description you wish, up to 255 characters in length, and it will appear in the list, but will not affect how the program operates. Here is an example:

```
1 REM * MY FIRST PROGRAM *
```

RUN it, and you'll see that it didn't make any difference.

When we wrote statement 13Ø, we wrote it as a GOTO to itself. This caused the computer to continue to operate and to "hang." If you really do wish for the computer to come to a halt, replace statement 13Ø with either the END command or the STOP command:

```
13Ø END    or    13Ø STOP
```

Try it both ways. You'll see that the only perceptible difference is that with STOP you get a BREAK message and a prompt. Either command will stop the machine, but with STOP, it is possible to resume operation using another command instruction, CONT, which is short for CONTinue.

Given our fund-raising problem and the values we have been using, each time the program is run, the resulting answer will be precisely the same. But suppose we don't know the initial value of J and we want to adapt the program to allow *any* value. Here's what to do:

```
1Ø INPUT J
```

That's all. Now, instead of giving J an initial value of 8, the computer will ask you what you'd like J to be. It will give a prompt, followed by a question mark, followed by the cursor. You must then enter the value that you'd like J to be. Note that the INPUT statement caused the computer to stop temporarily to await an answer. If you change statement 13Ø to GOTO 5, it will stop at statement 1Ø every time. Try it, entering different values for J. Note that so long as you enter a number, you get an answer in return. Now try the same thing entering an alphabetic letter. You'll see that it will not permit you to do that, and will indicate the error to you.

INPUT is like PRINT because it allows a message to be displayed on the screen. Retype 1Ø as follows:

```
1Ø INPUT "ENTER AMOUNT CONTRIBUTED TO THE SMITH FUND";J
```

RUN it. You'll see that it takes the value you give it, J in this case, and returns an answer.

AN IMPERFECT MACHINE

Computers do not operate perfectly; they are subject to error. They are, however, subject to errors of a predictable nature, and because they are predictable, we can compensate for them. This situation can be demonstrated by multiplying a number by its reciprocal. Type in the following:

```
PRINT (1/3) * (3/1)
```

On paper, you would get the number 1. What results did you get from the computer? The computer is subject to a precision problem, because it is a decimal and not a fractional machine. For instance, the fraction ⅓ is written in decimal form as 0.3333333333 . . . and the 3's go on forever. Thus, on the computer the instruction yields other than 1. Interestingly, the statement PRINT (¼) * (⁴⁄₁) would work out the way you'd expect.

Note that we did the preceding instruction in the calculator mode. Although the calculator mode is immediate, that is it is not part of a running program, it can be used to check results. For instance, if you were to include a STOP instruction, you could then print any variable, check its results, and then continue, leaving everything in memory undisturbed and unchanged. If you wish to know the contents of any numeric variable, type PRINT and then one or more numeric variables (separated by a comma or semicolon) that you wish to see.

MEMORY COMMAND

The command PRINT MEM has already been mentioned. In the 4K system, the answer came back as 3583. "K" to the computer means 1024 (positions of memory), so 4K of memory means 4096 positions of memory. If that's the case, when we PRINT MEM, why is the number only 3583? Where did those remaining 513 positions of memory go? They are used by the computer to provide services to your program, and are considered as "overhead."

Recall that the REMarks statement occupies space in memory. Every statement you type takes up memory. A unit of memory is called a *byte,* and while there is a complex definition for it, you may consider it to be a single memory position which holds either an alphabetic character, a number, or a special character, such as punctuation. Since numbers are kept in binary, some numbers, very large numbers, are kept in two bytes, but generally it works as you would expect. But this is not the only overhead we should consider. Type the following:

```
NEW
PRINT MEM
```

With a 4K system, the answer you should get is, again, 3583. Type RUN. Since there is now no program in the computer (recall that you typed NEW), you'll get back a READY message. Now, type instruction 10 from the funds program:

```
10  J = 8
```

Then type PRINT MEM. The answer you get back should be 3574. Nine bytes were consumed by the statement. How? It seems like only five characters were used. Here's how the overhead is figured:

- Each line number (no matter if 1 or 1000) and the space following it occupy 3 bytes.
- When you hit the **ENTER** key, a *carriage return* character is generated in memory, although it is not displayed on the screen. That takes 1 byte.
- Each number, letter, and space in the instruction occupies 1 byte.

Thus, there is a 4-byte overhead for every statement, regardless of its length. This will become extremely important as our programs get larger, and you must find the means to compress them. In this case, the statement at 10 occupies 9 bytes—4 for overhead and 5 for the instruction. As you enter instructions, it's wise, once in awhile, to do a PRINT MEM command. As the number approaches zero, you have some indication of how much space you have left in memory for new instructions. And when memory space becomes limited, you must reduce the size of each instruction, and how to do that will be shown later.

ERROR CONDITIONS

As previously mentioned, there are three error conditions available in Level I TRS-80 systems: WHAT?, HOW?, and SORRY. Generaly, these three mean the following:

- *WHAT?* You've violated the syntax rules of the computer's ianguage. Perhaps you haven't placed punctuation properly or have omitted a quotation mark. In essence, the statement is incorrect. The nice thing about TRS-80 error messages is that they appear in precisely the same place as the error on the displayed instruction. Examine the statement and retype it, correcting the syntax error.
- *HOW?* You've asked TRS-80 to perform something it might otherwise be able to perform, but which is currently beyond its abilities. Generally HOW? is caused by reference to a statement number above 32767, which is the largest number that can be used in the TRS-80 system.
- *SORRY.* You've exceeded the memory capacity of the TRS-80. This is why you should use the PRINT MEM command frequently. When you get this message, before you do anything else, you must go back and compress the program.

MATH OPERATORS

In our little fund-raising program, we used some *math operators,* the symbols =, +, −,*, and/. The computer is, of course, a number machine and is decimally, not fractionally, oriented. When you begin to use or obtain very large or very small numbers, however, some strange things happen. TRS-80 uses *standard scientific notation* (also called *exponential notation* or more simply *E-notation*) in the presentation of very large or very small numbers.

To illustrate, let's examine the number 8 in our decimal system. In the decimal system, the number 8 is really 8. (eight, decimal point, or 8.0). What would 8 million look like? It would look like 8000000. (eight, six zeros, decimal point). In mathematical parlance, 8 million is:

$$8*10*10*10*10*10*10 \quad \text{or} \quad 8*10^{+6}$$

TRS-80, like many computers, would express this number in E-notation. Eight million would look like 8E+06. The numbers expressed after the E are indicative of direction and size. The + indicates that a multiplication has been performed. The number 6 indicates the power of 10 that has been used. What about very small numbers? The number .000008 would be expressed as:

$$8/1\emptyset/1\emptyset/1\emptyset/1\emptyset/1\emptyset/1\emptyset \quad \text{or} \quad 8*1\emptyset^{-6}$$

In the same manner, this would be expressed as 8E-06. The important thing is that the counting begins *at the decimal point.*

RELATIONAL OPERATORS

The computer is also a *logic* machine. It has a mechanical ability, or more specifically, an electronic ability, to reason. By *reason,* we mean the ability to make very simple decisions of the IF . . . THEN variety. In reasoning, the computer also uses its numbering abilities to compare numbers or characters to other numbers or characters. This happens because each number or character has a numerical value or weight. The number 2 is "heavier," that is larger, than the number 1. The letter B is "heavier" than the letter A. Each number, letter, and special character has a computer number assigned to it. Together, they are called the computer's *character set.*

Suppose that we have two numeric variables, A and B. Both contain a number, but it is not known what number is contained in either. The numbers may be alike, or they may be dissimilar. Variable A may be greater than variable B (that is, variable B is less than variable A). A may not be equal to B. B may be equal to or greater than A (which is, by definition, less than or equal to B). Got the picture? On the TRS-80, we express it by using these *relational operators:*

```
A  =  B      A is equal to B (and vice versa)
A  >  B      A is greater than B
A  <  B      A is less than B
A < > B      A is not equal to B
A > = B      A is greater than or equal to B
A < = B      A is less than or equal to B
```

These relational operators are customarily placed into an IF . . . THEN statement, like this:

```
1Ø B = 8
2Ø IF B > = 6 THEN 5Ø
```

In this instance, B contains the value 8 which is definitely greater than or equal to 6. The sequence will then proceed to statement 5Ø.

The use of the relational operators in the IF . . . THEN statement is a *conditional branching* situation. The first variable (or number) following the IF is compared to the second variable (or number), and a branch is taken to the THEN address if the condition is met. The statement could have been written like this with the same results:

```
2Ø IF 6 < = B THEN 5Ø
```

It is important to remember that the branching takes place conditionally upon the relationship of the first variable to the second variable, or more specifically, the contents of those variables. If the branching to the THEN statement address is not taken, the computer assumes that the condition has not been met, and the program proceeds with the statement that follows Statement 2Ø. The order of specification of the multiple symbols is not important. The pair $><$ functions just as well as the pair $<>$.

In our funds program, at statement 13Ø, we told the computer to GOTO. GOTO is an example of an *unconditional branch,* that is, one that requires no conditional operators. The GOTO is customarily used to return to an instruction at the beginning of a processs, and is called *looping.*

If you should forget to use THEN, use IF . . . GOTO. It works just as well. Let's try some of these in a program:

```
5 CLS
1Ø A = Ø
2Ø B = 5
30 C = 1Ø
4Ø IF A > B THEN 9Ø
5Ø PRINT "A NOT GREATER THAN B"
6Ø IF A > < B THEN 12Ø
7Ø PRINT "A IS EQUAL TO B"
8Ø GOTO 14Ø
9Ø IF A = C THEN 16Ø
```

```
100 PRINT "A IS GREATER THAN B BUT LESS THAN C"
110 GOTO 140
120 IF A > B THEN 90
130 PRINT "A IS LESS THAN B"
140 A = A + 1
150 GOTO 40
160 PRINT "A IS EQUAL TO C"
170 END
```

This little program exercises all but the greater than/ less than/ equal combinations, thus giving an indication of how the conditional branching systems work. Type it into the computer, and then RUN it. Your display should show:

```
A NOT GREATER THAN B
A IS LESS THAN B
A NOT GREATER THAN B
A IS LESS THAN B
A NOT GREATER THAN B
A IS LESS THAN B
A NOT GREATER THAN B
A IS LESS THAN B
A NOT GREATER THAN B
A IS LESS THAN B
A NOT GREATER THAN B
A IS LESS THAN B
A IS EQUAL TO B
A IS GEATER THAN B BUT LESS THAN C
A IS GREATER THAN B BUT LESS THAN C
A IS GREATER THAN B BUT LESS THAN C
A IS GREATER THAN B BUT LESS THAN C
A IS EQUAL TO C
```

Now you see it, now you don't. There is too much to be printed on the screen, and so the top part is lost. That feature, called *scrolling*, will always happen unless you slow the process down. The simplest way to do that (with the knowledge you now have) is to insert the following statement:

```
INPUT X:PRINT A,B,C
```

In this manner, the computer will come to rest after the numeric variable A becomes equal to B. All you have to do is to press **ENTER** , and the rest of the display will appear. RUN it again.

Do you see any problems? There is one! What do you think that it is?

It's time to *debug* our program (that is, eliminate the errors). You'll recall that we had set variable A to Ø, B to 5, and C to 1Ø. At 55, 75, 1Ø5, 135, and 165, type the following instruction:

```
75 INPUT X
```

Don't concern yourself with the colon (:) yet.

RUN the program. Each time it stops, record left to right on a piece of paper, the contents of A, B, and C. When you've done that, press **ENTER** . You should find the following, in two-line sets:

Line 1	Produces	*Line 2*		
A NOT GREATER THAN B		Ø	5	1Ø
A IS LESS THAN B		Ø	5	1Ø
A NOT GREATER THAN B		1	5	1Ø
A IS LESS THAN B		1	5	1Ø
A NOT GREATER THAN B		2	5	1Ø
A IS LESS THAN B		2	5	1Ø
A NOT GREATER THAN B		3	5	1Ø
A IS LESS THAN B		3	5	1Ø
A NOT GREATER THAN B		4	5	1Ø
A IS LESS THAN B		4	5	1Ø
A NOT GREATER THAN B		5	5	1Ø
A IS LESS THAN B		5	5	1Ø
A IS EQUAL TO B		6	5	1Ø

Line 1							*Line 2*		
A IS GREATER THAN B BUT LESS THAN C							7	5	10
A IS GREATER THAN B BUT LESS THAN C							8	5	10
A IS GREATER THAN B BUT LESS THAN C							9	5	10
A IS GREATER THAN B BUT LESS THAN C							10	5	10
⋆ A IS EQUAL TO C							11	5	10

The asterisks are not part of the display. Note the value of variable A at the positions indicated by those asterisks. Each one is more than the amount indicated in the line above it. In other words, with B = 5, A should also be 5. But it is 6! Why? With C = 10, A should also be 10. But it is 11. Why? The reason for this can be found at statement 140. Note that it increments variable A at the bottom of the loop. It is positioned after the condition it signifies. Thus, the first time through the instructions, A remains at 0 until it is incremented at Statement 140. The simplest way to handle this is to change statement 10 to A = 1. It's a minor thing, but important. An easier way around the problem will be presented later in this chapter.

Remember that each statement has a 4-byte overhead for statement numbers, carriage returns, etc. You can save substantial overhead by combining several statements into a single statement. The colon indicates to the computer that what follows is a new statement, just as if you had continued on to a new sequence number. It's a handy way to condense a program, but there is one proviso: instructions can only be referenced by the statement number. In a multiple instruction statement, you can reference only the first instruction. If you need to reference another instruction of the statement, it must have its own sequence number.

In addition, while we did use the INPUT statement with a Variable X, nothing was entered to X. Well, it didn't seem that way, because no number was typed. However, merely by hitting the **ENTER** key, a 0 was stored at X. Since X is not used, it makes no difference. In this instance, the INPUT statement was used just to bring the process to a temporary halt.

KEEPING A COPY OF THE PROGRAM

What if your programming is interrupted by such mundane activities as getting a night's sleep or going to work? The TRS-80 is equipped with a cassette tape recorder/player, the same kind you play music upon. If you haven't yet connected it to the computer, do so now. On the back of the keyboard there is a connector marked "TAPE." You have a cable which fits that connector and which has three plugs on the other end. The three plugs are connected as follows:

- The small gray plug is placed into the REM jack on the recorder. Along this line, the TRS-80 will pass commands from the computer to the recorder for moving the tape (START/STOP).
- The large gray plug is placed into the AUX jack on the recorder. The TRS-80 will pass the data from the computer to the recorder along this line.
- The black plug goes into the EAR jack. Along this line, the computer passes data from the recorder to the computer.

Be extremely careful to place the black plastic plug supplied with the recorder into the jack labeled MIC. This blocks out the condenser microphone that is built into the recorder.

As the TRS-80 system is structured, there are some mechanical things you must do in order to save your program by *dumping* it off onto cassette tape.

- You must depress *both* the PLAY and RECORD levers. You must operate the tape recorder just as if you were singing into the microphone.
- You must ensure that you *do not* record on the plastic leader to the tape. REWIND the tape, and then FAST FORWARD it beyond the plastic leader. It is possible to obtain leaderless tape. It is, however, considerably more expensive.

Many tapes will work on the recorder. However, purchase *audio*, not digital tapes. There is a considerable difference in their performance. For the run-of-the-mill programs, you can use a C-30 tape. However, for extremely important programs, pay the extra money and obtain C-1Ø or C-2Ø certified computer tapes. The tape's coating is more durable, there is no leader to worry about, and the error rate is slight. They *are* considerably shorter, however, and they are more expensive.

When you are ready to dump your program onto cassette tape, type:

CSAVE **ENTER**

CSAVE stands for *C*assette *SAVE*. When you have done this, the motor of the recorder will begin to move, and the program will be transferred to the tape. When transfer is complete, a READY message will appear on the screen.

The TRS-80 records on tape as audio signals, although if you were to play it back, it would sound terrible. You'll also find that the volume setting on

the recorder is very critical. Once you have the correct setting, *leave it alone*.

The TRS-80 user's manual mentions ground loops. A ground loop is a hum that is introduced into the tape by the proximity of two wires connected to the device. After you have dumped your program, rewind the tape, remove the black plug (not the plastic one), and put the recorder into PLAY. Remember, don't change the volume setting. You can hear what your program sounds like on the recording, and with a little practice, you'll be able to distinguish the program from the background hum. A certain amount of hum is natural, but if it is too loud, it can interfere with the program. For that reason, it is good practice to save the program on tape several times. If, after you've saved the program, you rewind it and play it again (disconnect the plug connected to the EAR jack) you'll hear the sound of the program, and at the place between the programs, you'll hear the hum.

What about loading the program to the computer from the tape? The means of loading the program is the instruction:

CLOAD ENTER

That stands for *C*assette *Load*. Make sure the PLAY button is depressed. When dumping onto the cassette tape, the volume control is not significant, but when loading the program back into the computer from the cassette tape, it is extremely important. Radio Shack advises a volume setting of 7 to 8. The precise setting is different with every recorder and depends upon the condition of the magnetic heads. If the heads have become coated with oxide from the tape, difficulty will be encountered when loading, and frequently it is necessary to clean the recording and playback heads on the cassette recorder. That can be done with a Q-TipTM and isopropyl alcohol. The setting recommended above is for the tapes you have dumped. There is a different setting for the tapes you have dumped. There is a different setting for the tapes that Radio Shack distributes. Directions on those tapes are included with each of the programs (e.g., Blackjack and Backgammon) distributed with the computer. Also important is the setting of the TONE switch. *Always* set it to HIGH. The system responds better to the treble sounds.

As the program is loading into the computer, two asterisks will appear on the screen. One of them is permanent, and the other blinks with each statement that has been loaded (when it finds the carriage return which is at the end of the statement). If the right-hand asterisk does not appear, the volume is probably too high. If the right-hand asterisk appears but does not blink, the most frequent reason is that the volume is too low. *Be careful!* Make very small changes in the volume, the recorder is *that* sensitive. Until you become familiar with your particular unit's sensitivity, this situation will tend to frustrate you. If you run into trouble, RESET and start again.

A couple of very important points about loading the program from tape. First, if the program does not load or loads incorrectly (you'll see "garbage" when you do a LIST), check the tape unit's recording head. It will probably need cleaning. After cleaning, blow on the head very softly. Secondly, if you do encounter loading problems, the chances are very high that the tape is perfectly OK. Clean the heads, and experiment with the volume settings before abandoning the project. Very often, the first copy of a program (the one on the "outside" of the tape) will give you load problems, due to electromagnetic interference in your home. Such interference is generated by radios, televisions, microwave ovens, nearby compressors, etc. This makes the second and possibly the third recording of the program extremely important. Does this seem like too much trouble? Well, this recorder costs less than $50. You could invest in an expensive recorder but it wouldn't do much better.

For maintaining your tapes, buy a demagnetizer (called a degausser). The package will advise you of the motions to use when "cleaning" a tape. Be very careful to avoid holding the demagnetizer close to other tapes you may not wish to "clean." After you've used the demagnetizer on a tape, move the tape at least 3 feet away before you turn the current off. In other words, get the tape out of its magnetic field before you change the composition of the magnetic field. In doing so, you may save yourself hours of work. If you do not do so, you may leave electrons on the tape which might "mix" with your programs, causing the programs to load incorrectly. Keep your tapes away from motors, toasters, or other appliances. And keep them out of the direct sunlight.

It's possible to record on both sides of a tape, but it is not recommended. In the early days of a tape's use, it will be OK to do so. As the tape gets older and worn, however, its ability to properly maintain signal integrity on both sides of the tape diminishes. If you can afford to place several copies of a single program on a tape, and then only one program to a tape, then by all means, do so.

LOOP CONTROL

You will recall from the previous discussion that when a sequence of instructions is repeated, the process is called *looping*. Occasionally it is necessary to control the number of times we go through the loop. The process is called *iteration*. The instruction which is used is called FOR instruction, and it works with the NEXT instruction. The pair of instructions surrounds the loop. For example:

```
FOR N = 1 TO 500
NEXT N
```

Note that the FOR instruction involves the use of a numeric variable (in this case N) and a range through which the count will be made (in this case from 1 to 500). Unless otherwise specified the increment is done by "1." This particular example functions strictly as a delay. The program into which this was inserted would merely delay while N was advanced to 500 from 1 by 1. After N reaches 500, the sequence of instructions would continue with the instruction which follows the NEXT N. Let's modify this concept just a little to see how the FOR . . . NEXT loop would be useful. Key the following into the computer:

```
10 CLS
20 FOR S = 0 TO 59
30 PRINT S
40 NEXT S
50 GOTO 10
```

Now RUN it. What happened? The program went like a bat out of you-know-where, didn't it? In fact, it's *still* going. And it will continue forever, unless interrupted. How could that possibly be useful? Who wants to count form 0 to 59 anyway? Anyone who wants to build a clock. Look over the above, and you'll see that what we've set up is a nifty way to count seconds. Unfortunately, however, it's moving too fast to be accurate. Add the following instructions:

```
32 ƀƀƀƀ FOR N = 1 TO 500
34 ƀƀƀƀ NEXT N
```

RUN the program again. What happened? It slowed down, didn't it? Hit **BREAK** and then **CLEAR** and RUN the program again. Time the computer against a wrist watch which has a sweep-second hand. A new number should appear on the screen every second. If the hand on the watch runs faster than the computer, decrease the count at statement 32. If the hand on the watch runs slower than the computer, increase the count at statement 32.

You'll note that four mandatory blanks (ƀ) were inserted in both statement 32 and statement 34. That is a concession to reading ease. Do a LIST and the instructions should look like this:

```
10 CLS
20 FOR S = 0 TO 59
30 PRINT S
32     FOR N = 1 TO 500
34     NEXT N
40 NEXT S
50 GOTO 10
```

How does it work? The first thing we've done is set up a controlled loop that begins at 0, increments by 1 until Variable S reaches 59, resets, and then starts over again. That controlled loop looks like this:

```
20 FOR S = 0 TO 59
  . . .
  . . .
40 NEXT S
```

In other words, those instructions which fall between statement 20 and statement 40 will be done a total of 60 times (0 to 59). Imbedded within the FOR . . . NEXT loop just mentioned is another FOR . . . NEXT loop. That one counts from 1 to 500. TRS-80 can perform approximately 500 single-step FOR . . . NEXT loops in one second. Thus, for every time through the "S" loop, the printing of the Variable S will be done at approximately one per second.

Thus, the "N" loop has been made subordinate to the "S" loop. This is called *nesting*. Loop "S" has a nested loop "N." Can that same principle be extended to the hour and minute hands? Certainly, by typing NEW and starting over. Type the following, observing the spacing given:

```
10 CLS
20 FOR H = 0 TO 23
30    FOR M = 0 TO 59
40       FOR S = 0 TO 59
50          PRINT AT 470, H; ":";M; ":";S
60             FOR N = 1 TO 500
```

```
70                      NEXT N
80           NEXT S
90      NEXT M
100 NEXT H
```

The spacing given allows you to determine how the FOR . . . NEXT loops are paired. This illustration is quoted directly from the Radio Shack Level I manual, with permission. The only thing different from that which has been previously discussed is the PRINT AT instruction. That will be dealt with completely later, but for the time being, PRINT AT is a means to display data at a specific place on the computer's display screen. While this arrangement of instructions occupies more positions of memory (because of the spaces), it *is* easier to debug.

That's all very nice, but unless you plan to wait up until midnight to run it, it won't keep accurate time. How should the clock be "set?" Type in the following:

```
12 INPUT "ENTER HOUR";A
14 INPUT "ENTER MINUTE";B
16 INPUT "ENTER SECOND";C
```

Retype statements 20, 30, and 40, substituting "A," "B," and "C" for the 0 in each case (the zero to the right of the equals sign). Also, let's calibrate it. Change statement 60 to read: FOR N = 1 TO 500:NEXT N. Adjust the 500 upwards or downwards, as necessary. Remove statement 70 and RUN it. Now let it run for 5 minutes or so.

At the end of some significant time, look at your watch. Does the time indicated on the screen match your watch? If you made the entry at the beginning of an hour, it's probably pretty close. But if you made your entry at 10 minutes to the hour or 10 seconds to the minute, you'll note that something just is not right. Let it run another 10 or 15 minutes. When you come back, you'll note that things have gone from bad to worse. Why? Probably the hour indicator is OK, because you haven't been gone that long. But no doubt the minutes have gained 15 or so more than they should have, and the seconds indicator is liable to be anywhere.

The reason why this has happened is that the FOR . . . NEXT loop increments from the initial value you gave it—which in this case was the hour (A), minute (B), and second (C)—continues through until it finds the higher value—and then it *resets to the initial value you gave it*. If you had made your entry at 10 minutes before the hour (50), that means you'll "burn up" an hour every time you have counted to 10. Obviously, that's not right. We want that 59 at the second and minute indicators to revert to Ø even though we have entered something else in the beginning. Here's what you should do to cause that to happen.

```
85  ␣␣␣␣␣␣␣␣␣␣␣␣␣C = Ø
95  ␣␣␣␣␣␣␣␣B = Ø
1Ø5  A = Ø
```

The mandatory spaces will cause the instruction to fit nicely with the rest of the program. RUN it again, entering the correct time to begin, and then check it again in five minutes or so. It should be pretty close, and all you'll have to do is to modify the count in statement 6Ø to more closely calibrate the clock.

Want to have a little fun? Try these changes:

```
20 FOR H = 23 TO A STEP -1
30    FOR M = 59 TO B STEP -1
40       FOR S = 59 TO C STEP -1
85          C = 59
95       B = 59
105 A = 23
```

You'll have to make the entries and RUN the program to see what it does. But note the changes in the FOR statements. The controlled loop can be incremented (+) or decremented (−) by adding the STEP modifier to the FOR statement. You'll see the value of this when the presentation of graphics is made later in the book.

Now, about that PRINT AT statement. The CRT screen is capable of displaying 16 lines of 64 characters. The characters on the first line are numbered left to right, from Ø to 63. Character 64 would be the first character of the second line (or line 1, since the lines are numbered Ø to 15). Character 128 would be the first character of the third line. Multiply 16 by 64 and you'll see that the screen can display a total of 1Ø24 characters—one fourth of the capacity of a 4K system (4Ø96). When we use a PRINT AT statement, we merely designate the precise position on the screen for data to appear. In our clock, the use of the PRINT AT allowed us to print the time in precisely the same place every time. In fact, you have to look pretty closely to determine if anything has been printed there at all, as it looks as though only the seconds are changing. In reality, the entire line is changing every time. Caution: when you use a PRINT AT statement, it "blanks out" everything which precedes it on the line. See figures 2 and 3. So, if you desire to print many things on a line, fill the screen from right to left. This will become very important when mixing words with graphics, to be discussed later in the book.

Note that the program is getting larger. Take a LIST and you'll see that there is more program than will fit on a single screen. If there is more to be seen, just press the "up arrow" (↑) and you will cause the listing to *scroll*. Also, at any time, while you're executing a program, you can cause the program to "freeze" merely by pressing any key. It is recommended, however, that you do so by pressing either the space bar or the up arrow. This is just good operational practice, as neither displays anything extraneous on the screen. Note that you do not need to LIST your programs from the beginning every time. If you wish to examine any given statement, just type LIST 5ØØ (or whatever the statement number is) and the screen display will begin from that point.

THE PRINT INSTRUCTION

PRINTing is really another way of saying that the computer must have a means to produce output. In this computer, PRINT is the means to produce output on the display screen. The PRINT instruction doesn't produce anything in hardcopy form, on paper. Not that it can't be used for that, but the addition of such a printer to the TRS-80 involves some additional supporting hardware, and considerable expense, although there are also low-cost printers available which can be connected to your computer directly. However, to use a printer with your TRS-80 you must obtain Level II. You can learn about them at Radio Shack or by reviewing the trade media.

There are several ways to display information upon the screen. Some of these ways have already been briefly discussed. At this point these methods will be further explained and demonstrated.

To begin our discussion of methods to display data, it is necessary to distinguish between a *physical line* and a *logical line* to be displayed. In simple terms, a physical line is a fixed area of space on the face of the screen. Characters Ø to 63 constitute one physical line on the tube face, just as do characters 64 to 127, etc., line by line through position 1Ø24. A logical line is that information which will be formated into contiguous positions in memory with the intent that they be displayed upon some physical line of the screen, no matter where it is to be located. For instance, recall the exercise where the clock was developed. Remember that the successive print lines filled each line on the screen and then the display began scroll on the screen until the 60th line had been displayed. The line which we had decided to print was the logical line. And a succession of logical lines were placed on a succession of physical lines. Contrast that to the PRINT AT that we did when we wanted the clock to be displayed in a single location. In this instance, the logical line and the physical line became the same. Unless either a CLS instruction is given (which locates the next PRINT instruction's output upon the first line of the screen), or an alternative method of varying the display of the output is employed, the PRINT instruction will continue to print on successive physical lines on the screen.

The subject of zoning in the presentation of data using the PRINT instruction has been previously discussed. You will recall that when commas were used in the instruction, the data appeared in one of the four zones of the screen. It now becomes important to try some other forms of formating.

As mentioned before, each physical line has a logical construction which consists of 64 characters. If a message is to be correctly spaced, the spacing must be planned in the construction of the message itself. Thus, if it is desired to present words on the screen, they must be enclosed in quotation marks. But the following PRINT statement contains an error. Can you spot it?

```
1Ø PRINT "THIS STATEMENT CONTAINS";"AN ERROR."
```

When the statement is printed on the screen, the following will appear:

```
THIS STATEMENT CONTAINSAN ERROR.
```

As can be seen, the statement placed on the screen caused two words to be run together. To correct it, a space must be imbedded into one of the items to be displayed. To illustrate, a mandatory space is included:

```
1Ø PRINT "THIS STATEMENT CONTAINSb";"AN ERROR."
```

And, of course, it no longer contains the error. The spacing of mixed lines is extremely important. Recall the PRINT line which was used in the clock example: PRINT H;":";M;":";S. If you observed the CRT, you may have noted that there were spaces surrounding the numeric variables. This space is customarily reserved for a sign, and positive signs (+) are not displayed. In this instance, the colon is enclosed within the quotation marks, meaning that it is part of the data to be displayed, *not* a separator between instructions.

The completion of the PRINT instruction forces a carriage return. Ordinarily, any PRINT instruction following the PRINT instruction with the carriage return will display on the next available line (unless PRINT AT is used). However, if the PRINT instruction is terminated by a semicolon, the carriage return is suppressed. For example:

```
1Ø PRINT "PRINTING THIS WAY ALLOWS YOU";
2Ø PRINT "b/TO BREAK UP THE INSTRUCTION";
3Ø PRINT "b/WITHOUT BREAKING UP THE LINE."
```

Type in the above program and RUN it to prove the point. Now go back and change the semicolons to colons. What happens? It's an error situation. The computer was expecting something else to be included in the statement. If you had omitted the trailing punctuation altogether, the printed output would appear on three successive physical lines, which you may wish anyway.

Another way to achieve printing is to construct the line so that the proportional spacing is built into the statement itself. Thus, three successive PRINT statements, constructed like the following, would produce alignment on the screen:

```
1Ø PRINT "COLUMNb/b/b/b/b/b/b/b/b/b/b/COLUMNb/b/b/b/b/b/b/b/b/b/COLUMN"
2Ø PRINT "HEADINGb/b/b/b/b/b/b/b/b/b/HEADINGb/b/b/b/b/b/b/b/b/HEADING"
3Ø PRINT "ONEb/b/b/b/b/b/b/b/b/b/b/b/TWOb/b/b/b/b/b/b/b/b/b/b/b/THREE"
```

It remains for you to determine how you wish to align the headings (left and right) and how wide you wish the "white" space to be between the printing. For any extensive amount of printing, this method is extremely wasteful of memory. Nevertheless, it is an effective way to generate print lines, and there are times when this approach seems desirable.

TABULATION

One interesting variation of the PRINT command is its ability to allow you to structure the screen into columns and to do so very easily. It could be done by zones, as before. But in the zone format, you're restricted to only four columns and spacing could become a problem. That problem is solved by the TAB subsection of the PRINT command. Consider the following:

```
10 PRINT TAB(10);"CHECK";TAB(20);"PERSON";TAB(30);"AMOUNT";TAB(40);"DATE OF"
20 PRINT TAB(9);"NUMBER";TAB(21);"PAID";TAB(31);"PAID";TAB(41)"CHECK"
```

If you'll enter these two statements and then RUN them, you'll see that the headings line up like this:

| CHECK | PERSON | AMOUNT | DATE OF |
| NUMBER | PAID | PAID | CHECK |

Then, in successive lines, you can align the data to be presented in the same manner. There are two important things to remember about TAB:

1. It is a separate operation in the PRINT command and *must* be preceded and followed by a semicolon.
2. It is descriptive of a position on the *logical* line, i.e., each line can hold 64 characters, numbered Ø to 63. Once you have determined an alignment, that TAB applies to every line. That is different from the PRINT AT command which will follow.

On the following page you will see a TRS-80 Video Display Worksheet (reprinted with permission from the Radio Shack Level I Manual). Included too is a worksheet aligned by character, which also serves well as a coding sheet. You will see on the first sheet the 1Ø24 positions to which reference was previously made. Using the PRINT AT command, it is possible to position your displayed output at any of the 1Ø24 positions, assuming there is sufficient space to accommodate the message.

- Note that the top row is identified as TAB and is numbered from Ø to 63. Using this identification, you can plan the positioning of your character data upon the screen.
- Note that there are 16 groups of three horizontal lines, beginning with the numbers Ø, 64, 128, 192, 256, 32Ø, 384, 448, 512, 576, 64Ø, 7Ø4, 768, 832, 896, and 96Ø.
- Note that there are 48 individual horizontal lines, numbered Ø to 47. Each is one-third the height of a letter. It is on one of these horizontal lines that the Y-Axis positioning will be provided in the graphics capability of the TRS-80. More on graphics in a later chapter.
- Note that there are 128 individual vertical lines, numbered Ø to 127. Each is one-half the width of a letter. It is on one of these vertical lines that the X-Axis positioning will be provided in the graphics capability of the TRS-80. Again, that is a subject for a later chapter.

Thus, it can be seen that each character displayed on the screen occupies 6 of what we'll call *character elements* in a 2-by-3 character element matrix. Now to PRINT AT.

If it is desired to place a message in a particular place without concern for determining horizontal or vertical spacing, it can be done with the PRINT AT command. Clear the machine and enter the following:

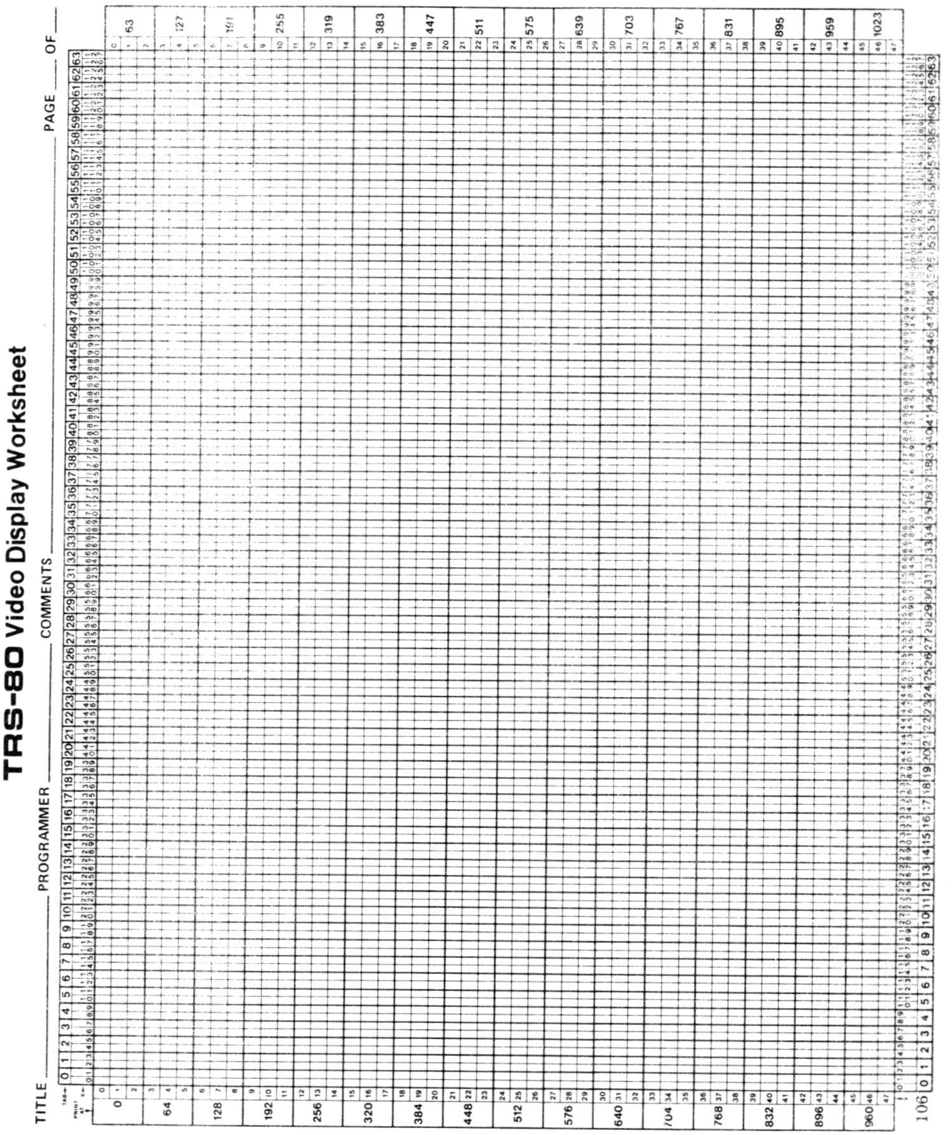

TRS-80 Video Display Worksheet

TITLE _____ PROGRAMMER _____ COMMENTS _____ PAGE ____ OF ____

Figure 2

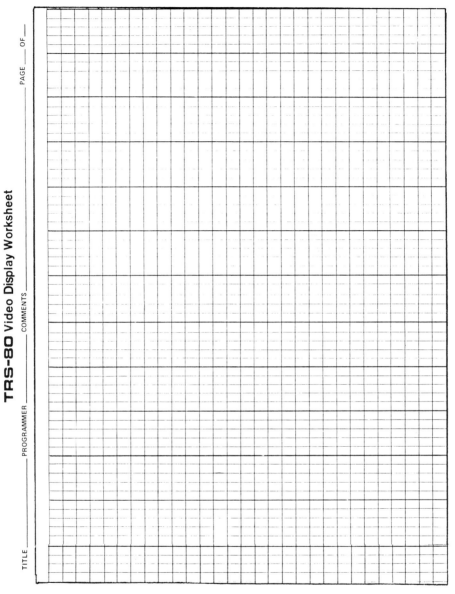

TRS-80 Video Display Worksheet

PROGRAMMER _____ COMMENTS _____ PAGE ___ OF ___

TITLE _____

Figure 3

```
10 PRINT AT 650,"POSITION 650"
```

RUN it and the point will be demonstrated. There are a couple of cautions to be observed when using the PRINT AT command:

- If you're using PRINT AT commands, position them on the screen line from right to left, placing the right-most field first, and working towards the left side of the line. This is the easiest way, particularly if the entire PRINT operation is not performed at one time. If it is to be performed at one time, merely terminate the PRINT AT command with a semicolon. While the positioning of the message is correct, the use of the command tends to obliterate any printing or graphics to the left *on the same line*. This can be a little frustrating, particularly if you must relocate a very complicated routine.
- One of the nice features of the PRINT AT command is its ability to utilize a *symbolic address*, as per the following example:

10 PRINT AT X, ''MESSAGE''

Of course, to use that, you must supply a value to X, a value which is neither less than zero nor greater than 1024, less the length of the message. You can even use a modified variable:

10 PRINT AT X + 10, ''MESSAGE''

Again, the *developed address* cannot exceed 1024 less the length of the message, which in this case is 7 characters. Thus, the developed address cannot be greater than 1017. Be sure to follow this address with a comma—*not* a semicolon.

You can use PRINT AT to ''blink'' a message, like this:

10 PRINT AT 650, ''POSITION 650''

30 PRINT AT 650, ''ƀƀƀƀƀƀƀƀƀƀƀƀƀ''

40 GOTO 10

Enter it and RUN. It will blink so fast that it will look like it isn't blinking at all. You should slow it down. Insert the following instruction:

20 FOR N = 1 TO 500:NEXT N

The speed of the flash can be controlled merely by changing the value in the FOR . . . NEXT loop.

Finally there is the PRINT# command, and it's use is to place data upon cassette tape. The PRINT# will be discussed later in the book after we've dealt with methods of handling data.

POSITIVE, NEGATIVE, AND ZERO

A computer is a sophisticated device, a number cruncher, but computers differ one from another. Such is the case with the difference between the Level I (the subject of this book) and Level II versions of the TRS-80. Many of the things which are designed to be within the capability of the Level II require some extra work to be done in Level I. One of these is the method to determine the sign of a number. With the SGN command in Level II, a number can be tested to determine if it is positive, negative, or zero. In Level I it is necessary to determine the relationship of the number to zero. If it's greater than zero, it's positive, if it's smaller than zero, it is negative. Here's how that is determined:

```
10 INPUT N
20 IF N < 0 GOTO 60
30 IF N = 0 GOTO 30
40 IF N > 0 GOTO 100
50 GOTO 10
60 PRINT "NUMBER IS NEGATIVE"
70 GOTO 10
30 PRINT "NUMBER IS ZERO"
90 GOTO 10
100 PRINT "NUMBER IS POSITIVE"
110 GOTO 10
```

Of course, it is not necessary to PRINT anything. This routine has been constructed in this manner to present the output of the test. RUN the little program, giving it an assortment of positive, negative, and zero values. On the negative values, it is necessary to precede the number by a minus sign.

MORE ABOUT RUN AND LIST

You know that any time you wish to execute the program, you have only to type RUN. The RUN command looks for the lowest numbered statement in the program and begins execution from there. If your program doesn't happen to begin at the lowest numbered statement, it will be necessary to insert at the lowest position a GOTO to where the program does begin. For that reason, it is generally a good practice to leave a few statement numbers available in the low numbers.

It may happen that when your program is complete you may wish to exercise only a portion of that program, such as the routine upon which you're working. When that is to be done, insert a STOP command at the end of the routine and then RUN the routine by specifying the initial statement you wish to exercise, like this:

```
RUN 100 (the number should be the first statement)
```

This will begin execution at statement 100 (or your number) and will continue until either the STOP command is encountered or the program comes to a natural end or breaking point, such as an INPUT command.

By now you recognize that the LIST command will display the program you are developing, all neatly sorted into ascending sequential statement sequence. The LIST command displays 12 lines and then you must hit the up arrow ($\leftarrow$) to scroll. This is a Level I technique only. But suppose you don't wish to scroll through your entire program. What then?

```
LIST 100 (or whatever statement number you choose)
```

And the list will begin at that number.

COMPACTION AND SHORTHAND

Throughout the text, mention has been made about making the program compact. More will be said about this in a later chapter, but for the time being, two options are available: compaction and shorthand.

Compaction is simply the removal of extra spaces from a statement. For instance, the following statement can be written two ways:

```
10 FOR N = 1 TO 500:NEXT N
```

or

```
10FORN=1TO500:NEXTN
```

The statement will work as well in its compacted form, each space not used is a position of memory which can be made available, but, of course, it is less readable. Throughout the balance of the book, the instructions will be shown in the most readable format.

The second option, for Level I users, is to use the shorthand dialect. *Microsoft*, the company which developed the BASIC Language for the TRS-80, devised a system where commands could be given using a single letter. The following figure details the commands and their shorthand equivalents:

Command/Statement	Abbreviation	Command/Statement	Abbreviation
PRINT	P.	TAB (after PRINT)	T.
NEW	N.	INT	I.
RUN	R.	GOSUB	GOS.
LIST	L.	RETURN	RET.
END	E.	READ	REA.
THEN	T.	DATA	D.
GOTO	G.	RESTORE	REST.
INPUT	IN.	ABS.	A.
MEM	M.	RND	R.
FOR	F.	SET	S.
NEXT	N.	RESET	R.
STEP (after FOR)	S.	POINT	P.
STOP	ST.	PRINT AT	P.A.
CONT	C.	CSAVE	CS.
		CLOAD	CL.

Figure 4.   Shorthand Dialect

Thus, the previous statements could have been written like this:

    1∅ F. N = 1 TO 5∅∅:N. N

        -or-

    1∅F.N = 1TO5∅∅:N. N

Some of the instructions in the list which have not yet appeared will be dealt with later, but all will be used at some point in the book. The shorthand dialect is a design feature of the Level I BASIC only. With only 4K, Radio Shack felt that it was necessary to cut corners.

MORE ON INPUT

There is one final gap to fill before proceeding to something new. While it would be nice to have the ability to position the cursor with a TAB or AT feature on the INPUT statement, that facility is not available. Thus, the positioning of input data and screen formating become somewhat critical. One of the ways to alleviate that difficulty is to use the multiple-formated INPUT statement, like this:

    1∅ INPUT A,B,C

This statement allows the collection of more than one item of data in a single INPUT statement. The only requirement is that the data, when entered, must be separated by commas, and must match the type of data expected. In the above illustration, three numeric values are expected.

Up to this point, only numeric data has been discussed, using the 26 numeric variables A through Z. But it is also possible to handle alphabetic data. In Level I you are restricted to only two alphabetic variables, each of 16 characters in length. The names of these variables are A$ and B$. You can INPUT them, PRINT them, or use them in any other instruction which would ordinarily be used to handle character data. However, when you use them and the sequence and degree to which you use them become very important, particularly where the data is mixed, as follows:

```
10 INPUT A$,A,B,C
```

The TRS-80 is very good about accepting only data which fits the type of variable, however, and if you violate the rules, you'll know about it immediately.

There are other ways to handle alphabetic data, which we'll cover in the discussion of DATA statements and arrays.

SUBROUTINES

Occasionally, when you have developed a particularly useful or complicated routine, you find that it's useful not only where it was planned, but also in several other places in the program. It could be rewritten each time it is needed, but that would be wasteful of time, memory, and efficiency. In addition, it would be difficult to debug. To address this concern, a *subroutine* is generally developed. The subroutine is a sequence of instructions that is developed once and then used as many times as necessary. Suppose you have the following timing loop:

```
1000 FOR N = 1 TO 500
```

If you desired to code this set of instructions each place they were required, you could do so—*or* you could code them once and then refer to them as required. You would refer to the subroutine with this instruction:

```
10 GOSUB 1000
```

And it would be necessary to add an instruction:

```
1020 RETURN
```

The subroutine at 1000 would function with each reference and then control would be returned to the statement which followed the instruction which had referenced it in the first place. For a three-statement subroutine, this might not be very important. But for a complex calculation subroutine, it would become very important indeed.

The single requirement for a subroutine is that it be allowed to find its RETURN statement, under normal circumstances. Other than normal circumstances would include coding developed to "break out" of the timing loop. It is possible to nest GOSUBs just as you nested FOR . . . NEXT statements. In other words, a subroutine can employ a second-level subroutine, just so long as the original RETURN is used.

MULTI-DIRECTIONAL BRANCHES

The TRS-80 BASIC has a very powerful statement for multiple logic path development. It is the ON . . . GOTO statement. Suppose you had displayed a selection of seven options (commonly called a *menu*) on the screen, like this:

```
10 PRINT "1. MONDAY"
20 PRINT "2. TUESDAY"
30 PRINT "3. WEDNESDAY"
40 PRINT "4. THURSDAY"
50 PRINT "5. FRIDAY"
60 PRINT "6. SATURDAY"
70 PRINT "7. SUNDAY"
80 INPUT "WHAT DAY IS IT?  (ENTER NUMBER)";N
```

In this instance, your program would be asking you for the day of the week. The entry in response to the question might cause certain things to happen within the program. The following logic could be used:

```
90 IF N < 1 GOTO 8000
100 IF N > 7 GOTO 8000
110 IF N = 1 GOTO 1000
120 IF N = 2 GOTO 2000
```

```
130 IF N = 3 GOTO 3000
140 IF N = 4 GOTO 4000
150 IF N = 5 GOTO 5000
160 IF N = 6 GOTO 6000
170 IF N = 7 GOTO 7000
180 GOTO 8000
```

At 1000, 2000, 3000, 4000, 5000, 6000, and 7000 the appropriate action would be taken based on the day of the week as indicated by the entry made in response to the question. The statement at 180 is a "do nothing" statement, as everything other than the numbers 1 through 7 have been rejected in Statements 90 and 100. But there is an easier way—more concise and more accurate. It is:

```
90 ON N GOTO 1000,2000,3000,4000,5000,6000,7000
100 GOTO 8000
```

Using the ON . . . GOTO combination allows the value of 1 to change control to statement 1000, the value of 2 to change control to statement 2000, etc. The only consideration is that the variable (N in this case) must contain the relative number required to change sequence to the appropriate place. In this illustration, anything *not* the numbers 1 through 7 is outside the range of the ON . . . GOTO, and is therefore not to be considered valid. In this case, statement 8000 would be a STOP or END. However, a common technique is to return to the menu, in which the new statement 100 would have to look like this:

```
100 CLS:GOTO 10
```

You can set the value of the variable to any value desired, so long as the ultimate value exists as a relative indicator for the ON . . . GOTO. If N were to have ranges not of 1 to 7 but of 11 to 17, you could code it like this:

```
90 ON N GOTO,,,,,,,,,,1000,2000,3000,4000,5000,6000,7000
```

In this manner, the commas would account for the first 10 numbers. Or, and certainly the better choice, it could be coded as follows:

```
90 ON N-10 GOTO 1000,2000,3000,4000,5000,6000,7000
```

GOSUB can be used in place of GOTO. However, each subroutine must have a RETURN statement.

HANDLING DATA

There are several ways for handling data on the TRS-80. The numeric variables (A through Z) are data, as discussed previously. Alphabetic data is stored in Level I in the variables A$ and B$. Thus, the management of alphabetic data is very important.

The restriction of 16 characters is not a serious restriction, provided you keep track of what you are doing. In some instances, alphabetic data can be *concatenated,* that is, joined together to effectively obtain a 32-character string of alphabetic data. In TRS-80 BASIC, it's done this way:

```
1Ø PRINT A$ + B$
```

In this instance, there is no addition between the two alphabetic variables, since it is impossible to add letters to letters. What happens is that the alphabetic strings are joined together and printed as if they were one string. For instance, the following instructions:

```
1Ø A$ = "HI,Ø"
2Ø B$ = "THERE!"
3Ø PRINT A$ + B$
```

will produce the message HI, THERE! on the screen.

As A$ and B$ have been used above, they are known as *constants.* A constant is a value which has been established in the program and is not generally changed. In Level I, the ability to store alphabetic constants is restricted by the availability of only two string variables, A$ and B$. But there is another way, the DATA statement, discussed below.

In addition to alphabetic (string) variables and numeric variables, there are three ways to store data in the Level I TRS-80:

- As a DATA statement, which is accessed by a READ instruction. The DATA statement is a *permanent* constant which can store both alphabetic and numeric data. Once set, they cannot be modified under the control of the program. This differs from the variables, which are, by definition, variable.
- As an element of an array (numeric only). Arrays will be discussed later in the book. While alphabetic data cannot be stored in a Level I array, the array can be used to reference alphabetic data which has been stored in DATA statements. More on this later.
- As a field written onto a cassette tape. Both kinds of data can be written onto the cassette tape, and, of course, read from the tape. Again, there will be more on this feature later in the book.

THE DATA STATEMENT

Consider the following:

```
DATA   42377,KEN,LORD,007328933,9,3,36
DATA   34984,ROBB,WARE,048273922,7,14,33
DATA   84379,TIM,SMITH,237743048,11,9,59
DATA   44736,KAREN,BROWN,023661578,11,12,61
```

Here we have structured some data which will be used by our program for whatever function it is designed to perform. From left to right, each DATA statement contains a sequence number, a first name, a last name, a social security number, and the month, day, and year of birth. Note that each line is structured in precisely the same manner as every other line. Note also that the first item is numeric, the next two are alphabetic, and the remaining four are numeric. Thus, in sequence, they can be described as:

```
A,A$,B$,B,C,D,E
```

Let's alter that statement slightly:

```
READ A,A$,B$,B,C,D,E
```

The above statement will read the very first DATA line. In order to read the four DATA lines which have been structured, the following must be done:

```
10 FOR N = 1 TO 4
20 READ A,A$,B$,B,C,D,E
-  -  -  -
90 NEXT N
```

What you do with the data located by these instructions should be included in the instructions between 20 and 90. While data about people might not be kept in a series of DATA lines, the structuring of tables in DATA lines, or possibly transformation tables could be placed there. For example:

```
1000 DATA "A","B","C","D","E","F","G","H","I"
1010 DATA "J","K","L","M","N","O","P","Q"
1020 DATA "R","S","T","U","V","W","X","Y","Z"
```

The above is a table which has been structured to contain the alphabet. Note that the table is entirely alphabetic. In the preceding table, the one that dealt with personal information, there were 7 variables. Each DATA line had been structured identically, in such a way that with each READ statement, corresponding data is obtained (the same *type* of data, but pertaining to another person). With the alphabet table, the format is different. Only two of the three are the same size. And there are 26 identical elements, each a letter of the alphabet.

The following would select the letter A from the table:

```
10 READ A$
```

The READ instruction could have been structured as 10 READ A$, B$. Had it been so structured, two letters, A and B, could have been read simultaneously. The letter B could have been obtained by simply issuing two successive READ instructions with the single alphabetic variable, A$. The limitation imposed by the presence of only two alphabetic variables, however, would at best allow us to read the alphabet only in pairs.

Using the same logic, the letter Z could be obtained by issuing 26 successive READ statements. But suppose that it is desired to obtain a letter on the basis of a number (in the range of 1 to 26) with the fewest possible instructions and structured in such a way that the routine will work with any number within the range. Consider the following:

```
10 CLS
20 INPUT "ENTER A NUMBER FROM 1 TO 26";N
30 FOR X = 1 TO N
40     READ A$
50 NEXT X
```

In the routine, a value for N is provided from the keyboard. A FOR . . . NEXT loop is then executed for the number of times indicated in N, the value supplied from the keyboard. When the Nth item of the DATA lines has been READ, A$ will contain the letter sought. Since the table is structured in alphabetic sequence, the letter obtained will correspond to the relative position in the table indicated by the number supplied.

DATA lines can be located anywhere in the program. They can be structured early in your program, late, or one at a time. Due to a concept of memory organization called memory mapping, they will end up in the same area of memory anyway. You, as the user of the computer, will not have to be concerned about the location of the data.

Once you have issued a READ instruction, the computer will advance to the next DATA line or item (depending upon the variables used in the READ instruction). It is not reset to the first DATA line. It is your responsibility to know what data you are treating and to keep track of your place in a variety of DATA items.

Assume that you have structured three distinct sets of DATA lines and you wish to read the third. With a FOR . . . NEXT loop you must read through all the preceding DATA until you find the data you are seeking.

If it becomes necessary to READ through the table from the beginning a second or subsequent time, the following instruction must be used:

RESTORE

RESTORE will direct the computer to return its internal pointer to the first DATA item.

DATA statements can be used to store a variety of data, but that data will be fixed (permanent) in nature. One such example of the use of the DATA statements would be to store the screen coordinates of a complicated graphics array. You'll find the methods to do this in a later chapter. Another example of the use of DATA statements might be the fixed elements of another table, such as an income tax table or a table of sales taxes. In essence, the DATA statements are used to establish data which cannot be internally modified in BASIC. Your responsibility in using DATA statements consists of knowing what data is where, how many READs to execute, and the restoration of the pointer to the beginning DATA statement if and when it becomes necessary to read them again.

ARRAYS

While the DATA statement is good for providing temporary input to a program in quantity, it is by no means the only way to introduce data to the system. Another is the use of an array. An array can be thought of as a series of mailboxes or pigeon holes in which items of data can be sorted. There are essentially two types of arrays: unidimensional and multidimensional. A multidimensional array, using the mailboxes as an example, looks like this:

Columns

R	100	00	01	02	03	04	05	06	07	08	09	10	. . . .	99
O	200	00	01	02	03	04	05	06	07	08	09	10	. . . .	99
W	300	00	01	02	03	04	05	06	07	08	09	10	. . . .	99
S	400	00	01	02	03	04	05	06	07	08	09	10	. . . .	99

Figure 5. Multidimensional array

In the example given, a two-dimensional array is shown, a function of rows and columns. Thus, the address of where data is located can be determined from a combination of rows and columns.

The unidimensional array is merely the same type of data structure, except that the boxes are sequentially numbered, like this:

01	02	03	04	05	06	07	08	09	10	11	12	13	14	15	16
17	18	19	20	21	22	23	24	25	26	27	28	29	30	31	32
33	34	35	36	37	38	39	40	41	42	43	44	45	46	47	48

Figure 6. Unidimensional array

In TRS-80 Level I BASIC, there is the restriction of a single unidimensional array, known as A(Sub). The (Sub) is the specific location within the array (also called a table), organized in much the same way as the example given relative to the DATA statements containing the alphabet. The instruction A(1) = 1, for instance, would store the number 1 in the first location of the table. The instruction A(26) = 26 would store the number 26 in its position. Therefore, we could "load" the array in this manner:

```
1Ø FOR N = 1 TO 26
2Ø      A(N) = N
3Ø NEXT N
```

Note: Do not confuse A(Sub) with variable A. Note also that in the instruction sequence, the value of N, since it cycles from 1 to 26, can also be used for the locator in the array. The DATA statements have not been duplicated. To prove the utility of this routine, insert a PRINT N,A(N) command at 25, as follows:

```
1Ø FOR N = 1 TO 26
2Ø      A(N) = N
25      PRINT N,A(N)
3Ø NEXT N
```

Thus, data can be loaded to and extracted from an array merely by knowing the location affected.

As mentioned, only numeric data can be loaded into the array. To get to the alphabetic data contained in the DATA lines, the contents of an element at A(Sub) would have to be used in a FOR . . . NEXT loop which controls a READ. The number contained in the array would then be the relative position in the table (alphabet) contained in the DATA lines. For example, if the value at A(Sub) was a 5, I would wish to perform 5 reads into the DATA statements in order to obtain the alphabetic data. That can be accomplished by placing a value into a variable, say X, and using X as the target value in the FOR . . . NEXT loop, like this:

```
X = A(Sub)
FOR N = 1 TO X
        READ A$
```

The really important thing about using an array, however, is to *know* what type of data resides where, when to retrieve it, and how to handle it once you have retrieved it.

The variable used to control a FOR . . . NEXT loop can also provide the location mechanism for extracting data from an array. Consider the following:

```
1Ø FOR N = 1 TO 13 STEP 2
2Ø       READ A$,B$
3Ø       PRINT A$,B$,A(N),A(N + 1)
4Ø NEXT N
```

In the routine, the data is extracted from both the DATA statements and the array in pairs, using the STEP factor of the FOR . . . NEXT loop. It could have been done as easily using the value of 1 to 26, omitting the STEP 2, and using only one of the two alphabetic variables. This would assume, of course, that the array has been preloaded, and would also require the presence of data in the DATA lines.

The illustration, as given, relies on the value of N from the FOR . . . NEXT loop to extract data. With a slight modification, the value of N can be used to extract the contents of the array, which can then be inserted in another FOR . . . NEXT loop which controls the reading of the DATA lines. It would work like this:

```
1Ø FOR N = 1 TO 26
2Ø      FOR L = 1 TO A(N)
3Ø          READ A$
4Ø          PRINT A$,N,L,A(N)
5Ø      NEXT L
6Ø      RESTORE
7Ø NEXT N
```

In this example, the search of the array is controlled by the value of N and then used to control, in turn, the reading of the DATA lines. After the data is printed, the process is continued, printing all the data up to the specific data sought, and then the pointer is placed back at the first DATA line with the RESTORE command.

It is good programming practice to move through an array with the help of a variable as the Sub element of the array call. There may be times, however, when a specific element of data is sought, and it can be called with the absolute location number. The use of the numeric variable permits the modification of that variable externally to the array call.

Look back to Figure 6. Note that there are 48, not 26, elements. No, there are not 22 new letters. With a little care, the computer can be convinced that an array is multidimensional rather than unidimensional. That is done with the use of *two* variables, one for horizontal movement and one for vertical movement.

If it is known that there are three rows of 16 data elements each, the first data element in the first row is accessed by a variable whose value is 1; the second row's first element with a variable whose value is 17; and the third row's first element with a variable whose value is 33. In the following examples, Variable V will be used for vertical movement and Variable H will be used for horizontal movement through the table depicted in Figure 6. The first thing to do is to initialize the variables:

```
1Ø H = 1:V = 1
```

In this instance, A(H) and A(V) point to precisely the same position in the array—element 1. Moving left to right, each increment of H will scan a line of 16 elements, as it has been constructed. Observe the following:

```
20 FOR H = 1 TO 16
30     PRINT A(H)
40 NEXT H
```

This sequence will scan the first line, and, of course, it would be possible just to keep going until H equals 48, assuming the FOR statement is adjusted to 48. That, however, assumes that it is known that the table is only and precisely 48 elements long. That is not necessarily known. Further, assuming that the array (table) has some structure, the type of data in the 1st, 17th, and 33rd elements bear some similarity, such as the field called employee number, but pertaining to three different people. Let's modify our thinking somewhat. Change, as follows:

```
10 H = 1:V = 0
```

Assume that the routine above will be used to print the array, modified slightly to the following:

```
20 FOR V = 0 TO 48 STEP 16
30     FOR H = 1 TO 16
40         PRINT A(V+H)
50     NEXT H
60 NEXT V
```

V is the controlling variable. It moves from 0 through 48 in STEP 16 (48 divided by 16 equals 3; there are three rows in the array). H is the scanning variable for each of the three rows. In this manner, this nested FOR loop structure will permit the extraction of all elements of the array, assuming that the length of the array is known precisely. What if it is not? The simplest means of handling this situation is this: when the array is being constructed, and after all data has been loaded, a *sentinel* line (customarily all 9's) is loaded at the end of the array. The addition of a check for the sentinel will allow you to build and utilize an array which may be variable or unknown in length:

```
35 IF A(V) = 9 GOTO 70
```

The selection of V for the check in this instance presupposes that there would not naturally be a 9 in that position. Of course, even this has no value if the 9 (in this instance) is not included in the 48 defined in the FOR statement at 20. What to do? If the array is being loaded from the keyboard, it's as simple as counting the array lines and storing that count into a variable which will be substituted for the 48 in the FOR statement. And, if the data is being read from tape, the tape can have a header record containing the row count—or checking a sentinel line located on the tape itself.

DATA ON CASSETTE TAPE

You will recall that earlier in the chapter CLOAD and CSAVE were discussed for loading and saving the program on tape. When you have used DATA lines for the storage of data in your program, you *must* take the CSAVE/CLOAD approach. For data which is developed and stored in an array, however, there are further considerations, as the array is *not* stored on tape with the program. Also, data may exceed the more than 800 elements available in an array in Level I, forcing you to store data on tape.

As with the use of CSAVE and CLOAD, be very careful about the mechanical controls of the tape recorder. To record upon the tape you must ensure that you are past any leader before you begin to write on the tape, and you must also ensure that the tape recorder has both the PLAY and RECORD levers depressed. When you are to read the data from the tape, ensure that the tape is rewound and that the PLAY lever is depressed.

Recall that it was important to know how much data had been written onto the tape, and therefore how much to read back in. This can be accomplished in one of two ways:

- The array ca.1 be scanned, looking for the sentinel line, and counting the lines until the sentinel line is found. This count can then be written into the first record to be stored on tape (the header record). The count can also be placed into a FOR . . . NEXT loop into which the writing instruction or the reading instruction has been placed. (Since the approximate size and physical configuration of the array are known quantities (the size being the distance between the first item and the last sentinel), scanning is done by breaking the array into logical groups and updating the appropriate counters to address the array group by group. When the group of sentinels is found, the scan is complete.)
- The array can be written to tape, including the sentinel line—or, assuming that the count is known, only the array needs to be written, recalling precisely the same amount of data when the data is read back into the computer.

The terms "read" and "write," have been used, for that is the function to be performed. However, the computer statements in BASIC are not "read" and "write." Instead, they are forms of other instructions, INPUT and PRINT. They differ only by the addition of a # (pound sign) following the command—PRINT # and INPUT #.

Since there are mechanical things which must be done before you write on the tape and read from it, it is generally good practice to prompt all actions with messages on the screen. In addition, it's good practice to ensure that that which is written to tape is the same as that which is read from it. In other words, don't read part of an array—read it all, and then deal with its contents. Further, recognizing the limitation of slightly more than 800 elements in an array, if there are considerably more items to be placed on tape, group them so that they can be moved about in array-sized groups. Finally, it should be mentioned that to the TRS-80 computer, the commands differ from their keyboard/display counterparts only by the *director,* which is the pound sign (#). In all other aspects, they are the same.

Recall the discussion of multiple inputs to the INPUT statement. They required that the inputs (*operands*) were separated by commas when INPUT from the keyboard. That is also true of INPUT #. For this reason, they must be written onto the tape at the time you perform the PRINT #, like this:

```
10 X = 1:Y = 2:Z = 3
20 PRINT # X;",";Y;",";Z
```

Study line 20 closely. Note that the operands of the PRINT # instruction *are themselves* separated by semicolons. But, note also that a comma is written onto the tape, in the appropriate place in the same manner as the variables X, Y, and Z.

At this point, a decision must be made as to how data will be written upon the tape. It is possible to write complete "records" or merely some consecutive data elements. There is a radical difference as to how the logic is to be structured. For instance, knowing that the matrix has a length of 48 elements, the routine can be written like this:

```
10 FOR N = 1 TO 48
20     PRINT # A(N)
30 NEXT N
```

This routine, which should be preceded by a prompt requesting the operator to depress the appropriate keys, will write 48 consecutive blocks onto tape. That's perfectly acceptable, provided it is known what is being written and, in turn, the INPUT # is structured in the same manner. If, on the other hand, it is desired to write 3 blocks or 16 elements each, there are some adjustments to be made.

This is how the routine to write 3 blocks of 16 elements upon tape would look:

```
10 H = 1
20 FOR N = 1 TO 3
30     PRINT # A(H);",";A(H+1);",";A(H+2);",";A(H+3);",";A(H+4);
       ",";A(H+5);",";A(H+6);",";A(H+7);",";A(H+8);",";A(H+9);
       ",";A(H+10);",";A(+11);",";A(H+12);",";A(H+13);",";
       A(H+14);",";A(H+15)
40 H = H + 16
50 NEXT N
```

As can be seen, while it's quite possible, it's much more involved and difficult. In Level I there is no ability to edit a statement—it must be completely retyped if there is an error. The length of the line shown is perfectly valid, as the maximum length of an instruction is 255 characters. They will overflow onto subsequent lines on the screen, but will work. Give careful consideration to other approaches to the problem, however, before you try that format.

Returning the tape to the beginning, the data can be INPUT # in a similar manner, except that it is not necessary to imbed the commas between operands (recall that they were written directly onto the tape). Here is the first example for INPUT #—in the data:

```
60 FOR N = 1 TO 48
70     INPUT # A(N)
80 NEXT N
```

Or the more complicated method:

```
60 H = 1
70 FOR N = 1 TO 3
80     INPUT # A(H),A(H+1),A(H=2),A(H+3),A(H+4),A(H+5),A(H+6)
       A(H+7),A(H+8),A(H+9),A(H+10),A(H+11),A(H+12),
       A(H+13),A(H+14),A(H+15)
90 H = H + 16
100 NEXT N
```

Important point: the data *must* be read from the tape in *precisely* the same manner as it was written onto the tape.

And there you have it. All that remains to be discussed are the graphics package and some of the more sophisticated mathematical functions and subroutines. That discussion will await a later chapter. In this chapter enough information has been presented to permit you to use the BASIC language in the performance of programming applications for the TRS-80. In the next chapter, these principles will be put to work.

3
Developing and Manipulating Data

The premise of this book, and indeed of the TRS-80 itself, is that the computer can perform useful work for you and your family, and that it will therefore be useful in the home. Hopefully, by the time you have completed this book, your imagination will have been stimulated toward developing useful and perhaps cost-effective applications for the use of your home computer. These could include a host of business-type applications, educational applications, home management applications, and even some entertainment. In later chapters, some financially oriented applications will also be developed. These are not complex, but they are extensive. Therefore, in this chapter, we will stick to the simpler applications—which can be developed in pieces, and which you'll be able to put to use. In the process, some useful techniques will be developed.

The predominant problem with Level I is that it is restricted to numeric data alone and cannot store alphabetic data in the array (table). In fairness to Radio Shack, it should be pointed out that the TRS-80 is not intended to be a replacement for a more sophisticated computer. Indeed, the microcomputer itself, as an entity, is intended largely for "number crunching." Only because it is recognized that the computer *must* handle *some* alphabetic data. A-String (A$) and B-String (B$) are included. This is sufficient *if* a little advance planning is done and if care is taken to be fully aware of the action taken.

THE BINARY SEARCH

One of the better techniques in common use in computer applications is the "binary search." Binary means "two" and the principle of the binary search assumes:

1. That whatever you're searching for is in some predetermined sequence, generally ascending.

2. That the field of search can be narrowed merely by using the "rule of halves," that is, dividing the object of the search into equal parts, determining the relationship of the item you're searching for to the midpoint, selecting the proper half, dividing it into two equal parts, and then continuing. In other words, a computerized 20 questions-type game.

That's how it works—now what is it? Suppose there is a very long list, such as a list of names, perhaps a thousand names long. If the list were in just any random sequence, it would be very difficult to find the name of a person, say John Smith. What you would do is to arrange the list in alphabetical sequence, beginning with A and ascending through the alphabet to Z. Now, when you wish to search the list for Smith, your eyes fall to the S's, you look at them one by one until you find Smith, and then, you look for John. Well, the computer works the same way, except that it cannot "see" the S's. So what happens is that the list must be put into alphabetic sequence and then divided right down the middle, between M and N. Now the name Smith is checked against N and found to be larger. It is known that Smith (S) falls somewhere between N and Z. The "bottom half" of the alphabet (A to M) is not searched. The next step is to split the upper half of the alphabet. The midpoint is now T. S (Smith) is smaller than T, so the upper quarter of the alphabet is no longer searched. It is known then that S falls somewhere between N and T. And so on.

While the development of games will be discussed in a later chapter, there is one game which can be developed at this point to expand upon the principle discussed above. It is known by the general title of "GUESS THE NUMBER." It goes like this:

```
10 CLS
20 INPUT "PICK A NUMBER FROM 1 TO 100";A
```

Of course, you *can* get "cute" and select 47.6593 and cause the program all sorts of troubles (unless you are prepared to deal with decimals). But that sort of thing can either be prevented (you'll learn how later) by using only the whole number part of the number, or it can be handled by including the appropriate logic. To illustrate the principles, we'll assume that you'll enter a whole number. Whatever number you have entered can now be found in the variable A.

If you enter the number, of course, the computer will "know" the number. Why pick a number if you can't protect it from the computer? True.

So, let's redo that statement, omitting the semicolon and the numeric variable A. It should look like this:

```
20 PRINT "PICK A NUMBER FROM 1 TO 100"
30 PRINT "PRESS ENTER WHEN YOU HAVE DECIDED ON THE NUMBER."
40 INPUT A
```

In this manner, the computer is not asking to know the number. It now resides in your head or on a piece of paper. And the INPUT A statement answered by the **ENTER** will generate a 0 at A, an automatic function of the machine when no number has been entered.

The computer does not know the number you have in mind, of course, but it does know the range it has offered you, and the midpoint of the range is 50. That is the next offering:

```
50 B = 50:D = 100:E = 0
60 CLS
70 GOSUB 500
```

At this point, the midpoint has been established, the screen has been cleared, and the linkage to a subroutine has been established. In the subroutine, the alternatives will be displayed. The reason for using a subroutine is that it will be used over and over. Let's examine the subroutine now:

```
500 PRINT TAB(30);"1.   GREATER THAN ";B
510 PRINT
520 PRINT "IS IT:";TAB(30);"2.   EQUAL TO ";B
530 PRINT
540 PRINT TAB (30);"3.   LESS THAN ";B
550 PRINT
560 INPUT "WHICH";A
570 C = C + 1
580 RETURN
```

In the subroutine, the relationship of the number to the midpoint (B) is examined, whatever that midpoint will become.

Back to the main routine: the selection has been made in the subroutine, but it is still not known, except that it is located at A and that it should contain the values 1, 2, or 3. If it contains any other number, the process must be repeated.

```
80 ON A GOTO ____,____,____
90 GOTO 60
```

Statement 80 will contain the address for "greater than" in the first space, the address for "equal to" in the second space, and the address for "less than" in the third. Of the three, the easiest one to deal with is the middle one—the "equal to:"

```
80 ON A GOTO ____,100,____
100 PRINT "HA! HA! I GUESSED YOUR NUMBER IN ONLY "
    ;C;"TRIES."
110 END
```

Note that statement 80 has been modified. Note also that statement 570 in the subroutine records the number of times the "guess" is made. That count is then displayed in statement 100.

Since the computer now knows that it wasn't equal, it knows that by definition the number is either higher or lower than the midpoint. If the number is less than what the computer has determined, then B must be divided by two, to get to the new midpoint. In this illustration, B would then become 25. If the number is larger than what the computer has determined, then the midpoint is determined by determining where the halfway point is between 50 and 100, or 75.

Theoretically, 50 could be multiplied by 1.5 to obtain 75. But that method would not work consistently. Thus, statement 50 contains the instruction D = 100. At this point, there are two ranges from which to select—0 to 50 and 50 to 100. Thus, if the top and bottom value of each range is added together and divided by two, the new midpoint will be determined. The same principle will continue to apply, except that the ranges must be adjusted when the decision has been made.

The new subroutines will be useful. The first one will be called the "upper half" subroutine and the second one will be called the "lower half" subroutine:

```
600 REM "UPPER HALF SUBROUTINE"
610 B = (B + D)/2
```

```
620 RETURN
700 REM "LOWER HALF SUBROUTINE"
710 B = (B + E)/2
720 RETURN
```

Look back again to statement 50 and you'll see that the bottom value of the range is held in variable E. All that is required when these subroutines are used is to ensure that the variables D and E are loaded with the proper range values at the time that one of these subroutines is called.

Back to statement 80:

```
80 ON A GOTO 120,100,_____
```

Beginning at statement 120, the "greater than" option is detailed. In the "greater than" situation, the new range is 50 to 100. Therefore, the first thing to do is to establish that range. The values cannot be arbitrarily "plugged" into those variables, however. Recall that the program is being developed to make the routines useful no matter what the numbers are. What is known, however, is that there is a new midpoint (B), by the logic expressed in statement 610. Before the old value of B is destroyed, however, the variable used for the bottom of the range (E) should be established with the value of variable B:

```
120 E = B
```

Now to determine the new midpoint:

```
130 GOSUB 600
```

Variable D does not need to be adjusted, as it is still the valid upper limit (in the upper half). At this point, the options are presented again, and the process will continue until the field is narrowed down:

```
140 GOTO 60
```

Back to statement 80:

```
80 ON A GOTO 120,100,150
```

At 150 the "less than" side of the question is treated. Now the range is from 0 to 50, although those values cannot be used directly, as explained before. The upper limit must be adjusted. The lower limit remains unchanged:

```
150 D = B
```

Now to find a new midpoint:

```
160 GOSUB 700
170 GOTO 60
```

That's just about all there is to it. There is one minor problem. When the ranges are such that the midpoint develops a decimal (e.g., half of 25 is 12.5), a specific position cannot be determined, and therefore, a number cannot be selected from the list. To ensure that that does not happen, a new instruction is required—the INTeger instruction. The INTeger instruction selects only the whole number portion of a number, disregarding the decimal fraction. It may not be absolutely precise, but it suits our purposes. Two instructions are required:

```
615 B = INT(B)
715 B = INT(B)
```

Here is the whole program as it has been completed:

```
10 CLS
20 PRINT "PICK A NUMBER FROM 1 TO 100"
30 PRINT "PRESS ENTER WHEN YOU HAVE DECIDED ON THE NUMBER."
40 INPUT A
50 B = 50:D = 100:E = 0
60 CLS
70 GOSUB 500
80 ON A GOTO 120,100,150
90 GOTO 60
100 PRINT "HA! HA! I GUESSED YOUR NUMBER IN ONLY ";C;"TRIES"
110 END
120 E = B
130 GOSUB 600
140 GOTO 60
150 D = B
```

```
150 GOSUB 700
170 GOTO 60
500 PRINT TAB(30);"1.  GREATER THAN ";B
510 PRINT
520 PRINT "IS IT:";TAB(30);"2.  EQUAL TO ";B
530 PRINT
540 PRINT TAB(30);"3.  LESS THAN ";B
550 PRINT
560 INPUT "WHICH";A
570 C = C + 1
580 RETURN
600 REM "UPPER HALF SUBROUTINE"
610 B = (B + D)/2
615 B = INT(B)
620 RETURN
700 REM "LOWER HALF SUBROUTINE"
710 B = (B + E)/2
715 B = INT (B)
720 RETURN
```

Note: do not be concerned about missing statement numbers. It still works. In fact, you will find that there will be instructions you will include for testing and you will remove those when you have determined that your program works.

Because of the division/integer principles used in this example, the maximum number which can be used is 99. Change statement 50 to modify the D value to 101 and it will work to 100.

Spend some time tracing the program through and using data which you supply. You'll find that it works not only for the upper half and the lower half, but also for the upper quarter of the lower half and the lower quarter of the upper half. The process continues until the range is extremely narrow. Once that is accomplished, finding the number that you "dreamed up" in the first place is not difficult. There are more sophisticated routines for "guessing the number," but this kind of example illustrates the principle the author had in mind and starts you into the kind of thinking required to write BASIC to determine the number dynamically. In other words, *you* might be able to figure from 1 to 100, but suppose that the selected number range had been from 10,000 to 10,000,000. That might be a little more difficult.

Taking the process a step further, this technique might be applied to searching a table for the presence of a number. Up to this point, an absolute match has been sought. To search a number table, we must remember that the number may or may not be on the table. We must make that determination.

The first step is to build the table. The table can be built from a data file stores on cassette tape, but even that would have to be built first. In order to illustrate the principle, we'll do a little simple construction of a table. Assume that the table consists of three data elements—a stock number (in the range of 1 to 1000), a description (which will be made uniform in each entry, for illustrative purposes), and a quantity-on-hand, in the range of 1 to 10,000. That is the range. The numbers will be generated randomly with the TRS-80's random number generator instruction. Format of the instruction is: $X = RND(N)$.

To see how the random number function works, key the following and RUN:

```
10 CLS
20 X = RND(1000)
30 PRINT X
40 FOR N = 1 TO 500:NEXT N
50 GOTO 20
```

RUN it long enough for it to be demonstrated that random numbers do indeed appear on the screen. The maximum value which can be "randomized" is 32767.

In this example, 100 table entries will be built with randomly selected stock numbers (1 to 1000), standard descriptions, and randomly selected quantities-on-hand (1 to 10,000). But there is a little problem. In Level I an array cannot be built containing an alphabetic variable—remember? The array is for the storage of numbers alone. To get around this problem, a randomly generated number will be generated in the range of 1 to 10, and ten description identifiers will be stored in DATA lines. Once that number has been generated, it will be inserted in a FOR . . . NEXT loop to control the number of READs in the DATA lines. Then the latter will be substituted (on the screen) for the former:

Review the following before proceeding:

```
10 FOR N = 1 TO 300 STEP 3
20      A(N) = RND(1000)
30      A(N+1) = RND(10)
40      A(N+2) = RND(10000)
50 NEXT N
60 CLS:C = 0
70 FOR N = 1 TO 300 STEP 3:C = C + 1
80      FOR X = 1 TO A(N+1)
90            READ A$
100     NEXT X
110     RESTORE
120     PRINT A(N),A$,A(N+2),C
130     FOR Z = 1 TO 500:NEXT Z
140 NEXT N
150 CLS
160 PRINT "END OF TABLE CONSTRUCT"
170 END
180 DATA "DESCRIPTION 1","DESCRIPTION 2","DESCRIPTION 3"
190 DATA "DESCRIPTION 4","DESCRIPTION 5","DESCRIPTION 6"
200 DATA "DESCRIPTION 7","DESCRIPTION 8","DESCRIPTION 9"
210 DATA "DESCRIPTION 10"
```

Again, it should be borne in mind that an arbitrary table with random values and artificial titles has been developed. From the above coding, it can be seen that the array is 100 units of 3 elements each. Thus, the FOR . . . NEXT loop is structured in 300 total elements, and each loop of N begins 3 array positions greater than the last. Statements 10 to 50 are the statements which build the table. Statement 20 randomly generates the stock number in the range of 1 to 1000. Statement 30 generates, randomly, the number of the description which will be appended to the displayed line.

Statements 180 to 210 contain descriptions sufficient to cover any number generated in statement 30. Statement 40 randomly generates the quantity-on-hand.

Statement 6Ø clears the screen and sets variable C to Ø. Variable C is used to count the number of table lines, and is displayed with the table lines in Statement 12Ø.

Once the table has been built, the statements from 8Ø to 21Ø are used to display it on the screen. It is constructed to locate all 300 elements in the same manner as the table was loaded.

Statements 8Ø to 1ØØ extract the randomly numbered description location number, which is then used in a controlled READ loop to locate the description (A$). Statement 11Ø restores the DATA pointer for the next time that it is needed.

At Statement 12Ø each element of the table is displayed, including the description selected on the basis of the randomly numbered description location number.

Statement 13Ø is merely a timer loop, to slow down the display to allow you to observe its function. When you are assured that it works, you may remove Statement 13Ø.

The rest should be self-explanatory, by this time. At this point, the really interesting things begin to happen. Recall that the premise for this discus-

Figure 7   Table Construct

sion was that a binary search could be done on the table to determine the presence or absence of a stock number. As it is presently constructed, however, it cannot do that, because the table exists in random order. In order to do a binary search, the stock numbers must be in ascending numerical sequence. This means that the table, to be useful, must be sorted.

There are many ways to perform a sort, but the easiest way is called the *exchange sort*. The exchange sort examines the array in pairs, changing their positions within the table until all elements are in the correct sequence. Array line 1 is compared to array line 2. If they are the same, the process compares array line 2 to array line 3. If they are not the same, the larger must be determined and placed, if necessary, into the second position of the pair. The process continues until no exchange needs to be made, after which the storing is complete.

Before the sort is added, the following instructions should be added to allow you to watch the routine as the numbers are generated; add them and RUN:

```
 7 CLS
 9 C = 0
42 C = C + 1
45 PRINT A(N),A(N+1),A(N+2),C
47 FOR Z = 1 TO 250:NEXT Z
55 FOR Z = 1 TO 500:NEXT Z
```

To include the sort, modify instruction 170 to the following:

```
170 FOR Z = 1 TO 500:NEXT Z:CLS:GOTO 300
```

And now, the sort:

```
300 V = 1:W = 4
310 FOR N = 1 TO 99
320     IF A(V) < = A(W) THEN 370
330     P = 1
340     R = A(V):S = A(V+1):T = A(V+2)
```

```
350     A(V) = A(W):A(V+1) = A(W+1):A(V+2) = A(W+2)
360     A(W) = R:A(W+1) = S:A(W+2) = T
370     V = V + 3:W = W + 3
380 NEXT N
390 IF P + 0 THEN 420
400 P = 0
410 GOTO 310
```

Here's how it works. Since the table lines are being examined in pairs, two pointers must be established, the first to the initial element of the first line and the second to the initial element of the second line. It is on this initial element that the sort is performed. That is accomplished in statement 300.

While there are 100 table lines, there are only 99 pairs, as follows:

$$1 - 2$$
$$2 - 3$$
$$3 - 4$$
$$\cdots$$
$$99 - 100$$

Thus, the control loop at statement 310 is established for 99 pairs. If that had been set at 100, the pointers would run off the end of the table, with unpredictable results.

At statement 320 the relationship of the *key field* of the first line to the *key field* of the second line is determined. A key field is that element of the array upon which sequencing is performed. If the key field of the first line is less than or equal to the key field of the second line, the lines are *already* in the proper sequence. The pointers can be updated (at statement 370) and the process continues to the next pair. If it is not, however, the lines must be exchanged. Whenever an exchange is performed, the program must be told that it has been done, because the sort will only come to an end when there are no more exchanges to be performed. That is accomplished in statement 330, by setting numeric variable P to 1. P will function as a *switch*. The position of the switch is tested after the loop is completed (statement 390).

At statements 340, 350, and 360, once it has been determined that the lines are in reverse order, it is necessary to shift the contents of the first line to a temporary storage location (in this case variables R, S, and T), move the contents of the second line to the locations, correspondingly, in the first line, and then move the items from temporary storage into the appropriate places in the second line. The pointers are then updated (at statement 370) and the process continues.

When the loop has been completed, and all table lines examined, the program checks to see if any exchanges have been made at any time during the sorting process. If no exchanges have been made, the table is now in the proper sequence, and the process can continue to the next step, statement 420. If an exchange has been made, however, the table must be reviewed again. So, the switch is returned to zero and the loop is begun again. Eventually, all table lines will be in the correct sequence, P will be 0, and the process will continue at statement 420.

The exchange sort is not the fastest type of sort, but it is very effective and very easily implemented on Level I TRS-80. Under tests, use of the sort routine found that on average between 85 to 90 passes of the table were made before the table was fully sorted. This can lead you to think that the program is not working, as the screen remains blank during the process. Thus, to ensure that it's working, and to provide useful information at the same time, instructions can be added which will display the sorting process. Statement 170 gets modified again:

```
170 FOR Z = 1 TO 500:NEXT Z:CLS:C = 0:Y = 0:GOTO 300
```

The addition of the initialization of variables C and Y are these: C will be used to count the total number of table lines accessed. N, which is part of the FOR . . . NEXT loop will be used to count the position within the table as the sorting process is done. And Y will be used to count the number of passes which have been made through the table. It should be pointed out that there is no absolute number which can be established for the number of passes through this particular table, since the numbers were generated randomly. In a more organized table, carefully established and changed only slightly, the sorting time would be diminished significantly. Insert the following instructions, RUN, and then go get a cup of coffee:

```
314 PRINT "STRING SORT","TOTAL","PER PASS","NR. PASSES"
315 PRINT
316 PRINT "ЬЬЬЬЬЬЬ",C,N,Y
344 PRINT "STRING SORT","TOTAL","PER PASS","NR. PASSES"
345 PRINT
346 PRINT "SORTING",C,N,Y
```

When it's run this time, it will look as though it's having a nervous breakdown, and it will seem that a great deal of time is required for it to finish. However, when tied to the routine which follows this discussion, you'll see that it does indeed work.

You could become easily annoyed at the amount of time that it takes. The author clocked it at more than 10 minutes. There has to be a better, shorter way. Within the constraints of what we have, the best way is to perform a *block sort*. Since the table has a range in the key field of 1—1000, 10 passes will be made through the table, extracting the numbers which lie within the first 100, then numbers in the second 100, and so on. In this manner, the number of strings which must be sorted are expanded to 10 smaller groups, which means that a low-numbered item which happens to be located at the end of the list during the random number generation would not have to work its way through the entire list to find its proper location. It would only have to work its way through its group.

The first step to obtain the block sort is:

```
305 GOSUB 1300
```

And then:

```
1300 G = 1:H = 101:K = 301
1310 FOR N = 1 TO 10
1320    FOR J = 1 TO 300 STEP 3
1330       IF (A(J) < G) + (A(J) > H) THEN 1360
1340       A(K) = A(J):A(K + 1) = A(J + 1):A(K + 2) = A(J + 2)
1350       K = K + 3
1360    NEXT J
1370    G = G + 100:H = H + 100
1380 NEXT N:K = 301
1390 FOR J = 1 TO 300 STEP 3
1400 A(J) = A(K):A(J + 1) = A(K + 1):A(J + 2) = A(K +2)
1410 K = K + 3
1420 NEXT J:CLS
1430 RETURN
```

Of course, as that is structured, there is merely a direct copy of the block-sorted table. It might be useful to use that return trip to effect some sorting. Before that is done, some display should be made on the screen to detail what is happening. Add the following instructions and make the suggested change:

```
1305 CLS:PRINT "BLOCK SORT, TABLE J TO TABLE K BY 100"
1355 GOSUB 1470
```

Change the THEN address in statement 1330 from 1360 to 1355.

```
1470 PRINT:PRINT AT 128,"LOWER","UPPER","TABLE J","TABLE K"
1480 PRINT:PRINT AT 192,G,H,J,K
1490 RETURN
```

And now, the changes for the second pass. Change statement 1380 as indicated and add the remaining instructions:

```
1380 NEXT N
1390 G = 1:H = 51:J = 1
1395 CLS:PRINT "BLOCK SORT, TABLE K TO TABLE J BY 50"
1400 FOR N = 1 TO 20
1410    FOR K = 301 TO 600 STEP 3
1420    IF (A(K) < G) + (A(K) > H) THEN 1450
1430    A(J) = A(K):A(J + 1) = A(K + 1):A(J + 2) = A(K + 2)
1440    J = J + 3
1450    GOSUB 1470:NEXT K
1460 NEXT N:RETURN
```

There is one new form of instruction located in this sequence. It's a "logical instruction"—located at 1330 and also at 1420. What the instruction does is to establish an OR situation—IF the first condition OR the second condition, then the action. The use of the parentheses is important, and the OR condition is signified by the + between the operands. One other logical operation, the AND, would be signified by an asterisk (*) in the same position.

Utilizing the block sort approach removes 80 to 90% of the sorting time. In the string sort (which follows the block sort) the author observed a minimum of 8 passes and a maximum of 13, as opposed to the 85 to 90 passes experienced in the pure exchange sort.

The following instructions are added to permit you to review the table visually before work is begun with it. Statements 420 to 500 are essentially a repeat of earlier instructions, but are inserted to allow viewing of the process:

```
420 RESTORE:C = 0:CLS
430 FOR N = 1 TO 300 STEP 3:C = C + 1
440     FOR X = 1 TO A(N+1)
450         READ A$
460     NEXT X
470 RESTORE
480 PRINT A(N),A$,A(N+2),C
490     FOR Z = 1 TO 1000:NEXT Z
500 NEXT N
```

Statement 490 has been inserted to slow the routine down to provide time to study the relationship between the elements. Once it has been determined that the routine is performing as it should, the count can either be reduced or the statement removed.

The table has been generated, reviewed, sorted, and revised. Now the table can be searched for a specific value. The same principles which were in use during the "guess the number" game should be used here. Recall that the variable B was used for the midpoint, D for the upper range value, and E for the lower range value. That will be done, but rather than just providing it with the initial values, we must develop it from the table:

```
510 B = A(151):D = A(298):E = A(1)
```

Recall that these table lines are in series of three elements. The range must be established based on the first element of the series of three. Thus, the first element of the middle line in the table is located at A(151). The first element of the table is located at A(1). And the first element of the last line is located at A(298). Important point—these are *actual* table entries. As B is developed, the chances are that B will not again be an actual table entry, except by accident (recall that the numbers were developed randomly).

The first thing to do with any large-sized table lookup is to map the table. The following is a map of the table which has been constructed:

Line	A(N)	A(N+1)	A(N+2)	Line	A(N)	A(N+1)	A(N+2)
1	1	2	3	2	4	5	6
3	7	8	9	4	10	11	12
5	13	14	15	6	16	17	18
7	19	20	21	8	22	23	24
9	25	26	27	10	28	29	30
11	31	32	33	12	34	35	36
13	37	38	39	14	40	41	42
15	43	44	45	16	46	47	48
17	49	50	51	18	52	53	54
19	55	56	57	20	58	59	60
21	61	62	63	22	64	65	66
23	67	68	69	24	70	71	72
25	73	74	75	26	76	77	78
27	79	80	81	28	82	83	84
29	85	86	87	30	88	89	90
31	91	92	93	32	94	95	96
33	97	98	99	34	100	101	102
35	103	104	105	16	106	107	108
37	109	110	111	38	112	113	114
39	115	116	117	40	118	119	120
41	121	122	123	42	124	125	126
43	127	128	129	44	130	131	132
45	133	134	135	46	136	137	138
47	139	140	141	48	142	143	144
49	145	146	147	50	148	149	150
51	151	152	153	52	154	155	156
53	157	158	159	54	160	161	162
55	163	164	165	56	166	167	168
57	169	170	171	58	172	173	174
59	175	176	177	60	178	179	180
61	181	182	183	62	184	185	186
63	187	188	189	64	190	191	192
65	193	194	195	66	196	197	198
67	199	200	201	68	202	203	204
69	205	206	207	70	208	209	210
71	211	212	213	72	214	215	216
73	217	218	219	74	220	221	222
75	223	224	225	76	226	227	228
77	229	230	231	78	232	233	234
79	235	236	237	80	238	239	240
81	241	242	243	82	244	245	246
83	247	248	249	84	250	251	252
85	253	254	255	86	256	257	258
87	259	260	261	88	262	263	264
89	265	266	267	90	268	269	270
91	271	272	273	92	274	275	276
93	277	278	279	94	280	281	282
95	283	284	285	96	286	287	288
97	289	290	291	98	292	293	294
99	295	296	297	100	298	299	300

Figure 8   Array Map

The advantage of mapping the table will become apparent shortly. The coding to handle the table binarily is easier to write than to explain, but when the table is searched binarily, versus sequentially, the number of search actions is diminished. On a table of only 100 lines, the difference in time is negligible. On larger tables, however, the technique will be beneficial. Both techniques will be presented, beginning with the sequential. The premise is that the table is already in ascending numeric sequence on the key field, Stock Number; note that statement 510 has been replaced:

SEQUENTIAL TABLE SEARCH

```
510 CLS
520 C = 0
525 INPUT "ENTER STOCK NUMBER (1 TO 1000)";A
530 A = INT(A)
540 FOR N = 1 TO 300 STEP 3
550     IF A = A(N) THEN 620
560     IF A(N) < A THEN 590
570     C = C + 1
580 NEXT N
590 CLS
600 PRINT "STOCK NUMBER"; A; "NOT ON FILE."
610 FOR Z = 1 TO 1000:NEXT Z:GOTO 510
620 CLS
630 PRINT "STOCK NUMBER","DESCRIPTION","QTY-ON-HAND","TABLE LINE"
640 PRINT
650 RESTORE
660 FOR Z = 1 TO A(N + 1)
670     READ A$
680 NEXT Z
690 PRINT A(N),A$,A(N + 2),C
700 FOR Z = 1 TO 1000:NEXT Z:GOTO 510
```

Here is the explanation:

At statement 520 the variable C, which is used to develop the line count (statement 570), for display in statement 690, is initialized.

Statements 525 and 530 seek the number from the keyboard and then strip any fraction.

Statement 540 sets up the FOR . . . NEXT loop to walk completely through the table, if necessary.

Statement 550 looks to match the console keyboard input to the table, looking for an equal. If it finds an equal, a heading is printed (statement

63Ø), the DATA lines are searched for a description which matches the code contained in the table (statements 65Ø to 68Ø), and it is presented.

If it is not equal, the program then checks to see if the point in the table where it should have been stored had it been on the table has been passed. In statement 56Ø, the table entry is compared to the keyboard input, and if the keyboard input is greater than the current table entry, it isn't there and will not be found on the table. The search is then interrupted and a message to that effect is printed. Note that the positioning of the message (in statement 6ØØ) is such that it isn't there on the table at all, and no "hit" is made, the result is the same. Had this table not been sorted and had remained in random order, this routine could still have been used, simply by removing statement 56Ø.

In both cases, a find and a no-find, a timer loop of 1ØØØ is established for the display, to give time to observe the message. The count can be increased or decreased, at statements 61Ø and 7ØØ.

BINARY TABLE SEARCH

So the search time of the two routines may be compared, both are included in the program. It will be later shown to invoke the choice of routines:

```
810 CLS
820 M = 151:B = 51:D = 101:E = 1:F = 0
825 INPUT "ENTER STOCK NUMBER (1 TO 1000)";A
830 A = INT(A)
840 IF A > A(M) THEN 960
850 IF A < A(M) THEN 1010
860 CLS
870 RESTORE
880 FOR N = 1 TO A(M+1)
890     READ A$
900 NEXT N
902 CLS
904 PRINT "STOCK NUMBER","DESCRIPTION","QTY-ON-HAND","TABLE LINE"
906 PRINT
910 PRINT A(M),A$,A(M+2),INT(B)
920 PRINT
930 FOR Z = TO 1000:NEXT Z:GOTO 810
950 REM "ABOVE MID-POINT"
960 GOSUB 1100
```

```
970 IF F = 1 GOTO 1050
980 IF D - E < 2 GOTO 1040
990 GOTO 840
1000 REM "BELOW MID-POINT"
1010 GOSUB 1200
1020 IF D - E < 2 GOTO 1040
1030 GOTO 840
1040 IF (A = A(M+3)) + (A = A(M-3)) THEN 850
1050 CLS
1060 PRINT "STOCK NUMBER";A;"NOT IN FILE"
1070 FOR Z = 1 TO 1000:NEXT Z:GOTO 810
1100 REM "UPPER LOCATOR SUBROUTINE"
1110 E = INT(B)
1120 B = B + (D - E)/2 + .5
1130 M = INT(B) * 3 + 1
1140 IF M = 301 THEN F = 1
1150 RETURN
1200 REM "LOWER LOCATOR SUBROUTINE"
1210 D = INT(B)
1220 B = B - (D - E)/2 - .5
1230 M = INT(B) * 3 + 1
1240 RETURN
```

As can be seen, this example will require some extensive explanation. If the table had been just a list of 100 values, the problem would be similar to the kind of thing encountered in the "guess the number" exercise. The table would be divided into halves, quarters, eights, etc., until the item sought was found—or no match whatsoever was found. But this table isn't a list of values, per se. It's a list of values *ordered in sets of three.* And so far as locating a value on the table, it is only the first value in the set of three values which is of interest. Thus, it becomes very important to ensure that when the table is addressed, it is that first value of the set of three which is found. The situation is further complicated by the fact that there are 100 lines of 3 elements, or 300 elements, which began at number 1 and proceed to number 300; in other words, relative to 1, not relative to 0. Thus, it must be ensured that the range is fully 100 lines.

The approach taken here is that of locating the line in the range of 1 to 100 and from that developing an element address compatible with the value of the stock number as located in A(N) in the table. Previously, the variable N had been used to control iteration (looping) and placement within the table. But under these circumstances, it's not possible to do both with the variable N. Therefore, the variable M has been substituted for the variable N when referring to a table element.

The majority of the selection logic of the binary search routine is contained in the two subroutines, at 1100 and 1200, respectively. It is worthy of note that the *first* search performed upon the table is not a function of either subroutine. Look at statement 810. Variable M, which will develop to be the location within the table of the first element of the series of three, is initially set at Line 51, first element. Its value is 151, and that can be verified by locating position 151 on the table map. At the same time, Line 51 is identified as a midpoint, by giving that value to variable B. Since the table is relative to 1, the range of the table is established as 1 (variable E) to 101 (variable D). Variable F is a flag bit which is turned on when movement is made outside the table (on the upper side only). That is turned on in statement 1140.

How the subroutines work is best explained by "walking through" each from the mid-point to the top and bottom of the range. On the left is the subroutine instruction. On the right are the results which have developed:

Upper Locator Subroutine

Instruction	What Develops
E = INT(B)	E = 51
B = B + (D - E)/2 + .5	B = 76.5
M = INT(B) * 3 + 1	M = 76 * 3 + 1 = 229

In the first iteration following the first search (assuming that this is the direction taken), the former midpoint (B) is established as the bottom of the range (E). The new midpoint (B) is developed by adding half of the difference of the range to the former midpoint, now the base (B). Had this table been four elements, and not three, the addition of the fraction would not have been necessary. But since fractions develop when dividing an odd-numbered range, the new midpoint is "rounded up" by the addition of .5 and then the integer portion is extracted. That integer portion is multiplied by 3 to determine the approximate position within the table, and then is incremented by 1 because the table is relative to 1. Had the table begun at 0, the addition of 1 would not have been necessary. The final number developed (229) can be found on the table map to be in the correct position.

Continuing:

Instruction	**What Develops**
E = B	E = 76
B = B + (D - E)/2 + .5	B = 89
M = INT(B) * 3 + 1	M = 89 * 3 + 1 = 268
E = B	E = 89
B = B + (D - E)/2 + .5	B = 94.5
M = INT(B) * 3 + 1	M = 94 * 3 + 1 = 283
E = B	E = 94
B = B * (D - E)/2 + .5	B = 98
M = INT(B) * 3 + 1	M = 98 * 3 + 1 = 295
E = B	E = 98
B = B + (D - E)/2 + .5	B = 100
M = INT(B) * 3 + 1	M = 100 * 3 + 1 = 301

Check the table map. Note that all but the last value of M correspond to a correct position within the map. The final value of M, 301, has been correctly developed, but is outside the range of the table. Thus it is rejected via the flag mechanism at statement 1140 and at statement 970. This is only necessary in the upper side, as the routine for the lower side does not drop to a value less than zero.

What about the lower side of the original midpoint? The logic is similar, except instead of rounding up with the .5, we now round down. And instead of adding the half of the difference, we now subtract it—recall that our original midpoint was 51—and also, we substitute D (upper limit of the range) for E.

Instruction	**What Develops**
D = INT(B)	D = 51
B = B - (D - E)/2 - .5	B = 25.5
M = INT(B) * 3 + 1	M = 25 * 3 + 1 = 76
D = INT(B)	D = 25
B = B - (D - E)/2 - .5	B = 12.5

```
M = INT(B) * 3 + 1                    M = 12 * 3 + 1 = 37

D = IMT(B)                            D = 12
B = B - (D - E)/2 - .5                B = 6
M = INT(B) * 3 + 1                    M = 6 * 3 + 1 = 19

D = INT(B)                            D = 6
B = B - (D - E)/2 - .5                B = 3
M = INT(B) * 3 + 1                    M = 3 * 3 + 1 + 10

D = INT(B)                            D = 3
B = B - (D - E)/2 - .5                B = 1.5
M = INT(B) * 3 + 1                    M = 1 * 3 + 1 = 4

D = INT(B)                            D = 1
B = B - (D - E)/2 - .5                B = .5
M = INT(B) * 3 + 1                    M = 0 * 3 + 1 = 1
```

And that's as far as it will go. It can never slip below 0. Of course, the actual number you will be developing will be a combination of uppers and lowers until you either find the stock number or have a "no-find." These iterations to the extremities of the table, however, prove that the routines work. In essence, this process is known as "desk checking." You can prove this by replacing the random number generator for A(N) with an incrementing counter which will give a range of stock numbers from 1 to 100. It can really be shaken down by incrementing that counter by 2, giving it a range of 2 to 200 and then trying a search on one of the numbers known not to be on the table.

As stated before, two options exist—the sequential search and the binary search. The selection process will work from the console, as follows:

```
502 CLS:PRINT "SELECT TYPE OF SEARCH":PRINT
504 PRINT "1. SEQUENTIAL":PRINT
506 PRINT "2. BINARY"
508 INPUT "WHICH";A
509 ON A GOTO 510,810:GOTO 502
```

That will do it. The following modification to the sequential search routine will permit viewing of the key numbers before the search is made—for testing purposes. Enter the following instructions:

```
511 N = 1
512 FOR L = 1 TO 5
513     FOR X = 1 TO 5
514         PRINT A(N),A(N + 3),A(N + 6),A(N + 9)
515         PRINT:N = N + 12
516     NEXT X
517         FOR Z = 1 TO 1000:NEXT Z
518     CLS
519 NEXT L
```

RUN the program, selecting first the sequential search. Note the time that it takes to return a reply. Take some notes when the key fields are displayed, as a basis for making your request. If there is not time to copy the numbers down, change the count in statement 517 to 5000.

As can be seen, it works. To change the search method to a binary search, the program must be run again. The following instructions will display the key field in the binary search routine:

```
811 N = 1
812 FOR L = 1 TO 5
813     FOR X = 1 TO 5
814         PRINT A(N),A(N + 3),A(N + 6),A(N + 9)
815         PRINT:N = N + 12
816     NEXT X
817         FOR Z = 1 TO 1000:NEXT Z
818     CLS
819 NEXT L
```

This coding is identical to that coding which appears in 511 through 519. Here is the program as it has been written:

```
7 CLS
9 C = 0
10 FOR N = 1 TO 330 STEP 3
20     A(N) = RND(1000)
```

```
30      A(N+1) = RND(1Ø)
40      A(N+2) = RND(1ØØØØ)
42      C = C + 1
45      PRINT A(N),A(N+1),A(N+2),C
47      FOR Z = 1 TO 25Ø:NEXT Z
5Ø NEXT N
55 FOR Z = 1 TO 5ØØ:NEXT Z
6Ø CLS:C = Ø
7Ø FOR N = 1 TO 3ØØ STEP 3:C = C + 1
8Ø      FOR X = 1 TO A(N+1)
9Ø          READ A$
1ØØ     NEXT X
11Ø RESTORE
12Ø PRINT A(N),A$,A(N+2),C
13Ø      FOR Z = 1 TO 5ØØ:NEXT Z
14Ø NEXT N
15Ø CLS
16Ø PRINT "END OF TABLE CONSTRUCT"
17Ø FOR Z = 1 TO 5ØØ:NEXT Z:CLS:C = Ø:Y = Ø:GOTO 3ØØ
18Ø DATA "DESCRIPTION 1","DESCRIPTION 2","DESCRIPTION 3"
19Ø DATA "DESCRIPTION 4","DESCRIPTION 5","DESCRIPTION 6"
2ØØ DATA "DESCRIPTION 7","DESCRIPTION 8","DESCRIPTION 9"
21Ø DATA "DESCRIPTION 1Ø"
3ØØ V = 1:W = 4
3Ø5 GOSUB 13ØØ
31Ø FOR N = 1 TO 99
314     PRINT "STRING SORT","TOTAL","PER PASS","NR. PASSES"
315     PRINT
316     PRINT "BBBBBBB",C,N,Y
32Ø     IF A(V) < = A(W) THEN 37Ø
33Ø     P = 1
34Ø     R = A(V):S = A(V+1):T = A(V+2)
344     PRINT "STRING SORT","TOTAL","PER PASS","NR. PASSES"
345     PRINT
346     PRINT "SORTING",C,N,Y,
```

```
350     A(V) = A(W):A(V+1) = A(W+1):A(V+2) = A(W+2)
360     A(W) = R:A(W+1) = S:A(W+2) = T
370     V = V + 3:W = W + 3
380 NEXT N
385 Y = Y + 1
390 IF P = Ø THEN 42Ø
4ØØ P = Ø
41Ø GOTO 31Ø
42Ø RESTORE"C = Ø:CLS
43Ø FOR N = 1 TO 3ØØ STEP 3:C = C + 1
44Ø     FOR X = 1 TO A(N+1)
45Ø         READ A$
46Ø     NEXT X
47Ø     RESTORE
48Ø     PRINT A(N),A$,A(N+2),C
49Ø     FOR Z = 1 TO 1ØØØ:NEXT Z
5ØØ NEXT N
5Ø2 CLS:PRINT "SELECT TYPE OF SEARCH":PRINT
5Ø4 PRINT "1. SEQUENTIAL":PRINT
5Ø6 PRINT "2. BINARY"
5Ø8 INPUT "WHICH";A
5Ø9 ON A GOTO 51Ø,81Ø:GOTO 5Ø2
51Ø CLS
511 N = 1
512 FOR L = 1 TO 5
513     FOR X = 1 TO 5
514         PRINT A(N),A(N + 3),A(N + 6),A(N + 9)
515         PRINT:N = N + 12
516     NEXT X
517         FOR Z = 1 TO 1ØØØ:NEXT Z
518     CLS
519 NEXT L
52Ø C = Ø
525 INPUT "ENTER STOCK NUMBER (1 TO 1ØØØ)";A
53Ø A = INT(A)
```

```
540 FOR N = 1 TO 300 STEP 3
550     IF A = A(N) THEN 620
560     IF A(N) < A THEN 590
570     C = C + 1
580 NEXT N
590 CLS
600 PRINT "STOCK NUMBER";A:"NOT ON FILE."
610 FOR Z = 1 TO 1000:NEXT Z:GOTO 520
620 CLS
630 PRINT "STOCK NUMBER","DESCRIPTION","QTY-ON-HAND","TABLE LINE"
640 PRINT
650 RESTORE
660 FOR Z = 1 TO A(N+1)
670     READ A$
680 NEXT Z
690 PRINT A(N),A$,A(N+2),C
700 FOR Z = 1 TO 1000:NEXT Z:GOTO 520
810 CLS
811 N = 1
812 FOR L = 1 TO 5
813     FOR X = 1 TO 5
814         PRINT A(N),A(N + 3),A(N + 6),A(N + 9)
815         PRINT:N = N + 12
816     NEXT X
817         FOR Z = 1 TO 1000:NEXT Z
818     CLS
819 NEXT L
820 M = 151:B = 51:D = 101:E = 1:F = 0
825 INPUT "ENTER STOCK NUMBER (1 TO 1000)";A
830 A = INT(A)
840 IF A > A(M) THEN 960
850 IF A < A(M) THEN 1010
860 CLS
870 RESTORE
880 FOR N = 1 TO A(M + 1)
```

```
890      READ A$
900 NEXT N
902 CLS
904 PRINT "STOCK NUMBER","DESCRIPTION","QTY-ON-HAND","TABLE LINE"
906 PRINT
910 PRINT A(M),A$,A(M+2),INT(B)
920 PRINT
930 FOR Z = 1 TO 1000:NEXT Z:GOTO 820
950 REM "ABOVE MID-POINT"
960 GOSUB 1100
970 IF F = 1 GOTO 1050
980 IF D - E < 2 GOTO 1040
990 GOTO 840
1000 REM "BELOW MID-POINT"
1010 GOSUB 1200
1020 IF D - E < 2 GOTO 1040
1030 GOTO 840
1040 IF (A = A(M+3)) + (A = A(M-3)) THEN 860
1050 CLS
1060 PRINT "STOCK NUMBER ";A;"NOT IN FILE"
1070 FOR Z = 1 TO 1000:NEXT Z:GOTO 820
1100 REM "UPPER LOCATOR SUBROUTINE"
1110 E = INT(B)
1120 B = B + (D - E)/2 + .5
1130 M = INT(B) * 3 + 1
1140 IF M = 301 THEN F = 1
1150 RETURN
1200 REM "LOWER LOCATOR SUBROUTINE"
1210 D = INT(B)
1220 B = B - (D - E)/2 - .5
1230 M = INT(B) * 3 + 1
1240 RETURN
1300 G = 1:H = 101:K = 301
1305 CLS:PRINT"BLOCK SORT, TABLE J TO TABLE K BY 100"
1310 FOR N = 1 TO 10
```

```
1320    FOR J = 1 TO 300 STEP 3
1330        IF (A(J) < G) + (A(J) > H) THEN 1355
1340        A(K) = A(J):A(K + 1) = A(J + 1):A(K + 2) = A(J + 2)
1350        K = K + 3
1355        GOSUB 1470
1360    NEXT J
1370    G = G + 100:H = H + 100
1380 NEXT N
1390 G = 1:H = 51:J = 1
1395 CLS:PRINT "BLOCK SORT, TABLE K TO TABLE J BY 50"
1400 FOR N = 1 TO 20
1410    FOR K = 301 to 500 STEP 3
1420        IF (A(K) < G) + (A(K) > H) THEN 1450
1430        A(J) = A(K):A(J + 1) = A(K + 1):A(J + 2) = A(K + 2)
1440        J = J + 3
1450        GOSUB 1470:NEXT K
1460 NEXT N:RETURN
1470 PRINT:PRINT AT 128,"LOWER","UPPER","TABLE J","TABLE K"
1480 PRINT:PRINT AT 192,G,H,J,K
1490 RETURN
```

While it may not be immediately obvious, this application is one which is most useful for an inventory situation. What possible relevance would that have to the home? With a little imagination, the routine could be used to keep track of your inventory of groceries. Try substituting the names of vegetables, meats, and canned goods for the descriptions in the data lines. The quantity should be reduced to something more reasonable, such as the range of 1 to 25. It's highly unlikely that there would be 10,000 cans of creamed corn in your kitchen cabinets.

As this program has been constructed, no particular attention has been given to the efficiency of the computer's memory usage. Coding and routines have been duplicated where they were required. There are many ways to increase the efficiency, and to decrease the operating time on the computer. One is the effective use of a subroutine.

In order to see clearly how the variables have been used throughout this program, it's useful to construct a documentation of the variables, where they were initially loaded, how they are used, the statement numbers at which they are located, and some general informative comments to give insight into the thought process involved in constructing the application, in addition to any REMark statements included in the program.

On the pages which follow is a table of one alphabetic string (A$) and of the numeric variables which have been used. Look it over. You should consider this information as you look to build efficiency into the program. The program, as written, works and has been tested by the author. But it is not the most efficiently organized table which could be built. It has been left as it was written as a means to provide discussion in the use of the variable table to assist in working out the "bugs."

VARIABLE	STATEMENT NUMBER	RANGE		CALCULATION	REFERENCE	COMMENTS
		FROM	TO			
A$	90				X	READ DESCRIPTION
	120				X	PRINT
	450				X	READ DESCRIPTION
	480				X	PRINT
	670				X	READ DESCRIPTION
	690				X	PRINT
	890				X	READ DESCRIPTION
	910				X	PRINT
A	508					INPUT - MENU
	509					SELECT VALUE
	520					STOCK NR.
	530			X		
	550					COMPARE
	560					COMPARE
	600					NO FIND MSG
	820					STOCK NR.
	830			X		
	840					COMPARE
	850					COMPARE
	1040					RANGE EXCLUSION
	1060					NO FIND MSG.
B	810				X	LOCATE TABLE POSITION
	910				X	PRINT POSITION
	1110			X		
	1120			X		
	1130			X		
	1210			X		
	1220			X		
	1230			X		
C	9					COUNTS DATA LINES
	42			X		
	60					INITIALIZE
	70			X		INCREMENT COUNTER

VARIABLE	STATEMENT NUMBER	RANGE FROM	RANGE TO	CALCULATION	REFERENCE	COMMENTS
C	170					INITIALIZE
	316					PRINT
	346					PRINT
	420					INITIALIZE
	430			X		INCREMENT COUNTER
	480					PRINT
	510					INITIALIZE
	570			X		INCREMENT COUNTER
	690					PRINT
D	810				X	LOCATE UPPER RANGE
	980				X	
	1120			X		
	1210			X		
	1220			X		
E	810				X	LOCATE LOWER RANGE
	980				X	
	1110			X		
	1120			X		
	1220			X		
F	810					INITIALIZE EOT FLAG
	970					CHECK FLAG
	1140					SET EOT FLAG
G	1300				X	INITIALIZE SORT STRING
	1330				X	RANGE CHECK
	1370					INCREMENT RANGE
	1420				X	RANGE CHECK
	1480					PRINT
H	1300				X	INITIALIZE SORT RANGE
	1330				X	RANGE CHECK
	1370					INCREMENT RANGE
	1420				X	RANGE CHECK
	1480					PRINT

VARIABLE	STATEMENT NUMBER	RANGE FROM	TO	CALCULATION	REFERENCE	COMMENTS
J	1320	1	300		X	SORT TABLE
	1330				X	
	1340				X	
	1360					LOOP
	1430				X	
	1440					INCREMENT LOCATOR
	1480					PRINT
K	1300				X	INITIALIZE 2D TABLE
	1340				X	
	1350					INCREMENT
	1410	301	600			LOOP THRU 2D TABLE
	1420				X	
	1430				X	
	1450					LOOP
	1480					PRINT
L	512	1	15			CONTROL DISPLAY
	519					LOOP
	812	1	15			CONTROL DISPLAY
	819					LOOP
M	810				X	LOCATE TABLE KEY
	840				X	
	850				X	
	880				X	
	910				X	
	1130			X		
	1140				X	CHECK RANGE
	1230				X	
N	10	1	300		X	TABLE CONTROL
	20				X	
	30				X	
	40				X	
	45				X	

	STATEMENT	RANGE		CALCULATION	REFERENCE	COMMENTS
VARIABLE	NUMBER	FROM	TO			
N	50				X	LOOP
	70	1	300		X	TABLE CONTROL
	80				X	LOCATE DESCRIPTION
	120				X	PRINT LINE
	140				X	LOOP
	310	1	99			PAIR LOOP CONTROL
	316					PRINT
	346					PRINT
	380					LOOP
	430	1	300		X	TABLE CONTROL
	480				X	
	500					LOOP
	511				X	
	514				X	
	515				X	INCREMENT
	540	1	300			TABLE CONTROL
	580					LOOP
	660				X	
	690				X	
	811				X	
	814				X	
	815				X	INCREMENT
	880	1	A(M+1)			CONTROL READ
	900					LOOP
	1310	1	10			SORT LOOP CONTROL
	1380					LOOP
	1400	1	20			SORT LOOP CONTROL
	1460					LOOP
P	330					PASS SWITCH - ON
	390					PASS SWITCH - OFF
	400					INITIALIZE
R	340					TEMP STORAGE
	360					TEMP STORAGE

VARIABLE	STATEMENT NUMBER	RANGE FROM	RANGE TO	CALCULATION	REFERENCE	COMMENTS
S	340					TEMP STORAGE
	360					TEMP STORAGE
T	340					TEMP STORAGE
	360					TEMP STORAGE
V	300				X	INITIALIZE PAIR
	320				X	
	340				X	
	350				X	
	370				X	INCREMENT
W	300				X	INITIALIZE PAIR
	320				X	
	350				X	
	360				X	
	370				X	INCREMENT
X	80	1	A(N+1)			LOCATE DESCRIPTION
	100					LOOP
	440	1	A(N+1)			LOCATE DESCRIPTION
	460					LOOP
	513	1	5			CONTROL DISPLAY
	516					LOOP
	813	1	5			CONTROL DISPLAY
	816					LOOP
Y	170					INITIALIZE
	316					PRINT-PASS COUNT
	346					PRINT-PASS COUNT
	385					INCREMENT
Z	47	1	250			TIMER
	55	1	500			TIMER
	130	1	500			TIMER
	170	1	500			TIMER
	490	1	1000			TIMER
	517	1	1000			TIMER

VARIABLE	STATEMENT NUMBER	RANGE FROM	RANGE TO	CALCULATION	REFERENCE	COMMENTS
Z	610	1	1000			TIMER
	660	1	A(N+1)			READ LOOP CONTROL
	680					LOOP
	700	1	1000			TIMER
	817	1	1000			TIMER
	930	1	1000			TIMER
	1070	1	1000			TIMER

When writing programs "on the run" the greatest mistake that can be made in the use of variables is to use more than are needed. Examine the table entries for variables F, L, P, R, S, T, and Y. With a little care, fewer than half that amount could have been used. When variables are used, and how they are used, are functions of the relationship of one variable to another. In the program, the variables indicated are used largely in many different areas of the program, in such a way that they cannot be confused with another variable. The same could be said for the two pairs, D and E, and G and H. In essence, these variables perform similar functions, so one pair could have been used for both functions. Examine statements 660 and 880. Note the use of variable X and variable Z. Since there is no conflict in their use, one could have been used in both places.

Another reason for building the variable table is to determine where subroutines can be used. Look at variable Z. The majority of the statements which use variable Z are oriented toward timing functions. While it is true that each occupies only one statement where it is used, there is still benefit in using a subroutine. Using the variable table, you'll become conscious of how many timing loops have been built into the program. In this program, 11 FOR . . . NEXT loops are modified. In a subroutine, only one modification would be required. With the exception of variable Z at statement 47, where 250 was arbitrarily assigned, the remaining timing loop counters are a function of the number of times the value 500 is used. The count could be standardized throughout the program, or the increments of time could be obtained by developing the appropriate number of subroutine calls (two GOSUBs of 500 each would produce 1000, if desirable). The time subroutine is largely a display-oriented concern—it has been entered to delay a display so it can be seen by the naked eye, a requirement if the program requires that data be read from the screen. The only other alternative is to bring the program to a stop, permitting resumption of activities (STOP/CONT). In Level II there is a function called INKEY$ which will permit the interruption of the timing process, but that facility is not available in Level I.

There is, of course, a valid argument for taking the other approach, that of using as many variables as possible. It helps to sort out what is being done by isolating the variable to the function in which it is located and on which it performs. In Level II, this is possible, as there are many more variables than in Level I. It's wise to try to conserve variables. The variable table is a useful item to post as the program is constructed.

One more concept should be examined. In the program just completed, the numbers which represented Stock Number, Quantity On Hand, and Description Identifier were randomly generated as a function of the RND instruction. To be really useful, however, facility should be included in the program to allow loading the table from the keyboard. Also, some facility should be included to store that table on cassette tape and to retrieve it when required. Therefore, the balance of this chapter will be devoted to the methods to:

- Build the table from the keyboard;
- Store the table onto cassette tape;
- Load the table from cassette tape;
- Make additions to, changes to, and deletions from the table; and
- Draw a listing of the entire table.

The first thing which must be done when handling any alphabetic data which is to become a logical part of any table is to establish that alphabetic data in DATA statements. Unfortunately, there is no way to do that under program control. The DATA statements must be entered as you would enter other program statements. Any item which will appear in the array must appear in numeric form. One of those items can be a relative position indicator for locating the alphabetic item in the DATA statements in a corresponding relative position. But the information must be placed in the DATA statements beforehand. If there is a number in the array for the item and that item is not in the DATA statement, the computer will either return incorrect results or will run out of DATA statements in search of the missing item. Thus, when making those entries, be particularly careful about the relative location of the data. Once done, the DATA statement will be part of the program saved on cassette tape with CSAVE and returned to memory (loaded) with CLOAD.

This is different from the data which will be loaded into or developed in the array A. When you do a CSAVE, the array is *not* stored with the program. Therefore, to save that data, it must be saved on a data cassette tape. It is possible to save both on the same cassette tape, but *always make it a habit to save the program* first. In actual practice, it's good business to save the program on one tape (and make several copies) and save the data on another tape (and also make several copies). Saving of the program is, of course, a function of CSAVE. Saving the array data, however, is a little different, as it must be done under program control. What follows is the method which can be used to save that data as many times as required. The routine will be placed in high memory, relative to the rest of the program.

It begins with an opening *menu* (a means of selecting options) which will offer the choice of routines to be performed. In actuality, this is the beginning of the program, despite the fact that it may not begin at the lowest number in the program sequence. Statement 1 has been "saved" to allow the program to GOTO the beginning—and this is the beginning. In addition to the five items previously listed, the opening menu will offer the sort. When the routine has been structured, the random number generator will be disconnected, but will be left in the program, should you wish to use it.

For purposes of this book, we'll proceed as if memory were unlimited. Compression can be worked into the program later.

Statement 2000 must be redone, with a couple of changes:

```
2000 ON A GOTO 2100,_____,_____,_____,_____,_____:GOTO 2000
```

At 2100 the building of the table will proceed. For simplicity, a table of only 10 times will be built, to minimize the amount of memory devoted to DATA statements. As previously stated, all DATA statements are read from the beginning. When a RESTORE is executed, the pointer is taken again to the top. If this program is structured *with* the sort module, there will be a slight problem, as routines must be established to bypass the 10 data items previously stored in DATA statements. It makes no difference where the DATA lines are stored in the program. In the computer's memory, all DATA statements end up together. Again, the DATA statements will contain the alphabetic description of the item, along with some indication of the relative location, as follows:

```
 1   TUNA FISH
 2   FROZEN PEAS
 3   CAKE MIX
 4   BEEF - LBS
 5   FISH - LBS
 6   DOG FOOD - CANS
 7   BREAD - LOAVES
 8   MILK - QTS
 9   CHEESE - OZS
10   SOUP - CANS
```

These translate to:

```
220 DATA "TUNA FISH","FROZEN PEAS","CAKE MIX","BEEF - LBS",
    FISH - LBS"
230 DATA "DOG FOOD - CANS","BREAD - LOAVES","MILK - QTS",
    "CHEESE - OZS"
240 DATA "SOUP - CANS"
1 GOTO 2000
2000 CLS:PRINT "SELECT THE FUNCTION YOU WISH TO PERFORM:"
2010 PRINT:PRINT TAB(5)"1.  BUILD THE TABLE"
2020 PRINT:PRINT TAB(5)"2.  STORE TABLE ON CASSETTE TAPE"
2030 PRINT:PRINT TAB(5)"3.  LOAD TABLE FROM CASSETTE TAPE"
2040 PRINT:PRINT TAB(5)"4.  TABLE MAINTENANCE AND RETRIEVAL"
2050 PRINT:PRINT TAB(5)"5.  LIST THE TABLE"
2060 PRINT:PRINT TAB(5)"6.  SORT THE TABLE"
2070 PRINT:INPUT "SELECT";A
```

Before proceeding, it should be remembered that no special efforts have been made at memory efficiency, and had such been made, there is a high probability that with the addition of the logic to perform the menu options, 4K would be easily exceeded.

The instruction which follows the menu looks like this:

```
2080 ON A GOTO _____,_____,_____,_____,_____,_____
```

Of course, the addresses are not yet known, but it is known that there are six options available. If memory size is a problem, it would be best to fractionalize the program into separate programs. Each should begin with the menu, as contained in 2000 to 2070, but the options that are not available within any given program should be disabled by entering 2000 into the appropriate positions. As the program is fractionalized, however, be very careful how the combinations are structured. Each of them must contain at least the options 2 or 3, in addition to any other function, as it will be necessary to story the data on tape in order to bring that data into another program. Unfortunately, TRS-80 (in BASIC) does not have the ability to combine two BASIC programs, though routines can be obtained in TRS-80 Assembler Language to do so. The combinations which are mandatory are:

$$1 - 2$$
$$3 - 4 - 2$$
$$3 - 5$$
$$3 - 6$$

The list could be as long as desired, provided that one keeps track of the relative position of each item within the DATA statements. That relative position will be entered from the keyboard, once the execution of the program is underway.

Since more timing loops will be needed, a timer subroutine will be developed. At this point, replace statements 47, 55, 130, 170, 490, 517, 610, 700, 930, and 1070 with: GOSUB 9900. Statement 9900 must be included in every version and combination of the program to be constructed:

```
9900 FOR Z = 1 TO 500:NEXT Z:RETURN
```

Now to build the table:

TABLE BUILD ROUTINE

```
2100 CLS:PRINT "TABLE BUILD ROUTINE":PRINT
2110 INPUT "HOW MANY ITEMS WILL APPEAR ON THE TABLE";A
2115 INPUT "HOW MANY UNIQUE DESCRIPTIONS HAVE YOU INCLUDED";P
2120 Q = INT(A * 1.2)
2130 J = 1:K = J + (A * 3) + 3
2140 PRINT:PRINT "SPACE HAS BEEN RESERVED FOR ";Q;"ITEMS"
2150 PRINT:PRINT "YOU WILL BE ADVISED OF REMAINING SPACE"
2160 PRINT:INPUT "PRESS ENTER WHEN YOU ARE PREPARED TO PROCEED";A
```

An explanation for the coding so far: At statement 2110 you are requested to tell the program how many items you'll be entering to the table—line items, that is. The program is structured to assume that you cannot count, however, in that the figure you give it is increased by 20% in statement 2120, and to ensure that you haven't slipped it a "mickey," only the integer portion is allowed. At statement 2115, you are asked to tell the program how many. The value developed at Q is used not only to define the table requirements, but also to structure the second table which will be used in the sort. That is done at 2130. Also at 2130 each table has been augmented by three additional elements, not available to you, which will hold an end-of-table sentinel—more on that later. At statement 2115, you are asked to tell the program how many DATA line items you have included in the program. If you're unsure, do a LIST on statement 2010 and count them. This is important, as that count will be used to verify that a corresponding DATA line item has been included for the item.

```
2165 L = 1
2170 CLS:PRINT "TABLE LINE";L
2180 RESTORE
2190 INPUT "ENTER RELATIVE DESCRIPTION INDICATOR NUMBER";A:PRINT
2200 IF A > P GOTO 2370
2210 INPUT "ENTER QUANTITY ON HAND";B:PRINT
2220 IF B > 100 GOTO 2390
2230 FOR N = 1 TO 10 + A
2240     READ A$
2250 ,NEXT N
2260 PRINT "ENTRY ACCEPTABLE":PRINT
2270 PRINT "STOCK NR.","DESCRIPTION","QTY-ON-HAND":PRINT
2280 PRINT L,A$,B
2290 PRINT:INPUT "IS IT CORRECT (Y/N)";B$
2300 IF B$ = "Y" THEN 2330
2310 PRINT:PRINT "TRANSACTION REJECTED - RE-ENTER"
2320 GOSUB 9900:GOTO 2170
2330 PRINT:PRINT "TRANSACTION ACCEPTED"
2340 A(J) = L:A(J + 1) = A:A(J + 2) = B
2350 J = J + 3
2360 GOSUB 9900:GOTO 2410
2370 PRINT:PRINT "INVALID DESCRIPTION - RE-DO"
2380 GOSUB 9900:PRINT:GOTO 2190
2390 PRINT:PRINT "INVALID QUANTITY - RE-DO"
2400 GOSUB 9900:PRINT:GOTO 2210
2410 PRINT:INPUT "WAS THAT THE LAST ITEM (Y/N)";B$
2420 IF B$ = "Y" THEN 2470
2430 Q = Q - 1
2440 IF Q = 0 THEN 2490
2450 PRINT:PRINT "NUMBER OF AVAILABLE TABLE LINES - ";Q:L = L + 1
2460 GOSUB 9900:GOTO 2170
2470 PRINT:PRINT "TABLE TERMINATED"
2480 A(J) = 999:A(J + 1) = 999:A(J + 2) = 999:GOSUB 9900:GOTO 2000
2490 PRINT:PRINT "OUT OF TABLE ROOM":GOTO 2470
```

At statement 2165, the line count is initialized. As this routine has been constructed, the table lines (Stock Number) have been assigned sequentially. If you have a need to have something other than a sequential number assigned to the table items, you will need to add a prompt and provide L via the INPUT route. Should you decide to do that, the prompt would have to be added at 2185. Statement 2165 will have to be removed, and the incrementation of L at statement 2450 will have to be removed.

At statement 2200 the input number is protected against the accidental inclusion of a number which will not match the DATA statements. If you do enter such a number, the entry is rejected and the prompt is repeated. At statement 2220 the quantity is checked against a maximum value of 100, a figure which was considered to be a reasonable upper extremity. If a higher number is required, statement 2220 should be altered.

Statement 2230 controls the READ of the 10 data items which comprise the original DATA lines in the system. If those have been removed, the number 10 can be removed from statement 2230.

As statements 2260 through 2290 the entry you have made is presented for your visual review prior to releasing it for inclusion in the table. If you reject the transaction, the process begins again. If you accept it, the transaction is loaded to the table at 2340.

The handling of descriptions which are invalid and quantities which exceed the number 100 are detailed in statements 2370—2400.

After each item you are asked if you wish to terminate the table load. If you do, or if you run out of the allocated table room, the table is terminated and the end-of-table sentinels are loaded into the space which is not available to you. The reason for the sentinels will become apparent in the routine which loads the table from cassette tape.

That's all there is to the Table Build Routine. The next is the routine for storing the table on cassette tape. Back to 2080:

```
2080 ON A GOTO 2100,2500,_____,_____,_____,_____
2500 CLS:PRINT "STORE TABLE ON CASSETTE TAPE ROUTINE":PRINT
2510 PRINT "INSURE THAT TAPE IS CONNECTED, POSITIONED, AND"
2520 PRINT "THAT THE PLAY AND RECORD LEVERS ARE DEPRESSED"
2530 PRINT:INPUT "PRESS ENTER WHEN READY TO PROCEED";A
2540 J = 1:CLS
2550 RESTORE
2560 FOR N = 1 TO A(J + 1) + 10
2570      READ A$
2580 NEXT N
2590 PRINT A(J),A$,A(J + 2):PRINT:GOSUB 9900
```

```
2600 PRINT # A(J);",";A(J + 1);",";A(J + 2)
2610 IF (A(J) = 999) * (A(J + 1) = 999) * (A(J) + 2) = 999) THEN 2630
2620 J = J + 3:GOTO 2550
2630 PRINT:PRINT "END OF STORE TABLE ON CASSETTE TAPE ROUTINE"
2640 PRINT:PRINT "IF YOU WISH TO RUN THE ROUTINE AGAIN,"
2650 PRINT:PRINT "MERELY REPEAT MENU SELECTION."
2660 PRINT:PRINT "TAPE MUST BE MANUALLY REWOUND BEFORE"
2670 PRINT:PRINT "IT CAN BE USED AS INPUT."
2680 GOSUB 9900:GOTO 2000
```

This routine should be reasonably straightforward. In statement 2560 the program accounts for the 10 extra DATA lines, as before, and reads forward to the DATA item which is indicated by the relative position indicator from the table. In statement 2590, the table item (with description) is displayed for verification that the routine is working. The table is written onto cassette tape at statement 2600, after which the table is checked to see if the sentinel record has been transferred. This is the AND condition in statement 2610. The rest of the routine should be self-explanatory.

Back to 2080:

```
2080 ON A GOTO 2100,2500,2700,_____,_____,_____
```

LOAD TABLE FROM CASSETTE TAPE ROUTINE

There is data out on cassette tape. That is known, for the routine to put it there was just completed, and the data is in the format required when the data is to be returned. In this routine, the data will be brought into memory for storage in the array. The routine is not complicated. In preparation for the MAINTENANCE and SORT routines, the span variables, J and K, must be set in this routine.

This routine will be merely a repetitive INPUT process, looking for the sentinel line, and displaying the data as it is accepted:

```
2700 CLS:PRINT "LOAD TABLE FROM CASSETTE ROUTINE":PRINT
2710 PRINT "INSURE THAT TAPE IS CONNECTED, POSITIONED, AND"
2720 PRINT "THAT THE PLAY LEVER ONLY IS DEPRESSED"
2730 PRINT:INPUT "PRESS ENTER WHEN READY TO PROCEED";A
2740 J = 1:CLS
2750 RESTORE
```

```
2760 INPUT # A(J),A(J + 1),A(J + 2)
2770 FOR N = 1 TO A(J + 1) + 10
2780    READ A$
2790 NEXT N
2800 PRINT A(J),A$,A(J+2):GOSUB 9900
2810 IF (A(J) = 999) * (A(J + 1) = 999) = 999) * (A(J + 2) = 999)
     THEN 2830
2820 J = J + 3:GOTO 2750
2830 PRINT:PRINT "END OF LOAD TABLE FROM CASSETTE TAPE ROUTINE"
2840 PRINT:INPUT "IF YOU WISH TO RUN THE ROUTINE AGAIN,"
2850 PRINT:PRINT "MERELY REPEAT MENU SELECTION."
2860 PRINT:PRINT "TAPE MUST BE MANUALLY REWOUND BEFORE"
2870 PRINT:PRINT "IT CAN BE USED AS INPUT."
2880 GOSUB 9900:GOTO 2000
```

That's the routine. If you compare them closely, you'll see that this routine is very much like the sequence of instructions which begin at statement 2500. In fact, about the only significant difference is the substitution of INPUT # for PRINT #. You will notice, however, that the arrangement of the search for A$ is different in this routine from the last.

TABLE MAINTENANCE AND RETRIEVAL ROUTINE

With the exception of the SORT, this routine is the most involved. The reason for this is that the routines required to search the table for an argument will be entered via the keyboard. For the sake of illustration, the search argument will be limited to the key field only—the Stock Nr. It is possible, however, to structure a variety of criteria for such an inquiry to the table. Among these are:

Inside range check (between parameters)
Outside range check (outside parameters)
First occurrence; last occurrence
AND conditions (this AND that)
OR conditions (this OR that)
Compound AND/OR conditions

Also to be included in this routine is the ability to call out a given table entry, make modifications to any element, or delete the entire entry. Further, there must be the facility to add an item to the table. Since there are many options offered, a series of screens containing menu selections must be presented.

Again, the process begins with 2080:

```
2080 ON A GOTO 2100,2500,2700,2900,___,_____
```

Concentrating first on the retrieval aspect, the initial menu should be presented as the way in:

```
2900 CLS:PRINT "TABLE MAINTENANCE AND RETRIEVAL ROUTINE"
2910 PRINT:PRINT "SELECT THE OPTION YOU WISH:"
2920 PRINT:PRINT "ƄƄƄƄƄ1.  RETRIEVAL"
2930 PRINT:PRINT "ƄƄƄƄƄ2.  MAINTENANCE"
2940 PRINT:INPUT "WHICH";A
2950 ON A GOTO 2960,_____:GOTO 2900
```

Statement 2950 cannot be completed until the maintenance portion of the routine is begun. There is, however, a monumental problem—it is not known how many data lines there will be. Therefore, there is no way to display the actual descriptions without running into other memory and receiving an error message. So, a sentinel must be added at the end of the DATA lines. Enter the following:

```
299 DATA "ZZZZZZZZZZ","ZZZZZZZZZZ"
```

Note that there are two strings of precisely 10 Z's. They will be used to compare or detect the end of the DATA lines (see statement 3070):

```
2960 CLS:PRINT "RETRIEVAL ROUTINE"
2970 PRINT:PRINT "ƄƄƄƄƄ1.  DISPLAY DESCRIPTIONS"
2980 PRINT:PRINT "ƄƄƄƄƄ2.  RETRIEVE TABLE ITEM"
2990 PRINT:INPUT "WHICH";A
3000 ON A GOTO 3005,_____:GOTO 2960
```

Again, statement 3000 cannot be completed until the retrieval portion is begun. The first thing to be done is to display the descriptions with a pause to take any notes:

```
3005 RESTORE
3010 FOR N = 1 TO 10
3020     READ A$
3030 NEXT N:CLS:B = 1:C = 2
3040 FOR N = 1 TO 5
3050     READ A$,B$
```

```
3060      PRINT B,A$,C,B$:PRINT
3070      IF (A$ = "ZZZZZZZZZZ") + (B$ = "ZZZZZZZZZZ") THEN 3120
3080      B = B + 1:C = C + 1
3090      PRINT:INPUT "PRESS ENTER TO CONTINUE";A
3100 NEXT N
3110 CLS:GOTO 3040
3120 PRINT:INPUT "DO YOU WISH MAINTENANCE AND RETRIEVAL MENU
     (Y/N)";A$
3130 IF A$ = "Y" THEN 2900
3140 GOTO 2000
```

That concludes the display of the descriptions and of their locations with-in the DATA lines. Note that after the first 10 DATA lines are bypassed, as before, the reading of the DATA lines is done in pairs, utilizing variables B and C to indicate the location of each pair. Because the reading is done in pairs and because an even-numbered set of DATA statements cannot be guaranteed, the two sets of Z's will be encountered—one or the other, or both—in the logical operation at 3070 (the OR option). The FOR . . . NEXT loop between 3040 and 3100 is structured to present the descriptions 10 at a time, and requiring manual entry at 3090 to continue to the next "page." The process continues in this manner until the "Z" sentinels are found, after which the option is given to return either to the MAINTE-NANCE/RETRIEVAL menu or back to the beginning.

RETRIEVAL

Time to complete statement 3000:

```
3000 ON A GOTO 3005,3200:GOTO 2960
```

In the retrieval, the opportunity to select only upon the key field, Stock Number, is presented. The rationale for this is that the number for which the search is conducted is known and the only interest is to know the quantity on hand. Here's how it proceeds:

```
3200 CLS:PRINT "RETRIEVAL ROUTINE"
3210 PRINT:PRINT "THIS ROUTINE ASSUMES THAT THERE IS"
3220 PRINT:PRINT "A VALID TABLE LOADED INTO MEMORY."
3230 PRINT:INPUT "HAS A TABLE BEEN LOADED (Y/N)";A$
3240 IF A$ < > "Y" GOTO 2000
```

```
3250 RESTORE:F = 0
3260 FOR N = 1 TO 10:READ A$:NEXT N
3270 CLS:INPUT "ENTER STOCK NUMBER";A
3280 A = INT(A)
3290 GOSUB 3420
3300 IF F = 0 GOTO 3350
3310 PRINT:PRINT "STOCK NR. ";A;"NOT IN TABLE":F = 0
3320 PRINT:INPUT "WAS THAT THE LAST RETRIEVAL (Y/N)";A$
3330 IF A$ = "Y" THEN 2000
3340 GOTO 3250
3350 FOR N = 1 TO A(J + 1)
3360     READ A$
3370 NEXT N
3380 PRINT:PRINT "STOCK NR.","DESCRIPTION","CODE","QTY-ON-HAND"
3390 PRINT:PRINT A(J + 1),A$,A(J + 2),A(J + 3)
3400 GOSUB 9900:GOTO 3320
3410 REM "TABLE SCAN ROUTINE"
3420 J = 1
3430 IF A(J) = A THEN F = 0
3440 IF (A(J) = 999) * (A(J + 1) = 999) * (A(J) + 2) = 999)
     THEN F = 1
3450 RETURN
```

This routine accepts a search argument from the keyboard and then reviews the table in search of a match. It may seem that this routine could have been written in the same manner as previous routines, but this one is slightly different, in that the search routine can be used by the maintenance routine. For this reason, it has been established as a subroutine at statements 3420 to 3450. At 3430 the match is sought. Not finding it, a check is made for the sentinels. The routine provides a return code in variable F—0 if a "hit" (the requested stock number has been found) and 1 for a "no-hit." The code is used to generate either the record which has been located or a message that the record is not on the table.

MAINTENANCE ROUTINE

Back to statement 2950:

```
2950 ON A GOTO 2960,3500:GOTO 2900
```

The routine to perform maintenance on the table can now be developed. Included in this routine will be the instructions to delete a record, replace a record, change any field within the record, or add a record. The addition of the record will be at the end of the table, but *before* the sentinels. The instructions to insert the new record anywhere in the table could now be developed, but that is not necessary at this point. The logic to ascertain if the record already exists on the table, to avoid duplication, follows:

```
3500 CLS:PRINT "TABLE MAINTENANCE ROUTINE"
3510 PRINT:PRINT "bbbbb1.  ADD A RECORD"
3520 PRINT:PRINT "bbbbb2.  CHANGE A RECORD"
3530 PRINT:PRINT "bbbbb3.  REPLACE A RECORD"
3540 PRINT:PRINT "bbbbb4.  DELETE A RECORD"
3550 ON A GOTO 3560,_____,_____,_____:GOTO 3500
3560 CLS:PRINT "ADD A RECORD"
3570 PRINT:INPUT "STOCK NR.";A:A = INT(A)
3580 PRINT:INPUT "DESCRIPTION INDICATOR";B:B = INT(B)
3590 RESTORE:FOR N = 1 TO 10:READ A$:NEXT N
3600 FOR N = 1 TO B
3610     READ A$
3620     IF A$ = "ZZZZZZZZZZ" THEN 3640
3630 NEXT N:GOTO 3670
3640 PRINT:PRINT "DESCRIPTION INDICATOR NOT IN DATA LINES"
3650 PRINT:PRINT "RE-ENTER"
3660 GOTO 3580
3670 PRINT"INPUT "QTY-ON-HAND";C:C - INT(C)
3680 IF C < 100 THEN C = 100
3690 CLS:PRINT "THIS IS THE RECORD YOU WISH TO ADD:"
3700 PRINT:PRINT A,B,A$,C
3710 PRINT:INPUT "IS IT CORRECT (Y/N)";A$
3720 IF A$ = "N" THEN 3560
3730 J = 1
3740 IF A = A(J) THEN 3780
3750 IF (A(J) = 999) * (A(J + 1) = 999) * (A(J + 2) = 999) THEN 3800
3760 J = J + 3
3770 GOTO 3740
```

```
3780 PRINT:PRINT "RECORD ALREADY EXISTS ON FILE"
3790 GOTO 3830
3800 A(J) = A:A(J + 1) = B:A(J + 2) = C
3810 A(J + 3) = 999:A(J + 4) = 999:A(J + 5) = 999
3820 GOTO 3790
3830 CLS:PRINT "PICK THE DESCRIPTION YOU WISH TO PROCEED:"
3840 PRINT:PRINT "ββββδ1.  ADD MORE RECORDS TO THE TABLE"
3850 PRINT:PRINT "βββδδ2.  RETURN TO THE MAINTENANCE ROUTINE"
3860 PRINT:PRINT "βββββ3.  RETURN TO MAINTENANCE/RETRIEVAL MENU"
3870 PRINT:PRINT "δδδδδ4.  RETURN TO INITIAL MENU"
3880 PRINT:INPUT "WHICH";A
3890 ON A GOTO 3560,3500,2900,2000:GOTO 3830
```

This routine is constructed to add a record to the end of the table. It will be out of sequence, of course, but the sort routine is available. In each case, the sentinel line is located, the new record is added to the table, and then the sentinel line is rewritten after the new record.

In developing the new record, it is constructed element by element, and then the entire new record is assembled and presented for review prior to actually updating the table. There is a comparison to determine if the record (stock number key field) is already on the table. If it is, the advice is given, and then an option is given as to which direction is to be taken next. The same is true of the description indicator code. The code DATA lines are scanned for the match—and if there is no match, advice is given.

Thus, only when the record is not a duplicate and the DATA lines have a corresponding alphabetic description, and the quantity does not exceed 100 (arbitrary) is the record written to the table.

RECORD CHANGE

The option is given to modify any table line within the table. To do so, a search must be made on the key field (stock number) of the item as it exists on the table. The fields to be modified are then selected, the change is made, is verified, and then the data is written back to the table. This differs from the replace routine which will follow, in that it does not allow change to only one field. However, the net result of performing a change to all elements is to produce a replacement record.

To get into this routine, a modification to the table maintenance routine menu selection must be made (statement 3550):

```
3550 ON A GOTO 3560,3900,_____,_____:GOTO 3500
3900 CLS:PRINT "CHANGE A RECORD"
3910 PRINT:INPUT "STOCK NR.";A:A = INT(A)
3920 RESTORE:FOR N = 1 TO 10:READ A$:NEXT N
3930 GOSUB 3420
3940 IF F = 0 THEN 3990
3950 PRINT:INPUT "STOCK NR.";A;"NOT IN TABLE":F = 0
3960 PRINT:INPUT "WAS THAT THE LAST CHANGE (Y/N)";A$
3970 IF A$ = "Y" then 2000
3980 GOTO 3900
3990 FOR N = 1 TO A(J + 1)
4000     READ A$
4010 NEXT N
4020 A = A(J):B = A(J + 1):C = A(J + 2)
4030 GOSUB 4300
4040 PRINT:PRINT "WHICH DO YOU WISH TO CHANGE:"
4050 PRINT:PRINT "ЬЬЬЬЬ1.  STOCK NR."
4060 PRINT:PRINT "ЬЬЬЬЬ2.  CODE"
4070 PRINT:PRINT "ЬЬЬЬЬ3.  QTY-ON-HAND"
4080 PRINT:PRINT "DESCRIPTION MUST BE CHANGED"
4090 PRINT "IN COMMAND MODE (DATA LINE) FOR LEVEL I."
4100 ON A GOTO 4110,4160,4260:GOTO 4040
4110 CLS:INPUT "ENTER NEW STOCK NR.";A:A = INT(A)
4120 GOSUB 4300
4130 GOTO 4230
4140 RESTORE:FOR N = 1 TO 10:READ A$:NEXT N
4150 PRINT:INPUT "ENTER NEW DESCRIPTION LOCATOR CODE";B:B = INT(B)
4160 FOR N = 1 TO B
4170     READ A$
4180     IF A$ = "ZZZZZZZZZZ" THEN 4220
4190 NEXT N
4200 GOSUB 4300
4210 GOTO 4230
4220 PRINT:PRINT "ENTER NEW QTY-ON-HAND";C:C = INT(C)
4230 PRINT:INPUT "IS NEW RECORD OK? (Y/N)";A$
```

```
4240 IF A$ <|> "Y" THEN 4040
4250 A(J) = A:A(J + 1) = B:A(J + 2) = C
4260 PRINT:INPUT "DO YOU WISH TO SORT? (Y/N);A$
4270 IF A$ = "Y" THEN 300
4280 GOTO 4340
4300 PRINT:PRINT "THE RECORD NOW LOOKS LIKE THIS:"
4310 PRINT:PRINT "STOCK NR.","DESCRIPTION","CODE","QTY-ON-HAND"
4320 PRINT:PRINT A,A$,B,C
4330 RETURN
4340 CLS:PRINT "PICK THE DIRECTION YOU WISH TO PROCEED:"
4350 PRINT:PRINT "ЬЬЬЬЬ1.  CHANGE MORE RECORDS."
4360 PRINT:PRINT "ЬЬЬЬЬ2.  RETURN TO MAINTENANCE ROUTINE"
4370 PRINT:PRINT "ЬЬЬЬЬ3.  RETURN TO MAINTENANCE/RETRIEVAL MENU"
4380 PRINT:PRINT "ЬЬЬЬЬ4.  RETURN TO INITIAL MENU"
4390 PRINT:INPUT "WHICH";A
4400 ON A GOTO 3900,3500,2900,2000
4410 GOTO 4340
```

In this routine, there is the opportunity to change any or all fields. When the change has been made, the new record is presented for approval before proceeding. About the only thing which is different from other routines is the ability to invoke the sort routine, per statement 4270.

Finally, there is presented a series of options for getting out of the routine and back to a menu which will service further needs.

REPLACE A RECORD

This routine is essentially the same as the change routine, except that the entire record must be changed before it is written back into place. The routine, as written, does not check against the table for duplications, but consider such a routine if several changes are to be made to the Stock Number fields.

```
3550 ON A GOTO 3560,3900,4450,____:GOTO 3500
4450 CLS:PRINT "REPLACE A RECORD"
4460 PRINT:INPUT "ENTER STOCK NR.";A
4470 J + 1
4480 IF A(J) = A THEN 4550
4490 IF (A(J) = 999) + A(J + 1) = 999) + (A(J + 2) = 999) THEN 4520
```

```
4500 J = J + 3
4510 GOTO 4480
4520 PRINT:PRINT "REQUESTED RECORD NOT IN TABLE"
4530 GOSUB 9900
4540 GOTO 4450
4550 RESTORE:FOR N = 1 TO 10:READ A$:NEXT N
4560 FOR N = 1 TO A(J + 1)
4570     READ A$
4580 NEXT N
4590 GOSUB 4300
4600 PRINT:PRINT "ENTER STOCK NR.";A(J)
4610 PRINT:PRINT "ENTER DESCRIPTION INDICATOR CODE";A(J + 1)
4620 PRINT:PRINT "ENTER QTY-ON-HAND";A(J + 2)
4630 CLS:PRINT "PICK THE DIRECTION YOU WISH TO PROCEED:"
4640 PRINT:PRINT "bbbbb1.  REPLACE MORE RECORDS"
4650 PRINT:PRINT "bbbbb2.  RETURN TO MAINTENANCE ROUTINE"
4660 PRINT:PRINT "bbbbb3.  RETURN TO MAINTENANCE/RETRIEVAL MENU"
4670 PRINT:PRINT "bbbbb4.  RETURN TO INITIAL MENU"
4680 PRINT:INPUT "WHICH";A
4690 ON A GOTO 4460,3500,2900,2000
4700 GOTO 4630
```

As can be seen, this is nothing more than a direct replacement, item for item, of a previous record. Again, the sequence will be incorrect if a stock number is changed. If the sort option is desired, enter the following instructions:

```
4622 PRINT:INPUT "DO YOU WISH TO SORT? (Y/N)";A$
4624 IF A$ = "Y" THEN 300
```

DELETE A RECORD

The simplest way to delete a record is to locate the record and then overlay it with a sentinel line. It begins again with statement 3550:

```
3550 ON A GOTO 3560,3900,4450,4750:GOTO 3500
4750 J = 1
4760 CLS:PRINT "DELETE A RECORD"
```

```
4770 PRINT:INPUT "ENTER STOCK NUMBER";A
4780 A = INT(A)
4790 IF A(J) = A THEN 4810
4800 IF (A(J) = 999) +(A(J + 1) = 999) + IF (A(J + 2) = 999)
     THEN 4840
4810 A(J) = 999:A(J + 1) = 999:A(J + 2) = 999
4820 J = J + 3
4830 GOTO 4770
4840 PRINT:PRINT "REQUESTED RECORD NOT ON FILE"
4850 GOSUB 9900
4860 CLS:PRINT "PICK THE DIRECTION YOU WISH TO PROCEED"
4870 PRINT:PRINT "bbbbb1.  DELETE MORE RECORDS"
4880 PRINT:PRINT "bbbbb2.  RETURN TO MAINTENANCE ROUTINE"
4890 PRINT:PRINT "bbbbb3.  RETURN TO MAINTENANCE/RETRIEVAL MENU"
4900 PRINT:PRINT "bbbbb4.  RETURN TO INITIAL MENU"
4910 PRINT:INPUT "WHICH;A
4920 ON A GOTO 4750,3900,4450,4750:GOTO 4860
```

Use "xxxxxxxxxx" to delete, and then sort.

Two more items remain on the original menu:

   List the table

   Sort the table

Actually, both have been accomplished in other parts of the program. Rather than duplicate them, make the final modification to statement 2080:

```
2080 ON A GOTO 2100,2500.2700,2900,420,300
```

The routine at 420 will perform the list—but be aware that in both cases, 420 and 300, previous routines are being entered. Each, of course, fits into other logic. If it is desired to make the routines independent, it will be necessary to copy the listing beginning at 420 into the statement range beginning at 5000. The sort does not require another routine, as the completion of the sort begins the process once again.

A quick estimate shows the program takes about 5.5K of memory. To fit it into a 4K Level I, the program must be condensed. To do this:

Consolidate the timer loops.

Consolidate the menu returns.

Combine instructions, where possible.

Remove as many REMarks as possible.

Remove as many spaces as practical. C = C + 1, for instance, can be written as C = C + 1.

With a little effort, this program can be brought back to 4K.

In reviewing the sort routine, it was found that "hits" were made in about 75% of the valid cases, owing to duplicates in the randomly generated number table. The result was that some adjustment needed to be made to compensate for the realignment for duplicate numbers. The following will take care of the majority of the cases:

```
831 IF A = A(M + 3) THEN 835
832 IF M - 3 < 0 THEN 840
833 IF A = A(M - 3) THEN 836
834 GOTO 840
835 M = M + 3:GOTO 860
836 M = M - 3:GOTO 860
```

Also, include the following:

```
1040 IF A = A(M + 3) THEN 1044
1041 IF M - 3 < 0 THEN 1050
1042 IF A = A(M - 3) THEN 1045
1043 GOTO 1050
1044 M = M + 3:GOTO 860
1045 M = M - 3:GOTO 860
```

These instructions check the lines on either side of the requested line, to adjust for any misalignment due to duplicates. Under the testing of the sort routine, it was found that the random number generator would generate as many as four identical stock numbers. Of course, a "normal" table might not have the same problem. With the generation, randomly, of four identical stock numbers, the two routines previously detailed should include the logic to handle (M + 6), (M + 9), (M + 12), (M − 6), (M − 9), and (M − 12).

Further, it should be borne in mind that the listing subroutine would have to have incorporated the routines necessary to bypass the first 10 DATA items.

This concludes the chapter and with it a fully explained and fairly sophisticated file maintenance and retrieval system. The reader now has the knowledge and the complete freedom to select the pieces required to perform the work desired.

Here is the entire program:

```
300 V = 1:W = 4
305 GOSUB 1300
310 FOR N = 1 TO 99
314     PRINT "STRING SORT","TOTAL","PER PASS","NR. PASSES"
315     PRINT
316     PRINT "bbbbb",C,N,Y
320     IF A(V) < = A(W) THEN 370
330     P = 1
340     R = A(V):S = A(V+1):T = A(V+2)
344     PRINT "STRING SORT","TOTAL","PER PASS","NR. PASSES"
345     PRINT
346     PRINT "SORTING",C,N,Y
350     A(V) = A(W):A(V+1) = A(W+1):A(V+2) = A(W + 2)
360     A(W) = R:A(W+1) = S:A(W+2) = T
370     V = V + 3:W = W + 3
380 NEXT N
385 Y = Y + 1
390 IF P = 0 THEN 420
400 P = 0
410 GOTO 310
420 RESTORE:C = 0:CLS
430 FOR N = 1 TO 300 STEP 3:C = C + 1
440     FOR X = 1 TO A(N+1)
450         READ A$
460     NEXT X
470     RESTORE
480     PRINT A(N),A$,A(N+2),C
490     FOR Z = 1 TO 1000:NEXT Z
500 NEXT N
502 CLS:PRINT "SELECT TYPE OF SEARCH":PRINT
504 PRINT "1. SEQUENTIAL":PRINT
506 PRINT "2. BINARY"
```

```
508 INPUT "WHICH";A
509 ON A GOTO 510,810:GOTO 502
510 CLS
511 N = 1
512 FOR L = 1 TO 5
513     FOR X = 1 TO 5
514         PRINT A(N),A(N + 3),A(N + 6),A(N + 9)
515         PRINT:N = N + 12
516     NEXT X
517         FOR Z = 1 TO 1000:NEXT Z
518     CLS
519 NEXT L
520 C = 0
525 INPUT "ENTER STOCK NUMBER (1 TO 1000)";A
530 A = INT(A)
540 FOR N = 1 TO 300 STEP 3
550 IF A = A(N) THEN 620
560 IF A(N) < A THEN 590
570 C = C + 1
580 NEXT N
590 CLS
600 PRINT "STOCK NUMBER";A:"NOT ON FILE."
610 FOR Z = 1 TO 1000:NEXT Z:GOTO 520
620 CLS
630 PRINT "STOCK NUMBER","DESCRIPTION","QTY-ON-HAND","TABLE LINE"
640 PRINT
650 RESTORE
660 FOR Z = 1 TO A(N+1)
670     READ A$
680 NEXT Z
690 PRINT A(N),A$,A(N+2),C
700 FOR Z = 1 TO 1000:NEXT Z:GOTO 520
810 CLS
811 N = 1
812 FOR L = 1 TO 5
813     FOR X = 1 TO 5
```

```
814     PRINT A(N),A(N +3),A(N + 6),A(N + 9)
815     PRINT:N = N + 12
816     NEXT X
817         FOR Z = 1 TO 1000:NEXT Z
818     CLS
819 NEXT L
820 M = 151:B = 51:D = 101:E = 1:F = 0
825 INPUT "ENTER STOCK NUMBER (1 TO 1000)";A
830 A = INT(A)
831 IF A = A(M + 3) THEN 835
832 IF M - 3 < 0 THEN 840
833 IF A = A(M - 3) THEN 836
834 GOTO 840
835 M = M + 3:GOTO 860
836 M = M - 3:GOTO 860
840 IF A > A(M) THEN 960
850 IF A < A(M) THEN 1010
860 CLS
870 RESTORE
880 FOR N = 1 TO A(M+1)
890     READ A$
900 NEXT N
902 CLS
904 PRINT "STOCK NUMBER","DESCRIPTION","QTY-ON-HAND","TABLE LINE"
906 PRINT
910 PRINT A(M),A$,A(M+2), INT(B)
920 PRINT
930 FOR Z = 1 TO 1000:NEXT Z:GOTO 820
950 REM "ABOVE MID-POINT"
960 GOSUB 1100
970 IF F = 1 GOTO 1050
980 IF D - E  < 2 GOTO 1040
990 GOTO 840
1000 REM "BELOW MID-POINT"
1010 GOSUB 1200
1020 IF D - E < 2 GOTO 1040
```

```
1030 GOTO 840
1040 IF A = A(M + 3) THEN 1044
1041 IF M - 3 < 0 THEN 1050
1042 IF A = A(M - 3) THEN 1045
1043 GOTO 1050
1044 M = M + 3:GOTO 860
1045 M = M - 3:GOTO 860
1050 CLS
1060 PRINT "STOCK NUMBER";A;"NOT IN FILE"
1070 FOR Z = 1 TO 1000:NEXT Z:GOTO 820
1100 REM "UPPER LOCATOR SUBROUTINE"
1110 E = INT(B)
1120 B = B + (D - E)/2 + .5
1130 M = INT(B) * 3 + 1
1140 IF M = 301 THEN F = 1
1150 RETURN
1200 REM "LOWER LOCATOR SUBROUTINE"
1210 D = INT(B)
1220 B = B - (D - E)/2 - .5
1230 M = INT(B) * 3 + 1
1240 RETURN
1300 G = 1:H = 101:K = 301
1305 CLS:PRINT "BLOCK SORT, TABLE J TO TABLE K BY 100"
1310 FOR N = 1 TO 10
1320     FOR J = 1 TO 300 STEP 3
1330     IF (A(J) < G) + (A(J) > H) THEN 1355
1340     A(K) = A(J):A(K + 1) = A(J + 1):A(K + 2) = A(J + 2
1350     K = K + 3
1355     GOSUB 1470
1360     NEXT J
1370     G = G + 100:H = H + 100
1380 NEXT N
1390 G = 1:H = 51:J = 1
1395 CLS:PRINT "BLOCK SORT, TABLE K TO TABLE J BY 50"
1400 FOR N = 1 TO 20
1410     FOR K = 301 TO 600 STEP 3
```

```
1420    IF (A(K) < G) + (A(K) > H) THEN 1450
1430    A(J) = A(K):A(J + 1) = A(K + 1):A(J + 2) = A(K + 2)
1440    J = J + 3
1450    GOSUB 1470:NEXT K
1460 NEXT N: RETURN
1470 PRINT:PRINT AT 128,"LOWER","UPPER","TABLE J","TABLE K"
1480 PRINT:PRINT AT 192,G,H,J,K
1490 RETURN
2000 CLS:PRINT "SELECT THE FUNCTION YOU WISH TO PERFORM:"
2010 PRINT:PRINT "1.   BUILD THE TABLE"
2020 PRINT:PRINT "2.   STORE TABLE ON CASSETTE TAPE"
2030 PRINT:PRINT "3.   LOAD TABLE FROM CASSETTE TAPE"
2040 PRINT:PRINT "4.   TABLE MAINTENANCE AND RETRIEVAL"
2050 PRINT:PRINT "5.  LIST THE TABLE"
2060 PRINT:PRINT "6.   SORT THE TABLE"
2070 PRINT:INPUT "SELECT";A
2080 ON A GOTO 2100,2500,2700,2900,420,300: GOTO 2000
2100 CLS:PRINT "TABLE BUILD ROUTINE":PRINT
2110 INPUT "HOW MANY ITEMS WILL APPEAR ON THE TABLE";A
2115 INPUT "HOW MANY UNIQUE DESCRIPTIONS HAVE YOU INCLUDED";P
2120 A = INT(A * 1.2)
2130 J = 1:K = J + A * 3 + 3
2140 PRINT:PRINT "SPACE HAS BEEN RESERVED FOR ";Q;"ITEMS"
2150 PRINT:PRINT "YOU WILL BE ADVISED OF REMAINING SPACE"
2160 PRINT:INPUT "PRESS ENTER WHEN YOU ARE PREPARED TO PROCEED";A
2165 L = 1
2170 CLS:PRINT "TABLE LINE";L
2180 RESTORE
2190 INPUT "ENTER RELATIVE DESCRIPTION INDICATOR NUMBER";A:PRINT
2200 IF A > P GOTO 2370
2210 INPUT "ENTER QUANTITY ON HAND";B:PRINT
2220 IF B > 100 GOTO 2390
2230 FOR N = 1 TO 10 + A
2240    READ A$
2250 NEXT N
2260 PRINT "ENTRY ACCEPTABLE":PRINT
```

```
2270 PRINT "STOCK NR.","DESCRIPTION","QTY-ON-HAND":PRINT
2280 PRINT L,A$,B
2290 PRINT:INPUT "IS IT CORRECT (Y/N)";B$
2300 IF B$ = "Y" THEN 2330
2310 PRINT:PRINT "TRANSACTION REJECTED - RE-ENTER"
2320 GOSUB 9900:GOTO 2170
2330 PRINT:PRINT "TRANSACTION ACCEPTED"
2340 A(J) = L:A(J + 1) = A:A(J + 2) = B
2350 J = J + 3
2360 GOSUB 9900:GOTO 2410
2370 PRINT:PRINT "INVALID DESCRIPTION - RE-DO"
2380 GOSUB 9900:PRINT:GOTO 2190
2390 PRINT:PRINT "INVALID QUANTITY - RE-DO"
2400 GOSUB 9900:PRINT:GOTO 2210
2410 PRINT:INPUT "WAS THAT THE LAST ITEM (Y/N)";B$
2420 IF B$ = "Y" THEN 2470
2430 Q = Q - 1
2440 IF Q = 0 THEN 2490
2450 PRINT:PRINT "NUMBER OF AVAILABLE TABLE LINES - ";Q:L = L + 1
2460 GOSUB 9900:GOTO 2170
2470 PRINT:PRINT "TABLE TERMINATED"
2480 A(J) = 999:A(J + 1) = 999:A(J + 2) = 999:GOSUB 9900:GOTO 2000
2490 PRINT:PRINT "OUT OF TABLE ROOM":GOTO 2470
2500 CLS:PRINT "STORE TABLE ON CASSETTE TAPE ROUTINE":PRINT
2510 PRINT "INSURE THAT TAPE IS CONNECTED, POSITIONED, AND"
2520 PRINT "THAT THE PLAY AND RECORD LEVERS ARE DEPRESSED"
2530 PRINT:INPUT "PRESS ENTER WHEN READY TO PROCEED";A
2540 J = 1:CLS
2550 RESTORE
2560 FOR N = 1 TO A(J + 1) + 10
2570     READ A$
2580 NEXT N
2590 PRINT A(J),A$,A(J + 2):PRINT:GOSUB 9900
2600 PRINT # A(J);",";A(J + 1);",";A(J + 2)
2610 IF (A(J) = 999) * (A(J + 1) = 999) * (A(J + 2) = 999) THEN 26.
2620 J = J + 3:GOTO 2550
```

```
2630 PRINT:PRINT "END OF STORE TABLE ON CASSETTE TAPE ROUTINE"
2640 PRINT:PRINT "IF YOU WISH TO RUN THE ROUTINE AGAIN,"
2650 PRINT:PRINT "MERELY REPEAT MENU SELECTION."
2660 PRINT:PRINT "TAPE MUST BE MANUALLY REWOUND BEFORE"
2670 PRINT:PRINT "IT CAN BE USED AS INPUT."
2680 GOSUB 9900:GOTO 2000
2700 CLS:PRINT "LOAD TABLE FROM CASSETTE ROUTINE":PRINT
2710 PRINT "INSURE THAT TAPE IS CONNECTED, POSITIONED, AND"
2720 PRINT "THAT THE PLAY LEVER ONLY IS DEPRESSED"
2730 PRINT:INPUT "PRESS ENTER WHEN READY TO PROCEED";A
2740 J = 1:CLS
2750 RESTORE
2760 INPUT # A(J),A(J + 1),A(J + 2)
2770 FOR N = 1 TO A(J + 1) + 10
2780    READ A$
2790 NEXT N
2800 PRINT A(J),A$,A(J+2):GOSUB 9900
2810 IF (A(J) = 999) * A(J + 1) = 999) * (A(J + 2) = 999) THEN 2830
2820 J = J + 3:GOTO 2750
2830 PRINT:PRINT "END OF LOAD TABLE FROM CASSETTE TAPE ROUTINE"
2840 PRINT:PRINT "IF YOU WISH TO RUN THE ROUTINE AGAIN,"
2850 PRINT:PRINT "MERELY REPEAT MENU SELECTION."
2860 PRINT:PRINT "TAPE MUST BE MANUALLY REWOUND BEFORE"
2870 PRINT:PRINT "IT CAN BE USED AS INPUT."
2880 GOSUB 9900:GOTO 2000
2900 CLS:PRINT "TABLE MAINTENANCE AND RETRIEVAL ROUTINE"
2910 PRINT:PRINT "SELECT THE OPTION YOU WISH:"
2920 PRINT:PRINT "ЬЬЬЬЬ1.  RETRIEVAL"
2930 PRINT:PRINT "ЬЬЬЬЬ2.  MAINTENANCE"
2940 PRINT:INPUT "WHICH";A
2950 ON A GOTO 2960,3500:GOTO 2900
2960 CLS:PRINT "RETRIEVAL ROUTINE"
2970 PRINT:PRINT "ЬЬЬЬЬ1.  DISPLAY DESCRIPTIONS"
2980 PRINT:PRINT "ЬЬЬЬЬ2.  RETRIEVE TABLE ITEM"
2990 PRINT:INPUT "WHICH";A
3000 ON A GOTO 3005,3200:GOTO 2960
```

```
3005 RESTORE
3010 FOR N = 1 TO 10
3020    READ A$
3030 NEXT N:CLS:B = 1:C = 2
3040 FOR N = 1 TO 5
3050    READ A$,B$
3060    PRINT B,A$,C,B$:PRINT
3070    IF (A$ = "ZZZZZZZZZZ") + (B$ = "ZZZZZZZZZZ") THEN 3120
3080    B = B + 1:C = C + 1
3090    PRINT:INPUT "PRESS ENTER TO CONTINUE";A
3100 NEXT N
3110 CLS:GOTO 3040
3120 PRINT:INPUT "DO YOU WISH MAINTENANCE AND RETRIEVAL MENU
     (Y/N)";A$
3130 IF A$ = "Y" THEN 2900
3140 GOTO 2000
3200 CLS:PRINT "RETRIEVAL ROUTINE"
3210 PRINT:PRINT "THIS ROUTINE ASSUMES THAT THERE IS"
3220 PRINT:PRINT "A VALID TABLE LOADED INTO MEMORY."
3230 PRINT:INPUT "HAS A TABLE BEEN LOADED (Y/N)";A$
3240 IF A$ < >"Y" GOTO 2000
3250 RESTORE:F = 0
3260 FOR N = 1 TO 10:READ A$:NEXT N
3270 CLS:INPUT "ENTER STOCK NUMBER";A
3280 A = INT(A)
3290 GOSUB 3420
3300 IF F = 0 GOTO 3350
3310 PRINT:PRINT "STOCK NR. ";A;"NOT IN TABLE":F = 0
3320 PRINT:INPUT "WAS THAT THE LAST RETRIEVAL (Y/N)";A$
3330 IF A$ = "Y" THEN 2000
3340 GOTO 3250
3350 FOR N = 1 TO A(J + 1)
3360    READ A$
3370 NEXT N
3380 PRINT:PRINT "STOCK NR.","DESCRIPTION","CODE","QTY-ON-HAND"
3390 PRINT:PRINT A(J + 1),A$,A(J + 2),A(J + 3)
```

```
3400 GOSUB 9900:GOTO 3320
3410 REM "TABLE SCAN ROUTINE"
3420 J = 1
3420 IF A(J) = A THEN F = 0
3440 IF (A(J) = 999) * (A(J + 1) = 999) * (A(J + 2) = 999)
     THEN F = 1
3450 RETURN
3500 CLS:PRINT "TABLE MAINTENANCE ROUTINE"
3510 PRINT:PRINT "ƀƀƀƀƀ1.  ADD A RECORD"
3520 PRINT:PRINT "ƀƀƀƀƀ2.  CHANGE A RECORD"
3530 PRINT:PRINT "ƀƀƀƀƀ3.  REPLACE A RECORD"
3540 PRINT:PRINT "ƀƀƀƀƀ4.  DELETE A RECORD"
3550 ON A GOTO 3560,3900,4450,4750:GOTO 3500
3560 CLS:PRINT "ADD A RECORD"
3570 PRINT:INPUT "STOCK NR.";A:A = INT(A)
3580 PRINT:INPUT "DESCRIPTION INDICATOR";B:B = INT(B)
3590 RESTORE:FOR N = 1 TO 10:READ A$:NEXT N
3600 FOR N = 1 TO B
3610    READ A$
3620     IF A$ = "ZZZZZZZZZZ" THEN 3640
3630 NEXT N:GOTO 3670
3640 PRINT:PRINT "DESCRIPTION INDICATOR NOT IN DATA LINES"
3650 PRINT:PRINT "RE-ENTER"
3660 GOTO 3580
3670 PRINT:INPUT "QTY-ON-HAND";C:C = INT(C)
3680 IF C > 100 THEN C = 100
3690 CLS:PRINT "THIS IS THE RECORD YOU WISH TO ADD:"
3700 PRINT:PRINT A,B,A$,C
3710 PRINT:INPUT "IS IT CORRECT (Y/N)";A$
3720 IF A$ = "N" THEN 3560
3730 J = 1
3740 IF A = A(J) THEN 3780
3750 IF (A(J) = 999) * (A(J + 1) = 999) * (A(J + 2) = 999) THEN 3800
3760 J = J + 3
3770 GOTO 3740
3780 PRINT:PRINT "RECORD ALREADY EXISTS ON FILE"
```

```
3790 GOTO 3900
3800 A(J) = A:A(J + 1) = B:A(J + 2) = C
3810 A(J + 3) = 999:A(J + 4) = 999:A(J + 5) = 999
3820 GOTO 3790
3900 CLS:PRINT "PICK THE DIRECTION YOU WISH TO PROCEED:"
3910 PRINT:PRINT "ᵇᵇᵇᵇᵇ1.  ADD MORE RECORDS TO THE TABLE"
3920 PRINT:PRINT "ᵇᵇᵇᵇᵇ2.  RETURN TO THE MAINTENANCE ROUTINE"
3930 PRINT:PRINT "ᵇᵇᵇᵇᵇ3.  RETURN TO MAINTENANCE/RETRIEVAL MENU'
3940 PRINT:PRINT "ᵇᵇᵇᵇᵇ4.  RETURN TO INITIAL MENU"
3950 PRINT:INPUT "WHICH";A
3960 ON A GOTO 3560,3500,2900,2000
3970 GOTO 3900
3900 CLS:PRINT "CHANGE A RECORD"
3910 PRINT:INPUT "STOCK NR.";A:A = INT(A)
3920 RESTORE:FOR N = 1 TO 10:READ A$:NEXT N
3930 GOSUB 3420
3940 IF F = 0 THEN 3990
3950 PRINT:PRINT "STOCK NR. ";A;"NOT IN TABLE":F = 0
3960 PRINT:INPUT "WAS THAT THE LAST CHANGE (Y/N)";A$
3970 IF A$ = "Y" then 2000
3980 GOTO 3900
3990 FOR N = 1 TO A(J + 1)
4000     READ A$
4010 NEXT N
4020 A = A(J):B = A(J + 1):C = A(J + 2)
4030 GOSUB 4300
4040 PRINT:PRINT "WHICH DO YOU WISH TO CHANGE:"
4050 PRINT:PRINT "ᵇᵇᵇᵇᵇ1.  STOCK NR."
4060 PRINT:PRINT "ᵇᵇᵇᵇᵇ2.  CODE"
4070 PRINT:PRINT "ᵇᵇᵇᵇᵇ3.  QTY-ON-HAND"
4080 PRINT:PRINT "DESCRIPTION MUST BE CHANGED"
4090 PRINT "IN COMMAND MODE (DATA LINE) FOR LEVEL I."
4100 ON A GOTO 4110,4160,4260:GOTO 4040
4110 CLS:INPUT "ENTER NEW STOCK NR.";A:A = INT(A)
4120 GOSUB 4300
4130 GOTO 4230
4140 RESTORE:FOR N = 1 TO 10:READ A$:NEXT N
```

```
4150 PRINT:INPUT "ENTER NEW DESCRIPTION LOCATOR CODE";B:B = INT(B)
4160 FOR N = 1 TO B
4170    READ A$
4180     IF A$ = "ZZZZZZZZZZ" THEN 4220
4190 NEXT N
4200 GOSUB 4300
4210 GOTO 4230
4220 PRINT:PRINT "ENTER NEW QTY-ON-HAND";C:C = INT(C)
4230 PRINT:INPUT "IS NEW RECORD OK? (Y/N)";A$
4240 IF A$ < > "Y" THEN 4040
4250 A(J) = A:A(J + 1) = B:A(J + 2) = C
4260 PRINT:INPUT "DO YOU WISH TO SORT? (Y/N);A$
4270 IF A$ = "Y" THEN 300
4280 GOTO 4340
4300 PRINT:PRINT "THE RECORD NOW LOOKS LIKE THIS:"
4310 PRINT:PRINT "STOCK NR.","DESCRIPTION","CODE","QTY-ON-HAND"
4320 PRINT:PRINT A,A$,B,C
4330 RETURN
4340 CLS:PRINT "PICK THE DIRECTION YOU WISH TO PROCEED:"
4350 PRINT:PRINT "ᑫᑫᑫᑫᑫ1.  CHANGE MORE RECORDS."
4360 PRINT:PRINT "ᑫᑫᑫᑫᑫ2.  RETURN TO MAINTENANCE ROUTINE"
4370 PRINT:PRINT "ᑫᑫᑫᑫᑫ3.  RETURN TO MAINTENANCE/RETRIEVAL MENU"
4380 PRINT:PRINT "ᑫᑫᑫᑫᑫ4.  RETURN TO INITIAL MENU"
4390 PRINT:INPUT "WHICH";A
4400 ON A GOTO 3900,3500,2900,2000
4410 GOTO 4340
4450 CLS:PRINT "REPLACE A RECORD"
4460 PRINT:INPUT "ENTER STOCK NR.";A
4470 J + 1
4480 IF A(J) + A THEN 4550
4490 IF (A(J) = 999) + A(J + 1) = 999) + (A(J + 2) = 999) THEN 4520
4500 J = J + 3
4510 GOTO 4480
4520 PRINT:PRINT "REQUESTED RECORD NOT IN TABLE"
4530 GOSUB 9900
4540 GOTO 4450
4550 RESTORE:FOR N = 1 TO 10:READ A$:NEXT N
```

```
4560 FOR N = 1 TO A(J + 1)
4570    READ A$
4580 NEXT N
4590 GOSUB 4300
4600 PRINT:PRINT "ENTER STOCK NR.";A(J)
4610 PRINT:PRINT "ENTER DESCRIPTION INDICATOR CODE";A(J + 1)
4620 PRINT:PRINT "ENTER QTY-ON-HAND";A(J + 2)
4622 PRINT:INPUT "DO YOU WISH TO SORT? (Y/N)";A$
4624 IF A$ = "Y" THEN 300
4630 CLS:PRINT "PICK THE DIRECTION YOU WISH TO PROCEED:"
4640 PRINT:PRINT "ƀƀƀƀ1.  REPLACE MORE RECORDS"
4650 PRINT:PRINT "ƀƀƀƀ2.  RETURN TO MAINTENANCE ROUTINE"
4660 PRINT:PRINT "ƀƀƀƀ3.  RETURN TO MAINTENANCE/RETRIEVAL MENU"
4670 PRINT:PRINT "ƀƀƀƀ4.  RETURN TO INITIAL MENU"
4680 PRINT:INPUT "WHICH";A
4690 ON A GOTO 4460,3500,2900,2000
4700 GOTO 4630
4750 J = 1
4760 CLS:PRINT "DELETE A RECORD"
4770 PRINT:INPUT "ENTER STOCK NUMBER";A
4780 A = INT(A)
4790 IF A(J) = A THEN 4810
4800 IF (A(J) = 999) +(A(J + 1) = 999) + IF (A(J + 2) = 999) THEN 484(
4810 A(J) = 999:A(J + 1) = 999:A(J + 2) = 999
4820 J = J + 3
4830 GOTO 4770
4840 PRINT:PRINT "REQUESTED RECORD NOT ON FILE"
4850 GOSUB 9900
4860 CLS:PRINT "PICK THE DIRECTION YOU WISH TO PROCEED"
4870 PRINT:PRINT "ƀƀƀƀ1.  DELETE MORE RECORDS"
4880 PRINT:PRINT "ƀƀƀƀ2.  RETURN TO MAINTENANCE ROUTINE"
4890 PRINT:PRINT "ƀƀƀƀ3.  RETURN TO MAINTENANCE/RETRIEVAL MENU"
4900 PRINT:PRINT "ƀƀƀƀ4.  RETURN TO INITIAL MENU"
4910 PRINT:INPUT "WHICH;A
4920 ON A GOTO 4750,3900,4450,4750:GOTO 4860
9900 FOR Z = 1 TO 500:NEXT Z:RETURN
```

4
Screen Graphics

The designers of the TRS-80 have included three instructions to cause lines to be drawn on the face of the screen of the CRT. Some people like to draw pictures, and more realistically, the use of graphics enhances the displayed reports, illustrations, and game displays.

Turn back to the Visual Display Planning Chart (Figure 2). Note that each horizontal line is divided into three graphics elements and that each vertical line is divided into two. Thus, there are 128 unique horizontal positions and 48 vertical positions, giving a total of 6144 positions which you can specifically affect upon the face of the screen.

The horizontal line is known as the *X-Axis*. The vertical is known as the *Y-Axis*. When using the graphics on the screen, it is not necessary to be concerned with the absolute address (Ø to 6143), but rather with the specific position on the X-Axis (Ø to 127) and the Y-Axis (Ø to 47).

Looking at the visual display sheet, note that X = Ø and Y = Ø are the coordinates of the single space in the upper left-hand corner. The command to "turn on" that position is:

```
5 CLS
1Ø SET (Ø,Ø)
2Ø GOTO 1Ø
```

The instruction takes the form SET (X,Y). The variables X and Y are used here because they correspond to what we have identified as the axes, but any variable will do, as in the following:

```
5 CLS
1Ø A = Ø:B = Ø
2Ø SET (A,B)
3Ø GOTO 1Ø
```

129

In the first illustration, above, the use of Ø,Ø in the operand of the instruction restricts that instruction to the double coordinates of zero, leaving no room for modification. In the second illustration, any set of values can be supplied to A and/or B and then the instruction can be executed with those values. The only restriction is that the value of A cannot exceed 127 and the value of B cannot exceed 47. In Level I, if these numbers are exceeded, the process "wraps" the screen; i.e., the figure runs off the screen at the right and reappears on the left. Since this is not permitted in Level II, limit the display to the boundaries at 127 and 47.

Try this:

```
1Ø FOR X = Ø TO 127
2Ø      SET (X,Ø)
3Ø NEXT X
4Ø GOTO 4Ø
```

When these are RUN, a horizontal line should be "painted" across the top of the screen, on Y-Axis line Ø. In this instance, the variable X has been used both for control of the FOR . . . NEXT loop and as one of the two operands of the SET instruction. Statement 4Ø is a must in any graphics program. If there were not an ending statement which branched to itself, the program would end and READY would be displayed.

Type NEW and enter the following:

```
1Ø FOR Y = Ø TO 47
2Ø      SET (Ø,Y)
3Ø NEXT Y
4Ø GOTO 4Ø
```

RUN it and there should be a line down the left side of the screen. Now, try to write a routine to do the same across the bottom and up the right side, drawing the bottom line from right to left. Try this:

```
1Ø FOR X = Ø TO 127
2Ø      SET (X,Ø)
3Ø NEXT X
4Ø FOR Y = Ø TO 47
5Ø      SET (Ø,Y)
6Ø NEXT Y
```

```
70 FOR X = 127 TO 0 STEP -1
80    SET (X,47)
90 NEXT X
100 FOR Y = 47 TO 0 STEP -1
110    SET (127,Y)
120 NEXT Y
130 GOTO 130
```

The screen should now be encased in a box when it's RUN. Make the following changes and RUN again:

```
10 FOR X = 0 TO 128 STEP 2
40 FOR Y = 0 TO 47 STEP 2
70 FOR X = 127 TO 0 STEP -2
100 FOR Y = 47 TO 0 STEP -2
```

Cute! That's fine, but one line was drawn at a time. This routine will draw them simultaneously:

```
5 X = 127:CLS
10 FOR N = 0 TO 127
20    SET (N,0)
30    SET (X,47)
40    X = X - 1
50 NEXT N
60 Y = 47
70 FOR N = 0 TO 47
80    SET (0,N)
90    SET (127,Y)
100    Y = Y - 1
110 NEXT N
120 GOTO 120
```

In this example, there are two measured FOR . . . NEXT loops. The problem is that only one can be specified, else the other would be a loop within a loop, resulting in the second line being drawn before the first one is completed. Also, since they operate in pairs and there is an identical number of positions to be "painted" in each, the size of the controlling FOR . . . NEXT loop is the same for both pairs, respectively. Even this does not draw all four lines simultaneously. It draws two pairs of lines, one pair at a time.

One of the difficulties with TRS-80 graphics is its inability to draw diagonal or curved lines. But this is no significant drawback. Again, it should be remembered that the TRS-80 is a *micro*computer—not the behemoth used to send the rocket to the moon.

Try the following:

```
10 Y = 0
20 FOR X = 0 TO 127 STEP 3
30    SET (X,Y)
40    Y = Y + 1
50 NEXT X
60 GOTO 60
```

This will give a diagonal line from top left to lower middle of the screen. Now try this:

```
70 Y = 0
80 FOR X = 127 TO 0 STEP -3
90    SET (X,Y)
100   Y = Y + 1
110 NEXT X
120 GOTO 120
```

This time, RUN 70. There should be a line from top right to bottom left. Now, remove statement 60 and RUN.

It stands to reason that if a light can be turned on, (a screen position is illuminated) it can also be turned off, i.e., a screen position can be darkened. The instruction for that is:

```
RESET (X,Y)
```

Using the same routine used above, try RESET. The following is structured to erase the lines after they have been painted:

```
115 Y = 0
120 FOR Z = 0 TO 127 STEP 3
130    RESET (X,Y)
```

```
140     Y = Y + 1
150 NEXT X
160 Y = Ø
170 FOR X = 127 TO Ø STEP -3
180     RESET (X,Y)
190     Y = Y + 1
```

RUN it and the display should show an "X" which is then erased. By itself, there's not much value to the X. Add the following:

```
210 FOR X = Ø TO 127
220     FOR Y = Ø TO 47
230         SET (X,Y)
240     NEXT Y
250 NEXT X
260 GOTO 26Ø
```

That should have painted the screen totally white. Now, let's have a little fun. Add:

```
26Ø X = RND(127)
27Ø Y = RND(47)
28Ø RESET (X,Y):GOTO 26Ø
```

This is an endless loop which will clear the screen in a random fashion, sort of a reverse snowstorm. If you would like to see a snowstorm occur, type NEW and enter the above instructions, changing RESET to SET.

Now that you have had a chance to see what happens when you use the SET and RESET commands, let's undertake a project which is a little more ambitious. The routine which follows this discussion will draw a picture, one that you will recognize.

A few things are worthy of note as this routine is constructed. In the routine there is extensive use of a single subroutine. This subroutine is quite different from those used previously, in that iteration control is exercised from outside the subroutine, while the iteration itself is performed within the subroutine. Note that the FOR . . . NEXT loop is inside the subroutine, but that it is constructed entirely of variables whose values are supplied from outside the routine. In this manner, the scope of the subroutine can be frequently changed. Likewise, the values of the SET command are supplied from outside the routine. In the example, variable R is used as the "from"

number in the FOR . . . NEXT loop; variable S is used as the "to" in the
FOR . . . NEXT loop; (both the aforementioned are for the Y coordinate of
the SET command). The FOR . . . NEXT variables for the X coordinate are
filled with the T and U variables. Why R,S,T,U? No reason. They could
just as easily have been A,B,C,D.

Note also that a new graphics instruction, POINT, has been introduced.
The function of POINT is merely to determine whether or not a position on
the screen has been illuminated. It is used to effect the reversal of the picture
to a negative image.

```
5 CLS
10 FOR X = 0 TO 127
20     FOR Y = 0 TO 40
30         SET (X,Y)
40     NEXT Y
50 NEXT X
100 R = 1:S = 3:T = 64:U = 126:GOSUB 500
110 T = 1:U = 62:GOSUB 500
120 R = 4:S = 6:GOSUB 500
130 R = 7:S = 9:T = 64:U = 126:GOSUB 500
140 T = 1:U = 62:GOSUB 500
150 R = 10:S = 12:GOSUB 500
160 R = 13:S = 15:GOSUB 500
170 T = 64:U = 126:GOSUB 500
180 R = 16:S = 17:T = 1:U - 62:GOSUB 500
190 R = 19:S = 21:T = 1:U = 126:GOSUB 500
200 R = 25:S = 27:GOSUB 500
210 R = 31:S = 33:GOSUB 500
220 R = 37:S = 39:GOSUB 500
230 FOR X = 10 TO 55 STEP 5
240     FOR Y = 3 TO 15 STEP 3
250         SET (X,Y)
260     NEXT Y
270 NEXT X
280 FOR Z = 1 TO 5000:NEXT Z
290 FOR Y = 1 TO 40
300     FOR X = 1 TO 126
```

```
310          IF POINT (X,Y) = 1 THEN 340
320          SET (X,Y)
330          GOTO 350
340          RESET (X,Y)
350      NEXT X
360 NEXT Y
370 FOR X = 0 TO 127
380      SET (X,0)
390      SET (X,40)
400 NEXT X
410 FOR Y = 0 TO 40
420      SET (0,Y)
430      SET (127,Y)
440 NEXT Y
450 GOTO 450
500 FOR Y = R TO S
510      FOR X = T TO U
520          RESET (X,Y)
530      NEXT X
540 NEXT Y
550 RETURN
```

That's it. After it's been entered and RUN, stand up, the display will show why.

A little explanation is in order. The loop from statement 10 to statement 50 paints the screen white. As constructed, it is very slow. Unfortunately, rapid screen cover is not possible in Level I. There are some minor changes which can speed it up. Change the following instruction:

```
10 FOR X = 0 TO 32
```

Add the following:

```
7 V = 64:W = 127:Z = 64
35      SET (W,Y)
36      SET (V,Y)
37      SET (Z,Y)
```

```
45      W = W - 1
46      V = V - 1
47      Z = Z + 1
```

This divides the screen into zones, filling zones 1 and 3 from left to right and zones 2 and 4 from right to left. The reason it is faster is because the loop is cut from 128 interactions to 33. It's faster yet with eight zones, as per this illustration:

In Statements 100 through 220 the values are supplied to the subroutine (statement 500) as previously mentioned. In each case only the variable which is different has been changed, for efficiency. Statement 110, for instance, depends upon the value for R and the value for S which have been established in statement 100. While this is more efficient, it is somewhat inflexible, in that instructions cannot be moved around. If you wish to move instructions around, you must set values for R, S, T, and U in every statement. This is mentioned because following this discussion we will have to have those values instruction by instruction.

You'll understand the reason for statements 230 through 270 when you see the display. Do not at this time panic with the STEP 5 and STEP 3 designations. They serve a very useful purpose.

Statement 280 is a timer—set the count to anything you like.

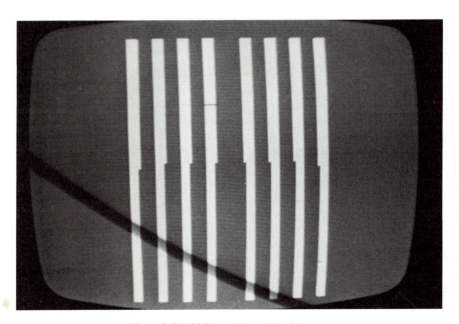

Figure 9. Rapid Screen Cover, Level I

The third graphics instruction is the POINT instruction. When the POINT instruction is used, designating the X,Y coordinates, a value is returned. That value is 1 if the position is lit (on) and Ø if the position is not lit (off). In the sequence between 31Ø and 34Ø, it is turned off if it is on, and on if it is off. In other words, the display is "negated," that is, changed from a positive image to a negative image. If Level II is installed, the statement looks like this:

```
IF POINT (X,Y) THEN RESET (X,Y) ELSE SET (X,Y)
```

Statements 37Ø to 44Ø merely draw a box around the picture.

It could be said that drawing a picture like this is of no practical value. But this has been a generalized approach to building a display. This one happened to make extensive use of straight lines, and therefore was a natural for the FOR . . . NEXT combination of instructions. On a very complicated permanent display, take another approach, as follows; make these changes:

Change:

```
1ØØ FOR N = 1 TO 13
11Ø      READ R,S,T,U
12Ø      GOSUB 5ØØ
13Ø NEXT N
```

Remove: statements 14Ø to 22Ø
Add:

```
6ØØ DATA 1,3,64,126
61Ø DATA 1,3,1,62
62Ø DATA 4,6,1,62
63Ø DATA 7,9,64,126
64Ø DATA 7,9,1,62
65Ø DATA 1Ø,12,1,62
66Ø DATA 13,15,1,62
67Ø DATA 13,15,64,126
68Ø DATA 16,17,1,62
69Ø DATA 19,21,1,126
7ØØ DATA 25,27,1,126
71Ø DATA 31,33,1,126
72Ø DATA 37,39,1,126
```

The net result is exactly the same. Instead of supplying values in the instructions themselves (100 to 220), the values are stored in DATA lines, and are extracted four at a time. With a little more work, all coordinates of the problem can be stored, even in random order, and the entire picture could be completed.

How is such a thing to be useful? There are a number of ways, for business, education, and planning. There is no limit. Let's pick one which at first may seem to be absurd—the layout of your favorite supermarket. Enter the following coding:

```
5 CLS
100 R = 0:S = 127:Y = 0:GOSUB 1000
110 R = 0:S = 127:Y = 47:GOSUB 1000
120 T = 0:U = 47:X = 0:GOSUB 1050
130 T = 0:U = 47:X = 127:GOSUB 1050
140 GOTO 140
1000 FOR X = R TO S
1010     SET (X,Y)
1020 NEXT X
1030 RETURN
1050 FOR Y = T TO U
1060     SET (X,Y)
1070 NEXT Y
1080 RETURN
```

RUN this much: Here the perimeter of the store is being built, and nothing more. Note that almost the same approach has been taken with the subroutines. Each has been constructed to require the supply of one of the coordinates from outside the subroutine, while the other, though keyed outside the subroutine, is a function of the FOR . . . NEXT loop on the inside of the subroutine. This is necessary as there are no nested FOR . . . NEXT loops in the subroutine. Note that in one subroutine the X variable is supplied while the Y variable is supplied in the other.

In the same manner as the line is drawn, there must be the facility to erase a line; time to locate the front door. The door in the illustration will be at the bottom right:

```
140 R = 100:S = 105:Y = 47:GOSUB 2000
150 GOTO 150
```

```
2000 FOR X = R TO S
2010     RESET (X,Y)
2020 NEXT X
2030 RETURN
2050 FOR Y = T TO U
2060     RESET (X,Y)
2070 NEXT Y
2080 RETURN
```

Both RESET routines have been constructed, although only one is used at this time.

Next, the location of those items which form the periphery, beginning with the office. Recall that the lines must be drawn around printing done on the screen, not the other way around. The labeling will be saved until later and then will be placed logically before the drawing of the floor plan.

```
150 R = 110:S = 127:Y = 40:GOSUB 1000
160 T = 40:U = 47:X = 110:GOSUB 1050
170 T = 42:U = 42:X = 110:GOSUB 2050
180 GOTO 180
```

Next, the Bakery Department:

```
180 R = 115:S = 127:Y = 30:GOSUB 1000
190 T = 30:U = 40:X = 115:GOSUB 1050
200 GOTO 200
```

As this routine is being developed, continue to "short circuit" the execution as is done in statement 200, replacing the statement and proceeding as the program is developed. RUN each phase to view the progress. Now to the Produce Department. The Produce Department will be on both sides of the aisle:

```
200 R = 115:S = 127:Y = 10:GOSUB 1000
210 T = 10:U = 30:X = 115:GOSUB 1050
220 R = 105:S = 110:Y = 15:GOSUB 1000
230 T = 15:U = 30:X = 110:GOSUB 1050
240 R = 105:S = 110:Y = 30:GOSUB 1000
250 T = 15:U = 30:X = 105:GOSUB 1050
```

```
260 T = 7:U = 8:X = 127:GOSUB 2050
270 GOTO 270
```

RUN this and note that a door has been included into the "back room." Now for the Delicatessen Department:

```
270 R = 90:S = 127:Y = 5:GOSUB 1000
280 T = 0:U = 5:X = 90:GOSUB 1050
290 GOTO 290
```

Now the Meat Department:

```
290 R = 30:S = 90:Y = 5:GOSUB 1000
300 T = 0:U = 5:X = 30:GOSUB 1050
310 GOTO 310
```

Time for another door to the "back room" and for the frozen meat counter; RUN these at each stage of the development:

```
310 R = 27:S = 29:Y = 0:GOSUB 2000
320 R = 0:S = 25:Y = 5:GOSUB 1000
330 T = 0:U = 5:X = 25:GOSUB 1050
340 T = 7:U = 8:X = 0:GOSUB 2050
350 GOTO 350
```

Note a second door to the "back room". Now how about the prepared meats (bologna, salami, kielbasa, etc.) counter?

```
350 R = 0:S = 10:Y = 10:GOSUB 1000
360 T = 10:U = 20:X = 10:GOSUB 1050
370 R = 0:S = 10:Y = 20:GOSUB 1000
380 GOTO 380
```

And the dairy:

```
380 R = 0:S = 10:Y = 35:GOSUB 1000
390 T = 10:U = 35:X = 10:GOSUB 1050
400 GOTO 400
```

Now a place for the prepared bakery goods:

```
400 R = 10:S = 20:Y = 42:GOSUB 1000
410 T = 35:U = 42:X = 10:GOSUB 1050
420 T = 42:U = 47:X = 20:GOSUB 1050
430 GOTO 430
```

For the magazines and greeting cards:

```
430 R = 15:S = 20:Y = 34:GOSUB 1000
440 R = 15:S = 20:Y = 40:GOSUB 1000
450 T = 34:U = 40:X = 15:GOSUB 1050
460 T = 34:U = 40:X = 20:GOSUB 1050
470 R = 20:S = 27:Y = 45:GOSUB 1000
480 T = 34:U = 47:X = 30:GOSUB 1050
490 T = 34:U = 45:X = 27:GOSUB 1050
500 R = 27:S = 30:Y = 34:GOSUB 1000
510 GOTO 510
```

The registers:

```
510 R = 36:S = 40:Y = 40:GOSUB 1000
520 R = 36:S = 40:Y = 38:GOSUB 1000
530 T = 38:U = 40:X = 36:GOSUB 1050
540 T = 38:U = 40:X = 40:GOSUB 1050
550 R = 46:S = 50:Y = 38:GOSUB 1000
560 R = 46:S = 50:Y = 40:GOSUB 1000
570 T = 38:U = 40:X = 46:GOSUB 1050
580 T = 38:U = 40:X = 50:GOSUB 1050
590 R = 56:S = 60:Y = 38:GOSUB 1000
600 R = 56:S = 60:Y = 40:GOSUB 1000
610 T = 38:U = 40:X = 56:GOSUB 1050
620 T = 38:U = 40:X = 60:GOSUB 1050
630 R = 66:S = 70:Y = 38:GOSUB 1000
640 R = 66:S = 70:Y = 40:GOSUB 1000
650 T = 38:U = 40:X = 56:GOSUB 1050
```

```
660 T = 38:U = 40:X = 60:GOSUB 1050
670 R = 76:S = 80:Y = 38:GOSUB 1000
680 R = 76:S = 80:Y = 40:GOSUB 1000
690 T = 38:U = 40:X = 76:GOSUB 1050
700 T = 38:U = 40:X = 80:GOSUB 1050
710 R = 86:S = 90:Y = 38:GOSUB 1000
720 R = 86:S = 90:Y = 40:GOSUB 1000
730 T = 38:U = 40:X = 86:GOSUB 1050
740 T = 38:U = 40:X = 90:GOSUB 1050
750 GOTO 750
```

And finally the aisles:

```
750 T = 10:U = 30:X = 15:GOSUB 1050
760 T = 10:U = 30:X = 20:GOSUB 1050
770 T - 10:U = 30:X = 25:GOSUB 1050
780 R = 15:S = 25:Y = 10:GOSUB 1000
790 R = 15:S = 25:Y = 30:GOSUB 1000
800 T = 10:U = 30:X = 30:GOSUB 1050
810 T = 10:U = 30:X = 35:GOSUB 1050
820 T = 10:U = 30:X = 40:GOSUB 1050
830 R = 30:S = 40:Y = 10:GOSUB 1000
840 R = 30:S = 40:Y = 30:GOSUB 1000
850 T = 10:U = 30:X = 45:GOSUB 1050
860 T = 10:U = 30:X = 50:GOSUB 1050
870 T = 10:U = 30:X = 55:GOSUB 1050
880 R = 45:S = 55:Y = 10:GOSUB 1000
890 R = 45:S = 55:Y = 30:GOSUB 1000
900 T = 10:U = 30:X = 60:GOSUB 1050
910 T = 10:U = 30:X = 65:GOSUB 1050
920 T = 10:U = 30:X = 70:GOSUB 1050
930 R = 60:S = 70:Y = 10:GOSUB 1000
940 R = 60:S = 70:Y = 30:GOSUB 1000
950 T = 10:U = 30:X = 75:GOSUB 1050
960 T = 10:U = 30:X = 80:GOSUB 1050
970 T = 10:U = 30:X = 85:GOSUB 1050
980 R = 75:S = 85:Y = 10:GOSUB 1000
```

```
99Ø R = 75:S = 85:Y = 3Ø:GOSUB 1ØØØ
995 GOTO 3ØØØ
3ØØØ T = 1Ø:U = 3Ø:X = 9Ø:GOSUB 1Ø5Ø
3Ø1Ø T = 1Ø:U = 3Ø:X = 95:GOSUB 1Ø5Ø
3Ø2Ø T = 1Ø:U = 3Ø:X = 1ØØ:GOSUB 1Ø5Ø
3Ø3Ø R = 9Ø:S = 1ØØ:Y = 1Ø:GOSUB 1ØØØ
3Ø4Ø R = 9Ø:S = 1ØØ:Y = 3Ø:GOSUB 1ØØØ
3Ø5Ø T = 1Ø:U = 13:X = 1Ø5:GOSUB 1Ø5Ø
3Ø6Ø T = 1Ø:U = 13:X = 11Ø:GOSUB 1Ø5Ø
3Ø7Ø R = 1Ø5:S = 11Ø:Y = 1Ø:GOSUB 1ØØØ
3Ø8Ø R = 1Ø5:S = 11Ø:Y = 13:GOSUB 1ØØØ
3Ø9Ø GOTO 3Ø9Ø
```

And there you have it, including a small counter at the end of the produce aisle. This concludes the drawing of the floor plan at your favorite supermarket. You should now have a pretty solid idea of how to perform one task using graphics. And you'd better CSAVE this one. About the toughest part of this particular exercise is that you get confused when looking at the program on the screen, as the numbers are quite similar.

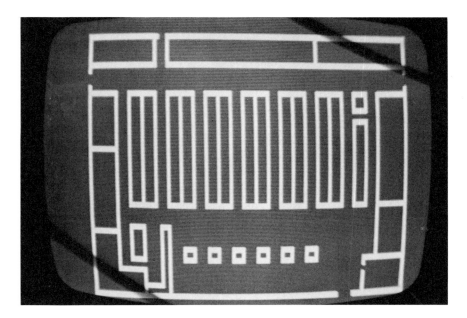

Figure 10. Supermarket Floor Plan

Should you care to label everything before you store the program off onto tape, do the following:

Add:

```
7 GOTO 4000
```

Change:

```
270 R = 90:S = 127:Y = 6:GOSUB 1000
290 R = 30:S = 90:Y = 6:GOSUB 1000
320 R = 0:S = 25:Y = 6:GOSUB 1000
```

These changes are to move the line so it does not conflict with the labels.

Add:

```
4000 PRINT
4010 PRINT "ЬЬFROZ. MT";TAB(30);"MEAT";TAB(50);"DELI"
4020 PRINT:PRINT:PRINT "  M";TAB(6);"A";TAB(13);"A";
4030 PRINT TAB(21);"A";TAB(28);"A";TAB(28);"A";
4040 PRINT TAB(36);"A";TAB(43);"A";TAB(51);"A";
4050 PRINT TAB(56);"A";TAB(60);"P"
4060 PRINT "ЬЬT";TAB(6);"I";TAB(13);"I";TAB(21);"I";
4070 PRINT TAB(28);"I";TAB(36);"I";TAB(43);"I";
4080 PRINT TAB(51);"I";TAB(56);"I";TAB(60);"R"
4090 PRINT TAB(6);"S";TAB(13);"S";TAB(21);"S";TAB(28);"S";
4100 PRINT TAB(36);"S";TAB(43);"S";TAB(51);"S";TAB(56);"S";
4110 PRINT TAB(60);"O"
4120 PRINT TAB(6);"L";TAB(13);"L";TAB(21);"L";TAB(28);"L";
4130 PRINT TAB(36);"L";TAB(43);"L";TAB(51);"L";TAB(56);"L";
4140 PRINT TAB(60);"D"
4150 PRINT "ЬЬD";TAB(6);"E";TAB(13);"E";TAB(21);"E";
4160 PRINT TAB(28);"E";TAB(36);"E";TAB(43);"E";TAB(51);"E";
4170 PRINT TAB(56);"E";TAB(60);"."
4180 PRINT "ЬЬR"
4190 PRINT "ЬЬY"
4200 PRINT TAB(11);"M";"A  I  S  L  E";TAB(60);"B"
4210 PRINT "ЬЬB";TAB(11);"A";TAB(60);"K"
4220 PRINT "ЬЬR";TAB(11);"G"
```

```
4230 PRINT "bbD";TAB(11);"S";TAB(20);"R  E  G  I  S";
4240 PRINT "T  E  R  S";TAB(58);"OFF"
4250 GOTO 100
```

Note that the instructions from 4000 to 4250 are established logically before the drawing of the graphics.

The use of graphics in home applications may be restricted to educational purposes, game development, planning applications, and for "prettying up" a display. It is highly unlikely that you'll be doing mechanical drawings, sewing pattern size adjustments, etc., with the TRS-80. It simply is not a multimillion dollar graphics system. Recall that it is impossible in Level I to establish a neatly formed curve, owing essentially to the shape of the graphics character.

To demonstrate this point, enter and RUN the following:

```
10 CLS
20 Y = 10
30 W = 64
100 FOR X = 64 TO 32 STEP -1
110    SET (X,Y)
```

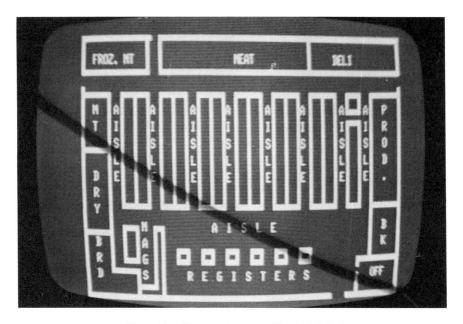

Figure 11.   Supermarket Floor Plan with Labels.

```
120      SET (W,Y)
130      SET (64,Y)
140      Y = Y + 1
150      W = W + 1
160 NEXT X
170 GOTO 170
```

Technically, that's a "curve," although at the moment, it looks like the business end of a pup tent. The construction of a curve with a greater degree of slope would require the use of distribution formulas. This particular "curve" begins at the midpoint and works in both directions and produces a result which is a "normal" distribution. But you get the idea.

The use of graphics for games is pretty straightforward. The drawing of any kind of playing field would make use of the graphics idea. For instance, enter and RUN the following:

```
10 CLS
20 Y = 14
30 FOR N = 1 TO 2
40      FOR X = 20 TO 100
50            SET (X,Y)
60      NEXT X
70      Y = Y + 10
80 NEXT N
90 X = 45
100 FOR N = 1 TO 2
110      FOR Y = 5 TO 32
120            SET (X,Y)
130            SET (X + 1,Y)
140      NEXT Y
150      X = X + 30
160 NEXT N
170 GOTO 170
```

You'll recognize the shape immediately, and there will be more about this game later in the book. The important thing to recognize here, however, is the spacing, and also the width of the vertical line, which is the reason for the instruction at 130.

Developing a picture on the screen, when all factors are known, is an easy task. Merely determine which graphics positions are to be lighted and, in one of the ways discussed, light it. Developing a picture based upon program logic is a bit more difficult. Drawing lines and "curves" based on the intermediate results of your own program takes some doing, because a procedure must be developed which is consistently accurate.

The following illustrates the point in a relatively easy to understand manner. It's a simple horserace, involving three races of four horses each. As constructed, the program allows the selection of "WIN," "PLACE," and "SHOW," but it is left to the reader to add the logic for placing bets and determining payoff. The program advances the horses based on the number received from a random number generator and moves the selected horse based upon the program itself. Try the following. Discussion will follow the routine:

```
10 RESTORE: C = 0
20 CLS
30 PRINT AT 15, "HⱮOⱮRⱮSⱮEⱮⱮRⱮAⱮCⱮE"
40 PRINT:PRINT "THE HORSES ARE:"
50 READ A$
60 PRINT:PRINT TAB(5) "1.Ɇ";A$
70 READ A$
80 PRINT TAB(5);"2.Ɇ";A$
90 READ A$
100 PRINT TAB(5);"3.Ɇ";A$
110 READ A$
120 PRINT TAB(5);"4.Ɇ";A$
130 PRINT:INPUT "PICK TO WIN";A(1)
140 IF (A(1) < 1) + (A(1) > 4) THEN 130
150 INPUT "PICK TO PLACE";A(2)
160 IF (A(2) < 1) + (A(2) > 4) THEN 150
170 IF A(1) = A(2) THEN 150
180 INPUT "PICK TO SHOW";A(3)
190 IF (A(3) < 1) + (A(3) > 4) THEN 180
200 IF (A(3) = A(1)) + (A(3) = A(2)) THEN 180
210 PRINT:INPUT "PRESS ENTER TO START RACE";A
220 CLS:C = C + 1:R = 6:S = 18:T = 30:U = 42:V = 0
230 G = 2:H = 2:I = 2:J = 2:GOSUB 1000:GOSUB 3100
```

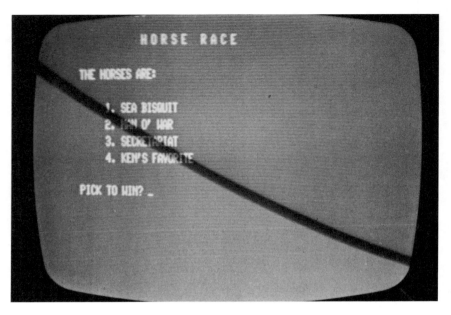

Figure 12   Horse Race Menu

```
240 GOSUB 3200:GOSUB 3300:GOSUB 3400
250 GOSUB 2000:GOTO 250
1000 CLS
1010 FOR Y=12 TO 36 STEP 12
1020     FOR X=0 TO 127
1030         SET (X,Y)
1040     NEXT X
1050 NEXT Y
1060 FOR X=0 TO 117 STEP 117
1070     FOR Y=0 TO 47 STEP 2
1080         SET (X,Y)
1090     NEXT Y
1100 NEXT X
1110 RETURN
2000 A = RND(4):A = INT(A)
2010 ON A GOTO 2020,2050,2080,2110:GOTO 2000
2020 G = G + 1
2030 IF G > 111 THEN 2140
```

```
2040 GOTO 2190
2050 H = H + 1
2060 IF H > 111 THEN 2200
2070 GOTO 2250
2080 I = I + 1
2090 IF I > 111 THEN 2260
2100 GOTO 2310
2110 J = J + 1
2120 IF J > 111 THEN 2320
2130 GOTO 2370
2140 V = V + 1
2150 IF V = 1 THEN PRINT AT 59, "WIN"
2160 IF V = 2 THEN PRINT AT 59, "PLACE"
2170 IF V = 3 THEN PRINT AT 59, "SHOW":G = -100
2180 GOTO 2380
2190 GOSUB 3100:GOTO 2380
2200 V = V + 1
2210 IF V = 1 THEN PRINT AT 378, "WIN"
2220 IF V = 2 THEN PRINT AT 378, "PLACE"
2230 IF V = 3 THEN PRINT AT 378, "SHOW":H = -100
2240 GOTO 2380
2250 GOSUB 3200:GOTO 2380
2260 V = V + 1
2270 IF V = 1 THEN PRINT AT 632, "WIN"
2280 IF V = 2 THEN PRINT AT 632, "PLACE"
2290 IF V = 3 THEN PRINT AT 632, "SHOW":I = -100
2300 GOTO 2380
2310 GOSUB 3300:GOTO 2380
2320 V = V + 1
2330 IF V = 1 THEN PRINT AT 890, "WIN"
2340 IF V = 2 THEN PRINT AT 890, "PLACE"
2350 IF V = 3 THEN PRINT AT 890, "SHOW":J = -100
2360 GOTO 2380
2370 GOSUB 3400
2380 IF V = 3 THEN 2400
2390 RETURN
```

```
2400 FOR Z = 1 TO 2000:NEXT Z
2410 CLS:INPUT "RUN AGAIN (Y/N)";A$
2420 IF A$ = "N" THEN 2450
2430 IF C = 3 THEN 10
2440 GOTO 20
2450 CLS:PRINT AT 0,"BYE"
2460 GOTO 2450
3100 REM "HORSE #1"
3105 IF G < 0 THEN 3170
3110 SET (G+6, R-1):RESET (G+5, R-1)
3115 SET (G,R):RESET (G-1,R):RESET (G-1,R+1)
3120 SET (G+1,R)
3125 SET (G+2,R)
3130 SET (G+3,R)
3135 SET (G+4,R)
3140 SET (G+5,R)
3145 SET (G,R+1)
3150 SET (G+2,R+1):RESET (G+1,R+1)
3155 SET (G+4,R+1):RESET (G+3,R+1)
3160 SET (G+2,R+2):RESET (G+1,R+2)
3165 SET (G+4,R+2):RESET (G+3,R+2)
3170 RETURN
3200 REM "HORSE #2"
3205 IF H < 0 THEN 3270
3210 SET (H+6,S+1):RESET (H+5,S+1)
3215 SET (H,S):RESET (H-1,S):RESET (H-1,S+1)
3220 SET (H+1,S)
3225 SET (H+2,S)
3230 SET (H+3,S)
3235 SET (H+4,S)
3240 SET (H+5,S)
3245 SET (H,S+1)
3250 SET (H+2,S+1):RESET (H+1,S+1)
3255 SET (H+4,S+1):RESET (H+3,S+1)
3260 SET (H+2,S+2):RESET (H+1,S+2)
```

```
3265 SET (H+4,S+2):RESET (H+3,S+2)
3270 RETURN
3300 REM "HORSE #3"
3305 IF I < 0 THEN 3370
3310 SET (I+6,T+1):RESET (I+5,T-1)
3315 SET (I,T):RESET (I-1,T):RESET (I-1, T+1)
3320 SET (I+1,T)
3325 SET (I+2,T)
3330 SET (I+3,T)
3335 SET (I+4,T)
3340 SET (I+5,T)
3345 SET (I,T+1)
3350 SET (I+2,T+1):RESET (I+1,T+1)
3355 SET (I+4,T+1):RESET (I+3,T+1)
3360 SET (I+2,T+2):RESET (I+1,T+2)
3365 SET (I+4,T+2):RESET (I+3,T+2)
3370 RETURN
3400 REM "HORSE #4"
3405 IF J < 0 THEN 3470
3410 SET (J+6,U=1):RESET (J+5,U=1)
3415 SET (J,U):RESET (J-1,U):RESET (J-1,U+1)
3420 SET (J+1,U)
3425 SET (J+2,U)
3430 SET (J+3,U)
3435 SET (J+4,U)
3440 SET (J+5,U)
3445 SET (J,U+1)
3450 SET (J+2,U+1):RESET (J+1,U+1)
3455 SET (J+4,U+1):RESET (J+3,U+1)
3460 SET (J+2,U+2):RESET (J+1,U+2)
3465 SET (J+4,U+2):RESET (J+3,U+2)
3470 RETURN
4000 DATA "SEA BISQUIT","MAN O' WAR","SECRETARIAT","KEN'S FAVORITE"
4010 DATA "LUCKY LADY","BLACK BEAUTY","RUN HORSE RUN","SLOW PLUG"
4020 DATA "SHARON'S SIREN","ALIDAR","PRINCE ALEX","HOLLY'S FOLLY"
```

You'll note that the names of each set of four horses are stored in the DATA lines of 4000 to 4020 and that they are read, in turn, by statements 50, 70, 90, 110. In this program only A$ is used, reading them one at a time. Note that the logic from statement 130 to statement 210 allows selection of "WIN," "PLACE," and "SHOW." Should you wish to add odds and payoffs to the program, those selections reside at A(1), A(2), and A(3) in the array. Note also that the logic at statements 140, 160, 170, 190, and 200 keeps you from selecting the same horse twice and from selecting a horse outside the range of 1 to 4.

In statement 220, variable C is used to count the number of the race. After the third race (statement 2430) the DATA lines are restored. Following that, the line position of the body of each horse is established as follows:

Horse #1	Line 6 (R)
Horse #2	Line 18 (S)
Horse #3	Line 30 (T)
Horse #4	Line 42 (U)

These are the "Y" variables which will be used in the SET commands (and RESET commands) in the subroutines at 3100, 3200, 3300, and 3400.

The "X" variables for each horse are established in statement 230, each beginning at X-position 2 (the starting line). The horses will be "inched" along their respective lines in the subroutine beginning at 2000 until they encounter X-position 111, the first being "WIN," the second to cross being "PLACE," and the third being "SHOW." The last one is "LOSER," but that is not displayed on the screen.

Subroutine 1000 draws the lines between the horses—identifying each one's "track." Note that subroutines 3100, 3200, 3300, and 3400 are structured identically, one for each horse. These are the routines to "light" the horses as they move across the screen. The logic includes instructions to "blank" out the trailing edge (at statements 10, 15, 50, 55, 60, and 65 of each subroutine). At 05 of each routine is the logic which keeps the horse from moving after he's crossed the finish line. Any negative number will do, but -100 has been used at 2170, 2230, 2290, and 2350. Subroutine 1000 also has the start and finish lines.

The subroutine at 2000 does all the work. Variable V is used to determine the order of crossing the finish line, and the appropriate "WIN," "PLACE," or "SHOW" message is displayed in the horse's track, to the right of the finish line, and that's it. A perfect example of modifying the display under program control, this one was presented for its simplicity and straightforwardness.

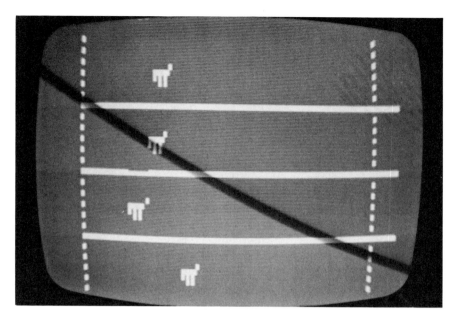

Figure 13   Horserace Display. Note that horse #3 was moving when the picture was taken (the disjointed head).

HIGH MARKS FOR TRS-80!

The next illustration takes an entirely different approach. This is the problem: the program will be constructed to plot the results of 10 tests on a graph. The graph will be 10 units on each side (10 by 10). The X-Axis will be the test number, while the Y-Axis will be the score (Ø to 1ØØ). The first step is to draw and label the graph:

```
1Ø CLS:GOTO 11Ø
2Ø X=11
3Ø FOR Y = Ø TO 35
4Ø    SET (X,Y)
5Ø NEXT Y
6Ø Y = 35
7Ø FOR X = 11 TO 115
8Ø    SET (X,Y)
9Ø NEXT X
1ØØ GOTO 18Ø
11Ø PRINT:PRINT "S6́1ØØ":PRINT "b́b́b́9Ø"
```

```
120 PRINT "Cƀƀ80":PRINT "ƀƀƀ70":PRINT "Oƀƀ60"
130 PRINT "ƀƀƀ50":PRINT "Rƀƀ40":PRINT "ƀƀƀ30"
140 PRINT "Eƀƀ20":PRINT "ƀƀƀ10":PRINT "ƀƀƀƀ0"
150 PRINT "TEST";TAB(7);"1";TAB(12);"2";TAB(17);"3";
    TAB(22);"4";TAB(27);"5";TAB(32);"6";TAB(37);
    "7";TAB(42);"8";TAB(47);"9";TAB(52);"10"
160 GOTO 20
```

The movement from statement 10 to statement 110 was necessary to place the printing before the graphics. RUN this much, just to ensure that it's working. The READY message is expected.

As previously mentioned, if all the points on a graphic display are known, there is no problem in developing the display. However, when accepting data to a program, the procedure must be developed so that it works consistently, regardless of the data provided. To do this requires an *algorithm*. An algorithm is only a formula or method which works consistently. In developing this program, many algorithms were tried before one which works consistently was discovered. The following example has been kept deliberately simple. It is presented for illustrative purposes and it does work consistently.

On the screen there is now a *matrix*, a 10 by 10 element set of "boxes" which represent the major points which can be derived. In the first DATA line (790, following), 10 scores have been placed. These 10 are for illustrative purposes. The routine will work correctly with any set of 10 numbers. The following routine extracts those scores from the DATA line and places them onto the array as what the statistician calls *class points*.

```
170 REM "LOAD ARRAY WITH SCORE COORDINATES"
180 L = 3:M =4:N = 5:P = 100:Q = 97:R = 94
200 FOR Z = 1 TO 11
210     A(L) = P:P = P - 10:A(L + 100)= L
```

Statement 190 was intentionally omitted. What has been done here is the division of each unit of 10 points into three segments (100, 97, 94). Each is decremented by 10 (the distance of variable Z), giving total coverage for 100 points. The reason for this is that there is not room on the screen for 100 vertical units, thus requiring that the plotted point is placed at the nearest valid coordinate. This, then, loads those plotting points to the array, and their relative position also to the array, removed by 100 array units. The following will complete the process, testing for negative numbers (variables Q and R):

```
220     L = L + 3
230     A(M) = Q:Q = Q - 10:A(M + 100) = M
240     IF Q < 0 THEN Q = 0
250     M = M + 3
260     A(N) = R:R = R - 10:A(N + 100) = N
270     IF R < 0 THEN R = 0
280     N = N + 3
290 NEXT Z
```

Now that it has been determined which class points are closest to the actual scores, the array can be scanned to determine where on the screen to place the points which represent the scores. The entire routine is presented, followed by the explanation:

```
300 L = 3:M = 4:N = 5
310 FOR X = 15 TO 110 STEP 10
320     READ A
330     FOR L = 3 TO 33
340         IF A = A(L) THEN 370
350         IF A < A(L) THEN NEXT L
360     IF A > A(L) THEN 380
370     Y = A(L + 100):GOTO 430
380     B = A(L) - A:B = INT(B)
390     IF B = -1 THEN Y = A(L+100)
400     IF B = -2 THEN Y = A(L+101)
410     IF B = -3 THEN Y = A(L+102)
420     IF B = -4 THEN Y = A(L+103)
430     SET (X,Y)
440 NEXT X
```

In 300 the original array pointers are restored. Each of the scores is read, one at a time (320), comparing its relationship to the predetermined spanning that had been defined. The 3 to 33 span in statement 330 corresponds to the places within the array where the points have been stored (3 points for each span of 10 points, or 33). Of course, 3 times 10 does not equal 33, but recall that the process begins at 3.

If one of the spanning points (4, 7, 10) is hit precisely (the equal condition, 340), then it is only necessary to extract the relative position (L + 100) and store it in the Y coordinate, to be used directly on the screen. However, if it's not equal, some manipulation must be done. If the score is less than the examined point, perhaps the next point is the one—or some distance between the two (see statement 35Ø). If it is greater, however, the next task is to determine how much greater. That determination is made in statement 38Ø.

Enter a problem: the difference may be either positive or negative, depending upon the Y-Axis relationship of the score to the predetermined spanning point. So, the number is made "pure" (changed to an integer—38Ø) and a determination is made as to its relative negative position (39Ø to 42Ø). Once that is known, and given that all possible paths have been accounted for, the point can be set—statement 43Ø.

Now the curves can be developed. Before that is done, here are the scores which are used in the illustration.

```
79Ø DATA 18, 78, 13, 96, 21, 5, 65, 87, 12, 1ØØ
```

As stated before, these can be any number, provided that 10 scores are placed in the DATA line.

As can be seen, the theoretical student alternates between brilliance and stupidity—just the sort of thing for plotting a sawtooth curve. This is done with a DATA line, but the program could be modified for entry of the ten factors from the keyboard. To do that, the scores must be stored in the array (suggest A(51) to A(6Ø)) and then the READ routine must be altered to access the array instead of the DATA line. If this is to be done, there are some other instructions to be deleted. Those instructions will be identified as they occur.

RUN the program and note that the points are indeed plotted. The DATA line approach was selected for illustrative purposes. As stated, it would be necessary to have an input command to load the array. To do so, zero the array first, at least the score points, in case you decide not to enter 10 scores, as the program is structured to handle all ten.

Getting the points of the graph plotted is not too difficult. The more difficult part remains, and the algorithmic approach is impractical. Note that while each of the 10 test incidences are separated by 10 elements of the X-Axis, the distance from the beginning of the graph (the zero point) and the first test is considerably shorter.

To accomplish the building of the curve, the following must be considered:

- Will the curve slope upwards, downwards, or remain horizontal?
- Each curve must span 10 horizontal graphic points (except for the initial curve) and all must be accounted for, despite the fact that there

may be no corresponding rise or fall. A change of 7 units over a horizontal span of 10 means that each would occupy .7 of the line, a physical impossibility.

To perform this, the POINT instruction must be used, examining the Y-Axis points a pair at a time. When the graph points are located, the difference between them will determine the slope of the line, as follows:

- A negative value means an increasing slope.
- A zero value indicates no slope (horizontal).
- A positive value indicates a decreasing slope.

The only problems which will be encountered will be in the relationship of the first Y-Axis point and the baseline (zero). The rest will follow in natural sequence:

```
45Ø REM "DEVELOP THE CURVES"
46Ø REM "FIRST THE ZERO BASELINE TO THE Y-AXIS"
47Ø FOR Y = Ø TO 33
48Ø     IF POINT (15,Y) = 1 THEN 5ØØ
49Ø NEXT Y
```

It is known that the first point is in the 15th X-Axis position, so it isn't necessary to scan for that. The scan, then, is strictly along the Y-Axis. When it is found, it will be highlighted:

```
5ØØ FOR Z = 1 TO 1ØØ:RESET (15,Y):SET (15,Y):NEXT Z:S = Y:F = Y
```

The FOR . . . NEXT loop merely flashes the point to draw attention. This instruction is in one other place in the program. F stands for "First Point" and S stands for "Second Point," the variables used as each pair of points is examined. At this point, it is known that the "from" coordinate is 33 (base Ø) and the "to" Y coordinate is the value of Y at the time the POINT command has discovered the point which was lit. F is set as a matter of course, particularly to enhance later coding. S is the second coordinate of the first pair, and becomes the first coordinate of the second and every subsequent pair.

The length of the rise or fall is developed in variable A. In the first case, the length is simply the difference between the place of the discovery of the point and 33. Thus:

```
51Ø A = 33 - Y:A = INT(A)
```

Next comes the determination of the unit of movement. Since there are only three spaces in this first point position, the length of the line (A) must be divided by three:

```
52Ø B = INT(A/3)
```

Thus, B is the distribution factor along the curve from Ø to Y. The curve must then be moved in increments (decrements or horizontals) of B until the span of 3 X-Axis points is satisfied. The same approach is used for the other points, but the spanning technique is different. Here's how it's done:

```
53Ø Y = 33:X = 13:B = B + 1
54Ø T = A/B:T = INT(T)
55Ø FOR P = 1 TO B
56Ø     FOR N = 1 TO T
57Ø         SET (X,Y)
58Ø         Y = Y - 1
59Ø     NEXT N
6ØØ     X = X + 1
61Ø NEXT P:X = X - 1
```

It was necessary to increment B to account for the difference between the number and its integer, to give a relatively equal break of the upward-climbing line (See instruction 58Ø). When A is divided by B, the result (T) becomes the loop control mechanism for the series of instructions above. At 61Ø it is necessary to decrement X, as it has moved one position beyond the valid point, by virtue of the fact that the incrementation of X follows the decrementation of Y.

With all these INTegers flying around, there is always the possibility of some difference between the final value of Y and the target address of S. This is addressed like this:

```
62Ø FOR P = Y TO S
63Ø     SET (X,Y)
64Ø     Y = Y - 1
65Ø NEXT P
```

That completes the line from the baseline to the first point. There are nine points to go, and the approach will be changed, as the routine to form the curves for the balance of the graph can be developed. Whenever a program is being written, it is frequently necessary to adjust pointers to get things started. That is true in this case, as the same position should not be POINTed twice. Thus, the Y pointer is moved once and the X pointer is moved twice, but in two separate increments—the second increment will become part of a loop:

```
660 Y = Y + 1:X = X + 1
670 X = X + 1:F = S:H = X:I = Y:E = E + 1
```

This is a unique situation, in that the first ten positions must be scanned (using X and Y variables) to locate the new plotting position and then the same ground must be covered with a curve or line. Thus, to preserve the location of the located point (which will become the new S (second)), the X and Y coordinates are stored off in H and I, respectively, after having identified the former second position (S) as the new first position (F). E, you will recall, is used for loop control. It is the factor which will limit the plotting to 10 points and no more:

```
680 FOR Y = 0 TO 33
690     IF POINT (X,Y) = 1 THEN 730
700 NEXT Y
710 X = X + 1
720 GOTO 680
730 FOR Z = 1 TO 100:RESET (X,Y):SET (X,Y):NEXT Z:S = Y
```

While it is known that the next point is 10 X-Axis positions away and that you could easily update this X coordinate by 10, the program would run a bit too fast. In this manner, the space between the test occurrences is scanned, one X-Axis position at a time until the new point is found. Then the point is "flashed" and the new second position (S) is stored. Now the rise and fall of the curve (commonly called the "slope") can be calculated and the spread (across 10 positions of the X-Axis) can be determined:

```
740 A = S - F:A = INT(A)
750 B = A/10
```

It's at this point that the slope is determined, and the mechanism for spanning the distance can be selected. When the slope of the line is upward, the second value (S) is a lower value of Y than the first value (F), with the result that A ends up negative. Then, when the slope of the line is less than 10 points, there develops a value of B which is fractional (or decimal). Thus:

```
76Ø IF B < 1 THEN 115Ø
77Ø B = INT(B)
78Ø GOTO 134Ø
```

And, of course, if the slope is fractional, taking the INTeger of B will produce a zero, with indeterminate effect upon the screen. So, statement 76Ø identifies the fact that it is fractional, with a change in sequence to 115Ø. Recall the DATA line at 79Ø. Instruction 78Ø moves around the DATA line at 79Ø. In fact, having to develop one DATA line, balance of the DATA lines can be developed at this time, beginning at statement 8ØØ. Note that there are 35 DATA lines, each looking somewhat like a binary number. Each contains a series of 1's and Ø's; 1Ø of them to each of the 35 lines. Each contains the "spread" of the slope. A Ø indicates no rise or fall, while a 1 indicates a rise or fall of one. Further down in the list, the number changes to 2's, 3's, and 4's. Looking at DATA line 8ØØ, note that there will be a rise of only one place, over a length of ten. It's important to recognize that there is a rise of 1 Y-Axis point for each "1" encountered. For the first nine positions, the line would be horizontal. The next position, the 1, will cause the line to be sloped, either above or below. Look at line 81Ø: in this instance, there are two rises in the line. Line 114Ø rises 35 places over a span of 10.

Here are the DATA lines in their entirety:

```
8ØØ DATA Ø,Ø,Ø,Ø,Ø,Ø,Ø,Ø,Ø,1          #1
81Ø DATA Ø,1,Ø,Ø,Ø,1,Ø,Ø,Ø,Ø          #2
82Ø DATA Ø,1,Ø,1,Ø,Ø,1,Ø,Ø.Ø          #3
83Ø DATA Ø,1,1,Ø,Ø,1,Ø,Ø,1,Ø          #4
84Ø DATA Ø,1,1,Ø,1,Ø,1,Ø,1,Ø          #5
85Ø DATA Ø,1,Ø,1,Ø,Ø,1,1,1,1          #6
86Ø DATA Ø,1,Ø,1,Ø,1,1,1,1,1          #7
87Ø DATA Ø,1,1,1,Ø,1,1,1,1,1          #8
88Ø DATA Ø,1,1,1,1,1,1,1,1,1          #9
89Ø DATA 1,1,1,1,1,1,1,1,1,1          #10
9ØØ DATA 1,2,1,1,1,1,1,1,1,1          #11
91Ø DATA 1,2,2,1,1,1,1,1,1,1          #12
92Ø DATA 1,2,2,2,1,1,1,1,1,1          #13
93Ø DATA 1,2,2,2,2,1,1,1,1,1          #14
94Ø DATA 1,2,2,2,2,2,1,1,1,1          #15
95Ø DATA 1,2,2,2,2,2,2,1,1,1          #16
96Ø DATA 1,2,2,2,2,2,2,2,1,1          #17
```

```
97Ø DATA 1,2,2,2,2,2,2,2,2,1          #18
98Ø DATA 1,2,2,2,2,2,2,2,2,2          #19
99Ø DATA 2,2,2,2,2,2,2,2,2,2          #20
1ØØØ DATA 2,3,2,2,2,2,2,2,2,2         #21
1Ø1Ø DATA 2,3,3,2,2,2,2,2,2,2         #22
1Ø2Ø DATA 2,3,3,3,2,2,2,2,2,2         #23
1Ø3Ø DATA 2,3,3,3,3,2,2,2,2,2         #24
1Ø4Ø DATA 2,3,3,3,3,3,2,2,2,2         #25
1Ø5Ø DATA 2,3,3,3,3,3,3,2,2,2         #26
1Ø6Ø DATA 2,3,3,3,3,3,3,3,2,2         #27
1Ø7Ø DATA 2,3,3,3,3,3,3,3,3,2         #28
1Ø8Ø DATA 2,3,3,3,3,3,3,3,3,3         #29
1Ø9Ø DATA 3,3,3,3,3,3,3,3,3,3         #30
11ØØ DATA 3,4,3,3,3,3,3,3,3,3         #31
111Ø DATA 3,4,4,3,3,3,3,3,3,3         #32
112Ø DATA 3,4,4,4,3,3,3,3,3,3         #33
113Ø DATA 3,4,4,4,4,3,3,3,3,3         #34
114Ø DATA 3,4,4,4,4,4,3,3,3,3         #35
```

Actually, lines 34 and 35 are not necessary, in that the problem defines a range of 33 vertical lines. But somebody is bound to try to enter a value above 1ØØ. The line will plot, but the POINT instruction will not find the point above 1ØØ, allowing the program to advance to the second subsequent point. The assignment of the relative spreads in lines 1 to 10 is purely arbitrary and can be changed. The others follow a formula. If the values in each DATA line are summed, that sum matches the relative line indicator given at the right. The number of positions on the slope is developed and then selected from the DATA lines.

```
115Ø X = H:Y = I:RESTORE
116Ø FOR N = 1 TO 1Ø:READ Q:NEXT N
```

The values of X and Y are restored. A bypass read of the scores to get at the DATA lines which contain the slope spreads is then performed. This first routine is devoted to those fractional amounts (B $<$ 1).

```
117Ø B = B * 1Ø:B = ABS(B)
```

Here the number is raised from a fractional position to a whole number position. And, a new instruction is introduced—the ABSolute instruction, which produces a number without a sign. B will now become the search control to find the appropriate DATA line—the relative line number:

```
1180 FOR N = 1 TO B
1190    READ A(201),A(202),A(203),A(204),A(205),A(206),
           A(207),A(208),A(209),A(210)
1200 NEXT N
```

Having located the appropriate relative line, the 10 values contained there are then extracted and placed into the array in 10 consecutively unused positions (zero-relative to 200). Now those 10 values are scanned and the lines are drawn:

```
1210 FOR N = 1 TO 10
1220    Q = N + 200
1230    IF A < 0 THEN 1280
1240    IF A > 0 THEN 1290
1250    SET (X,Y)
1260    X = X + 1
1270    GOTO 1300
1280    Y = Y - A(Q):GOTO 1250
1290    Y = Y + A(Q):GOTO 1250
1300 NEXT N
```

The only thing of significance to note is the test for the sign on variable A. The negative sign means that the slope will be upward, while the positive sign will mean that the slope will be downward.

Now the axis positions are updated, checking to see if the problem is completed. If not, the process begins again with the first instruction in the loop:

```
1310 X = X - 1:Y = Y + 1
1320 IF E = > 9 THEN 1550
1330 GOTO 670
```

At 1340 begins the routine for those slopes which rise more than 10 units of Y-Axis for each 10 X-Axis units horizontal spread. The procedure is nearly the same, except that B is not multiplied:

```
1340 X = H:Y = I:RESTORE
1350 FOR N = 1 TO B:READ Q:NEXT N
```

Instructions 1360 and 1370 were testing instructions and have been re-moved from the program.

```
1380 B = ABS(A)
1390 FOR N = 1 TO B
1400    READ A(201),A(202),A(203),A(204),A(205),
          A(206),A(207),A(208),A(209),A(210)
1410 NEXT N
1420 FOR N = 1 TO 10
1430    Q = N + 200
1440    IF A < THEN 1490
1450    IF A > 0 THEN 1500
1460    SET (X,Y)
1470    X = X + 1
1480    GOTO 1510
1490    Y = Y - A(Q):GOTO 1460
1500    Y = Y + A(Q):GOTO 1460
1510 NEXT N
1520 X = X - 1:Y = Y + 1
1530 IF E = > 9 THEN 1550
1540 GOTO 670
```

There it is. All that is now required is to draw the range lines:

```
1550 FOR Y = 4 TO 35 STEP 6
1560    FOR X = 15 TO 105 STEP 10
1570       SET (X,Y)
1580    NEXT X
1590 NEXT Y
1600 PRINT "PROGRAM ENDED"
1610 GOTO 1610
```

Here is the program in its entirety:

```
10 CLS:GOTO 110
20 X=11
30 FOR Y = 0 TO 35
40    SET (X,Y)
```

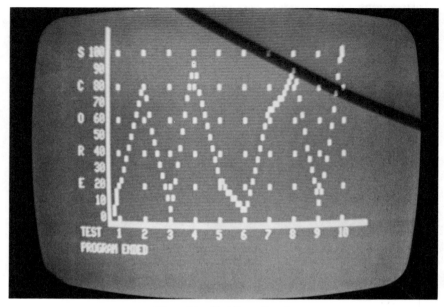

Figure 14.   Test Score Graph

```
50 NEXT Y
60 Y = 35
70 FOR X = 11 TO 115
80    SET (X,Y)
90 NEXT X
100 GOTO 180
110 PRINT:PRINT "Sb100":PRINT "bbb90"
120 PRINT "Cbb80":PRINT "bbb70":PRINT "Obb60"
130 PRINT "bbb50":PRINT "Rbb40":PRINT "bbb30"
140 PRINT "Ebb20":PRINT "bbb10":PRINT "bbbb0"
150 PRINT "TEST";TAB(7);"1";TAB(12);"2";TAB(17);"3";
    TAB(22);"4";TAB(27);"5";TAB(32);"6";TAB(37);
    "7";TAB(42);"8";TAB(47);"9";TAB(52);"10"
160 GOTO 20
170 REM "LOAD ARRAY WITH SCORE COORDINATES"
180 L = 3:M =4:N = 5:P = 100:Q = 97:R = 94
200 FOR Z = 1 TO 11
```

```
210     A(L) = P:P = P - 10:A(L + 100)= L
220     L = L + 3
230     A(M) = Q:Q = Q - 10:A(M + 100) = M
240     IF Q < 0 THEN Q = 0
250     M = M + 3
260     A(N) = R:R = R - 10:A(N + 100) = N
270     IF R < 0 THEN R = 0
280     N = N + 3
290 NEXT Z
300 L = 3:M = 4:N = 5
310 FOR X = 15 TO 110 STEP 10
320     READ A
330     FOR L = 3 TO 33
340         IF A = A(L) THEN 370
350         IF A < A(L) THEN NEXT L
360     IF A > A(L) THEN 380
370     Y = A(L + 100):GOTO 430
380     B = A(L) - A:B = INT(B)
390     IF B = -1 THEN Y = A(L+100)
400     IF B = -2 THEN Y = A(L+101)
410     IF B = -3 THEN Y = A(L+102)
420     IF B = -4 THEN Y = A(L+103)
430     SET (X,Y)
440 NEXT X
450 REM "DEVELOP THE CURVES"
460 REM "FIRST THE ZERO BASELINE TO THE Y-AXIS"
470 FOR Y = 0 TO 33
480     IF POINT (15,Y) = 1 THEN 500
490 NEXT Y
500 FOR Z = 1 TO 100:RESET (15,Y):SET (15,Y):NEXT Z:S = Y:F = Y
510 A = 33 - Y:A = INT(A)
520 B = INT(A/3)
530 Y = 33:X = 13:B = B + 1
540 T = A/B:T = INT(T)
550 FOR P = 1 TO B
```

```
560      FOR N = 1 TO T
570         SET (X,Y)
580         Y = Y - 1
590      NEXT N
600      X = X + 1
610 NEXT P:X = X - 1
620 FOR P = Y TO S
630     SET (X,Y)
640     Y = Y - 1
650 NEXT P
660 Y = Y + 1:X = X + 1
670 X = X + 1:F = S:H = X:I = Y:E = E + 1
680 FOR Y = 0 TO 33
690     IF POINT (X,Y) = 1 THEN 730
700 NEXT Y
710 X = X + 1
720 GOTO 680
730 FOR Z = 1 TO 100:RESET (X,Y):SET (X,Y):NEXT Z:S = Y
740 A = S - F:A = INT(A)
750 B = A/10
760 IF B < 1 THEN 1150
770 B = INT(B)
780 GOTO 1340
790 18,78,13,96,21,5,65,87,12,100
800 DATA 0,0,0,0,0,0,0,0,0,1
810 DATA 0,1,0,0,0,1,0,0,0,0
820 DATA 0,1,0,1,0,0,1,0,0.0
830 DATA 0,1,1,0,0,1,0,0,1,0
840 DATA 0,1,1,0,1,0,1,0,1,0
850 DATA 0,1,0,1,0,0,1,1,1,1
860 DATA 0,1,0,1,0,1,1,1,1,1
870 DATA 0,1,1,1,0,1,1,1,1,1
880 DATA 0,1,1,1,1,1,1,1,1,1
890 DATA 1,1,1,1,1,1,1,1,1,1
900 DATA 1,2,1,1,1,1,1,1,1,1
```

```
910 DATA 1,2,2,1,1,1,1,1,1,1
920 DATA 1,2,2,2,1,1,1,1,1,1
930 DATA 1,2,2,2,2,1,1,1,1,1
940 DATA 1,2,2,2,2,2,1,1,1,1
950 DATA 1,2,2,2,2,2,2,1,1,1
960 DATA 1,2,2,2,2,2,2,2,1,1
970 DATA 1,2,2,2,2,2,2,2,2,1
980 DATA 1,2,2,2,2,2,2,2,2,2
990 DATA 2,2,2,2,2,2,2,2,2,2
1000 DATA 2,3,2,2,2,2,2,2,2,2
1010 DATA 2,3,3,2,2,2,2,2,2,2
1020 DATA 2,3,3,3,2,2,2,2,2,2
1030 DATA 2,3,3,3,3,2,2,2,2,2
1040 DATA 2,3,3,3,3,3,2,2,2,2
1050 DATA 2,3,3,3,3,3,3,2,2,2
1060 DATA 2,3,3,3,3,3,3,3,2,2
1070 DATA 2,3,3,3,3,3,3,3,3,2
1080 DATA 2,3,3,3,3,3,3,3,3,3
1090 DATA 3,3,3,3,3,3,3,3,3,3
1100 DATA 3,4,3,3,3,3,3,3,3,3
1110 DATA 3,4,4,3,3,3,3,3,3,3
1120 DATA 3,4,4,4,3,3,3,3,3,3
1130 DATA 3,4,4,4,4,3,3,3,3,3
1140 DATA 3,4,4,4,4,4,3,3,3,3
1150 X = H:Y = I:RESTORE
1160 FOR N = 1 TO 10:READ Q:NEXT N
1170 B = B * 10:B = ABS(B)
1180 FOR N = 1 TO B
1190    READ A(201),A(202),A(203),A(204),A(205),A(206),
           A(207),A(208),A(209),A(210)
1200 NEXT N
1210 FOR N = 1 TO 10
1220    Q = N + 200
1230    IF A < 0 THEN 1280
1240    IF A > 0 THEN 1290
```

```
1250     SET (X,Y)
1260     X = X + 1
1270     GOTO 1300
1280     Y = Y-A(Q):GOTO 1250
1290     Y = Y+A(Q):GOTO 1250
1300 NEXT N
1310 X = X - 1:Y = Y + 1
1320 IF E =    9 THEN 1550
1330 GOTO 670
1350 FOR N = 1 TO B:READ Q:NEXT N
1380 B = ABS(A)
1390 FOR N = 1 TO B
1400     READ A(201),A(202),A(203),A(204),A(205),
             A(206),A(207),A(208),A(209),A(210)
1410 NEXT N
1420 FOR N = 1 TO 10
1430     Q = N + 200
1440     IF A < THEN 1490
1450     IF A > 0 THEN 1500
1460     SET (X,Y)
1470     X = X + 1
1480     GOTO 1510
1490     Y = Y - A(Q):GOTO 1460
1500     Y = Y + A(Q):GOTO 1460
1510 NEXT N
1520 X = X - 1:Y = Y + 1
1530 IF E = > 9 THEN 1550
1540 GOTO 670
1550 FOR Y = 4 TO 35 STEP 6
1560     FOR X = 15 TO 105 STEP 10
1570         SET (X,Y)
1580     NEXT X
1590 NEXT Y
1600 PRINT "PROGRAM ENDED"
1610 GOTO 1610
```

That was the graph for the 10 occurrences of test scores. It is significant in that it is the first kind of graphics routine discussed which develops and then displays results which have been developed in the program itself. Just how useful this particular application will be is a function of the kinds of applications you wish to develop for your TRS-80. Graphics are simply pictures which serve to convey a message.

USING GRAPHICS TO CONVEY A SCHEDULE

Few of us can write a program of moderate size or complexity without having to make some adjustments to the program. The program which follows is a scheduling program, built around planning for a meal. In its present form, it would be useful for the home. The principles, however, can be adapted to any scheduling situation. The application will work, no matter what data is provided to it. There are some limitations, which will be discussed, but the reader will find that the program works consistently.

A word of caution about this program before proceeding. First, it was developed on a 16K Level II TRS-80 and took about 6K of memory. If the system you are using is a Level I, you are encouraged to enter the program in shorthand and compress spaces. This will allow it to fit into 4K.

Next, this program was developed and tested piecemeal. In a few places there are double branches (GOTO's). The reason for this is that each new piece was added on at the point where the previous one halted. A Level II cross-reference listing can be used to work out these duplicates, when you get there.

Next, there are several identical or nearly identical statements and routines which could be placed into subroutines, saving memory. It may logically be asked why the author chose to present the program in this manner, rather than "cleaning it up" prior to publication. The reason is simple, but the program is not. While the program is more complex than others which have been presented, it is not difficult to understand, if you take the time to study it. To have worked in these efficiencies prior to its presentation would have removed the developmental approach used throughout this book. As the development and explanation are completed, some of the more difficult passages will be pointed out and several places where efficiencies can be incorporated will be identified. For the moment, it's important to understand the operation of the program.

As stated, this is a scheduling graph, developed to assist in the planning for the preparation and serving of a meal. It is presented in the form of what is called a *Gantt Chart*. Using information supplied to the program, and after the incorporation of some extensive editing, it builds a schedule for view and then tracks the time as it "ticks away." The program cannot force one to keep a schedule, of course, but it can be used to prompt action, ensuring that things are accomplished in time to serve the meal. As it's presented, however, bear in mind that the subject is scheduling, not just preparing dinner. Here's where it starts:

```
10 CLS
```

In this program, a variety of switches and pointers are used. A switch is a means to change direction based upon some reason. Think of it as a large model railroad set-up. You, from a remote location, change the direction of the train by changing a switch located in the track itself. In the program there are two kinds of switches; the *uni-stable* switches which are "thrown" once and remain thrown; and *bi-stable* or *flip-flop* switches which change back and forth. Each will be explained as it is encountered.

There is also a variety of pointers, used with the scanning of lines. Fifteen have been reserved, though only 13 have been used. The next instruction will be the method to insure that they are reset at the beginning of the program; the pointers will be discussed as they occur:

```
20 FOR N = 1 TO 15:A(N) = 0:NEXT N
```

This instruction can be omitted if you consistently hit the CLEAR button when your program begins.

It's title time:

```
30 PRINT TAB(20);"M E A L   P L A N N E R"
40 PRINT:PRINT "WHAT TIME WILL THE MEAL BE SERVED?"
50 PRINT "(ENTER HOUR - COMMA - MINUTE)"
60 PRINT:INPUT S,T:IF (S = 0) + (T < 0) THEN 10
70 IF S > 12 THEN 90
80 IF T < 60 THEN 110
90 PRINT "INVALID TIME PARAMETER - RE-ENTER"
100 FOR N = 1 TO 1000:NEXT N:GOTO 10
```

The routine above displays the title and asks for the time that the meal will be served. This is necessary, of course, for the planning of the schedule. The mishandling of the first INPUT question (variable S) will give a syntax error, so ensure that it is entered correctly. In statements 60, 70, and 80, steps are taken to ensure that the time is "pure," that it isn't in decimal form, negatively signed, or outside the boundaries of reason. This approach to editing will be typical throughout the application.

Next, the program needs to know the number of people who will be involved, as the time necessary to prepare something is a function of how many people will be served. The assumption is made that at least one person is to be served:

```
110 PRINT:INPUT "NUMBER OF PEOPLE TO BE SERVED";P:
    P = INT(P):IF P < 1 THEN P = 1:CLS
```

Every good meal starts off with an appetizer, and this meal is no exception:

```
120 PRINT:INPUT "APPETIZER (Y/N)";A$
130 IF A$ = "N" THEN 180
140 PRINT:INPUT "PREPARATION TIME PER PORTION (IN MINUTES)";R
150 IF R < 1 THEN R = 1
160 IF R > 10 THEN R = 10
170 A(1) = R * P
```

Note that a *default* time of 1 minute (see statement 150) has been assigned to the preparation of the appetizer (unless you have specified that there is no appetizer). But the program also restricts the maximum time allowable to 10 minutes per portion. That may or may not be reasonable. The product of the time for each portion times the number of people (in minutes) is stored in A(1).

The same approach is taken for the main course, except that a minimum of a half pound is required. The program rejects any weight which exceeds 20 pounds. That is followed by the cooking time required (not fewer than 10 minutes per pound and not more than 20 minutes per pound). The product of the two is the total main course time, and that is stored in A(2):

```
180 CLS:INPUT "WEIGHT OF MAIN COURSE (MEAT/FISH/POULTRY/OTHER)
    IN POUNDS";W:IF W < .5 THEN W = .5
190 IF W > 20 THEN 210
200 GOTO 230
210 PRINT:PRINT "NOT VALID FOR MORE THAN 20 LBS - RE-ENTER"
220 FOR N = 1 TO 1000:NEXT N:GOTO 180
230 PRINT:INPUT "COOKING TIME PER POUND (IN MINUTES)";C
240 IF C < 10 THEN C = 10
250 IF C > 20 THEN C = 20
260 A(2) = C * W
```

Now that the approach taken is evident, here is the rest of the "menu" for the meal. Note that the permissable parameters vary, but are always present:

```
270 CLS:INPUT "VEGETABLE (Y/N)";A$
280 IF A$ = "N" THEN 320
290 PRINT:INPUT "PREPARATION AND COOKING TIME (IN MINUTES)";A(3)
300 IF A(3) < 1 THEN A(3) = 1
310 IF A(3) > 30 THEN A(3) = 30
320 CLS:INPUT "BEVERAGE (Y/N)";A$
330 IF A$ = "N" THEN 410
340 PRINT:INPUT "HEATING/CHILLING TIME - PRESS ENTER IF ZERO";H
350 IF H < 1 THEN H = 1
360 IF H > 15 THEN H = 15
370 PRINT:INPUT "SERVING TIME PER PORTION (IN MINUTES)";I
380 IF I < 1 THEN I = 1
390 IF I > 5 THEN I = 5
400 A(4) = H * I
410 CLS:INPUT "DESSERT (Y/N)';A$
420 IF A$ = "N" THEN 540
430 PRINT:INPUT "TO BE COOKED (Y/N)";A$
440 IF A$ = "N" THEN 490
450 PRINT:INPUT "COOKING TIME (IN MINUTES)";A(5)
460 IF A(5) < 1 THEN A(5) = 1
470 IF A(5) > 60 THEN A(5) = 60
480 GOTO 540
490 PRINT:INPUT "PREPARATION TIME PER PORTION (IN MINUTES)";D
500 A(5) = D * P
510 IF A(5) < 1 THEN A(5) = 1
520 IF A(5) > 10 THEN A(5) = 10
```

At this point, the total time can be calculated and a graphic scale can be developed. The total time is the sum of all the times previously developed. That sum is stored in variable K, ensuring that a default of 1 hour exists, after converting the minutes to hours.

It has been determined that the scale will be 108 X-Axis units in length. Dividing that by the total number of hours developed will tell the length of an hour in X-Axis graphic units. Therefore, the time necessary to plot on the graph will be a function of the difference between the rightmost position on the screen (plus one) less the developed length of hours times the length of hours in graphic X-Axis units. To keep it in whole units, the INTeger is taken, after having rounded upward.

```
530 REM "CALCULATE THE TOTAL TIME IN HOURS"
540 K = (A(1) + A(2) + A(3) + A(4) + A(5))/60
550 IF K < 1 THEN K = 1
560 REM "DETERMINE GRAPH SCALE"
570 L = 100/K:L = INT(L):IF L < 1 THEN L = 1
580 X = 128-(K * L):X = INT(X):A(6) = X:K = INT(K + .5):CLS
```

That tells where the line will fall, but the presentation of the lines are withheld until the necessary printing is done. In the following, the category titles are positioned on the left side of the screen. There is a program title, and on line 3 begins the identification of each of the five courses of the meal:

```
590 PRINT:PRINT TAB (10);"M E A L    P R E P A R A T I O N
     S C H E D U L E":PRINT
600 PRINT "APPETIZER":PRINT
610 PRINT "MAIN COURSE":PRINT
620 PRINT "VEGETABLE":PRINT
630 PRINT "BEVERAGE":PRINT
640 PRINT "DESSERT"
```

Now the lines can be drawn across the bottom of the screen. The scale line will be on Y-Axis line 40. Of particular interest is statement 680, which prevents the running off the end of the screen if the calculations have gone awry. Note also that the scale is begun one position to the left of the actual scale. The reason for this is that it is the beginning of the leftward extension of the line as a point of hourly reference preceding the actual scale. More on this later. For the moment, the scale will be drawn from left to right.

```
650 FOR N = 1 TO K
660    FOR Z = 1 TO L
670       SET (X - 1, 40)
680       IF X = 127 THEN 780
```

```
69Ø            SET (X,4Ø)
7ØØ            X = X + 1
71Ø      NEXT Z
72Ø NEXT N
```

In the same manner as the line is arrested on the right side of the screen, the program also prevents shortfall, taking steps to "even" the right-hand margin:

```
73Ø IF X < 127 THEN 74Ø:GOTO 78Ø
74Ø FOR N = X TO 127
75Ø      SET (N,4Ø)
76Ø NEXT N
```

Note the use of variable X and variable N in the two routines. The reason for this is that it is wished to capture X at its present location, requiring it to be the "from" in the FOR statement at 74Ø. Unable to know which, both are stored, both are decremented once for "inclusive," the rightmost address is moved into A(7) (the leftmost is already in A(6)) defining the length of the developed line. A(14) is used to hold the leftmost position until later, when it will be used in a scan. A(6) will be incremented in later coding:

```
77Ø Y = 4Ø:A(7) = N - 1:A(6) = A(6) - 1:GOTO 8ØØ
78Ø Y = 4Ø:A(7) = X - 1:A(6) = A(6) = 1:A(14) = A(6)
```

Having identified the length of the line, the distance represented by one hour, and the specific ends of the line, the line can now be given "hash-marks" to indicate where the hours fall. This is done by placing a graphics mark above and below the scale line at the hour position. A check is also made to ensure that the time scale does not run off the left side of the screen (statement 82Ø) and the line is extended to the left. The leftward extension is merely to give the line completeness and extension out to and perhaps beyond the leftmost hash mark beyond the actual plotted time. This can be seen on the screen as a dotted line:

```
79Ø REM "A(6) LEFTMOST, A(7) RIGHTMOST POSITION OF LINE"
8ØØ FOR X = A(7) TO A(6) STEP - L
81Ø      SET (X,Y-1):SET (X,Y+1)
82Ø      IF X - L < 1 THEN 86Ø
83Ø      SET (X-L,Y-1):SET (X-L,Y+1)
```

```
84Ø     IF X - L - L < 1 THEN 86Ø
85Ø     SET (X - L - L,Y - 1):SET (X - L - L,Y + 1):
        IF(A(6) - G) < 1 THEN 88Ø
86Ø     SET (A(6) - G,Y):G = G + 2:IF (A(6)-G-4) < 1 THEN 88Ø
87Ø     SET (A(6)-G-4,Y)
88Ø NEXT X
89Ø X = A(6):SET (X,Y-1):SET (X,Y+1)
```

At this point the first switch is encountered—A(9). In is used at 9ØØ to permit the execution of the coding between 91Ø and 93Ø just once. There is a very basic decision to make. While graphics characters can be drawn at will, the positioning of time along the scale occupies space for the numbers to be displayed. If the line is 7 hours or less, the printing of the times can take place on one line. If the line is more than 7 hours, it must occupy two lines beneath the scale line. Any total time can be developed, but the actual time numbers will be clearly printed up to a total of 15 hours. It will still work (a maximum has been set) but the times displayed along the scale will not be discernable above 15 hours.

MEAL PREPARATION SCHEDULE

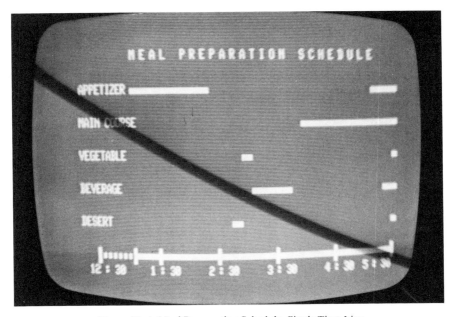

Figure 15.A Meal Preparation Schedule, Single Time Line

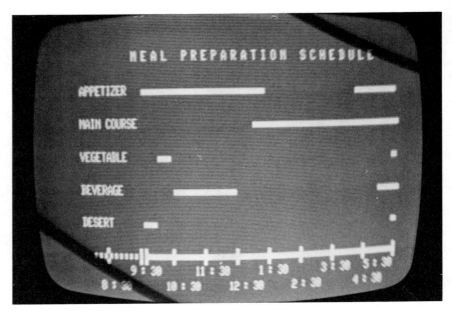

Figure 15.B Meal Preparation Schedule—Double Time Line

There are actually two printing routines—one lays out the time on one line beneath the scale line and one which lays it out on two lines, due to the compression of the line. They are located at 970 and 1270, respectively. Recall that the variable L was the length of the line which represented 1 hour—to get the two-line display, each line will be modified by 2 hours. Thus the doubling of L in instruction 930, giving a scale line and time line which looks like this:

	1:00		3:00		5:00		7:00		9:00
12:00		2:00		4:00		6:00		8:00	

When K is less than 8, the line looks like this:

12:00	1:00	2:00	3:00	4:00	5:00	6:00	7:00	8:00	9:00

Of course, in the example, the time spread is the same, due to the limitations of the page, but the double-lined example would continue on the left.

Because there are two possible formats, there are two routines. Some enterprising individual may find a way to combine them, but the author chose to keep them separate. In the situation where K is less than 8, only subroutine 970 is used. In the double-line situation, both 970 and 1270 are used, with the routine switching between them. The interesting thing to note at this point is that there is a very tight loop in instruction 940. If the process is to come to a halt, it does so as a function of what is determined within one of the subroutines.

```
900 IF A(9) = 1 THEN 940
910 A(9) = 1
920 IF K < = 7 THEN 950
930 L = L * 2
940 GOSUB 970:GOSUB 1270:GOTO 940
```

Looking at instruction 920, it can be seen that instructions 930 through 940 are for the double line. The single line format begins at 950 with actions on three switches—A(12), A(11), and A(10). Recall that there are two routines for printing—the first is used for single lines and for one half of the double lines. The second is for double lines only. Not knowing which will be entered first, and wishing to ensure that some instructions are bypassed when the entry is made, the switches are checked, and action taken accordingly. The reason for this action is as follows: while it was said that there are two print routines, there are in reality four—within each of the two there is a routine devoted exclusively to printing the rightmost time and a second routine which is used to generate the proper times towards the left of the screen. Also, note that within each of the four, there is yet another division of two separate routines. The reason for this is as follows: if it is wished to print the time in the format 5:00, then the double zero must be generated. A variable of 0 cannot be used, as it would print as 5:0, which would look a little strange. So, if a time of an even hour is entered early in the program, it must be detected and a :00 printed in its place. This may appear complicated, but it's more simple than it seems. Take time to study it and it should become obvious.

There is another set of considerations which relate to spacing. While the graphic lines can be drawn anywhere, only so many characters can be printed in the allotted space. The sequence of four instructions beginning at 1000 (and duplicated at 1300) measures and takes greatest advantage of that space. There is a point of scheduling beyond which the times can no longer be read on the scale. It will still work, but the display of the times will be obliterated. At first, it will look as if the printing preceding graphics rule has been broken. This is the exception. This printing has been done beneath the graphic lines and each print line is ended with a semicolon to suppress the roll-up (scrolling). This is done with the PRINT AT command with specific addresses given—951 and 952 for the first line and 1015 and 1016 for the second.

There are several references to the specific places on the print line. Since the movement is from right to left, a check is included at 1180 and at 1230 to ensure it doesn't extend beyond the screen's boundaries. The PRINT AT is modified by variables M, L, P, and E, and the time parameters S and T are adjusted to reflect the change in scale. The appropriate switches are set to move from one print routine to the other.

Look at statements 1200, 1220, 1490, and 1510. A computer can be made to do what is needed to do. The − 3 adjustment to P and E came about by experimentation. The negative 3 adjustment was made to have the display show what was wanted.

Here is the coding which has been explained above:

```
950 A(12) = 0:A(11) = 0:GOSUB 970
960 GOSUB 970:GOTO 960
970 IF A(12) = 1 THEN 1130
980 IF A(11) = 1 THEN 1130
990 A(10) = 1
1000 IF (S < 10) * (T = 0) THEN 1080
1010 IF (S < 10) * (T > 0) THEN 1100
1020 IF (S > = 10) * (T = 0) THEN 1040
1030 IF (S > = 10) * (T > 0) THEN 1060
1040 PRINT AT 951,S;":00";
1050 GOTO 1110
1060 PRINT AT 951,S;":";T;
1070 GOTO 1110
1080 PRINT AT 952,S;":00";
1090 GOTO 1110
1100 PRINT AT 952,S;":";T;
1110 M = INT(L / 2)
1120 IF A(12) < > 1 THEN 1250
1130 IF A(12) = 1 THEN 1160
1140 P = 959
1150 A(12) = 1
1160 S = S - 1:IF S = 0 THEN S = 12
1170 P = P - M
1180 IF P < = 896 THEN 1260
```

```
1190 IF T > Ø THEN 1220
1200 PRINT AT P - 3,S;":ØØ";
1210 GOTO 1230
1220 PRINT AT P - 3,S,":";T;
1230 IF P < = 9Ø5 THEN 126Ø
1240 RETURN
1250 A(12) = 1:P = 959:GOTO 1240
1260 GOTO 1540
1270 IF A(8) = 1 THEN 1420
1280 IF A(1Ø) = 1 THEN 142Ø
1290 A(11) = 1
1300 IF (S < 1Ø) * (T = Ø) THEN 1380
1310 IF (S < 1Ø) * (T > Ø) THEN 14ØØ
1320 IF (S > = 1Ø) * (T = Ø) THEN 1340
1330 IF (S > = 1Ø) * (T > Ø) THEN 136Ø
1340 PRINT AT 1Ø15,S;"ØØ";
1350 GOTO 1410
1360 PRINT AT 1Ø15,S;":";T;
1370 GOTO 1410
1380 PRINT AT 1Ø16,S;":ØØ";
1390 GOTO 1410
1400 PRINT AT 1Ø16,S;":";T;
1410 M = INT(L/2)
1420 IF A(8) = 1 THEN 1450
1430 E = 1Ø23:M = INT(L/4)
1440 A(8) = 1
1450 S = S - 1:IF S = Ø THEN S = 12
1460 E = E - M
1470 IF E < 896 THEN 1540
1480 IF T > Ø THEN 1510
1490 PRINT AT E - 3,S;":ØØ";
1500 GOTO 1520
1510 PRINT AT E - 3,S;":";T;
1520 IF E < 9Ø5 THEN 154Ø
1530 N = INT(L/2):RETURN
```

Once the time scale is done, then the coding must be done to plot the lines which represent the major elements of the meal onto the graph. Statements 1540 to 2100 are devoted to that purpose. Each of the routines has some similarity to the others. The scanning left address is stored in A(6) and manipulated. The length of the line is developed in V as a function of the ratio of the time stored, respectively, in A(1) through A(5)—the times developed for each portion of the meal. There are several instructions which are designed for keeping the line from running off the screen, specifically to the right. Where that occurs, the line is plotted against the right margin, rather than merely strung on from the last of the previous line.

Look at statement 1540 and examine variable V. The process is repeated several times as the line drawing is done. Variable K, of course, is the number of hours represented along the line, hashed in units of L. K exists in hours, so multiplying by 60 will convert that to minutes. Dividing the number for the meal unit by the time scale will produce a decimal, which is then multiplied by the length measures of L and K, converted to an integer, and protected against being zero. An arbitrary decision was made to devote one-fourth of the time for each unit (except for the main course) to serving the item, as it would do no good to have the vegetables cooked and waiting 1 hour before the meat was done. So it has been split up, with the three-fourths plotted in its appropriate place and its remaining one-fourth against the deadline time. That is true for each except A(2). The lines used are 10, 16, 22, 28, and 34, on the screen:

```
1540 V = (A(1)/(K*60)):V = V * L * K:V = INT(V):IF V < 1 THEN V = ⌐
1550 IF A(6) + V > 127 THEN A(6) = A(6) - V
1560 FOR X = A(6) TO A(6) + (3 * V)/4
1570     SET (X,10)
1580 NEXT X
1590 FOR X = 127 - V/4 TO 127
1600     SET (X,10)
1610 NEXT X
1620 A(6) = A(6) + V
1630 IF A(6) + V > 127 THEN A(6) = V
1640 V = (A(5)/(K*60)):V = V * L * K:V = INT(V):IF V < 1 THEN V =
1650 FOR X = A(6) TO A(6) + (3 * V)/4
1660     SET (X,34)
1670 NEXT X
1680 FOR X = 127 - V/4 TO 127
1690     SET (X,34)
```

```
1700 NEXT X
1710 A(6) = A(6) + V
1720 IF A(6) + V > 127 THEN A(6) = A(6) - V
1730 V = (A(3)/(K*60)):V = V * L * K:V = INT(V):IF V < 1 THEN V = 0
1740 FOR X = A(6) TO A(6) + (3 * V)/4
1750     SET (X,22)
1760 NEXT X
1770 FOR X = 127 - V/4 TO 127
1780     SET (X,22)
1790 NEXT X
1800 A(6) = A(6) + V
1810 IF A(6) + V > 127 THEN A(6) = A(6) - V
1820 V = (A(4)/(K*60)):V = V * L * K:V = INT(V):IF V < 1 THEN V = 0
1830 FOR X = A(6) TO A(6) + (3 * V)/4
1840     SET (X,28)
1850 NEXT X
1860 FOR X = 127 - V/4 TO 127
1870     SET (X,28)
1880 NEXT X
1890 A(6) = A(6) + V
1900 IF A(6) + V > 127 THEN A(6) = A(6) - V
1910 IF A(2) < 60 THEN 1930
1920 GOTO 1940
1930 GOSUB 2000:GOTO 1950
1940 V = (A(2)/(K*60)):V = V * L * K:V = INT(V):IF V < 1 THEN V = 0
1950 FOR X = A(6) TO A(6) + V
1960     SET (X,16)
1970     IF X = 127 THEN 1990
1980 NEXT X
1990 GOTO 2150
2000 V = (108*A(2))/60:A(6) = 127 - V
2010 IF A(1) < 2 THEN 2060
2020 IF A(3) < 2 THEN 2070
2030 IF A(4) < 2 THEN 2080
2040 IF A(5) < 2 THEN 2090
2050 GOTO 2100
```

```
2060 Y = 10:GOSUB 2110:GOTO 2020
2070 Y = 22:GOSUB 2110:GOTO 2030
2080 Y = 28:GOSUB 2110:GOTO 2040
2090 Y = 34:GOSUB 2110
2100 RETURN
2110 FOR X = A(14) TO 127
2120     RESET (X,Y)
2130 NEXT X
2140 RETURN
```

A(2) is always plotted against the right margin—statement 2000. As the SET instruction works, however, one place is always set, no matter if you store a 0 in it. Since there exists the possibility that some courses of the meal might be omitted, the routine from 2010 "wipes out" the lines which are not wanted. That routine continues through 2140.

The final stroke is a "timer" which obliterates the lines as the time "ticks" off. The time value is in statement 2180 and must be adjusted to reflect an accurate time measurement. Within this routine N will advance to 10 in about 30 seconds—that is, each position is "strobed" 10 times. Right now it's a "1" and it will move very fast. But figure the number of minutes involved in your process, multiply it by two to get the hours, and then multiply that by the number of hours which develops on your scale, and set that value into the TO parameter of the FOR instruction at 2180. The rest is history—enjoy your meal.

```
2150 REM "INSTR 2180 IS THE TIMER - APPROXIMATELY"
2160 REM "30 SECONDS FOR EACH 10.  RUN AND TIME"
2170 FOR X = A(14) TO 127
2180     FOR N = 1 TO 1
2190         GOSUB 2230
2200     NEXT N
2210 NEXT X
2220 GOTO 2290
2230 FOR Y = 10 TO 40 STEP 6
2240     IF (X < A(14) + 3) * (Y = 16) THEN 2270
2250     SET (X,Y)
2260     RESET (X,Y)
2270 NEXT Y
```

```
2280 RETURN
2290 CLS
2300 FOR N = 1 TO 3:PRINT:NEXT N
2310 PRINT TAB(20);"D I N N E R"
2320 FOR N = 1 TO 3:PRINT:NEXT N
2330 PRINT TAB(28);"I S"
2340 FOR N = 1 TO 3:PRINT:NEXT N
2350 PRINT TAB(20);"S E R V E D"
2360 GOTO 2360
```

Now let's look at the program in its entirety:

```
10 CLS
20 FOR N = 1 TO 15:A(N) = 0:NEXT N
30 PRINT TAB(20);"M E A L   P L A N N E R"
40 PRINT:PRINT "WHAT TIME WILL THE MEAL BE SERVED?"
50 PRINT "(ENTER HOUR - COMMA - MINUTE)"
60 PRINT:INPUT S,T:IF (S = 0) + (T < 0) THEN 10
70 IF S > 12 THEN 90
80 IF T < 60 THEN 110
90 PRINT "INVALID TIME PARAMETER - RE-ENTER"
100 FOR N = 1 TO 1000:NEXT N:GOTO 10
110 PRINT:INPUT "NUMBER OF PEOPLE TO BE SERVED";P:
    P = INT(0):IF P < 1 THEN P = 1:CLS
120 PRINT:INPUT "APPETIZER (Y/N)";A$
130 IF A$ = "N" THEN 180
140 PRINT:INPUT "PREPARATION TIME PER PORTION (IN MINUTES)";R
150 IF R < 1 THEN R = 1
160 IF R > 10 THEN R = 10
170 A(1) = R * P
180 CLS:INPUT "WEIGHT OF MAIN COURSE (MEAT/FISH/POULTRY/OTHER)
    IN POUNDS";W:IF W < .5 THEN W = .5
190 IF W > 20 THEN 210
200 GOTO 230
210 PRINT:PRINT "NOT VALID FOR MORE THAN 20 LBS - RE-ENTER"
220 FOR N = 1 TO 1000:NEXT N:GOTO 180
```

```
230 PRINT:INPUT "COOKING TIME PER POUND (IN MINUTES)";C
240 IF C < 10 THEN C = 10
250 IF C > 20 THEN C = 20
260 A(2) = C * W
270 CLS:INPUT "VEGETABLE (Y/N)";A$
280 IF A$ = "N" THEN 320
290 PRINT:INPUT "PREPARATION AND COOKING TIME (IN MINUTES)";A(3)
300 IF A(3) < 1 THEN A(3) = 1
310 IF A(3) > 30 THEN A(3) = 30
320 CLS:INPUT "BEVERAGE (Y/N)";A$
330 IF A$ = "N" THEN 410
340 PRINT:INPUT "HEATING/CHILLING TIME - PRESS ENTER IF ZERO";H
350 IF H < 1 THEN H = 1
360 IF H > 15 THEN H = 15
370 PRINT:INPUT "SERVING TIME PER PORTION (IN MINUTES)";I
380 IF I < 1 THEN I = 1
390 IF I > 5 THEN I = 5
400 A(4) = H * I
410 CLS:INPUT "DESSERT (Y/N)';A$
420 IF A$ = "N" THEN 540
430 PRINT:INPUT "TO BE COOKED (Y/N)";A$
440 IF A$ = "N" THEN 490
450 PRINT:INPUT "COOKING TIME (IN MINUTES)";A(5)
460 IF A(5) < 1 THEN A(5) = 1
470 IF A(5) > 60 THEN A(5) = 60
480 GOTO 540
490 PRINT:INPUT "PREPARATION TIME PER PORTION (IN MINUTES)";D
500 A(5) = D * P
510 IF A(5) < 1 THEN A(5) = 1
520 IF A(5) > 10 THEN A(5) = 10
530 REM "CALCULATE THE TOTAL TIME IN HOURS"
540 K = (A(1) + A(2) + A(3) + A(4) + A(5))/60
550 IF K < 1 THEN K = 1
560 REM "DETERMINE GRAPH SCALE"
570 L = 100/K:L = INT(L):IF L < 1 THEN L = 1
580 X = 128-(K * L):X = INT(X):A(6) = X:K = INT(K + .5):CLS
```

```
59Ø PRINT:PRINT TAB (1Ø);"M E A L   P R E P A R A T I O N
    S C H E D U L E":PRINT
6ØØ PRINT "APPETIZER":PRINT
61Ø PRINT "MAIN COURSE":PRINT
62Ø PRINT "VEGETABLE":PRINT
63Ø PRINT "BEVERAGE":PRINT
64Ø PRINT "DESSERT"
65Ø FOR N = 1 TO K
66Ø    FOR Z = 1 TO L
67Ø        SET (X - 1, 4Ø)
68Ø        IF X = 127 THEN 78Ø
69Ø        SET (X,4Ø)
7ØØ        X = X + 1
71Ø    NEXT Z
72Ø NEXT N
73Ø IF X < 127 THEN 74Ø:GOTO 78Ø
74Ø FOR N = X TO 127
75Ø    SET (N,4Ø)
76Ø NEXT N
77Ø Y = 4Ø:A(7) = N - 1:A(6) = A(6) - 1:GOTO 8ØØ
78Ø Y = 4Ø:A(7) = X - 1:A(6) = A(6) = 1:A(14) = A(6)
79Ø REM "A(6) LEFTMOST, A(7) RIGHTMOST POSITION OF LINE"
8ØØ FOR X = A(7) TO A(6) STEP - L
81Ø    SET (X,Y-1):SET (X,Y+1)
82Ø    IF X - L < 1 THEN 86Ø
83Ø    SET (X-L,Y-1):SET (X-L,Y+1)
84Ø    IF X - L - L < 1 THEN 86Ø
85Ø    SET (X - L - L,Y - 1):SET (X - L - L,Y + 1):
       IF(A(6) - G) <   THEN 88Ø
86Ø    SET (A(6) - G,Y):G = G + 2:IF (A(6)-G-4) < 1 THEN 88Ø
87Ø    SET (A(6)-G-4,Y)
88Ø NEXT X
89Ø X = A(6):SET (X,Y-1):SET (X,Y+1)
9ØØ IF A(9) = 1 THEN 94Ø
91Ø A(9) = 1
92Ø IF K < = 7 THEN 95Ø
```

```
930 L = L * 2
940 GOSUB 970:GOSUB 1270:GOTO 940
950 A(12) = 0:A(11) = 0:GOSUB 970
960 GOSUB 970:GOTO 960
970 IF A(12) = 1 THEN 1130
980 IF A(11) = 1 THEN 1130
990 A(10) = 1
1000 IF (S < 10) * (T = 0) THEN 1080
1010 IF (S < 10) * (T > 0) THEN 1100
1020 IF (S > = 10) * (T = 0) THEN 1040
1030 IF (S > = 10) * (T > 0) THEN 1060
1040 PRINT AT 951,S;":00";
1050 GOTO 1110
1060 PRINT AT 951,S;":";T;
1070 GOTO 1110
1080 PRINT AT 952,S;":00";
1090 GOTO 1110
1100 PRINT AT 952,S;":";T;
1110 M = INT(L / 2)
1120 IF A(12) <> 1 THEN 1250
1130 IF A(12) = 1 THEN 1160
1140 P = 959
1150 A(12) = 1
1160 S = S - 1:IF S = 0 THEN S = 12
1170 P = P - M
1180 IF P <= 896 THEN 1260
1190 IF T > 0 THEN 1220
1200 PRINT AT P - 3,S;":00";
1210 GOTO 1230
1220 PRINT AT P - 3,S,":";T;
1230 IF P < = 905 THEN 1260
1240 RETURN
1250 A(12) = 1:P = 959:GOTO 1240
1260 GOTO 1540
1270 IF A(8) = 1 THEN 1420
1280 IF A(10) = 1 THEN 1420
```

```
1290 A(11) = 1
1300 IF (S < 10) * (T = 0) THEN 1380
1310 IF (S < 10) * (T > 0) THEN 1400
1320 IF (S > = 10) * (T = 0) THEN 1340
1330 IF (S > = 10) * (T > 0) THEN 1360
1340 PRINT AT 1015,S;"00";
1350 GOTO 1410
1360 PRINT AT 1015,S;":";T;
1370 GOTO 1410
1380 PRINT AT 1016,S;":00";
1390 GOTO 1410
1400 PRINT AT 1016,S;":";T;
1410 M = INT(L/2)
1420 IF A(8) = 1 THEN 1450
1430 E = 1023:M = INT(L/4)
1440 A(8) = 1
1450 S = S - 1:IF S = 0 THEN S = 12
1460 E = E - M
1470 IF E < 896 THEN 1540
1480 IF T > 0 THEN 1510
1490 PRINT AT E - 3,S;":00";
1500 GOTO 1520
1510 PRINT AT E - 3,S;":";T;
1520 IF E < 905 THEN 1540
1530 N = INT(L/2):RETURN
1540 V = (A(1)/(K*60)):V = V * L * K:V = INT(V):IF V < 1 THEN V = 0
1550 IF A(6) + V > 127 THEN A(6) = A(6) - V
1560 FOR X = A(6) TO A(6) + (3 * V)/4
1570     SET (X,10)
1580 NEXT X
1590 FOR X = 127 - V/4 TO 127
1600     SET (X,10)
1610 NEXT X
1620 A(6) = A(6) + V
1630 IF A(6) + V > 127 THEN A(6) = V
1640 V = (A(5)/(K*60)):V = V * L * K:V = INT(V):IF V < 1 THEN V = 0
```

```
1650 FOR X = A(6) TO A(6) + (3 * V)/4
1660    SET (X,34)
1670 NEXT X
1680 FOR X = 127 - V/4 TO 127
1690    SET (X,34)
1700 NEXT X
1710 A(6) = A(6) + V
1720 IF A(6) + V > 127 THEN A(6) = A(6) - V
1730 V = (A(3)/(K*60)):V = V * L * K:V = INT(V):IF V < 1 THEN V = 0
1740 FOR X = A(6) TO A(6) + (3 * V)/4
1750    SET (X,22)
1760 NEXT X
1770 FOR X = 127 - V/4 TO 127
1780    SET (X,22)
1790 NEXT X
1800 A(6) = A(6) + V
1810 IF A(6) + V > 127 THEN A(6) = A(6) - V
1820 V = (A(4)/(K*60)):V = V * L * K:V = INT(V):IF V < 1 THEN V = 0
1830 FOR X = A(6) TO A(6) + (3 * V)/4
1840    SET (X,28)
1850 NEXT X
1860 FOR X = 127 - V/4 TO 127
1870    SET (X,28)
1880 NEXT X
1890 A(6) = A(6) + V
1900 IF A(6) + V > 127 THEN A(6) = A(6) - V
1910 IF A(2) < 60 THEN 1930
1920 GOTO 1940
1930 GOSUB 2000:GOTO 1950
1940 V = (A(2)/(K*60)):V = V * L * K:V = INT(V):IF V < 1 THEN V =
1950 FOR X = A(6) TO A(6) + V
1960    SET (X,16)
1970    IF X = 127 THEN 1990
1980 NEXT X
1990 GOTO 2150
2000 V = (108*A(2))/60:A(6) = 127 - V
```

```
2010 IF A(1) < 2 THEN 2060
2020 IF A(3) < 2 THEN 2070
2030 IF A(4) < 2 THEN 2080
2040 IF A(5) < 2 THEN 2090
2050 GOTO 2100
2060 Y = 10:GOSUB 2110:GOTO 2020
2070 Y = 22:GOSUB 2110:GOTO 2030
2080 Y = 28:GOSUB 2110:GOTO 2040
2090 Y = 34:GOSUB 2110
2100 RETURN
2110 FOR X = A(14) TO 127
2120     RESET (X,Y)
2130 NEXT X
2140 RETURN
2150 REM "INSTR 2180 IS THE TIMER - APPROXIMATELY"
2160 REM "30 SECONDS FOR EACH 10.  RUN AND TIME"
2170 FOR X = A(14) TO 127
2180     FOR N = 1 TO 1
2190         GOSUB 2230
2200     NEXT N
2210 NEXT X
2220 GOTO 2290
2230 FOR Y = 10 TO 40 STEP 6
2240     IF (X < A(14) + 3) * (Y = 16) THEN 2270
2250     SET (X,Y)
2260     RESET (X,Y)
2270 NEXT Y
2280 RETURN
2290 CLS
2300 FOR N = 1 TO 3:PRINT:NEXT N
2310 PRINT TAB(20);"D I N N E R"
2320 FOR N = 1 TO 3:PRINT:NEXT N
2330 PRINT TAB(28);"I S"
2340 FOR N = 1 TO 3:PRINT:NEXT N
2350 PRINT TAB(20);"S E R V E D"
2360 GOTO 2360
```

Finally, a different approach to graphics is presented. The following is the "cover sheet" to a TRS-80 demonstration given to the Meriden/Wallingford (Connecticut) Amateur Radio Club. All this routine does is to draw the emblem of the American Radio Relay League (ARRL) and present some general information. The routine is significant in that all X,Y coordinates are stored as DATA lines, are read, and then are displayed.

```
10 CLS
20 GOSUB 40
30 GOTO 30
40 RESTORE:CLS
50 PRINT AT 93, "MERIDEN/WALLINGFORD"
60 PRINT AT 229, "RADIO"
70 PRINT AT 358, "CLUB"
80 PRINT AT 334, "M"
90 PRINT AT 327, "A"
100 PRINT AT 398, "W"
110 PRINT AT 391, "R"
120 PRINT AT 480, "TRS/80 DEMO BY:"
130 PRINT AT 455, "R"
140 PRINT AT 462, "R"
150 PRINT AT 519, "L"
160 PRINT AT 526, "C"
170 PRINT AT 605, "KEN LORD - W1ETK"
180 FOR N = 1 TO 86
190     READ X,Y
200     SET (X,Y)
210 NEXT N
220 FOR N = 1 TO 80
230     READ X,Y
240     SET (X+7,Y)
250 NEXT N
260 RETURN
270 DATA 22,1,21,2,20,3,19,4,18,5,17,6,16,7,15,8,14,9,13,10,12,11,
        11,12,10,13,9,14,8,15,7,16,6,17,5,18,4,19,3,20,2,21,1,22,
        0,23
```

```
280 DATA 1,24,2,25,3,26,4,27,5,28,6,29,7,30,8,31,9,32,10,33,11,34,
        12,35,13,36,14,37,15,38,16,39,17,40,18,41,19,42,20,43,21,44
290 DATA 22,43,23,42,24,41,25,40,26,39,27,38,28,37,29,36,30,35,31,34
        32,33,33,32,34,31,35,30,36,29,37,28,38,27,39,26,40,25,41,24
        42,23,43,22
300 DATA 42,21,41,20,40,19,39,18,38,17,37,16,36,15,35,14,34,13,33,12
        32,11,31,10,30,9,29,8,28,7,27,6,26,5,25,4,24,3,23,2
310 DATA 13,7,14,7,15,7,16,7,17,7,13,8,17,8,14,9,15,9,16,9,15,10,15
        11
320 DATA 14,12,13,12,12,13,12,14,13,15,14,15,15,15,16,14,16,14,16,14
330 DATA 12,16,12,17,13,18,14,18,15,18,16,17
340 DATA 12,19,12,20,12,20,13,21,14,21,15,21,16,20
350 DATA 12,22,12,23,13,24,14,24,15,24,16,23,12,25
360 DATA 12,26,13,27,14,27,15,27,14,28,14,29
370 DATA 16,26,14,30
380 DATA 10,31,11,31,12,31,13,31,14,31,15,31,16,31,17,31,18,31,19,31
390 DATA 11,33,12,33,13,33,14,33,15,33,16,33,17,33,18,33
400 DATA 12,35,13,35,14,35,15,35,16,35,17,35
410 DATA 13,37,14,37,15,37,16,37,14,39,15,39
```

The graphics package on the TRS-80 is fun to use and worthwhile to enhance applications. Displays will be used in future chapters, particularly those dealing with games. While the graphics package is useful in Level I, it is much more so in Level II, where the graphics are significantly enhanced.

5
Using The TRS-80 For Education

One of the greatest uses for the home computer will be in the area of education. Educational theorists have predicted that in the upcoming years, schools as we know them will be radically changed—and much of that change will be attributable to the computer in the home, and its little sister, data communications. It is not inconceivable that in the not too distant future that the child's real teacher is someone whom the child will see once or twice a week, with other studies being concentrated around a computer—if not in the home, than certainly in the learning institutions. Already, in many schools in the land, there is some form of computing power available to students. Generally those students who are involved particularly in high school, are those who are more interested in the development of programs than the use of them. And a knowledge of computers has been essential for quite a few years for those high school students who intend to be science majors in college.

The computer as a teacher has certain distinct advantages over its human counterpart. Although the child will not be tempted to take an apple to the computer, under strict guidance the computer can become something that the human teacher is not—a tireless tutor. Using the computer it is possible to drill difficult subjects repetitively, many times beyond the patience of the human teacher. And it's a curious thing, but the majority of students will stick with the machine long after they have "turned off" a human teacher. To allow the student to get to that point—or more specifically to encourage him to make that kind of progress, some solid educational and psychological thinking must go into the programming of education packages for the computer. Yes, we may see the time when a microcomputer for each student is part of the work environment and its use solidly entrenched as part of the learning experience.

Several education-oriented alternatives are available for discussion, including those which concentrate solely upon repetitive and tireless drill, for example a speed-reading exercise, a multiplication exerciser, a geography test and a spelling exam.

Finally, for creative writers who think they'd like to attempt a book about this or another subject, a writer's dream (and reader's nightmare), a computerized buzzword generator is included.

It is in the area of text processing that the Level I machine falls seriously short, primarily because of the limitations upon alphabetic variables. Recall that there are only two, A$ and B$, each of which is limited to 16 characters. Thus, the ability to build text from the keyboard is severely limited in Level I. This is the reason for the DATA statement / READ statement combinations. The problem isn't the storage of data, per se. There is ample room in DATA statements or on cassette tape. The problem simply is one of the entry of variable length alphabetic data from the keyboard. With a little forward thinking, however, much of that limitation can be overcome.

The process will begin with the geography test. This is a multiple choice examination to test the student's knowledge of the capitals of each of the 50 United States. Note the extensive use of DATA statements. It's otherwise a very straightforward routine:

```
10 CLS
```

As stated, a considerable number of DATA statements are used. The next step will be to RESTORE the pointer to the head of those DATA lines. This is not necessary for the first time through, but statement 20 will be part of a loop:

```
20 RESTORE:P = 0:R = 0:W = 0:S = 0:0 = 0
```

In addition, some variables are initialized. Variable P will be used to develop right answer/wrong answer percentages. Variable R is the count of right answers. Variable W is the count of wrong answers. S is a switch for bypassing certain instructions when the student has selected the incorrect answer and it is desired to provide him with another opportunity to answer but not to affect the totals. And O (letter "O") is the counter which will denote the number of times the question is done "over." If the use of the letter O is difficult to distinguish, use another variable.

The next instructions merely position the title in the middle of the screen. A PRINT AT would have worked just as well, but constructing the routine this way is not a bad idea—you might wish to go back and add a message:

```
30 FOR N = 1 to 5:PRINT: NEXT N
40 PRINT TAB(15);"G E O G R A P H Y   T E S T"
50 GOSUB 1230:CLS
```

The subroutine at 1230 is just a timer, causing the display to pause. Shorten or lengthen the timer as necessary:

```
1230 FOR Z = 1 TO 500:NEXT X:RETURN
```

And now, the opening message:

```
60 PRINT "THIS WILL TEST YOUR KNOWLEDGE OF THE CAPITALS"
70 PRINT "OF STATES IN THE UNITED STATES OF AMERICA."
80 PRINT:PRINT "QUESTIONS WILL BE PRESENTED IN MULTIPLE-CHOICE
             FORMAT."
90 PRINT:PRINT "SIMPLY SELECT THE CORRECT ONE."
100 PRINT:PRINT "PRESS ENTER TO BEGIN."
110 INPUT A
```

Since there are 50 states to review, the next thing is to establish a FOR . . . NEXT loop which will travel through the 50 DATA lines. The data which will be used follows; the format used is:

- The state under examination. This is the value of A$ in statement 150.
- Four cities in the state, only one of which is the capital, the others being misleads. Due to the limitations of Level I, these four are read with a pair of READ instructions, each reading A$ and B$, at statements 160 and 190.
- The number of positions within those four cities which represent the correct answers. This will be compared to the student's input at statement 230.

```
730 DATA "ALABAMA","BIRMINGHAM","MONTGOMERY","TUSCALOOSA",ANNISTON",2
740 DATA "ALASKA","FAIRBANKS","JUNEAU","TOK JUNCTION","ANCHORAGE",2
750 DATA "ARIZONA","TUCSON","FLAGSTAFF","CASA GRANDE","PHOENIX",4
760 DATA "ARKANSAS","LITTLE ROCK","HARRISON","TEXARKANA","FT.
          SMITH",1
770 DATA "CALIFORNIA","LOS ANGELES","SACRAMENTO","SAN FRANCISCO",
          "SAN DIEGO",2
780 DATA "COLORADO","BOULDER","COLORADO SPRINGS","DENVER","FT.
          CARSON",3
790 DATA "CONNECTICUT","HARTFORD","WETHERSFIELD","NEW HAVEN",
          "DANBURY",1
800 DATA "DELAWARE","KENTON","DOVER","MILFORD","WILMINGTON",2
```

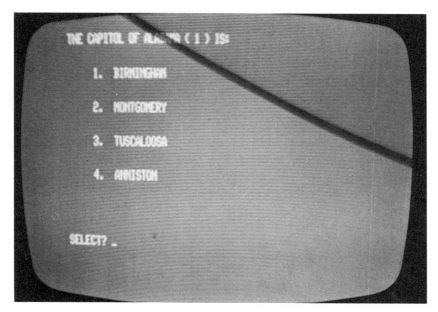

Figure 16.   Multiple Choice Test

```
81Ø DATA "FLORIDA","PENSACOLA","ORLANDO","TALLAHASSEE","MIAMI",3
82Ø DATA "GEORGIA","MACON","AUGUSTA","COLUMBUS","ATLANTA",4
83Ø DATA "HAWAII","HONOLULU","MOLOKAI","HILO","KAHULUI",1
84Ø DATA "IDAHO","BOISE","POCATELLO","IDAHO FALLS","NAMPA",1
85Ø DATA "ILLINOIS","CHAMPAIGN","PEORIA","CHICAGO","SPRINGFIELD",4
86Ø DATA "INDIANA","SOUTH BEND","INDIANAPOLIS","TERRE HAUTE",
        "LAFAYETTE",2
87Ø DATA "IOWA","SIOUX CITY","DES MOINES","WATERLOO","CEDAR RAPIDS",2
88Ø DATA "KANSAS","KANSAS CITY","SALINA","WICHITA","TOPEKA",4
89Ø DATA "KENTUCKY","FRANKFORT","PADUCAH","BOWLING GREEN",
        "LOUISVILLE",1
9ØØ DATA "LOUISIANA","NEW ORLEANS","BATON ROUGE","SHREVEPORT",
        "MONROE",2
91Ø DATA "MAINE","PORTLAND","BANGOR","AUGUSTA","LEWISTON",3
92Ø DATA "MARYLAND","BALTIMORE","TOWSON","ANNAPOLIS","ABERDEEN",3
93Ø DATA "MASSACHUSETTS","SPRINGFIELD","BOSTON","LEXINGTON",
        "WORCESTER",2
94Ø DATA "MICHIGAN","TROY","LANSING","FLINT","SAGINAW",2
1Ø9Ø DATA "OREGON","PORTLAND","EUGENE","SALEM","KLAMATH FALLS",3
```

```
 950 DATA "MINNESOTA","ST. PAUL","MINNEAPOLIS","DULUTH","ROCHESTER",1
 960 DATA "MISSISSIPPI","NATCHEZ","MERIDIAN","HATTIESBURG","JACKSON",4
 970 DATA "MISSOURI","SPRINGFIELD","INDEPENDENCE","JEFFERSON CITY",
         "COLUMBUS",3
 980 DATA "MONTANA","BOZEMAN","MISSOULA","BILLINGS","HELENA",4
 990 DATA "NEBRASKA","LEXINGTON","OMAHA","LINCOLN","GRAND ISLAND",3
1000 DATA "NEVADA","LAS VEGAS","CARSON CITY","RENO","HENDERSON",2
1010 DATA "NEW HAMPSHIRE","MANCHESTER","CONCORD","NASHUA",
         "PORTSMOUTH",2
1020 DATA "NEW JERSEY","ELIZABETH","NEWARK","TRENTON","CAMDEN",3
1030 DATA "NEW MEXICO","ALBUQUERQUE","LOS ALAMOS","ROSEWELL",
         "SANTA FE",4
1040 DATA "NEW YORK","ALBANY","SYRACUSE","NEW YORK CITY","BUFFALO",1
1050 DATA "NORTH CAROLINA","DURHAM","ASHVILLE","FAYETTEVILLE",
         "RALEIGH",4
1060 DATA "NORTH DAKOTA","BISMARK","GRAND FORKS","FARGO","MINOT",1
1070 DATA "OHIO","CLEVELAND","COLUMBUS","TOLEDO","CANTON",2
1080 DATA "OKLAHOMA","ENID","OKLAHOMA CITY","TULSA","STILLWATER",2
1100 DATA "PENNSYLVANIA","HARRISBURG","PITTSBURGH","PHILADELPHIA",
         "ERIE",1
1110 DATA "RHODE ISLAND","PAWTUCKET","CRANSTON","PROVIDENCE",
         "WARWICK",3
1120 DATA "SOUTH CAROLINA","COLUMBIA","GREENVILLE","CHARLESTON",
         "FLORENCE",1
1130 DATA "SOUTH DAKOTA","RAPID CITY","PIERRE","SIOUX FALLS",
         "ABERDEEN",2
1140 DATA "TENNESSEE","CHATTANOOGA","KNOXVILLE","MEMPHIS",
         "NASHVILLE",4
1150 DATA "TEXAS","FT. WORTH","HOUSTON","DALLAS","AUSTIN",4
1160 DATA "UTAH","OGDEN","SALT LAKE","PROVO","OREM",2
1170 DATA "VERMONT","BARRE","MONTPELIER","RUTLAND","BURLINGTON",2
1180 DATA "VIRGINIA","RICHMOND","ALEXANDRIA","ROANOKE",
         "NEWPORT NEWS",1
1190 DATA "WASHINGTON","TACOMA","SEATTLE","OLYMPIA","SPOKANE",3
1200 DATA "WEST VIRGINIA","WHEELING","CHARLESTON","HUNTINGTON",
         "PARKERSBURG",2
1210 DATA "WISCONSIN","MADISON","EAU CLAIRE","RACINE","WAUSAU",1
1220 DATA "WYOMING","CHEYENNE","CASPER","LARAMIE","SHERIDAN",1
```

That's the list. Now to the loop:

```
12Ø FOR N = 1 TO 5Ø
13Ø     CLS:O = Ø
14Ø     READ A$
15Ø     PRINT "THE CAPITAL OF ";A$;" (";N;") IS:":PRINT
16Ø     READ A$,B$
17Ø     PRINT TAB(5);"1.   ";A$:PRINT
18Ø     PRINT TAB(5);"2.   ";B$:PRINT
19Ø     READ A$,B$
2ØØ     PRINT TAB(5);"3.   ";A$:PRINT
21Ø     PRINT TAB(5);"4.   ";B$:PRINT
22Ø     READ B
23Ø     PRINT AT 7Ø4,"∅":INPUT "SELECT";A
```

As stated, the state is read first, followed by the cities, two at a time, followed by the number of the correct answer. The variable N in the capital line gives indication as to where you are in the DATA list.

In the following, S is used to bypass the counting of right or wrong answers in the case where the student has indicated the wrong answer. This allows you to get to the end of the test with an accurate count. The incorrect answer is detected at 24Ø and you take a side trip to post the wrong answer counter, set the switch, count the "take-over" (maximum permitted it three).

```
24Ø     IF A < > B THEN 41Ø
25Ø     IF S = 1 THEN 27Ø
26Ø     GOTO 3ØØ
27Ø     PRINT "CORRECT"
28Ø     GOSUB 123Ø
29Ø     GOTO 51Ø
```

One of the things you must consider in any educational situation is the psychological aspects of reward. In the following, a random number is generated, and that number is used to randomly select a reward for a correct answer. The range of numbers generated is seven, but there are only five standard options. The balance draw only the terse "CORRECT". It is taken to extremes, however, when a student has gained a large percentage of correct answers, with the messages contained in 36Ø and 37Ø.

```
300      C = RND(7):C = INT(C)
310      ON C GOTO 330,340,350,360,370
320      PRINT "CORRECT":GOTO 390
330      PRINT "VERY GOOD":GOTO 390
340      PRINT "EXCELLENT":GOTO 390
350      PRINT "OUTSTANDING":GOTO 390
360      IF R > 30 PRINT "YOU'RE A BRAIN!"
370      IF R > 40 PRINT "FANTASTIC"
380      GOTO 320
390      GOSUB 1230
```

At 400 the right answer counter is posted, the "over" counter is cleared, and the routine proceeds to the next state. There is a double timer involved here—at 390 and 500. If it is desired to shorten the pause, change the GOTO address in 400 to 510. The balance of the FOR . . . NEXT loop is devoted to the individual who has selected three incorrect answers out of four.

```
400      O = 0:R = R + 1:GOTO 500
410      IF S = 1 THEN 430
420      W = W + 1
430      S = 1:O = O + 1
440      IF O = 3 THEN 470
450      PRINT "TRY AGAIN"
460      GOTO 230
470      PRINT "YOU'RE GUESSING"
480      PRINT "THE ANSWER IS ";B
490      PRINT "LET'S GO ON";O = 0
500      GOSUB 1230
510      S = 0
520 NEXT N
```

This is the routine which posts the score—strictly an enumeration of the "rights" and "wrongs" and a percentage calculation of each; note that a check is done to see if the score is a perfect score (statement 550):

```
530 CLS
540 IF R = 50 THEN 1240
550 PRINT "CORRECT   ";R
```

```
560 PRINT "INCORRECT ";W:PRINT
570 P = INT(R/50 * 100)
580 PRINT "PERCENT CORRECT    ";P:PRINT
590 PRINT "PERCENT INCORRECT ";100 - P
```

Unless the student "flunks," the reward comes next. Grades of A, B, C, D, and F are awarded on the basis of percentage score in decades of 90-100, 80-89, 70-79, 60-69 and less than 60.

```
600 IF P > = 90 THEN A$ = "A":GOTO 650
610 IF P > - 80 THEN A$ = "B":GOTO 650
620 IF P > = 70 THEN A$ = "C":GOTO 650
630 IF P > = 60 THEN A$ = "D":GOTO 650
640 A$ = "F"
650 PRINT:PRINT "YOUR GRADE IS - - - ";A$
660 PRINT
670 INPUT "CARE TO TRY AGAIN (Y/N)";A$
680 IF A$ = "Y" THEN 10
690 PRINT:PRINT "GOODBYE - TRY AGAIN LATER"
700 IF P > 69 THEN 720
710 PRINT:PRINT "YOUR SCORE INDICATES THAT YOU NEED SOME MORE
    PRACTICE"
720 GOTO 720
```

And finally, the ultimate reward:

```
1240 CLS
1250 FOR N = 1 TO 5
1260     PRINT
1270 NEXT N
1280 PRINT TAB(8);"Y O U   G O T   T H E M   A L L   R I G H T !"
1290 PRINT:PRINT TAB(18);"C O N G R A T U L A T I O N S"
1300 FOR N = 1 TO 25:NEXT N
1310 GOTO 1240
```

As can be seen, the construction of a test involves some typing to get the DATA lines established. And since the DATA is being read with A$ and B$, the individual data item must not exceed 16 characters. However, the format of the program will not change, no matter the subject of the test. If the subject is to be changed, however, it will be necessary to modify the instructions at 40, 60, 70, 80, and 90. The size of the loop must be adjusted at 120 to reflect the actual count of the DATA lines.

Enter the program and try it. You might discover that you don't know all of the capitals of the 50 states yourself. The entire program, properly sequenced, follows:

```
10 CLS
20 RESTORE:P = 0:R = 0:W = 0:S = 0:0 = 0
30 FOR N = 1 to 5:PRINT: NEXT N
40 PRINT TAB(15);"G E O G R A P H Y   T E S T"
50 GOSUB 1230:CLS
60 PRINT "THIS WILL TEST YOUR KNOWLEDGE OF THE CAPITALS"
70 PRINT "OF STATES IN THE UNITED STATES OF AMERICA."
80 PRINT:PRINT "QUESTIONS WILL BE PRESENTED IN MULTIPLE-CHOICE
               FORMAT."
90 PRINT:PRINT "SIMPLY SELECT THE CORRECT ONE."
100 PRINT:PRINT "PRESS ENTER TO BEGIN."
110 INPUT A
120 FOR N = 1 TO 50
130     CLS:0 = 0
140     READ A$
150     PRINT "THE CAPITAL OF ";A$;" (";N;") IS:":PRINT
160     READ A$,B$
170     PRINT TAB(5);"1.   ";A$:PRINT
180     PRINT TAB(5);"2.   ";B$:PRINT
190     READ A$,B$
200     PRINT TAB(5);"3.   ";A$:PRINT
210     PRINT TAB(5);"4.   ";B$:PRINT
220     READ B
230     PRINT AT 704,"5":INPUT "SELECT";A
240     IF A < > B THEN 410
250     IF S = 1 THEN 270
260     GOTO 300
270     PRINT "CORRECT"
280     GOSUB 1230
290     GOTO 510
300     C = RND(7):C = INT(C)
310     ON C GOTO 330,340,350,360,370
320     PRINT "CORRECT":GOTO 390
```

```
330      PRINT "VERY GOOD":GOTO 390
340      PRINT "EXCELLENT":GOTO 390
350      PRINT "OUTSTANDING":GOTO 390
360      IF R > 30 PRINT "YOU'RE A BRAIN!"
370      IF R > 40 PRINT "FANTASTIC"
380      GOTO 320
390      GOSUB 1230
400      O = 0:R = R + 1:GOTO 500
410      IF S = 1 THEN 430
420      W = W + 1
430      S = 1:O = O + 1
440      IF O = 3 THEN 470
450      PRINT "TRY AGAIN"
460      GOTO 230
470      PRINT "YOU'RE GUESSING"
480      PRINT "THE ANSWER IS ";B
490      PRINT "LET'S GO ON";O = 0
500      GOSUB 1230
510      S = 0
520 NEXT N
530 CLS
540 IF R = 50 THEN 1240
550 PRINT "CORRECT ";R
560 PRINT "INCORRECT ";W:PRINT
570 P = INT(R/50 * 100)
580 PRINT "PERCENT CORRECT    ";P:PRINT
590 PRINT "PERCENT INCORRECT ";100 - P
600 IF P > = 90 THEN A$ = "A":GOTO 650
610 IF P > = 80 THEN A$ = "B":GOTO 650
620 IF P > = 70 THEN A$ = "C":GOTO 650
630 IF P > = 60 THEN A$ = "D":GOTO 650
640 A$ = "F"
650 PRINT:PRINT "YOUR GRADE IS - - - ";A$
660 PRINT
670 INPUT "CARE TO TRY AGAIN (Y/N)";A$
680 IF A$ = "Y" THEN 10
690 PRINT:PRINT "GOODBYE - TRY AGAIN LATER"
700 IF P > 69 THEN 720
710 PRINT:PRINI "YOUR SCORE INDICATES THAT YOU NEED SOME MORE
    PRACTICE"
720 GOTO 720
```

```
730 DATA "ALABAMA","BIRMINGHAM","MONTGOMERY","TUSCALOOSA",ANNISTON",2
740 DATA "ALASKA","FAIRBANKS","JUNEAU","TOK JUNCTION","ANCHORAGE",2
750 DATA "ARIZONA","TUCSON","FLAGSTAFF","CASA GRANDE","PHOENIX",4
760 DATA "ARKANSAS","LITTLE ROCK","HARRISON","TEXARKANA","FT.
        SMITH",1
770 DATA "CALIFORNIA","LOS ANGELES","SACRAMENTO","SAN FRANCISCO",
        "SAN DIEGO",2
780 DATA "COLORADO","BOULDER","COLORADO SPRINGS","DENVER","FT.
        CARSON",3
790 DATA "CONNECTICUT","HARTFORD","WETHERSFIELD","NEW HAVEN",
        "DANBURY",1
800 DATA "DELAWARE","KENTON","DOVER","MILFORD","WILMINGTON",2
810 DATA "FLORIDA","PENSACOLA","ORLANDO","TALLAHASSEE","MIAMI",3
820 DATA "GEORGIA","MACON","AUGUSTA","COLUMBUS","ATLANTA",4
830 DATA "HAWAII","HONOLULU","MOLOKAI","HILO","KAHULUI",1
840 DATA "IDAHO","BOISE","POCATELLO","IDAHO FALLS","NAMPA",1
850 DATA "ILLINOIS","CHAMPAIGN","PEORIA","CHICAGO","SPRINGFIELD",4
860 DATA "INDIANA","SOUTH BEND","INDIANAPOLIS","TERRE HAUTE",
        "LAFAYETTE",2
870 DATA "IOWA","SIOUX CITY","DES MOINES","WATERLOO","CEDAR RAPIDS",2
880 DATA "KANSAS","KANSAS CITY","SALINA","WICHITA","TOPEKA",4
890 DATA "KENTUCKY","FRANKFORT","PADUCAH","BOWLING GREEN",
        "LOUISVILLE",1
900 DATA "LOUISIANA","NEW ORLEANS","BATON ROUGE","SHREVEPORT",
        "MONROE",2
910 DATA "MAINE","PORTLAND","BANGOR","AUGUSTA","LEWISTON",3
920 DATA "MARYLAND","BALTIMORE","TOWSON","ANNAPOLIS","ABERDEEN",3
930 DATA "MASSACHUSETTS","SPRINGFIELD","BOSTON","LEXINGTON",
        "WORCESTER",2
940 DATA "MICHIGAN","TROY","LANSING","FLINT","SAGINAW",2
950 DATA "MINNESOTA","ST. PAUL","MINNEAPOLIS","DULUTH","ROCHESTER",1
960 DATA "MISSISSIPPI","NATCHEZ","MERIDIAN","HATTIESBURG","JACKSON",4
970 DATA "MISSOURI","SPRINGFIELD","INDEPENDENCE","JEFFERSON CITY",
        "COLUMBUS",3
980 DATA "MONTANA","BOZEMAN","MISSOULA","BILLINGS","HELENA",4
990 DATA "NEBRASKA","LEXINGTON","OMAHA","LINCOLN","GRAND ISLAND",3
1000 DATA "NEVADA","LAS VEGAS","CARSON CITY","RENO","HENDERSON",2
1010 DATA "NEW HAMPSHIRE","MANCHESTER","CONCORD","NASHUA",
        "PORTSMOUTH",2
```

```
1020 DATA "NEW JERSEY","ELIZABETH","NEWARK","TRENTON","CAMDEN",3
1030 DATA "NEW MEXICO","ALBUQUERQUE","LOS ALAMOS","ROSEWELL",
         "SANTA FE",4
1040 DATA "NEW YORK","ALBANY","SYRACUSE","NEW YORK CITY","BUFFALO",1
1050 DATA "NORTH CAROLINA","DURHAM","ASHVILLE","FAYETTEVILLE",
         "RALEIGH",4
1060 DATA "NORTH DAKOTA","BISMARK","GRAND FORKS","FARGO","MINOT",1
1070 DATA "OHIO","CLEVELAND","COLUMBUS","TOLEDO","CANTON",2
1080 DATA "OKLAHOMA","ENID","OKLAHOMA CITY","TULSA","STILLWATER",2
1090 DATA "OREGON","PORTLAND","EUGENE","SALEM","KLAMATH FALLS",3
1100 DATA "PENNSYLVANIA","HARRISBURG","PITTSBURGH","PHILADELPHIA",
         "ERIE",1
1110 DATA "RHODE ISLAND","PAWTUCKET","CRANSTON","PROVIDENCE",
         "WARWICK",3
1120 DATA "SOUTH CAROLINA","COLUMBIA","GREENVILLE","CHARLESTON",
         "FLORENCE",1
1130 DATA "SOUTH DAKOTA","RAPID CITY","PIERRE","SIOUX FALLS",
         "ABERDEEN",2
1140 DATA "TENNESSEE","CHATTANOOGA","KNOXVILLE","MEMPHIS",
         "NASHVILLE",4
1150 DATA "TEXAS","FT. WORTH","HOUSTON","DALLAS","AUSTIN",4
1160 DATA "UTAH","OGDEN","SALT LAKE","PROVO","OREM",2
1170 DATA "VERMONT","BARRE","MONTPELIER","RUTLAND","BURLINGTON",2
1180 DATA "VIRGINIA","RICHMOND","ALEXANDRIA","ROANOKE",
         "NEWPORT NEWS",1
1190 DATA "WASHINGTON","TACOMA","SEATTLE","OLYMPIA","SPOKANE",3
1200 DATA "WEST VIRGINIA","WHEELING","CHARLESTON","HUNTINGTON",
         "PARKERSBURG",2
1210 DATA "WISCONSIN","MADISON","EAU CLAIRE","RACINE","WAUSAU",1
1220 DATA "WYOMING","CHEYENNE","CASPER","LARAMIE","SHERIDAN",1
1230 FOR Z = 1 TO 500:NEXT X:RETURN
1240 CLS
1250 FOR N = 1 TO 5
1260 PRINT
1270 NEXT N
1280 PRINT TAB(8);"Y O U    G O T    T H E M    A L L    R I G H T !"
1290 PRINT:PRINT TAB(18);"C O N G R A T U L A T I O N S"
1300 FOR N = 1 TO 25:NEXT N
1310 GOTO 1240
```

REPETITIVE DRILL

One of the most advantageous ways to use the home computer in the field of education is with the repetitive drill. It could be a spelling exercise, a review of social studies, or mathematics. In fact, the computer will be a tireless tutor, allowing adaptation to any subject involving considerable amounts of rote learning. For illustration, that age-old nemesis, the multiplication table, has been selected. Recall your childhood—"one times one is one; two times one is two; three times one is . . . "

The concept of the program is relatively simple. Using the range of twelves (12 x 12), two factors are randomly generated, multiplied together, and then compared to the student's response. In this one the array is used to store the factors if the student misses the problem, allowing a post-test exercise review of the missed questions. It's a 20-question problem set:

```
10 FOR N = 1 TO 20:A(N) = 0:NEXT N:CLS:N = 0:R = 0:W = 0
20 GOSUB 920
30 PRINT TAB(10);"M U L T I P L I C A T I O N    D R I L L"
40 FOR Z = 1 TO 1000:NEXT Z
50 CLS
```

Note that it didn't start with a CLS. No reason, except to state that it only needs to be done before the display is used. Here are the opening messages:

```
60 PRINT "THIS WILL BE A FAST-PACED MULTIPLICATION TABLE EXERCISE"
70 PRINT:PRINT "YOU WILL RECEIVE 20 PROBLEMS FROM THE TABLE OF 12'S"
80 PRINT:PRINT "AT THE END I'LL TELL YOU YOUR SCORE AND WE'LL"
90 PRINT "REVIEW THE PROBLEMS YOU'VE MISSED, IF ANY."
100 PRINT:INPUT "PRESS ENTER TO BEGIN";X:CLS
```

There was no sigificance to the use of the variable X in statement 100. It was merely used to receive the object of the INPUT instruction, as an object of the INPUT instruction is required when the instruction is used. The actual process begins as follows:

```
110 FOR N = 1 TO 20
120     GOSUB 920
130     A = RND(12):A = INT(A):IF A < 1 THEN 130
140     B = RND(12):B = INT(B):IF B < 1 THEN 140
150     GOSUB 850
```

```
160     PRINT
170     C = A * B
180     INPUT "WHAT'S YOUR ANSWER";D
190     IF C = D THEN 250
200     GOSUB 920
210     PRINT "INCORRECT":PRINT
220     GOSUB 900:GOSUB 870
230     GOSUB 950
240 NEXT N:GOTO 330
```

Two factors are randomly generated and proven to be integers—and rejected if they are zero.

The subroutine at 920 is just a spacing option for the screen—as mentioned in a previous problem. The same thing could be accomplished with a PRINT AT. So why use this? Well, suppose that you wanted to vary the positioning on the screen, all that would be required would be the change of the number 5 to a variable and preloading the variable (statement 920):

```
920 CLS:PRINT N
930 FOR Z = 1 TO 5:PRINT:NEXT Z
940 RETURN
```

The subroutine at 850 is a standard message format for presenting the problem:

```
850 PRINT TAB(10);A;TAB(20);"TIMES";TAB(30);B;TAB(40);"EQUALS"
860 RETURN
```

The subroutine at 900 is the same standard message format except that it also contains the answer. The two messages (the one listed above and the one listed below) surround the student's answer on the screen.

```
900 PRINT TAB(10);A;TAB(20);"TIMES";TAB(30);B;TAB(40);
    "EQUALS";TAB(50);C
910 GOSUB 950:RETURN
```

The subroutine at 870 stores the incorrect factors into the array, and then only when a question has been missed:

```
87Ø A(N) = A
88Ø A(N + 2Ø) = B
89Ø RETURN
```

And the subroutine at 95Ø is just a timer:

```
95Ø FOR Z = 1 TO 1ØØØ:NEXT Z:RETURN
```

Statements 25Ø to 32Ø are the positive reinforcement messages for use on the screen. They are determined by a random number generator and are displayed following the student's answer:

```
25Ø P = RND(5):P = INT(P):IF P < 1 THEN 25Ø
26Ø ON P GOTO 27Ø,29Ø,3ØØ,31Ø,32Ø
27Ø PRINT "CORRECT":PRINT
28Ø GOSUB 9ØØ:GOTO 24Ø
29Ø PRINT "VERY GOOD":PRINT:GOTO 28Ø
3ØØ PRINT "EXCELLENT":PRINT:GOTO 28Ø
31Ø PRINT "SUPER":PRINT:GOTO 28Ø
32Ø PRINT "FANTASTIC":PRINT:GOTO 28Ø
```

No scorekeeping is accomplished until the 20th problem has been answered. Then the array is scanned to determine if any factors have been stored there, counting the ones which don't have any factors (the right answers), counting the ones which do have factors stored (the wrong answers), and calculating a percentage based on those findings:

```
33Ø CLS
34Ø FOR N = 1 TO 2Ø
35Ø     IF A(N) = Ø THEN R = R + 1
36Ø     IF A(N) <> Ø THEN W = W + 1
37Ø NEXT N
38Ø PRINT "NUMBER RIGHT IS - ";R:PRINT
39Ø PRINT "NUMBER WRONG IS - ";W:PRINT
4ØØ F = (R/2Ø * 1ØØ)
41Ø PRINT "PERCENTAGE RIGHT IS - ";F:PRINT
42Ø PRINT "PERCENTAGE WRONG IS - ";1ØØ - F
425 GOSUB 95Ø:CLS
```

Depending upon your desire to view the score, you may or may not elect to use statement 425.

Then, a grade is assigned:

```
430 IF F = 100 THEN 780
440 IF F > 90 THEN A$ = "A":GOTO 490
450 IF F > 80 THEN A$ = "B":GOTO 490
460 IF F > 70 THEN A$ = "C":GOTO 490
470 IF F > 60 THEN A$ = "D":GOTO 490
480 A$ = "F"
490 PRINT:PRINT "YOUR GRADE IS - ";A$
```

Then a goading message is printed to encourage the student to take the review. The review is merely a scan of the array, removing the factors and presenting them. The student is then given three opportunities to answer again the ones he missed. Then the answer is given and the program goes on to the next problem. Eventually, it will be cycled around again, and only goes to the end when all questions have been answered correctly.

```
500 IF F > 70 THEN 530
510 PRINT:PRINT "YOU CAN USE MORE PRACTICE"
520 GOSUB 950:GOSUB 920:CLS
530 PRINT:PRINT "LET'S REVIEW THE ONES YOU MISSED"
540 GOSUB 950
550 FOR N = 1 TO 20
560     IF A(N) = 0 THEN 690
570     A = A(N):B = A(N + 20)
580     GOSUB 850
590     C = A * B
600     INPUT "WHAT'S YOUR ANSWER";D
610     IF C = D THEN 660
620     PRINT "TRY AGAIN";T = T + 1:IF T = 3 THEN 640
630     GOTO 600
640     PRINT "WE'LL COME BACK TO THAT ONE"
650     PRINT "THE ANSWER IS ";D:GOTO 650
660     PRINT "CORRECT";A(N) = 0
670     FOR Z = 1 TO 500:NEXT Z
```

```
68Ø     CLS
69Ø NEXT N
7ØØ FOR N = 1 TO 2Ø
71Ø     IF A(N) < > Ø THEN 55Ø
72Ø NEXT N
73Ø PRINT:INPUT "WANT TO DO IT AGAIN (Y/N)";A$
74Ø IF A$ = "Y" THEN 1Ø
75Ø PRINT:PRINT "GOODBYE"
76Ø GOTO 76Ø
77Ø CLS
```

Finally, on the supposition that the student could get all the questions answered correctly the first time, a congratulatory message is flashed:

```
78Ø FOR N = 1 TO 5:PRINT:NEXT N
79Ø PRINT TAB(2Ø);"1 Ø Ø   P E R C E N T ! !"
8ØØ PRINT:PRINT TAB(18);"C O N G R A T U L A T I O N S"
81Ø FOR Z = 1 TO 2ØØ:NEXT Z
82Ø CLS
83Ø FOR Z = 1 TO 2ØØ:NEXT Z
84Ø GOTO 78Ø
```

Note that instruction 77Ø is never referenced. The reason is this: at the moment, the first congratulatory message is displayed at the bottom of the screen after the score. If it is wished to have it appear on a fresh screen, change the GOTO address in statement 43Ø to proceed to 77Ø.

It was not the author's intention to just present a program to perform multiplication drills. Rather, it was to show one approach to the problem. It will be up to the reader and his or her creativity to determine the kinds of problems best suited to home computer use. This particular one was easy to develop and operate, primarily because the numbers are randomly generated. The concept can be extended, using DATA lines or accepting DATA from cassette tape.

Here is the program in its entirety:

```
1Ø FOR N = 1 TO 2Ø:A(N) = Ø:NEXT N:CLS:N = Ø:R = Ø:W = Ø
2Ø GOSUB 92Ø
3Ø PRINT TAB(1Ø);"M U L T I P L I C A T I O N   D R I L L"
4Ø FOR Z = 1 TO 1ØØØ:NEXT Z
```

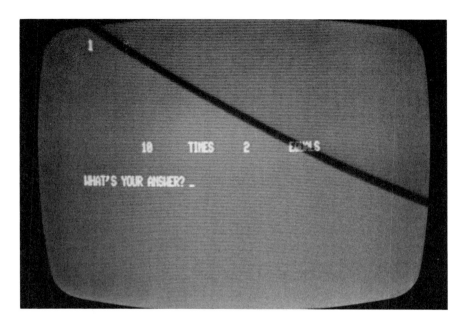

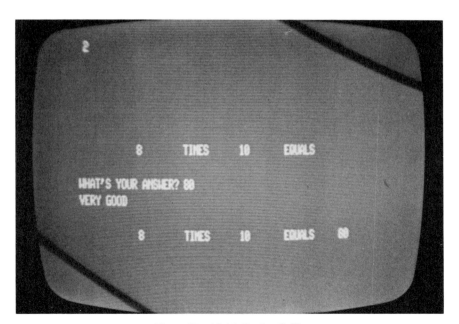

Figure 17.   Multiplication Drill

```
50 CLS
60 PRINT "THIS WILL BE A FAST-PACED MULTIPLICATION TABLE EXERCISE"
70 PRINT:PRINT "YOU WILL RECEIVE 20 PROBLEMS FROM THE TABLE OF 12's"
80 PRINT:PRINT "AT THE END I'LL TELL YOU YOUR SCORE AND WE'LL"
90 PRINT "REVIEW THE PROBLEMS YOU'VE MISSED, IF ANY."
100 PRINT:INPUT "PRESS ENTER TO BEGIN";X:CLS
110 FOR N = 1 TO 20
120     GOSUB 920
130     A = RND(12):A = INT(A):IF A < 1 THEN 130
140     B = RND(12):B = INT(B):IF B < 1 THEN 140
150     GOSUB 850
160     PRINT
170     C = A * B
180     INPUT "WHAT'S YOUR ANSWER";D
190     IF C = D THEN 250
200     GOSUB 920
210     PRINT "INCORRECT":PRINT
220     GOSUB 900:GOSUB 870
230     GOSUB 950
240 NEXT N:GOTO 330
250 P = RND(5):P = INT(P):IF P < 1 THEN 250
260 ON P GOTO 270,290,300,310,320
270 PRINT "CORRECT":PRINT
280 GOSUB 900:GOTO 240
290 PRINT "VERY GOOD":PRINT:GOTO 280
300 PRINT "EXCELLENT":PRINT:GOTO 280
310 PRINT "SUPER":PRINT:GOTO 280
320 PRINT "FANTASTIC":PRINT:GOTO 280
330 CLS
340 FOR N = 1 TO 20
350     IF A(N) = 0 THEN R = R + 1
360     IF A(N) <> 0 THEN W = W + 1
370 NEXT N
380 PRINT "NUMBER RIGHT IS - ";R:PRINT
390 PRINT "NUMBER WRONG IS - ";W:PRINT
400 F = (R/20 * 100)
410 PRINT "PERCENTAGE RIGHT IS - ";F:PRINT
420 PRINT "PERCENTAGE WRONG IS - ";100 - F
425 GOSUB 950:CLS
430 IF F = 100 THEN 780
```

```
440 IF F > 90 THEN A$ = "A":GOTO 490
450 IF F > 80 THEN A$ = "B":GOTO 490
460 IF F > 70 THEN A$ = "C":GOTO 490
470 IF F > 60 THEN A$ = "D":GOTO 490
480 A$ = "F"
490 PRINT:PRINT "YOUR GRADE IS - ";A$
500 IF F > 70 THEN 530
510 PRINT:PRINT "YOU CAN USE MORE PRACTICE"
520 GOSUB 950:GOSUB 920:CLS
530 PRINT:PRINT "LET'S REVIEW THE ONES YOU MISSED"
540 GOSUB 950
550 FOR N = 1 TO 20
560     IF A(N) = 0 THEN 690
570     A = A(N):B = A(N + 20)
580     GOSUB 850
590     C = A * B
600     INPUT "WHAT'S YOUR ANSWER";D
610     IF C = D THEN 660
620     PRINT "TRY AGAIN";T = T + 1:IF T = 3 THEN 640
630     GOTO 600
640     PRINT "WE'LL COME BACK TO THAT ONE"
650     PRINT "THE ANSWER IS ";D:GOTO 650
660     PRINT "CORRECT";A(N) = 0
670     FOR Z = 1 TO 500:NEXT Z
680     CLS
690 NEXT N
700 FOR N = 1 TO 20
710     IF A(N) < > 0 THEN 550
720 NEXT N
730 PRINT:INPUT "WANT TO DO IT AGAIN (Y/N)";A$
740 IF A$ = "Y" THEN 10
750 PRINT:PRINT "GOODBYE"
760 GOTO 760
770 CLS
780 FOR N = 1 TO 5:PRINT:NEXT N
790 PRINT TAB(20);"1 0 0   P E R C E N T ! !"
800 PRINT:PRINT TAB(18);"C O N G R A T U L A T I O N S"
810 FOR Z = 1 TO 200:NEXT Z
820 CLS
830 FOR Z = 1 TO 200:NEXT Z
```

```
840 GOTO 780
850 PRINT TAB(10);A;TAB(20);"TIMES";TAB(30);B;TAB(40);"EQUALS"
860 RETURN
870 A(N) = A
880 A(N + 20) = B
890 RETURN
900 PRINT TAB(10);A;TAB(20);"TIMES";TAB(30);B;TAB(40);
    "EQUALS";TAB(50);C
910 GOSUB 950:RETURN
920 CLS:PRINT N
930 FOR Z = 1 TO 5:PRINT:NEXT Z
940 RETURN
950 FOR Z = 1 TO 1000:NEXT Z:RETURN
```

THE "WRITER" WAY TO COMPOSE

Another of the ways that TRS-80 may be useful is in assisting the student to develop such school papers as essays and book reviews. There are several implementations of word processing systems, including one from Radio Shack.

The time is coming, and not too far in the future, when programs developed for the purpose will edit Johnny's language and give back a grammatically correct paper for submission. In the meantime, the TRS-80 can provide invaluable assistance in developing those papers in the first place.

What follows is a tongue-in-cheek indication of how some people write papers—a computerized buzzword generator. Essentially, the program selects randomly amongst a series of three lists of 10 words, two adjectives and a noun. As the opening of the program suggests, the words sound impressive, but mean absolutely nothing, and in some cases, don't even make much sense. The list is drawn from a little pocket card distributed many years ago by Honeywell, Inc., and deals primarily with words which have found fashionable use in the computer industry. Other such buzzword generators exist for education, medicine, etc.

Here is the program. Since it is so short, it will be presented first and explanation will follow:

```
10 CLS:PRINT "THIS IS A COMPUTERIZED BUZZWORD GENERATOR"
20 PRINT:PRINT "ABSOLUTELY NOTHING PRESENTED HERE MAKES ANY SENSE"
30 PRINT:PRINT "THE WORDS SOUND IMPRESSIVE, BUT MEAN ABSOLUTELY
   NOTHING"
```

```
40 PRINT "JUST THE SORT OF THING YOU'D LIKE TO INCLUDE IN A"
50 PRINT "PROPOSAL OR RESUME"
60 PRINT:PRINT "THE DOCUMENT FROM WHICH THIS WAS EXTRACTED"
70 PRINT "WAS PUBLISHED MANY YEARS AGO BY HONEYWELL, INC."
80 PRINT:PRINT "THE APPROACH CAN BE ADAPTED TO ANY FIELD OF
   ENDEAVOR"
90 FOR N = 1 TO 5000:NEXT N
100 RESTORE:CLS
110 B = RND(10):B = INT(B):IF B <   THEN 110
120 GOSUB 250
130 PRINT AT 488,A$
140 RESTORE B = 10:GOSUB 250
150 B = RND(10):B = INT(B):IF B < 1 THEN 150
160 GOSUB 250
170 PRINT AT 468,A$
180 RESTORE:B = 20:GOSUB 250
190 B = RND(10):B = INT(B):IF B < 1 THEN 190
200 GOSUB 250
210 PRINT AT 448,A$
220 FOR N = 1 TO 1000:NEXT N:GOTO 100
230 PRINT AT 832, " ":INPUT A
240 GOTO 100
250 FOR N = 1 TO B
260    READ A$
270 NEXT N
280 RETURN
290 DATA "OPTIONS"
300 DATA "FLEXIBILITY"
310 DATA "CAPABILITY"
320 DATA "MOBILITY"
330 DATA "PROGRAMMING"
340 DATA "CONCEPT"
350 DATA "TIME-PHASE"
360 DATA "PROJECTION"
370 DATA "HARDWARE"
380 DATA "CONTINGENCY"
390 DATA "MANAGEMENT"
400 DATA "ORGANIZATIONAL"
410 DATA "MONITORED"
```

```
420 DATA "RECIPROCAL"
430 DATA "DIGITAL"
440 DATA "LOGIC"
450 DATA "TRANSITIONAL"
460 DATA "INCREMENTAL"
470 DATA "THIRD GENERATION"
480 DATA "POLICY"
490 DATA "INTEGRATED"
500 DATA "TOTAL"
510 DATA "SYSTEMATIZED"
520 DATA "PARALLEL"
530 DATA "FUNCTIONAL"
540 DATA "RESPONSIVE"
550 DATA "OPTICAL"
560 DATA "SYNCHRONIZED"
570 DATA "COMPATIBLE"
580 DATA "BALANCED"
```

The program is really quite simple. The opening messages display on the screen, and then at statement 90 there is a timer which will give about 10 seconds for you to read the message, after which the program progresses. In keeping with information provided before, the print line is constructed from right to left. Thus, the words which appear on the right-hand side of the screen are defined in the first 10 DATA statements, from 290 to 380; those which are targeted for the center of the screen are contained in the next 10 DATA statements. Finally, those which will be displayed on the left side of the screen are in the last 10 DATA statements.

The process begins by generating a random number for B, at statement 110. At statements 250 through 270 there is a common READ subroutine. The number of DATA statements represented by B is read, with the final value existing at A$. Since the scope of the first 10 DATA statements is being examined, the selection is a direct representation of the value of B.

For the second and third selection, however, the pointer to the DATA lines has been RESTOREd and the first 10 DATA lines are bypassed to obtain the second group (at 140) and the first 20 DATA lines are bypassed to obtain the third group (at 190). The RESTORE options could be omitted and the bypass reads could be omitted and it would still work. It was left in to again demonstrate that it may often be necessary to bypass certain DATA statements. It's important to know precisely the location of DATA with which you are working. A more simple example is not available.

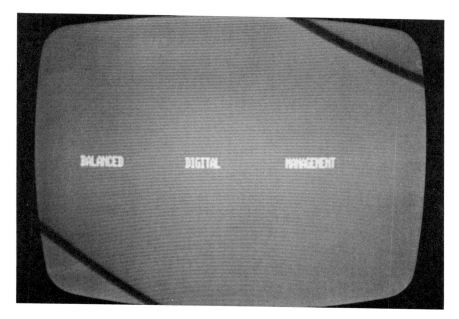

Figure 18.   Automated Buzzword Generator

ANOTHER KIND OF BUZZ

Another way to use the computer to exercise a student's learning capacity is with a spelling bee. Logically, the program to accomplish this is not dissimilar to the buzzword generator just discussed. Further, it has some of the aspects of the geography test presented before:

```
10 CLS
20 FOR N = 1 TO 100:A(N) = 0:NEXT N
30 R = 0:W = 0:S = 0:L = 0:V = 0
```

Standard clearing of ths array: here 100 array elements are being cleared to store 100 combinations of words. Actually, the array is used, as in the geography test, to keep track of any incorrect answers. Variable R is used to count the number right, and will be reset and used again when any missed questions are rereviewed. Variable W is used to count the number wrong, and will also be reset and used again when reviewing any questions which are missed.

```
40 FOR N = 1 TO 5:PRINT:NEXT N
50 PRINT TAB(20);"S P E L L I N G   B E E"
60 FOR Z = 1 TO 1000:NEXT Z
```

Statement 40 adjusts the print line to the top center of the screen. That is followed by the title of the program and a timer giving sufficient time to read it.

Before proceeding, here is the list of spelling words compiled for the exercise of the program. Note that each DATA line contains three words, one of which is the correctly spelled word, and then there is a fourth element, the correct answer. To change the list, the reader has only to replace the DATA lines from 690 to 800. Note the sentinel line in 810. Fewer words may be used or more may be inserted, so long as the sentinel line is present.

```
690 DATA "EXCELLENT","EXCELUNT","EXCELLANT","C"
700 DATA "CRISANTHENUM","CHRYSANTHENUM","CRISANTHEMUM","B"
710 DATA "NOURISH","NURISH","NOURISCH","C"
720 DATA "COMPOOTER","COMPUTOR","COMPUTER","A"
730 DATA "DATA","DATTA","DATER","C"
740 DATA "FRINDLY","FRIENDLY","FRENDLY","B"
750 DATA "AGGRAVATE","AGRAVATE","AGGRUVATE","C"
760 DATA "PERSUN","PURSON","PERSON","A"
770 DATA "TALLER","TAILOR","TAILER","B"
780 DATA "ALINEMENT","ALIGNMENT","ALINEMUNT","B"
790 DATA "CHIMNEY","CHIMINY","CHIMLY","C"
800 DATA "ELEPHANT","ELEFUNT","ELLIPHUNT","C"
810 DATA "ZZZZZ","ZZZZZ","ZZZZZ","ZZZZZ"
```

In each case, the program compares the correct answer against the student's response. As you observe the list, note that the list is laid out backwards, as it was with the buzzword generator, or rather it isn't exactly backwards—just answers A and C are reversed, because the printing is done from right to left. Since there are only two alphabetic variables, A$ and B$, it is necessary to go after the "C" answer first, followed by the "B" answer, followed by the "A." These, when displayed upon the screen, will line up under the appropriate headings, identified in statements 100, 110, and 120 below. If you want to change the words, as stated, you can. The upper limit is 100 questions. That is controlled by the following:

```
70 CLS
80 FOR N = 1  TO 100
90    PRINT AT 0,N
```

```
1ØØ     PRINT AT 365,"C"
11Ø     PRINT AT 345,"B"
12Ø     PRINT AT 325,"A"
13Ø     GOSUB 41Ø
14Ø NEXT N
```

The subroutine at 41Ø is the one which will do all the work. Note that a check for the sentinel, defined in DATA statement 81Ø, is made at 42Ø. In this manner, the list can be as long as desired, or as long as the reader has patience to key DATA statements into the program. Since there are four elements in each DATA line, they are read one at a time, displaying the first three in the appropriate places under the heading and storing the answer for comparison to the input provided by the student:

```
41Ø READ A$
42Ø IF A$ = "ZZZZZ" THEN 15Ø
43Ø PRINT AT 488,A$
44Ø READ A$
45Ø PRINT AT 468,A$
46Ø READ A$
47Ø PRINT AT 448,A$
48Ø READ B$
49Ø PRINT:PRINT
5ØØ INPUT "SELECT A, B, OR C";A$
51Ø IF A$ < > B$ THEN 57Ø
52Ø R = R + 1
53Ø PRINT:PRINT "CORRECT"
54Ø A(N) = Ø
55Ø FOR Z = 1 TO 5ØØ:NEXT Z
56Ø CLS:RETURN
```

As can be seen, B$ gets the answer, which is then checked against A$, as inputted by the student. If there is a match, the "number right" counter is incremented, the array position which would have held the number of the incorrect answer (had it been incorrect) is set to zero, and an exit is taken from the routine on the "correct side." As for the "incorrect side," the balance of that routine follows. Note that even though an exit has been taken from the routine itself, there is still a return to 56Ø to use the RETURN statement contained in the subroutine:

```
57Ø W = W + 1:S = 1
58Ø PRINT:PRINT "INCORRECT"
59Ø FOR Z = 1 TO 5ØØ:NEXT Z
6ØØ A(N) = N
61Ø GOTO 56Ø
```

Here the "number wrong" is incremented, the "incorrect" message is generated, the position is flagged in the array to indicate which had been answered incorrectly, and the process returns to the RETURN statement.

Having fulfilled the question base, it can now be determined what the score is and it can be printed. By the time the program has progressed to this point, variable N has incremented beyond the question positions, so 1 is subtracted from N and the result stored in B, which is used in the calculation to determine the percentage of accuracy. Note also that if none has been missed, the scorekeeping is avoided and a congratulatory message is displayed:

```
15Ø B = N - 1:CLS
16Ø PRINT "NUMBER RIGHT - ";R:PRINT
17Ø PRINT "NUMBER WRONG - ";W:PRINT
18Ø FOR Z = 1 TO 5ØØ:NEXT Z
19Ø P = INT(R/B * 1ØØ):IF P = 1ØØ THEN 62Ø
```

However, congratulations are given only if the 100% score is achieved on the first time through. That is controlled by variable S.

```
62Ø IF S < > Ø THEN 37Ø
63Ø CLS:IF L = 1Ø THEN 37Ø
64Ø FOR N = 1 TO 5:PRINT:NEXT N
65Ø PRINT TAB(2Ø);"1 Ø Ø    P E R C E N T ! !"
66Ø PRINT:PRINT TAB(18); "C O N G R A T U L A T I O N S"
67Ø FOR N = 1 TO 1ØØ:NEXT N:L = L + 1
68Ø GOTO 63Ø
```

Onward with the scorekeeping:

```
200 R = 0:W = 0
210 PRINT "PERCENTAGE RIGHT - ";P:PRINT
220 PRINT "PERCENTAGE WRONG - ";100 - P:PRINT
230 PRINT "TIME TO REVIEW"
240 FOR Z = 1 TO 1000:NEXT Z:CLS
```

When this has finished, the pointer is readjusted to the beginning of the array and a search is conducted to see if any numbers had been posted. If they have, the program reads to the first one, setting a bypass switch (variable V) and then the process continues as it had the first time through:

```
250 RESTORE
260 FOR N = 1 TO 100
270     PRINT AT 0,N
280     IF A(N) = 0 THEN 350
290     IF V = 1 THEN 340
300     FOR Z = 1 TO A(N)
310         READ A$:IF A$ = "ZZZZZ" THEN 150
320         FOR Q = 1 TO 3:READ A$:NEXT Q:V = 1          ·
330     NEXT Z
340     GOSUB 410
350 NEXT N
```

Finally, when all is said and done—and the program does not allow the student to "get away" from the lesson without first selecting the correct answer—then, and only then is the student asked if he/she would like to try it again.

```
360 CLS
370 INPUT "DO IT AGAIN (Y/N)";A$
380 IF A$ = "Y" THEN 10
390 PRINT:PRINT "G O O D B Y E"
400 GOTO 400
```

The following is a complete listing of the program:

```
10 CLS:RESTORE
20 FOR N = 1 TO 100:A(N) = 0:NEXT N
```

```
30 R = Ø:W = Ø:S = Ø:L = Ø:V = Ø
40 FOR N = 1 TO 5:PRINT:NEXT N
50 PRINT TAB(20);"S P E L L I N G   B E E"
60 FOR Z = 1 TO 1000:NEXT Z
70 CLS
80 FOR N = 1 TO 100
90      PRINT AT Ø,N
100      PRINT AT 365,"C"
110      PRINT AT 345,"B"
120      PRINT AT 325,"A"
130      GOSUB 410
140 NEXT N
150 B = N - 1:CLS
160 PRINT "NUMBER RIGHT - ";R:PRINT
170 PRINT "NUMBER WRONG - ";W:PRINT
180 FOR Z = 1 TO 500:NEXT Z
190 P = INT(R/B * 100):IF P = 100 THEN 620
195 IF W = Ø THEN 360
200 R = Ø:W = Ø
210 PRINT "PERCENTAGE RIGHT - ";P:PRINT
220 PRINT "PERCENTAGE WRONG - ";100 - P:PRINT
230 PRINT "TIME TO REVIEW"
240 FOR Z = 1 TO 1000:NEXT Z:CLS
250 RESTORE
260 FOR N = 1 TO 100
270      PRINT AT Ø,N
280      IF A(N) = Ø THEN 350
290      RESTORE
300      FOR Z = 1 TO A(N) - 1
310           READ A$:IF A$ = "ZZZZZ" THEN 150
320           FOR Q = 1 TO 3:READ A$:NEXT Q:V=1
330      NEXT Z
340      GOSUB 410
350 NEXT N
360 CLS:IF W = Ø THEN 150
370 INPUT "DO IT AGAIN (Y/N)";A$
380 IF A$ = "Y" THEN 10
390 PRINT:PRINT "G O O D B Y E"
400 GOTO 400
```

```
410 READ A$
420 IF A$ = "ZZZZZ" THEN 150
430 PRINT AT 488,A$
440 READ A$
450 PRINT AT 468,A$
460 READ A$
470 PRINT AT 448,A$
480 READ B$
490 PRINT:PRINT
500 INPUT "SELECT A, B, OR C";A$
510 IF A$ < >B$ THEN 570
520 R = R + 1
530 PRINT:PRINT "CORRECT"
540 A(N) = 0
550 FOR Z = 1 TO 500:NEXT Z
560 CLS:RETURN
570 W = W + 1:S = 1
580 PRINT:PRINT "INCORRECT"
590 FOR Z = 1 TO 500:NEXT Z
600 A(N) = N
610 GOTO 560
620 IF S < > 0 THEN 370
630 CLS:IF L = 10 THEN 370
640 FOR N = 1 TO 5:PRINT:NEXT N
650 PRINT TAB(20);"1 0 0   P E R C E N T ! !"
660 PRINT:PRINT TAB(18);"C O N G R A T U L A T I O N S"
670 FOR N = 1 TO 100:NEXT N:L = L + 1
680 GOTO 630
690 DATA "EXCELLENT","EXELUNT","EXCELLANT","C"
700 DATA "CRISANTHENUM","CHRYSANTHENUM","CRISANTHEMUM","B"
710 DATA "NOURISH","NURISH","NOURISCH","C"
720 DATA "COMPOOTER","COMPUTOR","COMPUTER","A"
730 DATA "DATA","DATTA","DATER","C"
740 DATA "FRINDLY","FRIENDLY","FRENDLY","B"
750 DATA "AGGRAVATE","AGRAVATE","AGGRUVATE","C"
760 DATA "PERSUN","PURSON","PERSON","A"
```

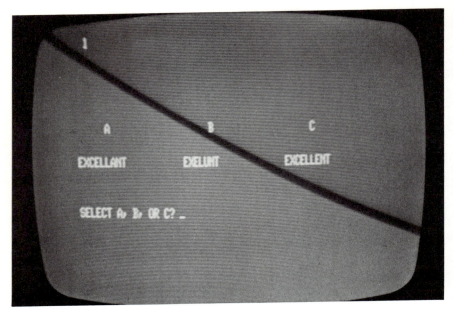

Figure 19.   Spelling Bee

```
77Ø DATA "TALER","TAILOR","TAILER","B"
78Ø DATA "ALINEMENT","ALIGNMENT","ALINEMUNT","B"
79Ø DATA "CHIMNEY","CHIMINY","CHIMLY","C"
8ØØ DATA "ELEPHANT","ELEFUNT","ELLIPHUNT","C"
81Ø DATA "ZZZZZ","ZZZZZ","ZZZZZ","ZZZZZ"
```

FASTER THAN A SPEEDING BULLET

The final educational activity to be discussed in this volume is that of speed reading. A very brief and commonly known text has been selected, and the activity has been structured using PRINT statements:

```
52Ø PRINT "THE LORD IS MY SHEPHERD; I SHALL NOT WANT.":GOSUB 72Ø
53Ø PRINT "HE MAKETH ME TO LIE DOWN IN GREEN PASTURES:':GOSUB 72Ø
54Ø PRINT "HE LEADETH ME BESIDE THE STILL WATERS.":GOSUB 72Ø
55Ø PRINT "HE RESTORETH MY SOUL.  HE LEADETH ME IN":GOSUB 72Ø
56Ø PRINT "THE PATHS OF RIGHTEOUSNESS FOR HIS NAME'S":GOSUB 72Ø
57Ø PRINT "SAKE.  YEA, THOUGH I WALK THROUGH THE":GOSUB 72Ø
58Ø PRINT "VALLEY OF DEATH.  I WILL FEAR NO EVIL:":GOSUB 72Ø
59Ø PRINT "FOR THOU ART WITH ME.  THY ROD AND THY":GOSUB 72Ø
```

```
600 PRINT "STAFF THEY COMFORT ME.  THOU PREPAREST A":GOSUB 720
610 PRINT "TABLE BEFORE ME IN THE PRESENCE OF MINE":GOSUB 720
620 PRINT "ENEMIES:  THOU ANOINTEST MY HEAD WITH OIL;":GOSUB 720
630 PRINT "MY CUP RUNNETH OVER.  SURELY GOODNESS AND":GOSUB 720
640 PRINT "MERCY SHALL FOLLOW ME ALL THE DAYS OF MY":GOSUB 720
650 PRINT "LIFE; AND I WILL DWELL IN THE HOUSE OF":GOSUB 720
660 PRINT "THE LORD FOR EVER.":GOSUB 720
```

Each line is structured in the 30–40 character range. The following opens the program:

```
10 CLS
20 T = 500
30 GOSUB 720
40 PRINT TAB(20):"S P E E D    R E A D I N G"
50 GOSUB 790
60 CLS
70 PRINT "THE FOLLOWING IS A PREPARED TEXT, EXCERPTED":PRINT
80 PRINT "FROM THE KING JAMES VERSION OF THE BIBLE.":PRINT
90 PRINT "YOU MAY SELECT A SPEED OR YOU MAY ELECT TO LET":PRINT
100 PRINT "THE COMPUTER SELECT A SPEED FOR YOU."
110 GOSUB 790:GOSUB 790
120 PRINT:INPUT "DO YOU WISH TO SELECT A SPEED (Y/N)",A$
130 IF A$ < > "Y" THEN 440
```

The variable T will be the display timer. At statement 20 it is loaded with a default value, the value it will receive if unchanged. Statement 790 is the general timer subroutine:

```
790 FOR N = 1 TO 1000:NEXT N:RETURN
```

If a speed is selected, the following selection of speeds is offered:

```
140 CLS:PRINT:PRINT "AVAILABLE SPEEDS ARE:":PRINT
150 PRINT TAB(5);"1.  6000 WPM"," 9.  600 WPM"
160 PRINT TAB(5);"2.  3000 WPM","10.  400 WPM"
170 PRINT TAB(5);"3.  2000 WPM","11.  300 WPM"
180 PRINT TAB(5);"4.  1500 WPM","12.  240 WPM"
190 PRINT TAB(5);"5.  1200 WPM","13.  200 WPM"
```

```
200 PRINT TAB(5);"6.  1000 WPM","14.  170 WPM"
210 PRINT TAB(5);"7.   850 WPM","15.  150 WPM"
220 PRINT TAB(5);"8.   750 WPM","16.  100 WPM"
230 PRINT:INPUT "SELECT";A:CLS
```

With each option, there is an associated time modification. Note that each is a function of the product of a factor to the default option. Remembering that 500 will hold the timer for about 1 second, and counting the number of characters on a line—dividing the number of characters by 5, you can closely hit the indicated reading speed.

With a normal, but lengthy, ON . . . GOTO, select one of 16 options and then swing right into the display:

```
240 ON A GOTO 250,260,270,280,290,300,310,320,330,340,350,360,370,
             380,390,400
250 T = 500 * .1:GOTO 410
260 T = 500 * .2:GOTO 410
270 T = 500 * .3:GOTO 410
280 T = 500 * .4:GOTO 410
290 T = 500 * .5:GOTO 410
300 T = 500 * .6:GOTO 410
310 T = 500 * .7:GOTO 410
320 T = 500 * .8:GOTO 410
330 T = 500 * 1:GOTO 410
340 T = 500 * 1.5:GOTO 410
350 T = 500 * 2.0:GOTO 410
360 T = 500 * 2.5:GOTO 410
370 T = 500 * 3:GOTO 410
380 T = 500 * 3.5:GOTO 410
390 T = 500 * 4:GOTO 410
400 T = 500 * 4.5
410 T = INT(T)
420 GOSUB 720
430 GOTO 520
```

520 is, of course, the printing routine. 720 is a screen spacing routine:

```
72Ø FOR N = 1 TO T:NEXT N
73Ø CLS
74Ø FOR N = 1 TO 7
75Ø     PRINT
76Ø NEXT N
77Ø PRINT TAB(1Ø);
78Ø RETURN
```

If the answer to the speed question (13Ø) was "N," the computer selects a speed, randomly, in the range of 300 to 600 words per minute. The 5/6 fraction in statement 460 is a function of the ratio of words per minute to the timing value:

```
 44Ø T = RND(5ØØ):T = INT(T)
 45Ø IF T  < 25Ø THEN 44Ø
 46Ø S = (5 * T)/6:S = INT(S)
 47Ø GOSUB 72Ø
 48Ø PRINT "THE COMPUTER HAS SELECTED";S;"WORDS PER MINUTE"
 49Ø GOSUB 79Ø
 5ØØ CLS
 51Ø GOSUB 72Ø
```

And all that remains are the closing remarks:

```
67Ø INPUT "WANT TO DO IT AGAIN (Y/N)";A$
68Ø IF A$ = "Y" THEN 1Ø
69Ø GOSUB 72Ø
7ØØ PRINT "G O O D B Y E"
71Ø GOTO 71Ø
```

The process can be speeded up by change statement 68Ø to GOTO 12Ø.

As can be seen, it's a simple program, but a powerful one if speed of reading is important. It will be a little work to load the text, but now you can see how it's done. The entire program follows:

```
1Ø CLS
2Ø T = 5ØØ
```

Figure 20.   Speed Reading Text

```
30 GOSUB 720
40 PRINT TAB(20):"S P E E D   R E A D I N G"
50 GOSUB 790
60 CLS
70 PRINT "THE FOLLOWING IS A PREPARED TEXT, EXCERPTED":PRINT
80 PRINT "FROM THE KING JAMES VERSION OF THE BIBLE.":PRINT
90 PRINT "YOU MAY SELECT A SPEED OR YOU MAY ELECT TO LET":PRINT
100 PRINT "THE COMPUTER SELECT A SPEED FOR YOU."
110 GOSUB 790:GOSUB 790
120 PRINT:INPUT "DO YOU WISH TO SELECT A SPEED (Y/N)",A$
130 IF A$ < > "Y" THEN 440
140 CLS:PRINT:PRINT "AVAILABLE SPEEDS ARE:":PRINT
150 PRINT TAB(5);"1.  6000 WPM"," 9.  600 WPM"
160 PRINT TAB(5);"2.  3000 WPM","10.  400 WPM"
170 PRINT TAB(5);"3.  2000 WPM","11.  300 WPM"
180 PRINT TAB(5);"4.  1500 WPM","12.  240 WPM"
190 PRINT TAB(5);"5.  1200 WPM","13.  200 WPM"
200 PRINT TAB(5);"6.  1000 WPM","14.  170 WPM"
210 PRINT TAB(5);"7.   850 WPM","15.  150 WPM"
220 PRINT TAB(5);"8.   750 WPM","16.  100 WPM"
```

```
230 PRINT:INPUT "SELECT";A:CLS
240 ON A GOTO 250,260,270,280,290,300,310,320,330,340,350,360,370,
              380,390,400
250 T = 500 * .1:GOTO 410
260 T = 500 * .2:GOTO 410
270 T = 500 * .3:GOTO 410
280 T = 500 * .4:GOTO 410
290 T = 500 * .5:GOTO 410
300 T = 500 * .6:GOTO 410
310 T = 500 * .7:GOTO 410
320 T = 500 * .8:GOTO 410
330 T = 500 * 1:GOTO 410
340 T = 500 * 1.5:GOTO 410
350 T = 500 * 2.0:GOTO 410
360 T = 500 * 2.5:GOTO 410
370 T = 500 * 3:GOTO 410
380 T = 500 * 3.5:GOTO 410
390 T = 500 * 4:GOTO 410
400 T = 500 * 4.5
410 T = INT(T)
420 GOSUB 720
430 GOTO 520
440 T = RND(500):T = INT(T)
450 IF T < 250 THEN 440
460 S = (5 * T)/6:S = INT(S)
470 GOSUB 720
480 PRINT "THE COMPUTER HAS SELECTED";S;"WORDS PER MINUTE"
490 GOSUB 790
500 CLS
510 GOSUB 720
520 PRINT "THE LORD IS MY SHEPHERD; I SHALL NOT WANT.":GOSUB 720
530 PRINT "HE MAKETH ME TO LIE DOWN IN GREEN PASTURES:':GOSUB 720
540 PRINT "HE LEADETH ME BESIDE THE STILL WATERS.":GOSUB 720
550 PRINT "HE RESTORETH MY SOUL.  HE LEADETH ME IN":GOSUB 720
560 PRINT "THE PATHS OF RIGHTEOUSNESS FOR HIS NAME'S":GOSUB 720
570 PRINT "SAKE.  YEA, THOUGH I WALK THROUGH THE":GOSUB 720
580 PRINT "VALLEY OF DEATH.  I WILL FEAR NO EVIL:":GOSUB 720
590 PRINT "FOR THOU ART WITH ME.  THY ROD AND THY":GOSUB 720
600 PRINT "STAFF THEY COMFORT ME.  THOU PREPAREST A":GOSUB 720
610 PRINT "TABLE BEFORE ME IN THE PRESENCE OF MINE":GOSUB 720
```

```
620 PRINT "ENEMIES:  THOU ANOINTEST MY HEAD WITH OIL;":GOSUB 720
630 PRINT "MY CUP RUNNETH OVER.  SURELY GOODNESS AND":GOSUB 720
640 PRINT "MERCY SHALL FOLLOW ME ALL THE DAYS OF MY":GOSUB 720
650 PRINT "LIFE; AND I WILL DWELL IN THE HOUSE OF":GOSUB 720
660 PRINT "THE LORD FOREVER.":GOSUB 720
670 INPUT "WANT TO DO IT AGAIN (Y/N)";A$
680 IF A$ = "Y" THEN 10
690 GOSUB 720
700 PRINT "G O O D B Y E"
710 GOTO 710
720 FOR N = 1 TO T:NEXT N
730 CLS
740 FOR N = 1 TO 7
750    PRINT
760 NEXT N
770 PRINT TAB(10);
780 RETURN
790 FOR N = 1 TO 1000:NEXT N:RETURN
```

6
Useful Applications for the Home

This chapter deals with such home computer applications as:

- shopping
- automotbile
- heating requirements
- chore planning
- grocery inventory
- activity schedule planning

(Financial applications appear in Chapter 8.)

SHOPPING

The application which follows can put a lot of order into your grocery shopping. In the application we have identified 129 categories of items in approximately 70 locations in our favorite supermarket, and have included the last known average prices of the items which are customarily purchased. The program is developed to accomodate a maximum of 150 items, numbered in the range of 1 to 150, but the processing has been restricted to 130 items for purposes of speeding up the handling of the DATA. Those places where an adjustment may be made to accomodate a larger number of items will be identified.

The format of the DATA statements is as follows:

Name	Variable
Item number	I
Description	A$
Unit of Measure	B$
Unit Price	P
Store Location	L

First you will need to:

- Map the store, assigning location numbers.
- Identify what items are placed in each location—at least the ones which interest you.
- Obtain the current average price of the specific group of items. If you wish to do it by brand name of item, you may wish to alter the description.

It is important, however, that all item numbers fall within the prescribed range and that there are no duplicates. Should your needs exceed the 150 items of which the application is capable, the range can be extended to at least 200 items, but not much futher in Level I.

First the DATA lines:

```
1100 DATA 1,"BABY FOOD","JAR",.35,27
1110 DATA 2,"BISQUICK","BOX",.97,13
1120 DATA 3,"CAKE MIX","BOX",.69,15
1130 DATA 4,"CEREAL","BOX ,1.04,34
1140 DATA 5,"COCOA","BOX",1.19,9
1150 DATA 6,"CONDIMENTS","BOX",.54,7
1160 DATA 7,"CRACKERS","BOX",.86,18
1170 DATA 8,"FLOUR","5 LB",1.27,25
1180 DATA 9,"JAM/JELLY","JAR",.49,16
1190 DATA 10,"PUDDING/GELATIN","PKG",.17,31
1200 DATA 11,"KETCHUP","JAR",.57,22
1210 DATA 12,"MAYONNAISE","JAR",.95,22
1220 DATA 13,"MILK, CANNED","CAN",.37,6
1230 DATA 14,"MILK,  POWDERED","PKG",1.39,11
1240 DATA 15,"MUSTARD","JAR",.37,44
1250 DATA 16,"NOODLES","PKG",.19,16
1260 DATA 17,"NUTS","PKG",.74,32
1270 DATA 18,"OLIVES","CAN",".69,26
1280 DATA 19,"PEANUT BUTTER","JAR",.95,21
1290 DATA 20,"PICKLES","JAR",".57,14
1300 DATA 21,"POP CORN","CAN",1.45,41
1310 DATA 22,"POTATO CHIPS","PKG",.69,4
1320 DATA 23,"RICE","PKG",.82,15
```

```
1330 DATA 24,"SALAD DRESSING","BOTTLE",.74,13
1340 DATA 25,"SALT","PKG",.52,36
1350 DATA 26,"SAUCES","JAR",.73,16
1360 DATA 27,"CRISCO","CAN",1.22,31
1370 DATA 28,"SOUPS","CAN",.37,12
1380 DATA 29,"SUGAR","5 LB",.90,18
1390 DATA 30,"SYRUP","BOTTLE",.67,14
1400 DATA 31,"TOPPINGS","CAN",.29,17
1410 DATA 32,"VINEGAR","BOTTLE",.47,22
1420 DATA 33,"YEAST","CAKE",".22,45
1430 DATA 34,"BREAD","LOAF",.75,55
1440 DATA 35,"CAKE","LOAF",1.42,54
1450 DATA 36,"COOKIES","PKG,1.19,53
1460 DATA 37,"DONUTS","DOZEN",1.42,52
1470 DATA 38,"PIES","EACH",1.69,51
1480 DATA 39,"ROLLS","PKG",.69,50
1490 DATA 40,"ASPARAGUS","CAN",.77,36
1500 DATA 41,"BEANS","CAN",.54,32
1510 DATA 42,"BEETS","CAN",.67,30
1520 DATA 43,"BROCCOLI","PKG",.37,48
1530 DATA 44,"CABBAGE","HEAD",.19,3
1540 DATA 45,"CARROTS","BUNCH",.37,3
1550 DATA 46,"CAULIFLOWER","PKG",.47,48
1560 DATA 47,"CELERY","BUNCH",.69,4
1570 DATA 48,"CORN","EAR",.12,2
1580 DATA 49,"CUCUMBER","EACH",.13,6
1590 DATA 50,"LETTUCE","HEAD",.69,3
1600 DATA 51,"MUSHROOMS","CAN",.45,45
1610 DATA 52,"ONIONS","BAG",.62,4
1620 DATA 53,"PEAS","PKG",.37,35
1630 DATA 54,"PEPPERS","BELL",.21,4
1640 DATA 55,"POTATOES","BAG",1.22,1
1650 DATA 56,"RADISHES","PKG",.27,5
1660 DATA 57,"SAUERKRAUT","CAN",.66,17
1670 DATA 58,"SPINACH","PKG",.42,34
```

```
1680 DATA 59,"SQUASH","PKG",.47,34
1690 DATA 60,"TOMATOES","PKG",.67,3
1700 DATA 61,"APPLES","BAG",.79,2
1710 DATA 62,"APRICOTS","CAN",.59,18
1720 DATA 63,"BANANAS","BUNCH",.69,3
1730 DATA 64,"BLUEBERRIES","PKG",.1.45,4
1740 DATA 65,"CHERRIES","BUNCH",.45,4
1750 DATA 66,"GRAPEFRUIT","EACH",.45,3
1760 DATA 67,"GRAPES","BUNCH",.69,5
1770 DATA 68,"LEMONS","EACH",.25,3
1780 DATA 69,"MELONS","EACH",.98,1
1790 DATA 70,"ORANGES","PKG",.98,2
1800 DATA 71,"PEACHES","CAN",.53,19
1810 DATA 72,"PEARS","CAN",.54,19
1820 DATA 73,"PINEAPPLE","CAN",.67,19
1830 DATA 74,"PRUNES","PKG",.82,25
1840 DATA 75,"BEER","6-PACK",2.37,33
1850 DATA 76,"COFFEE","JAR",4.35,29
1860 DATA 77,"FRUIT JUICES","CAN",.54,31
1870 DATA 78,"SOFT DRINKS","BOTTLE",".99,33
1880 DATA 79,"TEA","PKG",.69,34
1890 DATA 80,"BACON","LB",1.69,11
1900 DATA 81,"BEEF","LB",2.29,48
1910 DATA 82,"CHICKEN","LB",1.19,48
1920 DATA 83,"COLD CUTS","1/2 LB",1.69,49
1930 DATA 84,"FISH","LB",4.12,48
1940 DATA 85,"HOT DOGS","LB",1.39,51
1950 DATA 86,"HAM","5 lb",7.34,52
1960 DATA 87,"HAMBURGER","LB",1.39,48
1970 DATA 88,"LAMB","LB",2.29,48
1980 DATA 89,"LIVER","LB",1.17,48
1990 DATA 90,"PORK CHOPS","LB",2.32,48
2000 DATA 91,"ROAST","LB",2.19,48
2010 DATA 92,"SAUSAGE","PKG","1.69,49
2020 DATA 93,"SHRIMP","LB",3.29,47
2030 DATA 94,"SPARE RIBS","LB",1.12,48
```

```
2040 DATA 95,"STEAK","LB",2.23,48
2050 DATA 96,"T.V. DINNER","PKG",1.39,53
2060 DATA 97,"VEAL","LB",1.45,48
2070 DATA 98,"BUTTER","LB",1.49,66
2080 DATA 99,"CHEESE","1/2 LB",.89,63
2090 DATA 100,"COTTAGE CHEESE","LB",.82,65
2100 DATA 101,"CREAM","PINT",.79,62
2110 DATA 102,"EGGS","DOZ",.69,69
2120 DATA 103,"HALF-AND-HALF","CARTON",.54,66
2130 DATA 104,"ICE CREAM","1/2 GAL.",1.45,61
2140 DATA 105,"MARGARINE","LB",.69,63
2150 DATA 106,"MILK","1/2 GAL.",1.09,65
2160 DATA 107,"SOUR CREAM","1/2 PINT",.67,67
2170 DATA 108,"YOGURT","CONTAINER",.47,65
2180 DATA 109,"ALUMINUM FOIL","ROLL",.79,43
2190 DATA 110,"BLEACH","GAL",1.29,38
2200 DATA 111,"CANDY","BAR",".20,33
2210 DATA 112,"CIGARETTES","CARTON",6.30,16
2220 DATA 113,"CLEANSER","PKG",1.43,47
2230 DATA 114,"DETERGENT","PKG,.74,45
2240 DATA 115,"INSECTICIDE","SPRAY CAN",1.39,38
2250 DATA 116,"LIGHT BULBS","PKG OF 4",2.80,38
2260 DATA 117,"MATCHES, SAFETY","PKG",.27,30
2270 DATA 118,"PAPER TOWEL","ROLL",.77,49
2280 DATA 119,"DOG FOOD, DRY","10 LB",2.22,49
2290 DATA 120,"CAT FOOD, DRY",5 LB",1.14,49
2300 DATA 121,"POLISH","CAN",.92,34
2310 DATA 122,"SCOURING PADS","PKG",.59,20
2320 DATA 123,"BATH SOAP","BAR",.64,43
2330 DATA 124,"STARCH","PKG",.78,48
2340 DATA 125,"TOILET TISSUE","ROLL",.69,39
2350 DATA 126,"TOOTHPASTE","TUBE",.69,20
2360 DATA 127,"PAPER PLATES","PKG",.83,30
2370 DATA 128,"WAX","CAKE",.24,30
2380 DATA 129,"WAXED PAPER","ROLL",.76,40
2390 DATA 999,,,999,999
```

The data list is actually the largest part of the program. Note that the final data line is a sentinel line. Note also that the sentinel is assigned to the numeric fields only. The extra commas account for the alphabetic positions, without including the actual alphabetic data.

The program begins, as usual, by clearing the screen, positioning the title, and resetting variable E, which, as will be discussed later, is a "short list" switch.

```
1Ø CLS:RESTORE:E = Ø
2Ø FOR N = 1 TO 7:PRINT:NEXT N
3Ø PRINT TAB (2Ø);"S H O P P I N G   L I S T"
4Ø FOR N = 1 TO 6ØØ:A(N) = Ø:NEXT N
```

Statement 4Ø resets 600 positions of the array to zero; note that 600 is 150 times four. Thus, the plan is to store in the array four items of data relative to the grocery items which will be selected. The groups are organized like this:

ITEM NO.	QUANTITY DESIRED	EXTENDED PRICE	LOCATION

Figure 21.   Data Line Organization

As you will recall, each of the DATA lines has a unit price. As the list is displayed, the operator is asked how many of the selected items are desired. That answer is "plugged" into the second group. The product of that answer times the unit price is "plugged" into the third group. Item No. and Location are extracted directly from the DATA line.

The concept of how these groups are organized is extremely important, primarily because of the concept of "relative organization." Under relative organization, the corresponding positions of each group bear a relationship to the whole. That is, the first position of "Item No." the first position of "Quantity Desired," and the first position of "Extended Price," and the first position of "Location" all refer to the corresponding relative position within the DATA lines. This is the reason the DATA lines are numbered (I) beginning at one. It does happen that the position of the Item No. and the number of the item to which it refers are the same. That is true until the array is sorted, as will be discussed.

That principle can be illustrated in this manner:

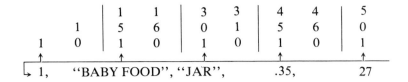

Figure 22.   Array Organization

With the inability, in Level I, to sort data (alphabetic), the requirement is to sort *pointers to data* instead. While a little more difficult to understand, it is a little more efficient in the use of computer execution time.

The process begins by establishing a heading and listing the first 10 DATA lines on the screen:

```
5Ø CLS
6Ø GOSUB 77Ø:GOSUB 8ØØ
```

Those subroutines follow:

```
77Ø PRINT "ITEM";TAB(1Ø);"DESCRIPTION";TAB(25);
78Ø PRINT "UNIT";TAB(35);"PRICE";TAB(45);"LOCATION"
79Ø PRINT:RETURN
8ØØ FOR Z = 1 TO 1Ø
81Ø    READ I,A$,B$,P,L
82Ø    IF I = 999 THEN 87Ø
83Ø    PRINT I;TAB(1Ø);A$;TAB(25);B$;TAB(35);
84Ø    PRINT "$";P;TAB(5Ø);L
85Ø NEXT Z
86Ø RETURN
87Ø PRINT:PRINT "LIST COMPLETE":E = 1
88Ø GOTO 86Ø
```

Next the ITEM No. is selected. Since each page of the list contains 10 items, there is also the facility to "page forward." This, then, is the reason for statement 7Ø.

```
7Ø A = Ø
8Ø PRINT AT 832, "ℓPRESS ENTER TO PAGE FORWARD - OR"
```

```
9Ø INPUT "ENTER NUMBER TO SELECT ITEM";A:A = INT(A)
1ØØ IF A > 13Ø THEN 8Ø
11Ø IF (A = Ø) * (E = Ø) THEN 5Ø
12Ø IF (A = Ø) * (E = 1) THEN 19Ø
```

In instruction 87Ø, E was set to 1 if the sentinel had been located before 10 lines had been displayed. Here the check is for the combination of A = Ø (page forward) *and* the absence of anything other than Ø in E (end of the list). If, at statement 11Ø, that pair of conditions exist, the process continues, displaying 10 items at a time. If an entry has not been made, but it is the end of the list, the program goes to 19Ø.

Note the range check at statement 1ØØ. You can legitimately increase that to 150 should you decide to expand the item selection. It can be changed to 200 with some other changes, which will be discussed.

The item is selected at statement 9Ø, and while it may not have been the item you meant, if it's valid, the program will proceed. Now the quantity must be entered. Note that there is INTeger protection on the entries, so it will be impossible to subdivide the unit of measure stored in the DATA lines.

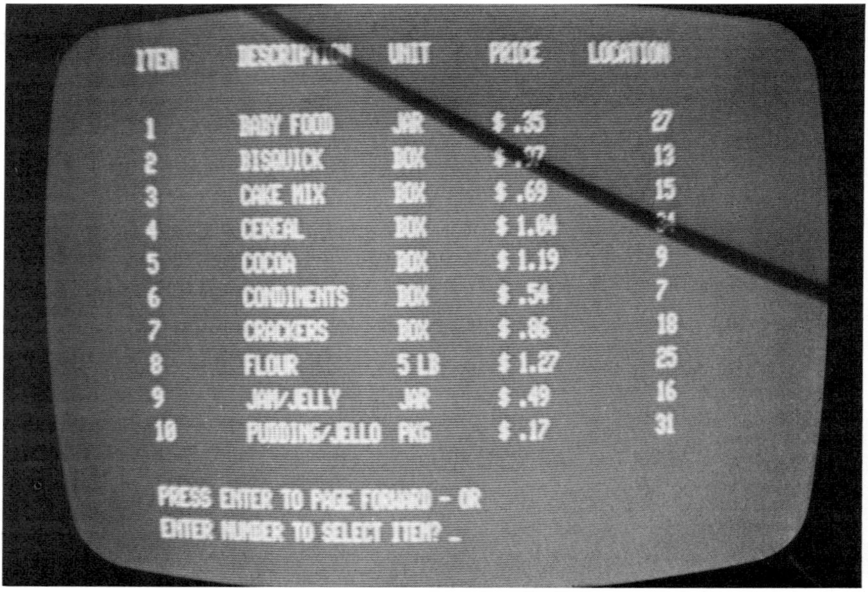

Figure 23.   Supermarket Inventory List

Note that the item number is stored in the array in the same relative position as its value (statement 140) and that the quantity desired is stored in the second group of the array.

```
130 REM "STORE ITEM NUMBER AND LOCATION"
140 A(A) = A
150 PRINT AT 832,"ƃ":INPUT "ENTER QUANTITY DESIRED";Q:Q = INT(Q)
160 REM "STORE QUANTITY DESIRED"
170 A(A + 150) = Q
180 GOTO 70
```

And then the process repeats. The space in the PRINT message (statement 150) is critical, as the instruction is used to position the INPUT statement beneath the displayed list. That position must be accounted for later in the program.

If you wish to expand the range from 150 to 200 items, you should make the following changes:

Where you Read	Substitute
N + 150	N + 200
N + 300	N + 400
N + 450	N + 600

When you've finished the list and find that you've forgotten something, you have only to go back through it. When you do, the following is important:

- If you select something which you had previously selected, you get the new selection and lose the old.
- You must page forward through the list before proceeding, by pressing the space bar.

```
190 CLS
200 PRINT "DID YOU MISS ANYTHING?"
210 PRINT:INPUT "DO YOU WISH TO REVIEW THE LIST (Y/N)";A$
220 IF A$ < > "Y" THEN 240
230 E = 0:RESTORE:GOTO 40
```

At this point, the price extensions are accomplished and the screen goes blank. To demonstrate that something is indeed occurring, some messages are included.

```
240 CLS:PRINT "DON'T GO AWAY":GOSUB 2400
250 PRINT "I'M FIGURING":GOSUB 2400
260 FOR N = 1 TO 130
270     CLS
280     IF A(N) = 0 THEN 340
290     RESTORE
300     PRINT AT 128, "STILL FIGURING"
310     GOSUB 1030
320     A(N + 450) = L
330     A(N + 300) = P * A(N + 150)
340 NEXT N
2400 FOR Z = 1 TO 1000:NEXT Z:RETURN
1030 FOR Z = 1 TO N
1040     READ I,A$,B$,P,L
1050     IF I = 999 THEN 1080
1060 NEXT Z
1070 RETURN
1080 PRINT "ITEM NOT ON LIST"
1090 GOTO 1070
```

At this point you are given the choice as to whether you want the list in item number sequence (original) or in location sequence (sorted). If you want it in item number sequence the numbers will stay in their assigned positions in the array, interspersed with array positions which contain the value of zero, placed there at the beginning of the program.

If you want it sorted, the sort is done by the "exchange" method, discussed earlier in the book. No attempt was made to speed up this sort, as it is not very lengthy. It should be pointed out, however, that when an exchange is effected, all corresponding positions in the other groups in the array are likewise rearranged. This will result in all zeros being low in the array and the item numbers being high.

```
350 PRINT "TIME TO PREPARE YOUR SHOPPING LIST."
360 PRINT "GET A PAPER AND PENCIL."
370 PRINT:PRINT "I WILL LIST, IN GROUPS OF TEN, THE ITEMS"
380 PRINT "YOU HAVE SELECTED"
390 PRINT:PRINT "AT THE END I WILL ESTIMATE YOUR BILL."
400 PRINT:PRINT "DO YOU WANT THE LIST SORTED INTO LOCATION"
```

```
410 INPUT "SEQUENCE (Y/N);A$
420 IF A$ < >"Y" THEN 590
430 FOR N = 1 TO 130
440     IF A(N + 450) < = A(N + 451) THEN 570
450     PRINT A(N + 450),A(N + 451),N
460     R = A(N):S = A(N + 150)
470     T = A(N + 300):U = A(N + 450)
480     A(N) = A(N + 1):A(N + 150) = A(N + 151)
490     A(N + 300) = A(N + 301):A(N + 450) = A(N + 451)
500     A(N + 1) = R:A(N + 151) = S
510     A(N + 301) = T:A(N + 451) = U
520     CLS:PRINT AT 0,"SORTING":F = 1
530     PRINT A(N + 450),A(N + 451),N
540 NEXT N
550 IF F = 0 THEN 590
560 F = 0:GOTO 430
570 CLS:PRINT AT 0,"bbbbbbb"
580 GOTO 540
```

Again it will be necessary to adjust statement 430 to change 130 to 150, and to adjust 430 through 530, as appropriate, to increase it to 200.

Here is the display routine; only the selected list is displayed this time:

```
590 CLS
600 PRINT "DON'T GO AWAY":GOSUB 2400
610 CLS:GOSUB 770
620 FOR N = 1 TO 130
630     IF A(N) = 0 THEN 660
640     RESTORE
650     GOSUB 890
660 NEXT N
890 FOR Z = 1 TO A(N)
900     READ I,A$,B$,P,L
910     IF I = 999 THEN 1010
920 NEXT Z
930 PRINT I;TAB(10);A$;TAB(25);A(N + 150)
940 PRINT TAB(35);A(N + 300);TAB(45);A(N + 450)
```

```
950 B = B + A(N + 300)
960 C = C + 1:IF C = 10 THEN 980
970 RETURN
980 INPUT "PRESS ENTER TO CONTINUE";C:C = 0
990 CLS:GOSUB 770
1000 GOTO 970
1010 PRINT:PRINT "ITEM NOT ON LIST"
1020 GOTO 970
670 PRINT:INPUT "ARE YOU READY FOR THE BILL (Y/N)";A$
680 IF A$ = "Y" THEN 710
690 PRINT "SORRY - IT'S YOURS ANYWAY"
700 GOSUB 2400
710 CLS
720 FOR N = 1 TO 7:PRINT:NEXT N
730 PRINT "ESTIMATED BILL","$";B
740 GOSUB 2400
750 PRINT "END OF SHOPPING LIST"
760 GOTO 760
```

All that needs to be done now is to present the estimated bill (accumulated at statement 950) and the process is complete.

Granted, it seems like an expensive way to maintain a shopping list, and it has to be copied to paper anyway. However, recall that the premise of this book is that the computer will be an integral part of the home. Inexpensive printers are available and no doubt a printer will ultimately be part of your home computer.

But perhaps you can see how, if this is tied to the store mapping project (from the graphics chapter) and the pantry inventory, discussed later in this chapter, the entire process can be simplified.

The entire program, in the proper sequence, is now presented:

```
10 CLS:RESTORE:E = 0
20 FOR N = 1 TO 7:PRINT:NEXT N
30 PRINT TAB (20);"S H O P P I N G   L I S T"
40 FOR N = 1 TO 600:A(N) = 0:NEXT N
50 CLS
60 GOSUB 770:GOSUB 800
70 A = 0
```

```
80 PRINT AT 832, "𝕓PRESS ENTER TO PAGE FORWARD - OR"
90 INPUT "ENTER NUMBER TO SELECT ITEM";A:A = INT(A)
100 IF A > 130 THEN 80
110 IF (A = 0) * (E = 0) THEN 50
120 IF (A = 0) * (E = 1) THEN 190
130 REM "STORE ITEM NUMBER AND LOCATION"
140 A(A) = A
150 PRINT AT 832,"𝕓":INPUT "ENTER QUANTITY DESIRED";Q:A = INT(Q)
160 REM "STORE QUANTITY DESIRED"
170 A(A + 150) = Q
180 GOTO 70
190 CLS
200 PRINT "DID YOU MISS ANYTHING?"
210 PRINT:INPUT "DO YOU WISH TO REVIEW THE LIST (Y/N)";A$
220 IF A$ < > "Y" THEN 240
230 E = 0:RESTORE:GOTO 40
240 CLS:PRINT "DON'T GO AWAY":GOSUB 2400
250 PRINT "I'M FIGURING":GOSUB 2400
260 FOR N = 1 TO 130
270     CLS
280     IF A(N) = 0 THEN 340
290     RESTORE
300     PRINT AT 128, "STILL FIGURING"
310     GOSUB 1030
320     A(N + 450) = L
330     A(N + 300) = P * A(N + 150)
340 NEXT N
350 PRINT "TIME TO PREPARE YOUR SHOPPING LIST."
360 PRINT "GET A PAPER AND PENCIL."
370 PRINT:PRINT "I WILL LIST, IN GROUPS OF TEN, THE ITEMS"
380 PRINT "YOU HAVE SELECTED"
390 PRINT:PRINT "AT THE END I WILL ESTIMATE YOUR BILL."
400 PRINT:PRINT "DO YOU WANT THE LIST SORTED INTO LOCATION"
410 INPUT "SEQUENCE (Y/N);A$
420 IF A$ < > "Y" THEN 590
430 FOR N = 1 TO 130
```

```
44Ø     IF A(N + 45Ø) < = A(N + 451) THEN 57Ø
45Ø     PRINT A(N + 45Ø),A(N + 451),N
46Ø     R = A(N):S = A(N + 15Ø)
47Ø     T = A(N + 3ØØ):U = A(N + 45Ø)
48Ø     A(N) = A(N + 1):A(N + 15Ø) = A(N + 151)
49Ø     A(N + 3ØØ) = A(N + 3Ø1):A(N + 45Ø) = A(N + 451)
5ØØ     A(N + 1) = R:A(N + 151) = S
51Ø     A(N + 3Ø1) = T:A(N + 451) = U
52Ø     CLS:PRINT AT Ø,"SORTING":F = 1
53Ø     PRINT A(N + 45Ø),A(N + 451),N
54Ø NEXT N
55Ø IF F = Ø THEN 59Ø
56Ø F = Ø:GOTO 43Ø
57Ø CLS:PRINT AT Ø,"▓▓▓▓▓▓▓"
58Ø GOTO 54Ø
59Ø CLS
6ØØ PRINT "DON'T GO AWAY":GOSUB 24ØØ
61Ø CLS:GOSUB 77Ø
62Ø FOR N = 1 TO 13Ø
63Ø     IF A(N) = Ø THEN 66Ø
64Ø     RESTORE
65Ø     GOSUB 89Ø
66Ø NEXT N
67Ø PRINT:INPUT "ARE YOU READY FOR THE BILL (Y/N)";A$
68Ø IF A$ = "Y" THEN 71Ø
69Ø PRINT "SORRY - IT'S YOURS ANYWAY"
7ØØ GOSUB 24ØØ
71Ø CLS
72Ø FOR N = 1 TO 7:PRINT:NEXT N
73Ø PRINT "ESTIMATED BILL","$";B
74Ø GOSUB 24ØØ
75Ø PRINT "END OF SHOPPING LIST"
76Ø GOTO 76Ø
77Ø PRINT "ITEM";TAB(1Ø);"DESCRIPTION";TAB(25);
78Ø PRINT "UNIT";TAB(35);"PRICE";TAB(45);"LOCATION"
79Ø PRINT:RETURN
```

```
800 FOR Z = 1 TO 10
810     READ I,A$,B$,P,L
820     IF I = 999 THEN 870
830     PRINT I;TAB(10);A$;TAB(25);B$;TAB(35);
840     PRINT "$";P;TAB(50);L
850 NEXT Z
860 RETURN
870 PRINT:PRINT "LIST COMPLETE":E = 1
880 GOTO 860
890 FOR Z = 1 TO A(N)
900     READ I,A$,B$,P,L
910     IF I = 999 THEN 1010
920 NEXT Z
930     PRINT I;TAB(10);A$;TAB(25);A(N + 150)
940     PRINT TAB(35);A(N + 300);TAB(45);A(N + 450)
950     B = B + A(N + 300)
960     C = C + 1:IF C = 10 THEN 980
970 RETURN
980 INPUT "PRESS ENTER TO CONTINUE";C:C = 0
990 CLS:GOSUB 770
1000 GOTO 970
1010 PRINT:PRINT "ITEM NOT ON LIST"
1020 GOTO 970
1030 FOR Z = 1 TO N
1040     READ I,A$,B$,P,L
1050     IF I = 999 THEN 1080
1060 NEXT Z
1070 RETURN
1080 PRINT "ITEM NOT ON LIST"
1090 GOTO 1070
1100 DATA 1,"BABY FOOD","JAR",.35,27
1110 DATA 2,"BISQUICK","BOX",.97,13
1120 DATA 3,"CAKE MIX","BOX",.69,15
1130 DATA 4,"CEREAL","BOX",1.04,34
1140 DATA 5,"COCOA","BOX",1.19,9
1150 DATA 6,"CONDIMENTS","BOX",.54,7
```

```
1160 DATA 7,"CRACKERS","BOX",.86,18
1170 DATA 8,"FLOUR","5 LB",1.27,25
1180 DATA 9,"JAM/JELLY","JAR",.49,16
1190 DATA 10,"PUDDING/JELLO","PKG",.17,31
1200 DATA 11,"KETCHUP","JAR",.57,22
1210 DATA 12,"MAYONNAISE","JAR",.95,22
1220 DATA 13,"MILK, CANNED","CAN",.37,6
1230 DATA 14,"MILK, POWDERED","PKG",1.39,11
1240 DATA 15,"MUSTARD","JAR",.37,44
1250 DATA 16,"NOODLES","PKG",.19,16
1260 DATA 17,"NUTS","PKG",.74,32
1270 DATA 18,"OLIVES","CAN",".69,26
1280 DATA 19,"PEANUT BUTTER","JAR",.95,21
1290 DATA 20,"PICKLES","JAR",".57,14
1300 DATA 21,"POP CORN","CAN",1.45,41
1310 DATA 22,"POTATO CHIPS","PKG",.69,4
1320 DATA 23,"RICE","PKG",.82,15
1330 DATA 24,"SALAD DRESSING","BOTTLE",.74,13
1340 DATA 25,"SALT","PKG",.52,36
1350 DATA 26,"SAUCES","JAR",.73,16
1360 DATA 27,"SHORTENING","CAN",1.22,31
1370 DATA 28,"SOUPS","CAN",.37,12
1380 DATA 29,"SUGAR","5 LB",.90,18
1390 DATA 30,"SYRUP","BOTTLE",.67,14
1400 DATA 31,"TOPPINGS","CAN",.29,17
1410 DATA 32,"VINEGAR","BOTTLE",.47,22
1420 DATA 33,"YEAST","CAKE",".22,45
1430 DATA 34,"BREAD","LOAF",.75,55
1440 DATA 35,"CAKE","LOAF",1.42,54
1450 DATA 36,"COOKIES","PKG,1.19,53
1460 DATA 37,"DONUTS","DOZEN",1.42,52
1470 DATA 38,"PIES","EACH",1.69,51
1480 DATA 39,"ROLLS","PKG",.69,50
1490 DATA 40,"ASPARAGUS","CAN",.77,36
1500 DATA 41,"BEANS","CAN",.54,32
1510 DATA 42,"BEETS","CAN",.67,30
```

```
1520 DATA 43,"BROCCOLI","PKG",.37,48
1530 DATA 44,"CABBAGE","HEAD",.19,3
1540 DATA 45,"CARROTS","BUNCH",.37,3
1550 DATA 46,"CAULIFLOWER","PKG",.47,48
1560 DATA 47,"CELERY","BUNCH",.69,4
1570 DATA 48,"CORN","EAR",.12,2
1580 DATA 49,"CUCUMBER","EACH",.13,6
1590 DATA 50,"LETTUCE","HEAD",.69,3
1600 DATA 51,"MUSHROOMS","CAN",.45,45
1610 DATA 52,"ONIONS","BAG",.62,4
1620 DATA 53,"PEAS","PKG",.37,35
1630 DATA 54,"PEPPERS","BELL",.21,4
1640 DATA 55,"POTATOES","BAG",1.22,1
1650 DATA 56,"RADISHES","PKG",.27,5
1660 DATA 57,"SAUERKRAUT","CAN",.66,17
1670 DATA 58,"SPINACH","PKG",.42,34
1680 DATA 59,"SQUASH","PKG",.47,34
1690 DATA 60,"TOMATOES","PKG",.67,3
1700 DATA 61,"APPLES","BAG",.79,2
1710 DATA 62,"APRICOTS","CAN",.59,18
1720 DATA 63,"BANANAS","BUNCH",.69,3
1730 DATA 64,"BLUEBERRIES","PKG",.1.45,4
1740 DATA 65,"CHERRIES","BUNCH",.45,4
1750 DATA 66,"GRAPEFRUIT","EACH",.45,3
1760 DATA 67,"GRAPES","BUNCH",.69,5
1770 DATA 68,"LEMONS","EACH",.25,3
1780 DATA 69,"MELONS","EACH",.98,1
1790 DATA 70,"ORANGES","PKG",.98,2
1800 DATA 71,"PEACHES","CAN",.53,19
1810 DATA 72,"PEARS","CAN",.54,19
1820 DATA 73,"PINEAPPLE","CAN",.67,19
1830 DATA 74,"PRUNES","PKG",.82,25
1840 DATA 75,"BEER","6-PACK",2.37,33
1850 DATA 76,"COFFEE","JAR",4.35,29
1860 DATA 77,"FRUIT JUICES","CAN",.54,31
1870 DATA 78,"SOFT DRINKS","BOTTLE",".99,33
```

```
1880 DATA 79,"TEA","PKG",.69,34
1890 DATA 80,"BACON","LB",1.69,11
1900 DATA 81,"BEEF","LB",2.29,48
1910 DATA 82,"CHICKEN","LB",1.19,48
1920 DATA 83,"COLD CUTS","1/2 LB",1.69,49
1930 DATA 84,"FISH","LB",4.12,48
1940 DATA 85,"HOT DOGS","LB",1.39,51
1950 DATA 86,"HAM","5 lb",7.34,52
1960 DATA 87,"HAMBURGER","LB",1.39,48
1970 DATA 88,"LAMB","LB",2.29,48
1980 DATA 89,"LIVER","LB",1.17,48
1990 DATA 90,"PORK CHOPS","LB",2.32,48
2000 DATA 91,"ROAST","LB",2.19,48
2010 DATA 92,"SAUSAGE","PKG","1.69,49
2020 DATA 93,"SHRIMP","LB",3.29,47
2030 DATA 94,"SPARE RIBS","LB",1.12,48
2040 DATA 95,"STEAK","LB",2.23,48
2050 DATA 96,"T.V. DINNER","PKG",1.39,53
2060 DATA 97,"VEAL","LB",1.45,48
2070 DATA 98,"BUTTER","LB",1.49,66
2080 DATA 99,"CHEESE","1/2 LB",.89,63
2090 DATA 100,"COTTAGE CHEESE","LB",.82,65
2100 DATA 101,"CREAM","PINT",.79,62
2110 DATA 102,"EGGS","DOZ",.69,69
2120 DATA 103,"HALF-AND-HALF","CARTON",.54,66
2130 DATA 104,"ICE CREAM","1/2 GAL.",1.45,61
2140 DATA 105,"MARGARINE","LB",.69,63
2150 DATA 106,"MILK","1/2 GAL.",1.09,65
2160 DATA 107,"SOUR CREAM","1/2 PINT",.67,67
2170 DATA 108,"YOGURT","CONTAINER",.47,65
2180 DATA 109,"ALUMINUM FOIL","ROLL",.79,43
2190 DATA 110,"BLEACH","GAL",1.29,38
2200 DATA 111,"CANDY","BAR",".20,33
2210 DATA 112,"CIGARETTES","CARTON",6.30,16
2220 DATA 113,"CLEANSER","PKG",1.43,47
2230 DATA 114,"DETERGENT","PKG,.74,45
```

```
2240 DATA 115,"INSECTICIDE","SPRAY CAN",1.39,38
2250 DATA 116,"LIGHT BULBS","PKG OF 4",2.80,38
2260 DATA 117,"MATCHES, SAFETY","PKG",.27,30
2270 DATA 118,"PAPER TOWEL","ROLL",.77,49
2280 DATA 119,"DOG FOOD, DRY","10 LB",2.22,49
2290 DATA 120,"CAT FOOD, DRY","5 LB",1.14,49
2300 DATA 121,"POLISH","CAN",.92,34
2310 DATA 122,"SCOURING PADS","PKG",.59,20
2320 DATA 123,"BATH SOAP","BAR",.64,43
2330 DATA 124,"STARCH","PKG",.78,48
2340 DATA 125,"TOILET TISSUE","ROLL",.69,39
2350 DATA 126,"TOOTHPASTE","TUBE",.69,20
2360 DATA 127,"PAPER PLATES","PKG",.83,30
2370 DATA 128,"WAX","CAKE",.24,30
2380 DATA 129,"WAXED PAPER","ROLL",.76,40
2390 DATA 999,,,999,999
2400 FOR Z = 1 TO 1000:NEXT Z:RETURN
```

PANTRY INVENTORY

Using what has been learned thus far, let's vary the theme slightly. Suppose an inventory system could be established which could be posted on a periodic basis and which, upon request, could automatically generate a shopping list. That is very possible, with some minor changes in orientation of the shopping application and some additional logic. The following is just an example. As the program is presented, it takes about 6K of memory, so shorthand must be used to bring it within the 4K range of your Level I machine. In addition, the list should be tailored to your specific needs.

The first thing which must be done is the expansion of the DATA lines. Using the same DATA lines as used in the shopping application, an additional numeric value is added. This value is the minimum amount you wish to have on hand before the program initiates a request for replenishment. The new field will be variable M, or "minimum." Since the data lines are the same as the shopping list, only a few are shown here for illustration. The entire list will be shown at the end:

```
2320 DATA 1,"BABY FOOD","JAR",.35,27,3
2330 DATA 2,"BISQUICK","BOX",.97,13,2
2340 DATA 3,"CAKE MIX","BOX",.69,15,2
```

```
2350 DATA 4,"CEREAL","BOX",1.04,34,4
2360 DATA 5,"COCOA","BOX",1.19,9,5
2370 DATA 6,"CONDIMENTS","BOX",.54,7,3
2380 DATA 7,"CRACKERS","BOX",.86,18,1
2390 DATA 8,"FLOUR","5 LB",1.27,25,2
```

The program begins just like the previous program, except that there is a menu option:

```
10 CLS:RESTORE:E = 0
20 FOR N = 1 TO 7:PRINT:NEXT N
30 PRINT TAB (15);"P A N T R Y   I N V E N T O R Y"
40 FOR N = 1 TO 750:A(N) = 0:NEXT N
50 CLS
60 PRINT "SELECT THE DESIRED OPTION:":PRINT
70 PRINT TAB(5);"1.  POST INVENTORY USAGE":PRINT
80 PRINT TAB(5);"2.  REPLENISH INVENTORY":PRINT
90 PRINT TAB(5);"3.  INITIALIZE INVENTORY":PRINT
100 INPUT "WHICH";C
110 ON C GOTO 120,580,2100:GOTO 50
```

Here are three options. The first, POST INVENTORY USAGE, allows you to take a known amount of inventory and to make adjustments to it. The REPLENISH INVENTORY allows you to replace the inventory items, without concern for the minimum quantities established in the DATA lines. Those quantities end up on the file on a cassette tape. Once that tape has been read back into the program, the necessary "orders" will be generated to fill the inventory amount to the established minimums you have placed in the DATA lines, assuming that the amount is less than the minimum.

The third option, INITIALIZE INVENTORY, is the one which will be discussed first, as it builds a data tape of inventory on hand, to the extent that you have indicated minimum levels, you can then adjust it from there. Here is the initialization routine:

```
2100 CLS:RESTORE
2110 PRINT "PLACE A FRESH TAPE IN THE TAPE DRIVE.":PRINT
2120 PRINT "ENSURE THAT IT HAS MOVED PAST THE LEADER.":PRINT
2130 PRINT "DEPRESS BOTH PLAY AND RECORD BUTTONS.":PRINT
2140 INPUT "PRESS ENTER WHEN READY.";C
```

```
2150 CLS
2160 PRINT "I N V E N T O R Y   I N I T I A L I Z A T I O N"
2170 PRINT "MINIMUM BALANCE OF EACH ITEM BEING PLACED ON TAPE"
2180 PRINT "ITEM #","BALANCE"
2190 FOR N = 1 TO 130
2200     READ I,A$,B$,P,L,M
2210     PRINT # I;",";M
2250     PRINT I,M
2260 NEXT N
2270 CLS
2280 PRINT "REWIND THE TAPE.  IT IS NOT NECESSARY TO WAIT"
2290 PRINT "UNTIL THE REWIND IS COMPLETE."
2300 INPUT "PRESS ENTER WHEN READY";C
2310 GOTO 10
```

Note that the coding of statements 2220, 2230, and 2240 is missing. Do not be concerned—nothing is missing from the program. As was previously mentioned, these programs have been developed on the author's Level II machine. In addition to the PRINT AT vs. PRINT @ differences between the levels, there is also a difference in the INPUT # and PRINT # commands. To get the instructions to work on the Level II machine, other instructions had to be included. Those instructions were removed when the text was prepared.

The routine simply reads the DATA lines and places the ITEM NO. and the BALANCE numbers on tape. Be prepared for a lengthy process, as the data-to-tape process is not very speedy, particularly since it is constructed to write only two variables to the tape at a time. Data is displayed upon the screen as it is being written to tape. It will scroll, and was included to advise you that the program is working properly. The use of variable C is arbitrary. Variable A could have been used, as in the last program.

Option 1—the POST INVENTORY option, can function from either the DATA lines or from the data tape, and that option is presented in statement 120. It's just a simple read-from-tape routine. Note that again the data is displayed upon the screen so you can be assured that something is happening.

```
120 CLS:INPUT "WILL THERE BE AN INPUT TAPE (Y/N)";A$
130 IF A$ < > "Y" THEN 250
140 PRINT:PRINT "LOAD THE PANTRY INVENTORY TAPE AND PRESS PLAY"
```

```
15Ø PRINT:INPUT "PRESS ENTER WHEN READY";C
16Ø CLS:PRINT "READING THE TAPE"
17Ø PRINT "ITEM #","BALANCE"
18Ø FOR N = 1 TO 13Ø
19Ø     INPUT # A(N),A(N + 6ØØ)
23Ø     PRINT A(N),A(N + 6ØØ)
24Ø NEXT N
```

Again, the missing statements are the Level II considerations, which have been moved.

The next routine is a direct copy from the previous program. As this program was developed, this routine fits in several places. No attempt was made to compress all those routines int ɔ a single subroutine, but if memory is tight, place the following sequence of instructions into a subroutine, don't forget RETURN. (Just a reminder that a subroutine must be terminated by a RETURN.) The other references to the coding will become apparent as the application is developed. The message has been altered to make it more indicative of the process being accomplished.

```
25Ø CLS
26Ø GOSUB 176Ø:GOSUB 179Ø
27Ø A = Ø
28Ø PRINT AT 832,"ɃPRESS ENTER TO PAGE FORWARD - OR"
29Ø INPUT "ENTER NUMBER TO SELECT ITEM";A:A = INT(A)
3ØØ IF A > 13Ø THEN 28Ø
31Ø IF (A = Ø) ★ (E = Ø) THEN 25Ø
32Ø IF (A = Ø) ★ (E = 1) THEN 39Ø
33Ø REM "STORE ITEM NUMBER"
34Ø A(A) = A
35Ø PRINT AT 832,"Ƀ":INPUT "ENTER QUANTITY USED";Q:Q = INT(Q)
36Ø REM "STORE DEFAULT QUANTITY TO BE REORDERED"
37Ø A(A + 15Ø) = Q:A(A + 6ØØ) = A(A + 6ØØ) - Q
38Ø GOTO 27Ø
39Ø CLS
4ØØ PRINT "DID YOU MISS ANYTHING?"
41Ø PRINT:INPUT "DO YOU WISH TO REVIEW THE LIST (Y/N)";A$
42Ø IF A$ < > "Y" THEN 44Ø
43Ø E = Ø:RESTORE:GOTO 25Ø
```

Because there is not the ability to affect memory directly in the sequence of things presented on the screen—that is, a screen line cannot be tested for the presence of alphabetic characters—it now becomes necessary to review the DATA lines and compare them to the inventory usage figures. This time a common READ subroutine has been used. The only other thing of significance is that the program will not permit the reduction of inventory by more than that which has been stored in the minimum balance field, variable M:

```
44Ø CLS:PRINT "DON'T GO AWAY":GOSUB 362Ø
45Ø PRINT "I'M FIGURING":GOSUB 362Ø
46Ø FOR N = 1 TO 13Ø
47Ø     CLS
48Ø     IF A(N) = Ø THEN 56Ø
49Ø     RESTORE
5ØØ     PRINT AT 128,"STILL FIGURING"
51Ø     GOSUB 2Ø3Ø
52Ø     A(N + 45Ø) = L
53Ø     IF A(N + 6ØØ) > = M THEN 56Ø
54Ø     IF A(N + 6ØØ) < M THEN A(M + 6ØØ) = M
55Ø     PRINT "SUBSTITUTING REORDER FOR USAGE":GOSUB 362Ø
56Ø NEXT N
57Ø GOTO 133Ø
2Ø3Ø FOR Z = 1 TO N
2Ø4Ø     READ I,A$,B$,P,L,M
2Ø5Ø     IF I = 999 THEN 2Ø8Ø
2Ø6Ø NEXT Z
2Ø7Ø RETURN
2Ø8Ø PRINT "ITEM NOT ON LIST"
2Ø9Ø GOTO 2Ø7Ø
```

The replenishment routine is a little more lengthy, but very straight-foward, as it merely repeats the logic previously prepared—the data is read from the tape, modified from the keyboard, and rewritten to the tape:

```
58Ø CLS
59Ø PRINT "IN ORDER TO REPLENISH INVENTORY, YOU SHOULD"
6ØØ PRINT "FIRST LOAD THE PANTRY INVENTORY TAPE.  IF"
```

```
610 PRINT "YOU HAVE ALREADY DONE THAT, IT WILL NOT BE"
620 PRINT "NECESSARY TO DO SO NOW.  IF YOU HAVE NOT ALREADY"
630 PRINT "DONE SO, YOU MUST AT THIS TIME."
640 PRINT:INPUT HAVE YOU ALREADY LOADED THE TAPE (Y/N)";A$
650 IF A$ = "Y" THEN 770
660 PRINT:INPUT "PRESS ENTER WHEN TAPE IS READY";C
670 CLS:PRINT "ITEM # ","BALANCE"
680 FOR N = 1 TO 130
690    INPUT # A(N),A(N + 600)
730    PRINT A(N),A(N + 600)
740 NEXT N
750 CLS:PRINT "REWIND THE TAPE.  PRESS ENTER WHEN READY."
760 INPUT "NOT NECESSARY TO WAIT FOR THE REWIND.";C
770 CLS
780 GOSUB 1760:GOSUB 1790
790 A = 0
800 PRINT AT 832,"bPRESS ENTER TO PAGE FORWARD - OR"
810 INPUT "ENTER NUMBER TO SELECT ITEM";A:A = INT(A)
820 IF A  >130 THEN 800
830 IF (A = 0) * (E = 0) THEN 770
840 IF (A = 0) * (E = 1) THEN 910
850 REM "STORE THE AMOUNT TO BE ADDED"
860 A = A(A)
870 PRINT AT 832,"b":INPUT "ENTER THE AMOUNT TO BE ADDED TO
    INVENTORY";Q
880 Q = INT(Q)
890 A(A + 600) = A( + 600) + Q
900 GOTO 790
910 CLS
920 PRINT "TIME TO STORE OFF THE CURRENT INVENTORY BALANCE"
930 GOSUB 3620
940 PRINT:PRINT "PLACE A FRESH TAPE IN THE TAPE DRIVE"
950 PRINT:PRINT "INSURE THAT IT HAS MOVED PAST THE LEADER."
960 PRINT:PRINT "DEPRESS BOTH PLAY AND RECORD"
```

```
970 PRINT:INPUT "PRESS ENTER WHEN READY.";C
980 CLS:PRINT "ITEM #","BALANCE"
990 FOR N = 1 TO 130
1000    PRINT # A(N);",";A(N + 600)
1040 NEXT N
```

The balance of the active portion of the program is precisely the same logic as was presented in the previous program—checking for balances, but instead of offering *you* the option to order, the computer will do it for you. You are permitted, however, to modify those figures:

```
1050 CLS
1060 PRINT "NOW FOR SOME AUTOMATED SHOPPING"
1070 PRINT:PRINT "BE PATIENT WHILE I FIGURE WHAT WE NEED"
1080 FOR N = 1 TO 130
1090    PRINT AT 128, "I'M MAKING A LIST"
1100    IF A(N) = 0 THEN 1170
1110    RESTORE
1120    PRINT AT 128, "I'M STILL WORKING"
1130    GOSUB 2030
1140    IF A(N + 600) < M THEN A(N + 150) = M
1150    IF A(N + 600) > = M THEN A(N + 150) = A(N + 600)
1160    A(N + 300) = P * A(N + 150)
1170 NEXT N
1180 CLS
1190 INPUT "IS THERE ANY ITEM UPON WHICH YOU'D LIKE TO CHECK
     (Y/N)";A$
1200 IF A$ < > "Y" THEN 1330
1210 CLS:GOSUB 1760:GOSUB 1790
1220 A = 0
1230 PRINT AT 832,"PRESS ENTER TO PAGE FORWARD - OR"
1240 INPUT "ENTER NUMBER TO SELECT";A:A = INT(A)
1250 IF A > 130 THEN 1230
1260 IF (A = 0) * (E = 0) THEN 1210
1270 IF (A = 0) * (E = 1) THEN 1330
```

```
1280 A = A(A)
1290 PRINT AT 832," ":INPUT "ENTER THE AMOUNT YOU WISH TO (+)
     INCREASE OR (-) DECREASE"
1300 Q = INT(Q)
1310 A(N + 150) = Q:A(N + 300) = P * A(N + 150)
1320 GOTO 1220
1330 CLS
1340 PRINT "TIME TO PREPARE YOUR SHOPPING LIST."
1350 PRINT "GET A PAPER AND PENCIL."
1360 PRINT:PRINT "I WILL LIST, IN GROUPS OF TEN, THE ITEMS"
1370 PRINT "YOU HAVE SELECTED"
1380 PRINT:PRINT "AT THE END I WILL ESTIMATE YOUR BILL."
1390 PRINT:PRINT "DO YOU WANT THE LIST SORTED INTO LOCATION"
1400 INPUT "SEQUENCE (Y/N)";A$
1410 IF A$ < > "Y" THEN 1580
1420 FOR N = 1 TO 130
1430     IF A(N + 450) < = A(N + 451) THEN 1560
1440     PRINT A(N + 450),A(N + 451),N
1450     R = A(N):S = A(N + 150)
1460     T = A(N + 300):U = A(N + 450)
1470     A(N) = A(N + 1):A(N + 150) = A(N + 151)
1480     A(N + 300) = A(N + 301):A(N + 450) = A(N + 451)
1490     A(N + 1) = R:A(N + 151) = S
1500     A(N + 301) = T:A(N + 451) = U
1510     CLS:PRINT AT 0,"SORTING":F = 1
1520     PRINT A(N + 450),A(N + 451),N
1530 NEXT N
1540 IF F = 0 THEN 1580
1550 F = 0:GOTO 1420
1560 CLS:PRINT AT 0,"bbbbbbb"
1570 GOTO 1530
```

Finally, the presentation of the bill. Also, the inclusion of a couple of general purpose routines which are used in several places in the program.

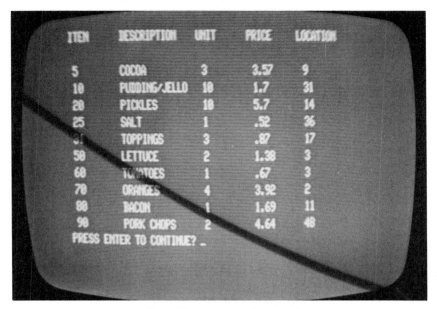

Figure 24. Automated shopping list.

```
1580 CLS
1590 PRINT "DON'T GO AWAY":GOSUB 3620
1600 CLS:GOSUB 1760
1610 FOR N = 1 TO 130
1620    IF A(N) = 0 THEN 1650
1630    RESTORE
1640    GOSUB 1880
1650 NEXT N
1660 PRINT:INPUT "ARE YOU READY FOR THE BILL (Y/N)";A$
1670 IF A$ = "Y" THEN 1700
1680 PRINT "SORRY - IT'S YOURS ANYWAY"
1690 GOSUB 3620
1700 CLS
1710 FOR N = 1 TO 7:PRINT:NEXT N
1720 PRINT "ESTIMATED BILL","$";B
1730 GOSUB 3620
```

```
1740 PRINT "END OF SHOPPING LIST"
1750 GOTO 1750
1760 PRINT "ITEM";TAB(10);"DESCRIPTION";TAB(25);
1770 PRINT "UNIT";TAB(35);"PRICE";TAB(45);"LOCATION";TAB(55);
     "MINIMUM"
1780 PRINT:RETURN
1790 FOR Z = 1 TO 10
1800    READ I,A$,B$,P,L,M
1810    IF I = 999 THEN 1860
1820    PRINT I;TAB(10);A$;TAB(25);B$;TAB(35);
1830    PRINT "$";P;TAB(47);L;TAB(57);M
1840 NEXT Z
1850 RETURN
1860 PRINT:PRINT "LIST COMPLETE":E = 1
1870 GOTO 1850
1880 FOR Z = 1 TO A(N)
1890    READ I,A$,B$,P,L,M
1900    IF I = 999 THEN 2010
1910 NEXT Z
1920    PRINT I;TAB(10);A$;TAB(25);A(N + 150);
1930    PRINT TAB(35);A(N + 300);TAB(45);A(N + 450);
1940    PRINT TAB(57);A(N + 600)
1950    B = B + A(N + 300)
1960    C = C + 1:IF C = 10 THEN 1980
1970 RETURN
1980 INPUT "PRESS ENTER TO CONTINUE";C:C = 0
1990 CLS:GOSUB 1760
2000 GOTO 1970
2010 PRINT:PRINT "ITEM NOT ON LIST"
2020 GOTO 1970
```

Here is the program in its entirety:

```
10 CLS:RESTORE:E = 0
20 FOR N = 1 TO 7:PRINT:NEXT N
30 PRINT TAB (15);"P A N T R Y    I N V E N T O R Y"
```

```
40 FOR N = 1 TO 750:A(N) = 0:NEXT N
50 CLS
60 PRINT "SELECT THE DESIRED OPTION:":PRINT
70 PRINT TAB(5);"1.  POST INVENTORY USAGE":PRINT
80 PRINT TAB(5);"2.  REPLENISH INVENTORY":PRINT
90 PRINT TAB(5);"3.  INITIALIZE INVENTORY":PRINT
100 INPUT "WHICH";C
110 ON C GOTO 120,580,2100:GOTO 50
120 CLS:INPUT "WILL THERE BE AN INPUT TAPE (Y/N)";A$
130 IF A$ <> "Y" THEN 250
140 PRINT:PRINT "LOAD THE PANTRY INVENTORY TAPE AND PRESS PLAY"
150 PRINT:INPUT "PRESS ENTER WHEN READY";C
160 CLS:PRINT "READING THE TAPE"
170 PRINT "ITEM #","BALANCE"
180 FOR N = 1 TO 130
190 INPUT # A(N),A(N + 600)
230     PRINT A(N),A(N + 600)
240 NEXT N
250 CLS
260 GOSUB 1760:GOSUB 1790
270 A = 0
280 PRINT AT 832,"PRESS ENTER TO PAGE FORWARD - OR"
290 INPUT "ENTER NUMBER TO SELECT ITEM";A:A = INT(A)
300 IF A > 130 THEN 280
310 IF (A = 0) * (E = 0) THEN 250
320 IF (A = 0) * (E = 1) THEN 390
330 REM "STORE ITEM NUMBER"
340 A(A) = A
350 PRINT AT 832,"":INPUT "ENTER QUANTITY USED";Q:Q = INT(0)
360 REM "STORE DEFAULT QUANTITY TO BE REORDERED"
370 A(A + 150) = Q:A(A + 600) = A(A + 600) - Q
380 GOTO 270
390 CLS
400 PRINT "DID YOU MISS ANYTHING?"
410 PRINT:INPUT "DO YOU WISH TO REVIEW THE LIST (Y/N)";A$
420 IF A$ <> "Y" THEN 440
```

```
430 E = Ø:RESTORE:GOTO 25Ø
440 CLS:PRINT "DON'T GO AWAY":GOSUB 362Ø
450 PRINT "I'M FIGURING":GOSUB 362Ø
460 FOR N = 1 TO 13Ø
470     CLS
480     IF A(N) = Ø THEN 56Ø
490     RESTORE
500     PRINT AT 128,"STILL FIGURING"
510     GOSUB 2Ø3Ø
520     A(N + 45Ø) = L
530     IF A(N + 6ØØ)>= M THEN 56Ø
540     IF A(N + 6ØØ) < M THEN A(M + 6ØØ) = M
550     PRINT "SUBSTITUTING REORDER FOR USAGE":GOSUB 362Ø
560 NEXT N
570 GOTO 133Ø
580 CLS
590 PRINT "IN ORDER TO REPLENISH INVENTORY, YOU SHOULD"
600 PRINT "FIRST LOAD THE PANTRY INVENTORY TAPE.  IF"
610 PRINT "YOU HAVE ALREADY DONE THAT, IT WILL NOT BE"
620 PRINT "NECESSARY TO DO SO NOW.  IF YOU HAVE NOT ALREADY"
630 PRINT "DONE SO, YOU MUST AT THIS TIME."
640 PRINT:INPUT HAVE YOU ALREADY LOADED THE TAPE (Y/N)";A$
650 IF A$ = "Y" THEN 77Ø
660 PRINT:INPUT "PRESS ENTER WHEN TAPE IS READY";C
670 CLS:PRINT "ITEM #Ø","BALANCE"
680 FOR N = 1 TO 13Ø
690     INPUT # A(N),A(N + 6ØØ)
730     PRINT A(N),A(N + 6ØØ)
740 NEXT N
750 CLS:PRINT "REWIND THE TAPE.  PRESS ENTER WHEN READY."
760 INPUT "NOT NECESSARY TO WAIT FOR THE REWIND.";C
770 CLS
780 GOSUB 176Ø:GOSUB 179Ø
790 A = Ø
800 PRINT AT 832,"ØPRESS ENTER TO PAGE FORWARD - OR"
```

```
810 INPUT "ENTER NUMBER TO SELECT ITEM";A:A = INT(A)
820 IF A  >130 THEN 800
830 IF (A = 0) * (E = 0) THEN 770
840 IF (A = 0) * (E = 1) THEN 910
850 REM "STORE THE AMOUNT TO BE ADDED"
860 A = A(A)
870 PRINT AT 832,"b":INPUT "ENTER THE AMOUNT TO BE ADDED TO
    INVENTORY";Q
880 Q = INT(Q)
890 A(A + 600) = A( + 600) + Q
900 GOTO 790
910 CLS
920 PRINT "TIME TO STORE OFF THE CURRENT INVENTORY BALANCE"
930 GOSUB 3620
940 PRINT:PRINT "PLACE A FRESH TAPE IN THE TAPE DRIVE"
950 PRINT:PRINT "INSURE THAT IT HAS MOVED PAST THE LEADER."
960 PRINT:PRINT "DEPRESS BOTH PLAY AND RECORD"
970 PRINT:INPUT "PRESS ENTER WHEN READY.";C
980 CLS:PRINT "ITEM #b","BALANCE"
990 FOR N = 1 TO 130
1000    PRINT # A(N);",";A(N + 600)
1040 NEXT N
1050 CLS
1060 PRINT "NOW FOR SOME AUTOMATED SHOPPING"
1070 PRINT:PRINT "BE PATIENT WHILE I FIGURE WHAT WE NEED"
1080 FOR N = 1 TO 130
1090    PRINT AT 128,"I'M MAKING A LIST"
1100    IF A(N) = 0 THEN 1170
1110    RESTORE
1120    PRINT AT 128, "I'M STILL WORKING"
1130    GOSUB 2030
1140    IF A(N + 600) < M THEN A(N + 150) = M
1150    IF A(N + 600) > = M THEN A(N + 150) = A(N + 600)
1160    A(N + 300) = P * A(N + 150)
1170 NEXT N
```

```
1180 CLS
1190 INPUT "IS THERE ANY ITEM UPON WHICH YOU'D LIKE TO CHECK
     (Y/N)";A$
1200 IF A$ < > "Y" THEN 1330
1210 CLS:GOSUB 1760:GOSUB 1790
1220 A = Ø
1230 PRINT AT 832,"bPRESS ENTER TO PAGE FORWARD - OR"
1240 INPUT "ENTER NUMBER TO SELECT";A:A = INT(A)
1250 IF A > 130 THEN 1230
1260 IF (A = Ø) * (E = Ø) THEN 1210
1270 IF (A = Ø) * (E = 1) THEN 1330
1280 A = A(A)
1290 PRINT AT 832,"b":INPUT "ENTER THE AMOUNT YOU WISH TO (+)
     INCREASE OR (-) DECREASE"
1300 Q = INT(Q)
1310 A(N + 150) = Q:A(N + 300) = P * A(N + 150)
1320 GOTO 1220
1330 CLS
1340 PRINT "TIME TO PREPARE YOUR SHOPPING LIST."
1350 PRINT "GET A PAPER AND PENCIL."
1360 PRINT:PRINT "I WILL LIST, IN GROUPS OF TEN, THE ITEMS"
1370 PRINT "YOU HAVE SELECTED"
1380 PRINT:PRINT "AT THE END I WILL ESTIMATE YOUR BILL."
1390 PRINT:PRINT "DO YOU WANT THE LIST SORTED INTO LOCATION"
1400 INPUT "SEQUENCE (Y/N)";A$
1410 IF A$ < > "Y" THEN 1580
1420 FOR N = 1 TO 130
1430    IF A(N + 450) < = A(N + 451) THEN 1560
1440    PRINT A(N + 450),A(N + 451),N
1450    R = A(N):S = A(N + 150)
1460    T = A(N + 300):U = A(N + 450)
1470    A(N) = A(N + 1):A(N + 150) = A(N + 151)
1480    A(N + 300) = A(N + 301):A(N + 450) = A(N + 451)
1490    A(N + 1) = R:A(N + 151) = S
1500    A(N + 301) = T:A(N + 451) = U
```

```
1510    CLS:PRINT AT Ø,"SORTING":F = 1
1520    PRINT A(N + 45Ø),A(N + 451),N
1530 NEXT N
1540 IF F = Ø THEN 158Ø
1550 F = Ø:GOTO 142Ø
1560 CLS:PRINT AT Ø,"XXXXXXXX"
1570 GOTO 1530
1580 CLS
1590 PRINT "DON'T GO AWAY":GOSUB 362Ø
1600 CLS:GOSUB 176Ø
1610 FOR N = 1 TO 13Ø
1620    IF A(N) = Ø THEN 165Ø
1630    RESTORE
1640    GOSUB 188Ø
1650 NEXT N
1660 PRINT:INPUT "ARE YOU READY FOR THE BILL (Y/N)";A$
1670 IF A$ = "Y" THEN 17ØØ
1680 PRINT "SORRY - IT'S YOURS ANYWAY"
1690 GOSUB 362Ø
1700 CLS
1710 FOR N = 1 TO 7:PRINT:NEXT N
1720 PRINT "ESTIMATED BILL","$";B
1730 GOSUB 362Ø
1740 PRINT "END OF SHOPPING LIST"
1750 GOTO 175Ø
1760 PRINT "ITEM";TAB(1Ø);"DESCRIPTION";TAB(25);
1770 PRINT "UNIT";TAB(35);"PRICE";TAB(45);"LOCATION";TAB(55);
     "MINIMUM"
1780 PRINT:RETURN
1790 FOR Z = 1 TO 1Ø
1800    READ I,A$,B$,P,L,M
1810    IF I = 999 THEN 186Ø
1820    PRINT I;TAB(1Ø);A$;TAB(25);B$;TAB(35);
1830    PRINT "$";P;TAB(47);L;TAB(57);M
1840 NEXT Z
```

```
1850 RETURN
1860 PRINT:PRINT "LIST COMPLETE":E = 1
1870 GOTO 1850
1880 FOR Z = 1 TO A(N)
1890     READ I,A$,B$,P,L,M
1900     IF I = 999 THEN 2010
1910 NEXT Z
1920     PRINT I;TAB(10);A$;TAB(25);A(N + 150);
1930     PRINT TAB(35);A(N + 300);TAB(45);A(N + 450);
1940     PRINT TAB(57);A(N + 600)
1950     B = B + A(N + 300)
1960     C = C + 1:IF C = 10 THEN 1980
1970 RETURN
1980 INPUT "PRESS ENTER TO CONTINUE";C:C = 0
1990 CLS:GOSUB 1760
2000 GOTO 1970
2010 PRINT:PRINT "ITEM NOT ON LIST"
2020 GOTO 1970
2030 FOR Z = 1 TO N
2040     READ I,A$,B$,P,L,M
2050     IF I = 999 THEN 2080
2060 NEXT Z
2070 RETURN
2080 PRINT "ITEM NOT ON LIST"
2090 GOTO 2070
2100 CLS:RESTORE
2110 PRINT "PLACE A FRESH TAPE IN THE TAPE DRIVE.":PRINT
2120 PRINT "ENSURE THAT IT HAS MOVED PAST THE LEADER.":PRINT
2130 PRINT "DEPRESS BOTH PLAY AND RECORD BUTTONS.":PRINT
2140 INPUT "PRESS ENTER WHEN READY.";C
2150 CLS
2160 PRINT "I N V E N T O R Y   I N I T I A L I Z A T I O N"
2170 PRINT "MINIMUM BALANCE OF EACH ITEM BEING PLACED ON TAPE"
2180 PRINT "ITEM #","BALANCE"
2190 FOR N = 1 TO 130
```

```
2200      READ I,A$,B$,P,L,M
2210      PRINT # I;",";M
2250      PRINT I,M
2260 NEXT N
2270 CLS
2280 PRINT "REWIND THE TAPE.  IT IS NOT NECESSARY TO WAIT"
2290 PRINT "UNTIL THE REWIND IS COMPLETE."
2300 INPUT "PRESS ENTER WHEN READY";C
2310 GOTO 10
2320 DATA 1,"BABY FOOD","JAR",.35,27,3
2330 DATA 2,"BISQUICK","BOX",.97,13,2
2340 DATA 3,"CAKE MIX","BOX",.69,15,2
2350 DATA 4,"CEREAL","BOX",1.04,34,4
2360 DATA 5,"COCOA","BOX",1.19,9,5
2370 DATA 6,"CONDIMENTS","BOX",.54,7,3
2380 DATA 7,"CRACKERS","BOX",.86,18,1
2390 DATA 8,"FLOUR","5 LB",1.27,25,2
2400 DATA 9,"JAM/JELLY","JAR",.49,16,5
2410 DATA 10,"PUDDING/JELLO","PKG",.17,31,10
2420 DATA 11,"KETCHUP","JAR",.57,22,2
2430 DATA 12,"MAYONNAISE","JAR",.95,22,2
2440 DATA 13,"MILK,  CANNED","CAN",.37,6,4
2450 DATA 14,"MILK,  POWDERED","PKG",1.39,11,2
2460 DATA 15,"MUSTARD","JAR",.37,44,2
2470 DATA 16,"NOODLES","PKG",.19,16,4
2480 DATA 17,"NUTS","PKG",.74,32,14
2490 DATA 18,"OLIVES","CAN",".69,26,3
2500 DATA 19,"PEANUT BUTTER","JAR",.95,21,4
2510 DATA 20,"PICKLES","JAR",".57,14,6
2520 DATA 21,"POP CORN","CAN",1.45,41,2
2530 DATA 22,"POTATO CHIPS","PKG",.69,4,3
2540 DATA 23,"RICE","PKG",.82,15.,1
2550 DATA 24,"SALAD DRESSING","BOTTLE",.74,13,9
2560 DATA 25,"SALT","PKG",.52,36,2
2570 DATA 26,"SAUCES","JAR",.73,16,6
```

```
2580 DATA 27,"SHORTENING","CAN",1.22,31,1
2590 DATA 28,"SOUPS","CAN",.37,12,25
2600 DATA 29,"SUGAR","5 LB",.90,18,3
2610 DATA 30,"SYRUP","BOTTLE",.67,14,2
2620 DATA 31,"TOPPINGS","CAN",.29,17,4
2630 DATA 32,"VINEGAR","BOTTLE",.47,22,2
2640 DATA 33,"YEAST","CAKE",".22,45,4
2650 DATA 34,"BREAD","LOAF",.75,55,6
2660 DATA 35,"CAKE","LOAF",1.42,54,3
2670 DATA 36,"COOKIES","PKG,1.19,53,6
2680 DATA 37,"DONUTS","DOZEN",1.42,52,3
2690 DATA 38,"PIES","EACH",1.69,51,2
2700 DATA 39,"ROLLS","PKG",.69,50,4
2710 DATA 40,"ASPARAGUS","CAN",.77,36,1
2720 DATA 41,"BEANS","CAN",.54,32,2
2730 DATA 42,"BEETS","CAN",.67,30,4
2740 DATA 43,"BROCCOLI","PKG",.37,48,1
2750 DATA 44,"CABBAGE","HEAD",.19,3,2
2760 DATA 45,"CARROTS","BUNCH",.37,3,3
2770 DATA 46,"CAULIFLOWER","PKG",.47,48,1
2780 DATA 47,"CELERY","BUNCH",.69,4,2
2790 DATA 48,"CORN","EAR",.12,2,12
2800 DATA 49,"CUCUMBER","EACH",.13,6,3
2810 DATA 50,"LETTUCE","HEAD",.69,3,2
2820 DATA 51,"MUSHROOMS","CAN",.45,45,3
2830 DATA 52,"ONIONS","BAG",.62,4,2
2840 DATA 53,"PEAS","PKG",.37,35,100
2850 DATA 54,"PEPPERS","BELL",.21,4,6
2860 DATA 55,"POTATOES","BAG",1.22,1,2
2870 DATA 56,"RADISHES","PKG",.27,5,3
2880 DATA 57,"SAUERKRAUT","CAN",.66,17,1
2890 DATA 58,"SPINACH","PKG",.42,34,1
2900 DATA 59,"SQUASH","PKG",.47,34,3
2910 DATA 60,"TOMATOES","PKG",.67,3,2
2920 DATA 61,"APPLES","BAG",.79,2,3
```

```
2930 DATA 62,"APRICOTS","CAN",.59,18,2
2940 DATA 63,"BANANAS","BUNCH",.69,3,2
2950 DATA 64,"BLUEBERRIES","PKG",1.45,4,65
2960 DATA 65,"CHERRIES","BUNCH",.45,4,3
2970 DATA 66,"GRAPEFRUIT","EACH",.45,3,3
2980 DATA 67,"GRAPES","BUNCH",.69,5,2
2990 DATA 68,"LEMONS","EACH",.25,3,6
3000 DATA 69,"MELONS","EACH",.98,1,4
3010 DATA 70,"ORANGES","PKG",.98,2,6
3020 DATA 71,"PEACHES","CAN",.53,19,12
3030 DATA 72,"PEARS","CAN",.54,19,12
3040 DATA 73,"PINEAPPLE","CAN",.67,19,12
3050 DATA 74,"PRUNES","PKG",.82,25,1
3060 DATA 75,"BEER","6-PACK",2.37,33,24
3070 DATA 76,"COFFEE","JAR",4.35,29,4
3080 DATA 77,"FRUIT JUICES","CAN",.54,31,48
3090 DATA 78,"SOFT DRINKS","BOTTLE",".99,33,48
3100 DATA 79,"TEA","PKG",.69,34,2
3110 DATA 80,"BACON","LB",1.69,11,6
3120 DATA 81,"BEEF","LB",2.29,48,10
3130 DATA 82,"CHICKEN","LB",1.19,48,10
3140 DATA 83,"COLD CUTS","1/2 LB",1.69,49,5
3150 DATA 84,"FISH","LB",4.12,48,10
3160 DATA 85,"HOT DOGS","LB",1.39,51,10
3170 DATA 86,"HAM","5 lb",7.34,52,5
3180 DATA 87,"HAMBURGER","LB",1.39,48,10
3190 DATA 88,"LAMB","LB",2.29,48,5
3200 DATA 89,"LIVER","LB",1.17,48,5
3210 DATA 90,"PORK CHOPS","LB",2.32,48,6
3220 DATA 91,"ROAST","LB",2.19,48,10
3230 DATA 92,"SAUSAGE","PKG","1.69,49,10
3240 DATA 93,"SHRIMP","LB",3.29,47,25
3250 DATA 94,"SPARE RIBS","LB",1.12,48,3
3260 DATA 95,"STEAK","LB",2.23,48,12
3270 DATA 96,"T.V. DINNER","PKG",1.39,53,6
```

```
3280 DATA 97,"VEAL","LB",1.45,48,5
3290 DATA 98,"BUTTER","LB",1.49,66,5
3300 DATA 99,"CHEESE","1/2 LB",.89,63,12
3310 DATA 100,"COTTAGE CHEESE","LB",.82,65,1
3320 DATA 101,"CREAM","PINT",.79,62,1
3330 DATA 102,"EGGS","DOZ",.69,69,2
3340 DATA 103,"HALF-AND-HALF","CARTON",.54,66,2
3350 DATA 104,"ICE CREAM","1/2 GAL.",1.45,61,4
3360 DATA 105,"MARGARINE","LB",.69,63,6
3370 DATA 106,"MILK","1/2 GAL.",1.09,65,4
3380 DATA 107,"SOUR CREAM","1/2 PINT",.67,67,1
3390 DATA 108,"YOGURT","CONTAINER",.47,65,12
3400 DATA 109,"ALUMINUM FOIL","ROLL",.79,43,2
3410 DATA 110,"BLEACH","GAL",1.29,38,2
3420 DATA 111,"CANDY","BAR",".20,33,12
3430 DATA 112,"CIGARETTES","CARTON",6.30,16,2
3440 DATA 113,"CLEANSER","PKG",1.43,47,6
3450 DATA 114,"DETERGENT","PKG,.74,45,12
3460 DATA 115,"INSECTICIDE","SPRAY CAN",1.39,38,2
3470 DATA 116,"LIGHT BULBS","PKG OF 4",2.80,38,12
3480 DATA 117,"MATCHES, SAFETY","PKG",.27,30,2
3490 DATA 118,"PAPER TOWEL","ROLL",.77,49,6
3500 DATA 119,"DOG FOOD, DRY","10 LB",2.22,49,10
3510 DATA 120,"CAT FOOD, DRY",5 LB",1.14,49,10
3520 DATA 121,"POLISH","CAN",.92,34,2
3530 DATA 122,"SCOURING PADS","PKG",.59,20,4
3540 DATA 123,"BATH SOAP","BAR",.64,43,6
3550 DATA 124,"STARCH","PKG",.78,48,2
3560 DATA 125,"TOILET TISSUE","ROLL",.69,39,24
3570 DATA 126,"TOOTHPASTE","TUBE",.69,20,2
3580 DATA 127,"PAPER PLATES","PKG",.83,30,2
3590 DATA 128,"WAX","CAKE",.24,30,2
3600 DATA 129,"WAXED PAPER","ROLL",.76,40,2
3610 DATA 999,,,999,999,999
3620 FOR Z = 1 TO 1000:NEXT Z:RETURN
```

USES FOR RECREATION

With the increased interest in skiing, there is much concern for the effective temperature, as modified by the wind chill factor. The following program will, given the known temperature and wind speed (close to the options given), and advise you of the effective temperature:

```
10 CLS
20 FOR N = 1 TO 5 PRINT:NEXT N
30 PRINT TAB(15);"W I N D   C H I L L   C H A R T":PRINT:PRINT
40 PRINT "DATA PROVIDED COURTESY OF THE TRAVELERS WEATHER"
50 PRINT "SERVICE, HARTFORD, CONNECTICUT"
60 FOR N = 1 TO 1500:NEXT N
70 CLS:PRINT "SELECT THE TEMPERATURE CLOSEST TO THE ACTUAL
   TEMPERATURE"
80 PRINT
90 PRINT 35,30,25,20,15,10,0,-5,-10,-15,-20,-25,-30,-35
100 PRINT
110 INPUT "ENTER NEGATIVE NUMBERS PRECEEDED BY A MINUS SIGN";T
120 P = ABS(T)
130 Q = P / 5:Q = INT(Q)
140 R = Q * 5
150 IF P = R THEN 180
160 PRINT "DON'T GET CUTE"
170 GOTO 60
```

The chart for this application was obtained from a local weather service, and the formula is a closely guarded secret. It remains for the theoretical mathematicians amongst our readers to derive the formula—but why bother?

Note that there is a selection of 15 "actual" temperatures, each a multiple of five. The instructions from 120 to 150 protect the program from the entry of temperatures which are not offered on the menu. Instruction 120 removes the sign (if the number is negative). The absolute number is then divided by 5 and the integer portion taken—statement 130. At 140 the integer is remultiplied by 5 and the product verified against the absolute value of the original input. Note that variables P, Q, and R are used as a "lock." They are used again after the wind-speed determination, below:

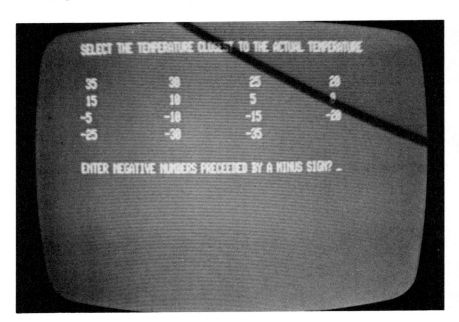

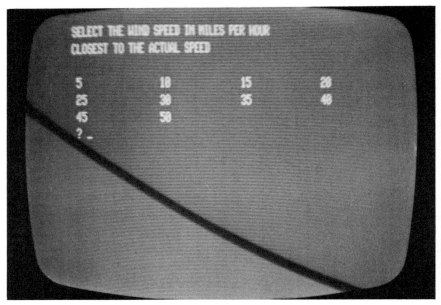

Figure 25 A and B   Windchill Factors

```
180 CLS:PRINT "SELECT THE WIND SPEED IN MILES PER HOUR"
190 PRINT "CLOSEST TO THE ACTUAL SPEED"
200 PRINT
210 PRINT 5,10,15,20,25,30,35,40,45,50
220 INPUT " ";W
230 P = ABS(W)
240 Q = P / 5:Q = INT(Q)
250 R = Q * 5
260 IF P = R THEN 280
270 GOTO 180
```

From this point on, the program is a straightforward logical examination of the matrix of temperatures and wind speeds within the range permitted by the chart.

```
280 IF (T = 35) * (W = 5)  THEN C = 33:GOTO 1780
290 IF (T = 35) * (W = 10) THEN C = 21:GOTO 1780
300 IF (T = 35) * (W = 15) THEN C = 16:GOTO 1780
310 IF (T = 35) * (W = 20) THEN C = 12:GOTO 1780
320 IF (T = 35) * (W = 25) THEN C =  7:GOTO 1780
330 IF (T = 35) * (W = 30) THEN C =  5:GOTO 1780
340 IF (T = 35) * (W = 35) THEN C =  3:GOTO 1780
350 IF (T = 35) * (W = 40) THEN C =  1:GOTO 1780
360 IF (T = 35) * (W = 45) THEN C =  1:GOTO 1780
370 IF (T = 35) * (W = 50) THEN C =  0:GOTO 1780
380 IF (T = 30) * (W = 5)  THEN C = 27:GOTO 1780
390 IF (T = 30) * (W = 10) THEN C = 16:GOTO 1780
400 IF (T = 30) * (W = 15) THEN C = 11:GOTO 1780
410 IF (T = 30) * (W = 20) THEN C =  3:GOTO 1780
420 IF (T = 30) * (W = 25) THEN C =  0:GOTO 1780
430 IF (T = 30) * (W = 30) THEN C = -2:GOTO 1780
440 IF (T = 30) * (W = 35) THEN C = -4:GOTO 1780
450 IF (T = 30) * (W = 40) THEN C = -4:GOTO 1780
460 IF (T = 30) * (W = 45) THEN C = -6:GOTO 1780
470 IF (T = 30) * (W = 50) THEN C = -7:GOTO 1780
480 IF (T = 25) * (W = 5)  THEN C = 21:GOTO 1780
```

```
49Ø IF (T = 25) * (W = 1Ø) THEN C =  9:GOTO 178Ø
5ØØ IF (T = 25) * (W = 15) THEN C =  1:GOTO 178Ø
51Ø IF (T = 25) * (W = 2Ø) THEN C = -4:GOTO 178Ø
52Ø IF (T = 25) * (W = 25) THEN C = -7:GOTO 178Ø
53Ø IF (T = 25) * (W = 3Ø) THEN C = -11:GOTO 178Ø
54Ø IF (T = 25) * (W = 35) THEN C = -13:GOTO 178Ø
55Ø IF (T = 25) * (W = 4Ø) THEN C = -15:GOTO 178Ø
56Ø IF (T = 25) * (W = 45) THEN C = -17:GOTO 178Ø
57Ø IF (T = 25) * (W = 5Ø) THEN C = -17:GOTO 178Ø
58Ø IF (T = 2Ø) * (W = 5)  THEN C = -17:GOTO 178Ø
59Ø IF (T = 2Ø) * (W = 1Ø) THEN C =  2:GOTO 178Ø
6ØØ IF (T = 2Ø) * (W = 15) THEN C = -6:GOTO 178Ø
61Ø IF (T = 2Ø) * (W = 2Ø) THEN C = -9:GOTO 178Ø
62Ø IF (T = 2Ø) * (W = 25) THEN C = -15:GOTO 178Ø
63Ø IF (T = 2Ø) * (W = 3Ø) THEN C = -18:GOTO 178Ø
64Ø IF (T = 2Ø) * (W = 35) THEN C = -2Ø:GOTO 178Ø
65Ø IF (T = 2Ø) * (W = 4Ø) THEN C = -22:GOTO 178Ø
66Ø IF (T = 2Ø) * (W = 45) THEN C = -24:GOTO 178Ø
67Ø IF (T = 2Ø) * (W = 5Ø) THEN C = -24:GOTO 178Ø
68Ø IF (T = 15) * (W = 5)  THEN C = 12:GOTO 178Ø
69Ø IF (T = 15) * (W = 1Ø) THEN C = -2:GOTO 178Ø
7ØØ IF (T = 15) * (W = 15) THEN C = -11:GOTO 178Ø
71Ø IF (T = 15) * (W = 2Ø) THEN C = -17:GOTO 178Ø
72Ø IF (T = 15) * (W = 25) THEN C = -22:GOTO 178Ø
73Ø IF (T = 15) * (W = 3Ø) THEN C = -24:GOTO 178Ø
74Ø IF (T = 15) * (W = 35) THEN C = -27:GOTO 178Ø
75Ø IF (T = 15) * (W = 4Ø) THEN C = -29:GOTO 178Ø
76Ø IF (T = 15) * (W = 45) THEN C = -31:GOTO 178Ø
77Ø IF (T = 15) * (W = 5Ø) THEN C = -31:GOTO 178Ø
78Ø IF (T = 1Ø) * (W = 5)  THEN C =  7:GOTO 178Ø
79Ø IF (T = 1Ø) * (W = 1Ø) THEN C = -9:GOTO 178Ø
8ØØ IF (T = 1Ø) * (W = 15) THEN C = -18:GOTO 178Ø
81Ø IF (T = 1Ø) * (W = 2Ø) THEN C = -24:GOTO 178Ø
82Ø IF (T = 1Ø) * (W = 25) THEN C = -29:GOTO 178Ø
83Ø IF (T = 1Ø) * (W = 3Ø) THEN C = -33:GOTO 178Ø
84Ø IF (T = 1Ø) * (W = 35) THEN C = -35:GOTO 178Ø
```

```
850  IF (T = 10) * (W = 40)   THEN C = -36:GOTO 1780
860  IF (T = 10) * (W = 45)   THEN C = -38:GOTO 1780
870  IF (T = 10) * (W = 50)   THEN C = -38:GOTO 1780
880  IF (T = 5)  * (W = 5)    THEN C =  1:GOTO 1780
890  IF (T = 5)  * (W = 10)   THEN C = -15:GOTO 1780
900  IF (T = 5)  * (W = 15)   THEN C = -25:GOTO 1780
910  IF (T = 5)  * (W = 20)   THEN C = -32:GOTO 1780
920  IF (T = 5)  * (W = 25)   THEN C = -37:GOTO 1780
930  IF (T = 5)  * (W = 30)   THEN C = -41:GOTO 1780
940  IF (T = 5)  * (W = 35)   THEN C = -43:GOTO 1780
950  IF (T = 5)  * (W = 40)   THEN C = -45:GOTO 1780
960  IF (T = 5)  * (W = 45)   THEN C = -46:GOTO 1780
970  IF (T = 5)  * (W = 50)   THEN C = -47:GOTO 1780
980  IF (T = 0)  * (W = 5)    THEN C =  -6:GOTO 1780
990  IF (T = 0)  * (W = 10)   THEN C = -22:GOTO 1780
1000 IF (T = 0)  * (W = 15)   THEN C = -33:GOTO 1780
1010 IF (T = 0)  * (W = 20)   THEN C = -40:GOTO 1780
1020 IF (T = 0)  * (W = 25)   THEN C = -45:GOTO 1780
1030 IF (T = 0)  * (W = 30)   THEN C = -49:GOTO 1780
1040 IF (T = 0)  * (W = 35)   THEN C = -52:GOTO 1780
1050 IF (T = 0)  * (W = 40)   THEN C = -54:GOTO 1780
1060 IF (T = 0)  * (W = 45)   THEN C = -54:GOTO 1780
1070 IF (T = 0)  * (W = 50)   THEN C = -56:GOTO 1780
1080 IF (T = -5) * (W = 5)    THEN C = -11:GOTO 1780
1090 IF (T = -5) * (W = 10)   THEN C = -27:GOTO 1780
1100 IF (T = -5) * (W = 15)   THEN C = -40:GOTO 1780
1110 IF (T = -5) * (W = 20)   THEN C = -46:GOTO 1780
1120 IF (T = -5) * (W = 25)   THEN C = -52:GOTO 1780
1130 IF (T = -5) * (W = 30)   THEN C = -56:GOTO 1780
1140 IF (T = -5) * (W = 35)   THEN C = -60:GOTO 1780
1150 IF (T = -5) * (W = 40)   THEN C = -62:GOTO 1780
1160 IF (T = -5) * (W = 45)   THEN C = -63:GOTO 1780
1170 IF (T = -5) * (W = 50)   THEN C = -63:GOTO 1780
1180 IF (T = -10) * (W = 5)   THEN C = -15:GOTO 1780
1190 IF (T = -10) * (W = 10)  THEN C = -31:GOTO 1780
1200 IF (T = -10) * (W = 15)  THEN C = -45:GOTO 1780
```

```
1210 IF (T = -10) * (W = 20)  THEN C = -52:GOTO 1780
1220 IF (T = -10) * (W = 25)  THEN C = -58:GOTO 1780
1230 IF (T = -10) * (W = 30)  THEN C = -63:GOTO 1780
1240 IF (T = -10) * (W = 35)  THEN C = -67:GOTO 1780
1250 IF (T = -10) * (W = 40)  THEN C = -69:GOTO 1780
1260 IF (T = -10) * (W = 45)  THEN C = -70:GOTO 1780
1270 IF (T = -10) * (W = 50)  THEN C = -70:GOTO 1780
1280 IF (T = -15) * (W = 5)   THEN C = -20:GOTO 1780
1290 IF (T = -15) * (W = 10)  THEN C = -38:GOTO 1780
1300 IF (T = -15) * (W = 15)  THEN C = -51:GOTO 1780
1310 IF (T = -15) * (W = 20)  THEN C = -60:GOTO 1780
1320 IF (T = -15) * (W = 25)  THEN C = -67:GOTO 1780
1330 IF (T = -15) * (W = 30)  THEN C = -70:GOTO 1780
1340 IF (T = -15) * (W = 35)  THEN C = -72:GOTO 1780
1350 IF (T = -15) * (W = 40)  THEN C = -76:GOTO 1780
1360 IF (T = -15) * (W = 45)  THEN C = -78:GOTO 1780
1370 IF (T = -15) * (W = 50)  THEN C = -79:GOTO 1780
1380 IF (T = -20) * (W = 5)   THEN C = -26:GOTO 1780
1390 IF (T = -20) * (W = 10)  THEN C = -45:GOTO 1780
1400 IF (T = -20) * (W = 15)  THEN C = -60:GOTO 1780
1410 IF (T = -20) * (W = 20)  THEN C = -68:GOTO 1780
1420 IF (T = -20) * (W = 25)  THEN C = -75:GOTO 1780
1430 IF (T = -20) * (W = 30)  THEN C = -78:GOTO 1780
1440 IF (T = -20) * (W = 35)  THEN C = -83:GOTO 1780
1450 IF (T = -20) * (W = 40)  THEN C = -87:GOTO 1780
1460 IF (T = -20) * (W = 45)  THEN C = -87:GOTO 1780
1470 IF (T = -20) * (W = 50)  THEN C = -88:GOTO 1780
1480 IF (T = -25) * (W = 5)   THEN C = -31:GOTO 1780
1490 IF (T = -25) * (W = 10)  THEN C = -52:GOTO 1780
1500 IF (T = -25) * (W = 15)  THEN C = -65:GOTO 1780
1510 IF (T = -25) * (W = 20)  THEN C = -76:GOTO 1780
1520 IF (T = -25) * (W = 25)  THEN C = -83:GOTO 1780
1530 IF (T = -25) * (W = 30)  THEN C = -87:GOTO 1780
1540 IF (T = -25) * (W = 35)  THEN C = -90:GOTO 1780
1550 IF (T = -25) * (W = 40)  THEN C = -94:GOTO 1780
1560 IF (T = -25) * (W = 45)  THEN C = -94:GOTO 1780
```

```
1570 IF (T = -25) * (W = 50)  THEN C = -96:GOTO 1780
1580 IF (T = -30) * (W = 5)   THEN C = -35:GOTO 1780
1590 IF (T = -30) * (W = 10)  THEN C = -58:GOTO 1780
1600 IF (T = -30) * (W = 15)  THEN C = -70:GOTO 1780
1610 IF (T = -30) * (W = 20)  THEN C = -81:GOTO 1780
1620 IF (T = -30) * (W = 25)  THEN C = -89:GOTO 1780
1630 IF (T = -30) * (W = 30)  THEN C = -94:GOTO 1780
1640 IF (T = -30) * (W = 35)  THEN C = -98:GOTO 1780
1650 IF (T = -30) * (W = 40)  THEN C = -101:GOTO 1780
1660 IF (T = -30) * (W = 45)  THEN C = -101:GOTO 1780
1670 IF (T = -30) * (W = 50)  THEN C = -103:GOTO 1780
1680 IF (T = -35) * (W = 5)   THEN C = -41:GOTO 1780
1690 IF (T = -35) * (W = 10)  THEN C = -64:GOTO 1780
1700 IF (T = -35) * (W = 15)  THEN C = -78:GOTO 1780
1710 IF (T = -35) * (W = 20)  THEN C = -88:GOTO 1780
1720 IF (T = -35) * (W = 25)  THEN C = -96:GOTO 1780
1730 IF (T = -35) * (W = 30)  THEN C = -101:GOTO 1780
1740 IF (T = -35) * (W = 35)  THEN C = -105:GOTO 1780
1750 IF (T = -35) * (W = 40)  THEN C = -107:GOTO 1780
1760 IF (T = -35) * (W = 45)  THEN C = -108:GOTO 1780
1770 IF (T = -35) * (W = 50)  THEN C = -110:GOTO 1780
```

Depending upon the combinations which have been entered, a value is assigned to C, which is then displayed with a message:

```
1780 CLS
1790 FOR N = 1 TO 5:PRINT:NEXT N
1800 PRINT TAB(10);"THE WIND CHILL TEMPERATURE IS:":PRINT
1810 PRINT TAB(30);C;"DEGREES"
```

And then, just to make light of the situation, some nonsense messages have been added to the screen. They are not integral to the program. Instructions 1820 to 1980 can be omitted:

```
1820 PRINT
1830 IF C < -100 THEN PRINT "WELCOME TO THE ANTARTIC":GOTO 1980
1840 IF C < -90 THEN PRINT "TIME TO RENT A DOG SLED":GOTO 1980
1850 IF C < -80 THEN PRINT "LET'S BUILD AN IGLOO":GOTO 1980
```

```
1860 IF C < -70 THEN PRINT "NORTH TO ALASKA!":GOTO 1980
1870 IF C < -60 THEN PRINT "A HEAT WAVE IN SIBERIA":GOTO 1980
1880 IF C < -50 THEN PRINT "WANT TO GO SHOPPING IN HUDSON'S BAY?":
     GOTO 1980
1890 IF C < -40 THEN PRINT "WELCOME TO THE DEEP FREEZE":GOTO 1980
1900 IF C < -30 THEN PRINT "MOBIL 1 WEATHER":GOTO 1980
1910 IF C < -20 THEN PRINT "FROSTBITE CITY":GOTO 1980
1920 IF C < -10 THEN PRINT "A HOT TIME AT THE OLD ICE HOUSE":
     GOTO 1980
1930 IF C < 0 THEN PRINT "ICE CARNIVAL TIME AT DARTMOUTH":GOTO 1980
1940 IF C > 30 THEN PRINT "SKI THE AUSTRIAN ALPS":GOTO 1980
1950 IF C > 20 THEN PRINT "GATHER ICE CUBES FOR APRES-SKI":
     GOTO 1980
1960 IF C > 10 THEN PRINT "B R R R R R R ":GOTO 1980
1970 IF C > 0 THEN PRINT "NO SCHOOL TODAY"
1980 PRINT
1990 INPUT "PRESS ENTER TO RETURN TO THE BEGINNING";A
2000 GOTO 70
```

As can be seen, the program is simple, but useful. Because it is not logically complex, it will not be repeated in its entirety. If the program is to be of greater use, however, it should be augmented to cover the temperatures and wind speeds which fall between those that have been stated. Give a brief example of how this might be done.

The next effort pursued in this book will help you to accomplish statement 1950 of the previous program:

RECIPE — RECIPE

One of the software programs available directly from Radio Shack is one to assist you to modify recipes. Thus, if you have a recipe for 2 people and you are to feed 15, it will provide the extensions for you. If one of the ingredients happens to be a teaspoon of salt (recipe for 2) then the computer program will tell you that 7.5 teaspoons of salt are required. And, since 3 teaspoons are equal to 1 tablespoon, 7.5 teaspoons will become 2.5 tablespoons. That logic is not duplicated here, but if you think about it, the process is as simple as multiplying the units of measure by the number of portions to be served and dividing the product by any consolidation of the measurement.

Figure 26   Too Cold!

The following is a *really important* recipe program, called *BAR-TENDER*. The program presents 24 cocktail recipes, based on a pair of menus presented at the beginning of the program. In developing this program a basic decision must be made. Should the recipes be placed on and retrieved from cassette tape? Should they be placed into DATA lines? At this point the 16-character limitation of A$ and B$ becomes obvious. Thus, it was decided to create PRINT lines with the recipes. The DATA lines are used, however, to present the menu, as follows:

```
2040 DATA " 1.  ALEXANDER"," "
2050 DATA " 2.  ANGEL'S KISS"," "
2060 DATA " 3.  BLOODY MARY"," "
2070 DATA " 4.  CHAMPAGNE ","COCKTAIL"
2080 DATA " 5.  CREME DE MENTHE ","FRAPPE"
2090 DATA " 6.  DAIQUIRI"," "
2100 DATA " 7.  GIMLET"," "
2110 DATA " 8.  GIN AND TONIC"," "
2120 DATA " 9.  GIN RICKY"," "
2130 DATA "10.  GRASSHOPPER"," "
```

```
2140 DATA "11. MANHATTAN"," "
2150 DATA "12. MARTINI"," "
2160 DATA "13. MINT JULEP"," "
2170 DATA "14. OLD FASHIONED"," "
2180 DATA "15. PINK LADY"," "
2190 DATA "16. PLANTER'S PUNCH"," "
2200 DATA "17. ROB ROY"," "
2210 DATA "18. SCREWDRIVER"," "
2220 DATA "19. SIDECAR"," "
2230 DATA "20. SINGAPORE SLING"," "
2240 DATA "21. STINGER"," "
2250 DATA "22. TOM COLLINS"," "
2260 DATA "23. WARD 8"," "
2270 DATA "24. WHISKEY SOUR"," "
```

Of particular importance to these DATA lines is the inclusion of the second parameter. This is necessary because of the 16-character limitation, and is required for items 4 and 5. Because it *is* required for those two, it is also required for all the others, even though the parameter may not be used. The reason for this is the READ instruction at statement 80.

OK, let's open it up:

```
10 CLS:A = 0
20 FOR N = 1 TO 15
30     PRINT: TAB(20);"B A R T E N D E R"
40 NEXT N
50 GOSUB 2030:GOSUB 2030
```

Variable A is the variable which will receive the menu selection. Since the same variable will be used to "page forward" from menu (first half) to menu (second half), it must be set to 0. Statement 2030 is the timer. The routine from 20 to 40 displays the title for the entire height of the screen.

```
2030 FOR N = 1 TO 500:NEXT N:RETURN
```

As constructed, there are 24 recipes, presented 12 at a time. The tracking of which page is being displayed is done by setting the variable P to either 1 or 2.

```
60 RESTORE:P = 1:CLS
70 FOR N = 1 TO 12
80     READ A$,B$:A = 0
90     PRINT TAB(5);A$ + B$
100 NEXT N
```

Note statement 90. The A$ + B$ is a technique for combining two alphabetic fields. Look back at statements 2070 and 2080. Note that both have a trailing space in the first data item, permitting proper spacing when printed.

The program is constructed as a series of interlocking subroutines. The boundaries of the subroutine which begins at 150 are between 150 and 1980. At statements 120 and 130 you will have to make some modifications if you plan to add to the recipe list. A change to the mechanism in handling P will be necessary. Instead of merely changing P from 1 to 2 and back again, it will be necessary to increment P linearly, and to add instructions via another switch to switch between the movement to statements 60 and 70.

```
110 GOSUB 150
120 IF P = 2 THEN 60
130 CLS:P = 2
140 GOTO 70
```

Figure 27   Bartender

Also included is the paging mechanism. If no number has been entered to A, the program checks which page is being dealt with, and behaves accordingly:

```
150 PRINT:PRINT "PRESS ENTER TO PAGE FORWARD"
160 INPUT "SELECT";A
170 IF (A = Ø) * (P = 1) THEN 130
180 IF (A = Ø) * (P = 2) THEN 60
```

Now there is an entry in response to the question. An ON GOTO could have been constructed, but the 24 entries required would have made the statement unwieldy. So, one ON GOTO is constructed for each half (of 12), subtracting 12 from the value of the second half to permit use of the relative positioning of 1 to 12.

```
190 IF P = 2 THEN 220
200 ON A GOTO 250,310,360,440,520,570,630,700,770,840,900,970
210 GOTO 70
220 CLS
230 ON A - 12 GOTO 1030,1130,1210,1280,1360,1430,1490,1560,1640,
    1700,1780,1860
240 GOTO 60
```

And now, the individual recipes. You may find it desirable to modify any recipe to suit your individual taste. Each recipe makes use of a standard routine to locate the name of the drink and a second standard routine which merely contains a heading:

```
1940 RESTORE
1950 FOR N = 1 TO A
1960     READ A$,B$
1970 NEXT N
1980 RETURN
1990 CLS
2000 PRINT TAB(20);"R E C I P E   F O R :"
2010 PRINT:PRINT A$ + B$
2020 PRINT:PRINT:RETURN
```

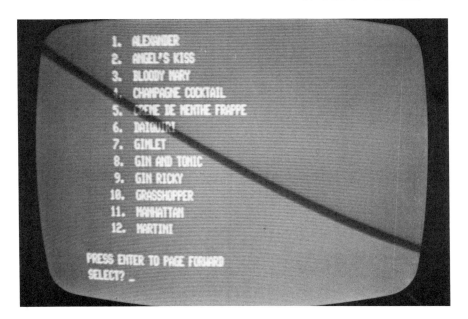

Figure 28.   The Menu

Recipe for an Alexander:

```
250 GOSUB 1940:GOSUB 1990
260 PRINT "1/2 OZ. FRESH CREAM":PRINT
270 PRINT "3/4 OZ. CREME DE CACAO":PRINT
280 PRINT "1 1/2 OZ. GIN OR BRANDY":PRINT:PRINT
290 PRINT "SHAKE WELL WITH CRACKED ICE, STRAIN."
300 GOTO 1920
```

Recipe for an Angel's Kiss:

```
310 GOSUB 1940:GOSUB 1190
320 PRINT "3/4 PONY GLASS FILLED WITH CREME DE CACAO":PRINT
330 PRINT "FLOAT HEAVY CREAM ON TOP":PRINT:PRINT
340 PRINT "DECORATE WITH CHERRY ON A TOOTHPICK":PRINT
350 GOTO 1920
```

Recipe for a Bloody Mary:

```
360 GOSUB 1940:GOSUB 1990
370 PRINT "1 1/2 OZ. VODKA"
380 PRINT "3 OZ. TOMATO JUICE"
390 PRINT "1/3 JIGGER LEMON JUICE":PRINT
400 PRINT "DASH WORCESTERSHIRE SAUCE":PRINT
410 PRINT "SALT AND PEPPER TO TASTE":PRINT
420 PRINT "SHAKE WITH ICE, STRAIN."
430 GOTO 1920
```

Recipe for a Champagne Cocktail:

```
440 GOSUB 1940:GOSUB 1990
450 PRINT "1 LUMP SUGAR":PRINT
460 PRINT "DASH ANGOSTURA BITTERS":PRINT
470 PRINT "CHILLED CHAMPAGNE":PRINT:PRINT
480 PRINT "SATURATE LUMP OF SUGAR WITH DASH OF BITTERS"
490 PRINT "ADD ICE CUBES, FILL WITH CHAMPAGNE"
500 PRINT "TOP WITH TWIST OF LEMON PEEL"
510 GOTO 1920
```

Recipe for a Crème de Menthe Frappé:

```
520 GOSUB 1940:GOSUB 1990
530 PRINT "FILL COCKTAIL GLASS WITH FINE ICE":PRINT
540 PRINT "ADD GREEN CREME DE MENTHE":PRINT
550 PRINT "SERVE WITH SHORT STRAWS":PRINT
560 GOTO 1920
```

Recipe for a Daiquiri:

```
570 GOSUB 1940:GOSUB 1990
580 PRINT "JUICE OF 1/2 LIME OR LEMON":PRINT
590 PRINT "1 TSP. POWDERED SUGAR":PRINT
600 PRINT "1 1/2 OZ. LIGHT BARCARDI RUM":PRINT:PRINT
610 PRINT "SHAKE WITH CRACKED ICE AND WHEN SHAKER FROSTS,
    STRAIN":PRINT
620 GOTO 1920
```

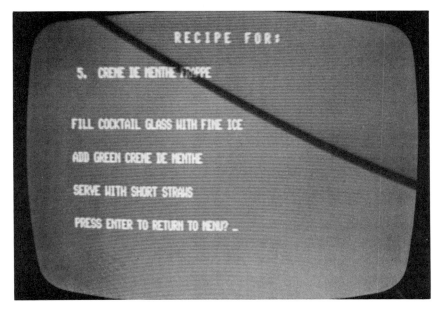

Figure 29.   The Recipe

Recipe for a Gimlet:

```
630 GOSUB 1940:GOSUB 1990
640 PRINT "3 PARTS DRY GIN":PRINT
650 PRINT "1 PART LIME JUICE":PRINT
660 PRINT "DASH PLAIN SODA":PRINT:PRINT
670 PRINT "SHAKE GIN AND JUICE WITH ICE":PRINT
680 )RI6T  ,TRAIN.  TOP WITH SODA"
690 GOTO 1920
```

Recipe for a Gin and Tonic:

```
700 GOSUB 1940:GOSUB 1990
710 PRINT "JUICE AND RIND OF 1/4 LIME":PRINT
720 PRINT "1 1/2 OZ. DRY GIN":PRINT
730 PRINT "QUININE WATER (TONIC)":PRINT:PRINT
740 PRINT "PUT LIME, GIN, ICE CUBES IN 8 OZ. GLASS":PRINT
750 PRINT "FILL WITH TONIC"
760 GOTO 1920
```

Recipe for a Gin Ricky:

```
770 GOSUB 1940:GOSUB 1990
780 PRINT "JUICE AND RIND OF 1/2 LIME":PRINT
790 PRINT "1 1/2 OZ. GIN":PRINT
800 PRINT "SODA":PRINT:PRINT
810 PRINT "ADD ICE, JUICE AND RIND OF LIME TO TALL GLASS"
820 PRINT "ADD GIN, FILL WITH SODA, STIR, TOP WITH CHERRY"
830 GOTO 1920
```

Recipe for a Grasshopper:

```
840 GOSUB 1940:GOSUB 1990
850 PRINT "1 OZ. CREME DE MENTHE":PRINT
860 PRINT "1 OZ. CREME DE CACAO":PRINT
870 PRINT "3/4 OZ. FRESH CREAM":PRINT:PRINT
880 PRINT "SHAKE WELL WITH ICE.  STRAIN INTO CHAMPAGNE GLASS'
890 GOTO 1920
```

Recipe for a Manhattan:

```
900 GOSUB 1940:GOSUB 1990
910 PRINT "1/4 SWEET VERMOUTH":PRINT
920 PRINT "3/4 BOURBON OR RYE":PRINT
930 PRINT "DASH ANGOSTURA BITTERS":PRINT:PRINT
940 PRINT "STIR WITH CRACKED ICE":PRINT
950 PRINT "SERVE WITH CHERRY"
960 GOTO 1920
```

Recipe for a Martini:

```
970 GOSUB 1940:GOSUB 1990
980 PRINT "1/2 DRY VERMOUTH":PRINT
990 PRINT "3/4 GIN":PRINT:PRINT
1000 PRINT "STIR WITH CRACKED ICE, STRAIN":PRINT
1010 PRINT "POUR INTO COCKTAIL GLASS.  ADD OLIVE"
1020 GOTO 1920
```

Recipe for a Mint Julep:

```
1030 GOSUB 1940:GOSUB 1990
1040 PRINT "SEVERAL MINT SPRIGS":PRINT
1050 PRINT "1 TSP. SUGAR":PRINT
1060 PRINT "DASH WATER":PRINT
1070 PRINT "BOURBON":PRINT
1080 PRINT "CRUSH MINT, ADD SUGAR, WATER IN 12 OZ. GLASS"
1090 PRINT "FILL TO TOP WITH CRACKED ICE.  POUR BOURBON INTO"
1100 PRINT "ONE HALF INCH OF THE TOP OF THE GLASS.  STIR UNTIL"
1110 PRINT "GLASS FROSTS."
1120 GOTO 1920
```

Recipe for an Old Fashioned:

```
1130 GOSUB 1940:GOSUB 1990
1140 PRINT "1 LUMP SUGAR":PRINT
1150 PRINT "DASH ANGOSTURA BITTERS":PRINT
1160 PRINT "SPLASH OF PLAIN SODA":PRINT
1170 PRINT "1 1/2 OZ. BOURBON":PRINT
1180 PRINT "MUDDLE SUGAR, BITTERS, SODA"
1190 PRINT "ADD 2 ICE CUBES, CHERRY, ORANGE SLICE"
1200 GOTO 1920
```

Recipe for a Pink Lady:

```
1210 GOSUB 1940:GOSUB 1990
1220 PRINT "1/2 OZ. GRENADINE":PRINT
1230 PRINT "1 1/4 OZ. GIN":PRINT
1240 PRINT "1/2 OZ. LEMON JUICE":PRINT
1250 PRINT "1 EGG WHITE":PRINT:PRINT
1260 PRINT "SHAKE WITH CRACKED ICE AND STRAIN."
1270 GOTO 1920
```

Recipe for Planter's Punch:

```
1280 GOSUB 1940:GOSUB 1990
1290 PRINT "1 TSP. SUGAR":PRINT
```

```
1300 PRINT "1 JIGGER JAMAICA RUM":PRINT
1310 PRINT "1 OZ. LEMON OR LIME JUICE":PRINT
1320 PRINT:PRINT "SHAKE WITH FINE ICE.  POUR UNSTRAINED INTO"
1330 PRINT "10 OZ. GLASS.  TOP WITH SLICE OF ORANGE, LEMON,"
1340 PRINT "CHERRY, AND SPRIG OF FRESH MINT"
1350 GOTO 1920
```

Recipe for a Rob Roy:

```
1360 GOSUB 1940:GOSUB 1990
1370 PRINT "1 PART SWEET VERMOUTH":PRINT
1380 PRINT "2 PARTS SCOTCH":PRINT
1390 PRINT "DASH ANGOSTURA BITTERS":PRINT:PRINT
1400 PRINT "STIR WITH CRACKED ICE, STRAIN, SERVE WITH"
1410 PRINT:PRINT "TWIST OF LEMON."
1420 GOTO 1920
```

Recipe for a Screwdriver:

```
1430 GOSUB 1940:GOSUB 1990
1440 PRINT "2 OZ. VODKA":PRINT
1450 PRINT "ORANGE JUICE":PRINT
1460 PRINT:PRINT "PUT 2 ICE CUBES IN 6 OZ. GLASS.":PRINT
1470 PRINT "ADD VODKA.  FILL WITH JUICE.  STIR"
1480 GOTO 1920
```

Recipe for a Sidecar:

```
1490 GOSUB 1940:GOSUB 1990
1500 PRINT "1/2 OZ. LEMON JUICE":PRINT
1510 PRINT "1 1/2 OZ. BRANDY":PRINT
1520 PRINT "1/2 OZ. COINTREAU":PRINT:PRINT
1530 PRINT "SHAKE ALL INGREDIENTS WELL WITH CRACKED ICE.":PRINT
1540 PRINT "STRAIN INTO A WELL-CHILLED COCKTAIL GLASS"
1550 GOTO 1920
```

Recipe for a Singapore Sling:

```
1560 GOSUB 1940:GOSUB 1990
1570 PRINT "JUICE OF 1/2 LEMON":PRINT
1580 PRINT "1/2 OZ. BENEDICTINE":PRINT
1590 PRINT "1/2 OZ. CHERRY BRANDY":PRINT
1600 PRINT "2 OZ. GIN":PRINT
1610 PRINT "DECORATE WITH ORANGE SLICE.  TOP WITH SODA"
1620 PRINT "STIR.  SERVE WITH STRAW."
1630 GOTO 1920
```

Recipe for a Stinger:

```
1640 GOSUB 1940:GOSUB 1990
1650 PRINT "2 PARTS BRANDY":PRINT
1660 PRINT "1 PART WHITE CREME DE MENTHE":PRINT
1670 PRINT:PRINT "SHAKE WELL WITH CRACKED ICE.  STRAIN.":PRINT
1680 PRINT "POUR INTO COCKTAIL GLASS."
1690 GOTO 1920
```

Recipe for a Tom Collins:

```
1700 GOSUB 1940:GOSUB 1990
1710 PRINT "1 TSP. POWDERED SUGAR":PRINT
1720 PRINT "1 1/2 OZ. GIN":PRINT
1730 PRINT "1/2 JIGGER LEMON JUICE":PRINT
1740 PRINT "PLAIN SODA":PRINT
1750 PRINT "DISSOLVE SUGAR IN JUICE.  ADD ICE CUBES,"
1760 PRINT "GIN, SODA, AND STIR WELL."
1770 GOTO 1920
```

Recipe for a Ward 8:

```
1780 GOSUB 1940:GOSUB 1990
1790 PRINT "1/2 OZ. LEMON JUICE":PRINT
1800 PRINT "1/2 OZ. ORANGE JUICE":PRINT
1810 PRINT "2 OZ. RYE":PRINT
```

```
1820 PRINT "4 DASHES GRENADINE":PRINT
1830 PRINT "SHAKE WITH CRACKED ICE.  SERVE WITHOUT STRAINING."
1840 PRINT "TOP WITH ORANGE SLICE."
1850 GOTO 1920
```

Recipe for a Whiskey Sour:

```
1860 GOSUB 1940:GOSUB 1990
1870 PRINT "1/2 JIGGER LEMON JUICE":PRINT
1880 PRINT "1 TSP. POWDERED SUGAR":PRINT
1890 PRINT "1 1/2 OZ. BOURBON":PRINT:PRINT
1900 PRINT "SHAKE WITH CRACKED ICE.  STRAIN.  SERVE WITH":PRINT
1910 PRINT "CHERRY AND ORANGE SLICE."
1920 INPUT "PRESS ENTER TO RETURN TO MENU";B
1930 GOTO 60
```

Because the program is so straightforward, it will not be presented here in its entirety. Just enter the instructions as they have been encountered in the illustration.

It is not the intention of the book to encourage anyone to drink, particularly a young reader. The program was presented as an example of one technique which might be useful in the home environment. The same routines could be used in any application where alternate sets of directions can be established. One more caution: don't spill on the keyboard!

SIXTY-EIGHT DEGREES, PLEASE

A computer in the home, in addition to providing a source of entertainment, education, or life enrichment, should also provide some very solid savings in home operating costs. TRS-80 can provide some of that today, and the chances are, as interface capabilities are added, that those savings will be multiplied many times.

One of the ways the TRS-80 can help in managing home operating costs is with the ability to calculate, and to some extent predict, fuel oil consumption. It could be asked "Why bother?" Well, if you are a vendor of fuel, the answer is "So I'll know when to deliver the fuel." But for the homeowner, faced with the ever-increasing cost of fuel oil, to say nothing of the restriction of the supply, the ability to track and predict usage and costs may be an invaluable asset. At the very least, the ability to budget for the winter's needs may be critical. The key is a device known as the "degree day."

The temperature at which a person sets the thermostat in his home is, of course, a matter of personal choice, commensurate with a person's ability and willingness to pay for fuel and the availability of a supply. We all know what is happening to the latter. In general, when the heating season begins, oil is consumed as the temperature drops beneath 65 degrees. Each day there is a high temperature and a low temperature, which are announced on the radio or published in the local newspaper. The half-way point between them is the average or "mean" temperature. Studies show that for each degree the mean temperature varies from the 65-degree mark, a quart of oil is burned. Or stated more clearly, for each 4 degrees variance beneath the 65-degree mark, you can expect to burn 1 gallon of oil, assuming that you keep the thermostat within a "normal" range.

The key to degree-day forecasting is the establishment of a "normal" year. For degree-day calculations, the "year" runs from July 1 to June 30. In the program which follows, degree-day data for July 1, 1977 through June 30, 1978, as provided through the courtesy of the Traveler's Weather Service, Hartford, CT, are loaded to DATA lines. It would be quite impossible here to give "normal" year for every area of the country. For this program to be useful to you, it will be necessary for you to obtain the data from a local weather service or from the U.S. Weather Service office nearest to you. All that needs to be done then is to load the DATA lines with the pertinent data in the format described below.

In evaluating how to approach the problem for execution on TRS-80 Level I, it was decided to place all the data in DATA statements, primarily because of the amount of time required for execution of the program. The alternative would have been to store the data on cassette tape, a lengthy process.

Note that the DATA lines are structured to include first the number representing the month of the year, followed by 365 days of history, in sets of five, each of the five broken into three parts, as follows:

MONTH	DAY OF MONTH	DEGREE DAYS

Figure 30. Data Line Organization

As slated, these DATA statements are loaded with 1977-1978 data. For purposes of your use, that data may be construed as "normal."

```
1070 DATA 7,1,0,7,2,0,7,3,0,7,4,0,7,5,0
1080 DATA 7,6,0,7,7,0,7,8,0,7,9,0,7,10,0
1090 DATA 7,11,0,7,12,0,7,13,0,7,14,0,7,15,0
```

```
1100 DATA 7,16,0,7,17,0,7,18,0,7,19,0,7,20,0
1110 DATA 7,21,0,7,22,0,7,23,0,7,24,0,7,25,0
1120 DATA 7,26,0,7,27,0,7,28,0,7,29,0,7,30,0
1130 DATA 7,31,0,8,1,0,8,2,0,8,3,0,8,4,0
1140 DATA 8,5,0,8,6,0,8,7,0,8,8,0,8,9,0
1150 DATA 8,10,0,8,11,0,8,12,0,8,13,0,8,14,0
1160 DATA 8,15,0,8,16,0,8,17,0,8,18,0,8,19,0
1170 DATA 8,20,1,8,21,1,8,22,1,8,23,1,8,24,1
1180 DATA 8,25,1,8,26,1,8,27,1,8,28,1,8,29,1
1190 DATA 8,30,1,8,31,1,9,1,1,9,2,1,9,3,1
1200 DATA 9,4,1,9,5,2,9,6,2,9,7,2,9,8,2
1210 DATA 9,9,2,9,10,2,9,11,3,9,12,3,9,13,3
1220 DATA 9,14,3,9,15,3,9,16,4,9,17,4,9,18,4
1230 DATA 9,19,4,9,20,5,9,21,5,9,22,5,9,23,5
1240 DATA 9,24,6,9,25,6,9,26,6,9,27,7,9,28,7
1250 DATA 9,29,7,9,30,8,10,1,8,10,2,8,10,3,9
1260 DATA 10,4,9,10,5,10,10,6,10,10,7,10,10,8,10
1270 DATA 10,9,11,10,10,11,10,11,11,10,12,12,10,13,12
1280 DATA 10,14,12,10,15,13,10,16,13,10,17,13,10,18,14
1290 DATA 10,19,14,10,20,14,10,21,15,10,22,15,10,23,15
1300 DATA 10,24,16,10,25,16,10,26,17,10,27,17,10,28,17
1310 DATA 10,29,18,10,30,18,10,31,18,11,1,18,11,2,19
1320 DATA 11,3,19,11,4,20,11,5,20,11,6,20,11,7,21
1330 DATA 11,8,21,11,9,21,11,10,22,11,11,22,11,12,23
1340 DATA 11,13,23,11,14,24,11,15,24,11,16,25,11,17,25
1350 DATA 11,18,26,11,19,26,11,20,26,11,21,27,11,22,27
1360 DATA 11,23,28,11,24,28,11,25,29,11,26,30,11,27,31
1370 DATA 11,28,30,11,29,31,11,30,32,12,1,32,12,2,33
1380 DATA 12,3,33,12,4,34,12,5,34,12,6,35,12,7,35
1390 DATA 12,8,35,12,9,36,12,10,36,12,11,37,12,12,37
1400 DATA 12,13,37,12,14,37,12,15,38,12,16,38,12,17,38
1410 DATA 12,18,38,12,19,39,12,20,39,12,21,39,12,22,39
1420 DATA 12,23,39,12,24,40,12,25,40,12,26,40,12,27,40
1430 DATA 12,28,40,12,29,40,12,30,40,12,31,40,1,1,40
1440 DATA 1,2,40,1,3,40,1,4,40,1,5,40,1,6,40
```

```
1450 DATA 1,7,40,1,8,40,1,9,40,1,10,40,1,11,40
1460 DATA 1,12,41,1,13,41,1,14,41,1,15,41,1,16,41
1470 DATA 1,17,41,1,18,40,1,19,40,1,20,40,1,21,40
1480 DATA 1,22,40,1,23,40,1,24,40,1,25,40,1,26,40
1490 DATA 1,27,40,1,28,40,1,29,40,1,30,40,1,31,40
1500 DATA 2,1,40,2,2,40,2,3,40,2,4,40,2,5,40,
1510 DATA 2,6,40,2,7,39,2,8,39,2,9,39,2,10,39
1520 DATA 2,11,39,2,12,39,2,13,38,2,14,38,2,15,38
1530 DATA 2,16,38,2,17,38,2,18,38,2,19,37,2,20,37
1540 DATA 2,21,37,2,22,36,2,23,36,2,24,36,2,25,35
1550 DATA 2,26,35,2,27,35,2,28,35,3,1,34,3,2,34
1560 DATA 3,3,33,3,4,33,3,5,33,3,6,32,3,7,32
1570 DATA 3,8,32,3,9,31,3,10,31,3,11,31,3,12,30
1580 DATA 3,13,30,3,14,30,3,15,29,3,16,29,3,17,28
1590 DATA 3,18,28,3,19,28,3,20,27,3,21,27,3,22,26
1600 DATA 3,23,26,3,24,26,3,25,25,3,26,25,3,27,24
1610 DATA 3,28,24,3,29,23,3,30,23,3,31,23,4,1,22
1620 DATA 4,2,22,4,3,21,4,4,21,4,5,21,4,6,20
1630 DATA 4,7,20,4,8,19,4,9,19,4,10,19,4,11,18
1640 DATA 4,12,18,4,13,17,4,14,17,4,15,17,4,16,16
1650 DATA 4,17,16,4,18,15,19,15,4,20,15,4,21,14
1660 DATA 4,22,14,4,23,13,4,24,13,4,25,13,4,26,13
1670 DATA 4,27,12,4,28,12,4,29,12,4,30,11,5,1,11
1680 DATA 5,2,11,5,3,11,5,4,10,5,5,10,5,6,10
1690 DATA 5,7,9,5,8,9,5,9,9,5,10,8,5,11,8
1700 DATA 5,12,8,5,13,7,5,14,7,5,15,7,5,16,7
1710 DATA 5,17,6,5,18,6,5,19,6,5,20,6,5,21,5
1720 DATA 5,22,5,5,23,5,5,24,5,5,25,4,5,26,4
1730 DATA 5,27,4,5,28,3,5,29,3,5,30,3,5,31,2
1740 DATA 6,1,2,6,2,2,6,3,2,6,4,2,6,5,1
1750 DATA 6,6,1,6,7,1,6,8,1,6,9,1,6,10,1
1760 DATA 6,11,1,6,12,1,6,13,1,6,14,1,6,15,1
1770 DATA 6,16,0,6,17,0,6,18,0,6,19,0,6,20,0
1780 DATA 6,21,0,6,22,0,6,23,0,6,24,0,6,25,0
1790 DATA 6,26,0,6,27,0,6,28,0,6,29,0,6,30,0
```

In addition, the months are presented, along with the number of days in each. More on this later.

```
950 DATA "JUL","Y",31
960 DATA "AUG","UST",31
970 DATA "SEP","TEMBER",30
980 DATA "OCT","OBER",31
990 DATA "NOV","EMBER",30
1000 DATA "DEC","EMBER",31
1010 DATA "JAN","UARY",31
1020 DATA "FEB","RUARY",28
1030 DATA "MAR","CH",31
1040 DATA "APR","IL",30
1050 DATA "MAY"," ",31
1060 DATA "JUN","E",30
```

The opening menu is very simple—just two options, followed by a request for cost data. That cost data will be used later for cost record/protection.

```
10 CLS:RESTORE
20 PRINT TAB(20);"D E G R E E   D A Y   F O R E C A S T"
30 PRINT:PRINT "DO YOU WISH TO:"
40 PRINT:PRINT TAB(5),"1.  CALCULATE USAGE AND COST HISTORY"
50 PRINT:PRINT TAB(5);"2.  PROJECT USAGE AND COST"
60 PRINT:INPUT "SELECT";A
70 IF (A < 1) + (A > 2) THEN 10
80 PRINT:INPUT "ENTER COST PER GALLON";P
90 IF (P < .40) + (P > .99) THEN 10
100 ON A GOTO 110,430:GOTO 10
```

The approach taken is to load the degree-day data to the array. The relative position within the array will account for the actual day. Again, you are reminded that the year is organized, for these purposes, in a July 1 to June 30 sequence, 365 days. The assumption is made that you will modify the specific date to change the degree day data as required, saving the entire program via CSAVE. It's faster in this manner, and the "normal" year will change from year to year. If you wish to keep the DATA lines as an indicator of trend, then it will be necessary to store them as data onto tape and read them back in when needed.

A couple things have been built into this program which are not used by the program as it is written. They are:

- The division of the month name in the DATA lines.
- The loading of the calendar, which follows immediately hereafter.

These were placed in the program in the anticipation that the reader may wish to expand the program to:

- Search on a month's abbreviation.
- Include routines to store on cassette tape other than the "normal" year, as defined by the DATA statements. This is possible through the use of array positions 1—12 and 101—465. This will allow the storage of not only a "normal" year, but also another year for comparison purposes.

```
110 CLS
120 PRINT "DON'T GO AWAY - I'M WORKING"
130 FOR N = 1 TO 12
140    READ A$,B$,C
150    A(N) = C
160 NEXT N
170 PRINT:PRINT "CALENDAR LOADED"
180 PRINT:PRINT
190 PRINT "STILL WORKING"
200 FOR N = 1 TO 365
210    READ A,B,C
220    A(N + 100) = C
230 NEXT N
240 PRINT:PRINT "DEGREE DAYS LOADED TO ARRAY"
250 FOR N = 1 TO 1500:NEXT N
```

Now for the first option:

```
260 CLS:RESTORE
270 PRINT TAB(20); "U S A G E   H I S T O R Y":J = 1
280 PRINT "MONTH","GALLONS","DEGREE DAYS","COST"
```

```
290 FOR N = 1 TO 12
300     READ A$,B$,C
310         FOR Z = J TO C - 1 + J
320             U = U + A(Z + 100)
330         NEXT Z
340     J = C + J
350     G = U / 4:L = L + G
360     F = P * G:M = M + F:K = K + U
370     PRINT A$ + B$,G,U,"$";F
380     F = 0:U = 0
390 NEXT N
400 PRINT "TOTALS",L,K,"$";M
410 INPUT "PRESS ENTER TO RETURN TO THE BEGINNING";A
420 GOTO 10
```

The instructions at 310 and 320 increment through the array, accumulating the degree days to a length defined by C, the number of days in the

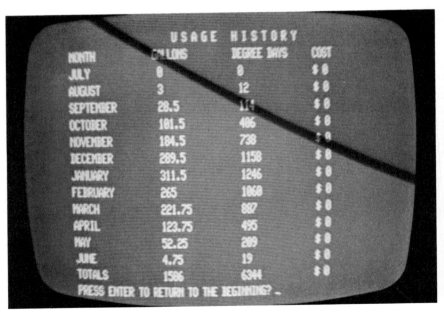

Figure 31.   Fuel Usage History
(Note that no cost factor was entered)

month. It was chosen to start variable J at 1, necessitating the adjustment of C by − 1 (270 and 310). It could have just as easily been Ø and C, respectively.

At 350 the number of gallons is calculated (degree days divided by 4) and a running total of gallons is kept. Cost is calculated, degree days and costs are accumulated at 360, and the line representing the month is displayed at 400. In the illustration above, a zero cost has been loaded.

The second option is a little more detailed:

```
430 CLS:RESTORE
440 PRINT:PRINT "DO YOU WISH A 30, 60, OR 90 DAY FORECAST?"
450 INPUT "ENTER NUMBER";A
460 Q = A / 30:Q = INT(Q):CLS
470 PRINT:PRINT "WHICH MONTH IS IT NOW?"
480 PRINT
490 FOR N = 1 TO 12
500    READ A$,B$,C
510    PRINT N;".    ";A$ + B$
520 NEXT N
530 RESTORE
540 PRINT:INPUT "SELECT";A:A = INT(A)
550 IF (A > 12) + (A < 1) THEN 430
560 IF A + Q > 12 THEN A = A -12
570 FOR N = 1 TO A + Q
580    READ A$,B$,C
590    D = D + C
600 NEXT N
610 H = N
620 IF D > 365 THEN D = 365
630 RESTORE
640 FOR N = 1 TO 12
650    READ A$,B$,C
660 NEXT N
670 CLS:PRINT "DON'T GO AWAY - I'M DISTRIBUTING DATA"
680 GOSUB 860
690 PRINT:PRINT "OK.  THAT'S DONE.  I'M CALCULATING NOW"
700 FOR N = 1 TO D
```

```
710     U = U + A(N + 100)
720 NEXT N
730 G = U / 4
740 F = P * G
750 CLS
760 RESTORE
770 FOR N = 1 TO H - 1
780     READ A$,B$,C
790 NEXT N
800 PRINT "PROJECTION THROUGH ";A$ + B$;":"
810 PRINT
820 PRINT U;"DEGREE DAYS"
830 PRINT G;"GALLONS"
840 PRINT "COST - $";F
850 GOTO 410
860 RESTORE
870 FOR N = 1 TO 12
880     READ A$,B$,C
890 NEXT N
900 FOR N = 1 TO 365
910     READ A,B,C
920     A(N + 100) = C
930 NEXT N
940 RETURN
```

Initially you are allowed the option to select a 30, 60 or 90-day forecast. However, the logic to "wrap around" the year-end (June to July) has not been included. You can do so if you wish, but it is really not necessary. A 90-day forecast beginning with July will be as valid as one which is begun in June. The "forecasting" ability of this program is based upon its ability to scan forward in the "normal" year. For simplicity, until you obtain a statistics degree, this will give you a relative indicator of trend.

Statement 460 forces an integer, probably in the 1 to 3 range. If it does not, either higher or lower, there is no serious harm. It is short-circuited at 550 and 560. Thus 1, 2, or 3 is added to the number of the month selected from the screen (statement 570), and the total number of days (array positions) is accumulated at variable D.

The range of the examination is stored at H, for use later on, an action which is necessary due to the RESTORE/READ actions at 630 and 650. H will be used again at 770.

The routine at 630 to 660 is merely a bypass operation—to get at the degree-day data, which is then loaded into the array in the subroutine at 860. You'll note that there is another RESTORE and bypass at 860. Why, then, are the instructions at 630 to 660 necessary? For *this* program they are not, but it is in this routine where you'll insert the logic to call out the monthly abbreviations, should you choose to use them. They should be inserted between what is now 650 and 660.

Beyond that, the calculations are similar to the first routine, except that the scope of the calculations is diminished by the length you have selected for the projection.

Again, it is assumed that you will modify the specific dates, as reflected in the DATA lines. If you'll do that, you'll have part "current" data and part "normal" data. If you choose to place your current data onto tape, you must then INPUT # the data back into memory, compare it to the "normal" data as stored in the DATA lines and build your trend as a function of the variation of "current" to "normal!" If you do modify the DATA lines, be sure to CSAVE. And, you might also consider constructing a graph, now that you know how.

Here is the program in its entirety:

```
10 CLS:RESTORE
20 PRINT TAB(20);"D E G R E E    D A Y    F O R E C A S T"
30 PRINT:PRINT "DO YOU WISH TO:"
40 PRINT:PRINT TAB(5),"1.  CALCULATE USAGE AND COST HISTORY"
50 PRINT:PRINT TAB(5);"2.  PROJECT USAGE AND COST"
60 PRINT:INPUT "SELECT";A
70 IF (A < 1) + (A > 2) THEN 10
80 PRINT:INPUT "ENTER COST PER GALLON";P
90 IF (P  < .40) + (P  > .99) THEN 10
100 ON A GOTO 110,430:GOTO 10
110 CLS
120 PRINT "DON'T GO AWAY - I'M WORKING"
130 FOR N = 1 TO 12
140    READ A$,B$,C
150    A(N) = C
160 NEXT N
```

```
170 PRINT:PRINT "CALENDAR LOADED"
180 PRINT:PRINT
190 PRINT "STILL WORKING"
200 FOR N = 1 TO 365
210     READ A,B,C
220     A(N + 100) = C
230 NEXT N
240 PRINT:PRINT "DEGREE DAYS LOADED TO ARRAY"
250 FOR N = 1 TO 1500:NEXT N
260 CLS:RESTORE
270 PRINT TAB(20); "U S A G E   H I S T O R Y":J = 1
280 PRINT "MONTH","GALLONS","DEGREE DAYS","COST"
290 FOR N = 1 TO 12
300     READ A$,B$,C
310         FOR Z = J TO C - 1 + J
320             U = U + A(Z + 100)
330         NEXT Z
340     J = C + J
350     G = U / 4:L = L + G
360     F = P * G:M = M + F:K = K + U
370     PRINT A$ + B$,G,U,"$";F
380     F = 0:U = 0
390 NEXT N
400 PRINT "TOTALS",L,K,"$";M
410 INPUT "PRESS ENTER TO RETURN TO THE BEGINNING";A
420 GOTO 10
430 CLS:RESTORE
440 PRINT:PRINT "DO YOU WISH A 30, 60, OR 90 DAY FORECAST?"
450 INPUT "ENTER NUMBER";A
460 Q = A / 30:Q = INT(Q):CLS
470 PRINT:PRINT "WHICH MONTH IS IT NOW?"
480 PRINT
490 FOR N = 1 TO 12
500     READ A$,B$,C
510     PRINT N;".   ";A$ + B$
520 NEXT N
```

```
530 RESTORE
540 PRINT:INPUT "SELECT";A:A = INT(A)
550 IF (A > 12) + (A < 1) THEN 430
560 IF A + Q > 12 THEN A = A -12
570 FOR N = 1 TO A + Q
580    READ A$,B$,C
590    D = D + C
600 NEXT N
610 H = N
620 IF D > 365 THEN D = 365
630 RESTORE
640 FOR N = 1 TO 12
650    READ A$,B$,C
660 NEXT N
670 CLS:PRINT "DON'T GO AWAY - I'M DISTRIBUTING DATA"
680 GOSUB 860
690 PRINT:PRINT "OK.  THAT'S DONE.  I'M CALCULATING NOW"
700 FOR N = 1 TO D
710    U = U + A(N + 100)
720 NEXT N
730 G = U / 4
740 F = P * G
750 CLS
760 RESTORE
770 FOR N = 1 TO H - 1
780    READ A$,B$,C
790 NEXT N
800 PRINT "PROJECTION THROUGH ";A$ + B$;":"
810 PRINT
820 PRINT U;"DEGREE DAYS"
830 PRINT G;"GALLONS"
840 PRINT "COST - $";F
850 GOTO 410
860 RESTORE
870 FOR N = 1 TO 12
880    READ A$,B$,C
```

```
890 NEXT N
900 FOR N = 1 TO 365
910     READ A,B,C
920     A(N + 100) = C
930 NEXT N
940 RETURN
950 DATA "JUL","Y",31
960 DATA "AUG","UST",31
970 DATA "SEP","TEMBER",30
980 DATA "OCT","OBER",31
990 DATA "NOV","EMBER",30
1000 DATA "DEC","EMBER",31
1010 DATA "JAN","UARY",31
1020 DATA "FEB","RUARY",28
1030 DATA "MAR","CH",31
1040 DATA "APR","IL",30
1050 DATA "MAY"," ",31
1060 DATA "JUN","E",30
1070 DATA 7,1,0,7,2,0,7,3,0,7,4,0,7,5,0
1080 DATA 7,6,0,7,7,0,7,8,0,7,9,0,7,10,0
1090 DATA 7,11,0,7,12,0,7,13,0,7,14,0,7,15,0
1100 DATA 7,16,0,7,17,0,7,18,0,7,19,0,7,20,0
1110 DATA 7,21,0,7,22,0,7,23,0,7,24,0,7,25,0
1120 DATA 7,26,0,7,27,0,7,28,0,7,29,0,7,30,0
1130 DATA 7,31,0,8,1,0,8,2,0,8,3,0,8,4,0
1140 DATA 8,5,0,8,6,0,8,7,0,8,8,0,8,9,0
1150 DATA 8,10,0,8,11,0,8,12,0,8,13,0,8,14,0
1160 DATA 8,15,0,8,16,0,8,17,0,8,18,0,8,19,0
1170 DATA 8,20,1,8,21,1,8,22,1,8,23,1,8,24,1
1180 DATA 8,25,1,8,26,1,8,27,1,8,28,1,8,29,1
1190 DATA 8,30,1,8,31,1,9,1,1,9,2,1,9,3,1
1200 DATA 9,4,1,9,5,2,9,6,2,9,7,2,9,8,2
1210 DATA 9,9,2,9,10,2,9,11,3,9,12,3,9,13,3
1220 DATA 9,14,3,9,15,3,9,16,4,9,17,4,9,18,4
1230 DATA 9,19,4,9,20,5,9,21,5,9,22,5,9,23,5
1240 DATA 9,24,6,9,25,6,9,26,6,9,27,7,9,28,7
```

```
1250 DATA 9,29,7,9,30,8,10,1,8,10,2,8,10,3,9
1260 DATA 10,4,9,10,5,10,10,6,10,10,7,10,10,8,10
1270 DATA 10,9,11,10,10,11,10,11,11,10,12,12,10,13,12
1280 DATA 10,14,12,10,15,13,10,16,13,10,17,13,10,18,14
1290 DATA 10,19,14,10,20,14,10,21,15,10,22,15,10,23,15
1300 DATA 10,24,16,10,25,16,10,26,17,10,27,17,10,28,17
1310 DATA 10,29,18,10,30,18,10,31,18,11,1,18,11,2,19
1320 DATA 11,3,19,11,4,20,11,5,20,11,6,20,11,7,21
1330 DATA 11,8,21,11,9,21,11,10,22,11,11,22,11,12,23
1340 DATA 11,13,23,11,14,24,11,15,24,11,16,25,11,17,25
1350 DATA 11,18,26,11,19,26,11,20,26,11,21,27,11,22,27
1360 DATA 11,23,28,11,24,28,11,25,29,11,26,30,11,27,31
1370 DATA 11,28,30,11,29,31,11,30,32,12,1,32,12,2,33
1380 DATA 12,3,33,12,4,34,12,5,34,12,6,35,12,7,35
1390 DATA 12,8,35,12,9,36,12,10,36,12,11,37,12,12,37
1400 DATA 12,13,37,12,14,37,12,15,38,12,16,38,12,17,38
1410 DATA 12,18,38,12,19,39,12,20,39,12,21,39,12,22,39
1420 DATA 12,23,39,12,24,40,12,25,40,12,26,40,12,27,40
1430 DATA 12,28,40,12,29,40,12,30,40,12,31,40,1,1,40
1440 DATA 1,2,40,1,3,40,1,4,40,1,5,40,1,6,40
1450 DATA 1,7,40,1,8,40,1,9,40,1,10,40,1,11,40
1460 DATA 1,12,41,1,13,41,1,14,41,1,15,41,1,16,41
1470 DATA 1,17,41,1,18,40,1,19,40,1,20,40,1,21,40
1480 DATA 1,22,40,1,23,40,1,24,40,1,25,40,1,26,40
1490 DATA 1,27,40,1,28,40,1,29,40,1,30,40,1,31,40
1500 DATA 2,1,40,2,2,40,2,3,40,2,4,40,2,5,40,
1510 DATA 2,6,40,2,7,39,2,8,39,2,9,39,2,10,39
1520 DATA 2,11,39,2,12,39,2,13,38,2,14,38,2,15,38
1530 DATA 2,16,38,2,17,38,2,18,38,2,19,37,2,20,37
1540 DATA 2,21,37,2,22,36,2,23,36,2,24,36,2,25,35
1550 DATA 2,26,35,2,27,35,2,28,35,3,1,34,3,2,34
1560 DATA 3,3,33,3,4,33,3,5,33,3,6,32,3,7,32
1570 DATA 3,8,32,3,9,31,3,10,31,3,11,31,3,12,30
1580 DATA 3,13,30,3,14,30,3,15,29,3,16,29,3,17,28
1590 DATA 3,18,28,3,19,28,3,20,27,3,21,27,3,22,26
1600 DATA 3,23,26,3,24,26,3,25,25,3,26,25,3,27,24
```

```
1610 DATA 3,28,24,3,29,23,3,30,23,3,31,23,4,1,22
1620 DATA 4,2,22,4,3,21,4,4,21,4,5,21,4,6,20
1630 DATA 4,7,20,4,8,19,4,9,19,4,10,19,4,11,18
1640 DATA 4,12,18,4,13,17,4,14,17,4,15,17,4,16,16
1650 DATA 4,17,16,4,18,15,19,15,4,20,15,4,21,14
1660 DATA 4,22,14,4,23,13,4,24,13,4,25,13,4,26,13
1670 DATA 4,27,12,4,28,12,4,29,12,4,30,11,5,1,11
1680 DATA 5,2,11,5,3,11,5,4,10,5,5,10,5,6,10
1690 DATA 5,7,9,5,8,9,5,9,9,5,10,8,5,11,8
1700 DATA 5,12,8,5,13,7,5,14,7,5,15,7,5,16,7
1710 DATA 5,17,6,5,18,6,5,19,6,5,20,6,5,21,5
1720 DATA 5,22,5,5,23,5,5,24,5,5,25,4,5,26,4
1730 DATA 5,27,4,5,28,3,5,29,3,5,30,3,5,31,2
1740 DATA 6,1,2,6,2,2,6,3,2,6,4,2,6,5,1
1750 DATA 6,6,1,6,7,1,6,8,1,6,9,1,6,10,1
1760 DATA 6,11,1,6,12,1,6,13,1,6,14,1,6,15,1
1770 DATA 6,16,0,6,17,0,6,18,0,6,19,0,6,20,0
1780 DATA 6,21,0,6,22,0,6,23,0,6,24,0,6,25,0
1790 DATA 6,26,0,6,27,0,6,28,0,6,29,0,6,30,0
```

AW, BUT MOM . . . GEE WHIZ!

Ever had any trouble getting the kids to do chores around the house? Do your kids accuse you of playing favorite or of picking on them when you have things to be done? Let TRS-80 take the criticism!

The following is a program which randomly selects the child and randomly assigns two tasks to him or her. It's set up for five children and 10 tasks, but both can be modified to suit your needs.

First, the cast of characters:

```
1500 DATA "KAREN"
1510 DATA "TIMMY"
1520 DATA "MICHAEL"
1530 DATA "MATTHEW"
1540 DATA "KATHLEEN"
```

These are the children of the author and of an associate, and we can testify from personal experience that doing chores at home is just not at the head of their individual priority lists.

And the tasks we want them to do:

```
1550 DATA "DISHES"
1560 DATA "GARBAGE"
1570 DATA "LAUNDRY"
1580 DATA "VACUUM"
1590 DATA "RUBBISH"
1600 DATA "LAWN"
1610 DATA "WINDOWS"
1620 DATA "BASEMENT"
1630 DATA "GARAGE"
1640 DATA "GROCERIES"
```

Here is the opening screen:

```
10 CLS:RESTORE
20 PRINT TAB(20);"C H O R E   R E M I N D E R"
30 PRINT:PRINT "HAVING TROUBLE GETTING THE KIDS TO DO THE CHORES?"
40 PRINT:PRINT "LET TRS-80 DO THE TASK FOR YOU.  IT REMOVES THE"
50 PRINT "ANGER AND THE HOUNDING."
60 PRINT:PRINT "THE PROGRAM AUTOMATICALLY SELECTS THE NAMES OF"
70 PRINT "ONE OF FIVE CHILDREN AND THEN AUTOMATICALLY SELECTS"
80 PRINT "TWO TASKS FOR HIM OR HER TO PERFORM.  AND IT WILL BE"
90 PRINT "DIFFERENT EACH TIME YOU RUN IT."
100 PRINT:INPUT "PRESS ENTER TO BEGIN",A
```

Since there is some internal gyrating to be done, and the screen will be blank, the following is put on the screen to keep the viewer occupied:

```
110 CLS
120 FOR N = 1 TO 500:NEXT N
130 PRINT:PRINT:PRINT:PRINT "I'M THINKING"
140 FOR N = 1 TO 500:NEXT N
150 PRINT:PRINT:PRINT:PRINT "I'M THINKING"
160 FOR N = 1 TO 500:NEXT N
170 PRINT:PRINT:PRINT:PRINT "DON'T RUSH ME!"
180 FOR N = 1 TO 500:NEXT N
```

The children are selected, one at a time, via a random number generator, in the range of 1 to 5:

```
135Ø R = RND(5)
136Ø R = INT(R)
137Ø IF R < 1 THEN 135Ø
138Ø RETURN
```

These numbers are loaded into the first five positions of the array, with steps taken in each case to insure that no duplicates have been selected:

```
19Ø GOSUB 135Ø:A(1) = R
2ØØ GOSUB 135Ø
21Ø IF R = A(1) THEN 2ØØ
22Ø A(2) = R
23Ø GOSUB 135Ø
24Ø FOR N = 1 TO 2
25Ø    IF R = A(N) THEN 23Ø
26Ø NEXT N
27Ø A(3) = R
28Ø GOSUB 135Ø
29Ø FOR N = 1 TO 3
3ØØ    IF R = A(N) THEN 28Ø
31Ø NEXT N
32Ø A(4) = R
33Ø GOSUB 135Ø
34Ø FOR N = 1 TO 4
35Ø    IF R = A(N) THEN 33Ø
36Ø NEXT N
37Ø A(5) = R
```

The numbers placed into the array will be used later as a guide for searching the name portion of the DATA lines.

The random number generation for the chores is similar, except that the first five data lines (names) are rejected:

```
139Ø R = RND(15)
14ØØ R = INT(R)
141Ø IF R < 6 THEN 139Ø
142Ø RETURN
```

And then the assignment to the array is done in a similar manner, ensuring that there are no duplicates:

```
380 GOSUB 1390
390 A(6) = R
400 GOSUB 1390
410 IF R = A(6) THEN 400
420 A(7) = R
430 GOSUB 1390
440 FOR N = 6 TO 7
450     IF R = A(N) THEN 430
460 NEXT N
470 A(8) = R
490 FOR N = 6 TO 8
500     IF R = A(N) THEN 480
510 NEXT N
520 A(9) = R
530 GOSUB 1390
540 FOR N = 6 TO 9
550     IF R = A(N) THEN 530
560 NEXT N
570 A(10) = R
580 GOSUB 1390
590 FOR N = 6 TO 10
600     IF R = A(N) THEN 580
610 NEXT N
620 A(11) = R
630 GOSUB 1390
640 FOR N = 6 TO 11
650     IF R = A(N) THEN 630
660 NEXT N
670 A(12) = R
680 GOSUB 1390
690 FOR N = 6 TO 12
700     IF R = A(N) THEN 680
710 NEXT N
```

```
720 A(13) = R
730 GOSUB 1390
740 FOR N = 6 TO 13
750     IF R = A(N) THEN 730
760 NEXT N
770 A(14) = R
780 GOSUB 1390
790 FOR N = 6 TO 14
800     IF R = A(N) THEN 780
810 NEXT N
820 A(15) = R
```

Now the people are selected and the tasks for each have been selected as well, both done randomly. The following is a pause to give a message to "Mom."

```
830 CLS
840 PRINT "I HAVE ASSIGNED THE TASKS."
850 PRINT:PRINT "I WOULD SUGGEST THAT YOU GET PAPER AND PE
860 PRINT:GOSUB 1460
1460 PRINT:PRINT:INPUT "PRESS ENTER TO CONTINUE";A
1470 RETURN
```

Now display the computer's selections:

```
1430 PRINT "CHORES FOR: ";A$
1440 PRINT
1450 RETURN
870 CLS
880 R = A(1):GOSUB 1300
890 GOSUB 1430
900 R = A(6):GOSUB 1300
910 GOSUB 1480
920 R = A(7):GOSUB 1300
930 GOSUB 1480
940 GOSUB 1460
950 CLS
```

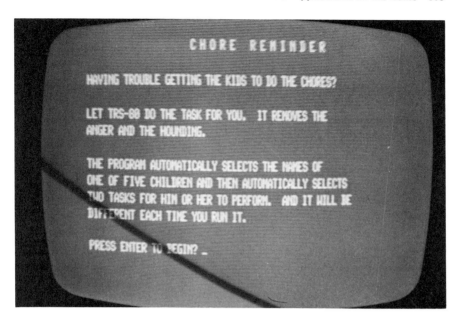

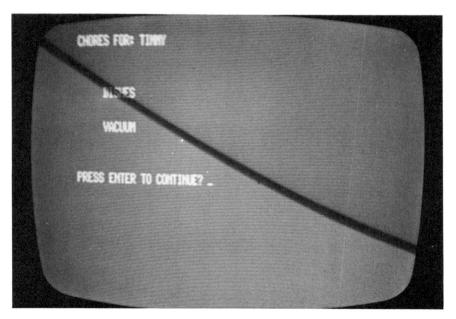

Figure 32.   Chore Reminder

```
960 R = A(2):GOSUB 1300
970 GOSUB 1430
980 R = A(8):GOSUB 1300
990 GOSUB 1480
1000 R = A(9):GOSUB 1300
1010 GOSUB 1480
1020 GOSUB 1460
1030 CLS
1040 R = A(3):GOSUB 1300
1050 GOSUB 1430
1060 R = A(10):GOSUB 1300
1070 GOSUB 1480
1080 R = A(11):GOSUB 1300
1090 GOSUB 1480
1100 GOSUB 1460
1110 CLS
1120 R = A(4):GOSUB 1300
1130 GOSUB 1430
1140 R = A(12):GOSUB 1300
1150 GOSUB 1480
1160 R = A(13):GOSUB 1300
1170 GOSUB 1480
1180 GOSUB 1460
1190 CLS
1200 R = A(5):GOSUB 1300
1210 GOSUB 1430
1220 R = A(14):GOSUB 1300
1230 GOSUB 1480
1240 R = A(15):GOSUB 1300
1250 GOSUB 1480
1260 GOSUB 1460
1480 PRINT:PRINT TAB(5);A$
1490 RETURN
1300 RESTORE
1310 FOR N = 1 TO R
```

```
1320    READ A$
1330 NEXT N
1340 RETURN
```

All that remains is the ability for you to perform the selection a subsequent time, if you need to do so:

```
1270 CLS
1280 INPUT "HIT ENTER TO EFFECT REASSIGNMENT";A
1290 GOTO 10
```

Now the kids will do their tasks cheerfully, right? Right! At least they won't blame *you* for assigning them.

Here's the whole program:

```
10 CLS:RESTORE
20 PRINT TAB(20);"C H O R E   R E M I N D E R"
30 PRINT:PRINT "HAVING TROUBLE GETTING THE KIDS TO DO THE CHORES?"
40 PRINT:PRINT "LET TRS-80 DO THE TASK FOR YOU.  IT REMOVES THE"
50 PRINT "ANGER AND THE HOUNDING."
60 PRINT:PRINT "THE PROGRAM AUTOMATICALLY SELECTS THE NAMES OF"
70 PRINT "ONE OF FIVE CHILDREN AND THEN AUTOMATICALLY SELECTS"
80 PRINT "TWO TASKS FOR HIM OR HER TO PERFORM.  AND IT WILL BE"
90 PRINT "DIFFERENT EACH TIME YOU RUN IT."
100 PRINT:INPUT "PRESS ENTER TO BEGIN",A
110 CLS
120 FOR N = 1 TO 500:NEXT N
130 PRINT:PRINT:PRINT:PRINT "I"M THINKING"
140 FOR N = 1 TO 500:NEXT N
150 PRINT:PRINT:PRINT:PRINT "I'M STILL THINKING"
160 FOR N = 1 TO 500:NEXT N
170 PRINT:PRINT:PRINT:PRINT "DON'T RUSH ME!"
180 FOR N = 1 TO 500:NEXT N
190 GOSUB 1350:A(1) = R
200 GOSUB 1350
210 IF R = A(1) THEN 200
220 A(2) = R
```

```
230 GOSUB 1350
240 FOR N = 1 TO 2
250     IF R = A(N) THEN 230
260 NEXT N
270 A(3) = R
280 GOSUB 1350
290 FOR N = 1 TO 3
300     IF R = A(N) THEN 280
310 NEXT N
320 A(4) = R
330 GOSUB 1350
340 FOR N = 1 TO 4
350     IF R = A(N) THEN 330
360 NEXT N
370 A(5) = R
380 GOSUB 1390
390 A(6) = R
400 GOSUB 1390
410 IF R = A(6) THEN 400
420 A(7) = R
430 GOSUB 1390
440 FOR N = 6 TO 7
450     IF R = A(N) THEN 430
460 NEXT N
470 A(8) = R
490 FOR N = 6 TO 8
500     IF R = A(N) THEN 480
510 NEXT N
520 A(9) = R
530 GOSUB 1390
540 FOR N = 6 TO 9
550     IF R = A(N) THEN 530
560 NEXT N
570 A(10) = R
580 GOSUB 1390
590 FOR N = 6 TO 10
```

```
600     IF R = A(N) THEN 580
610 NEXT N
620 A(11) = R
630 GOSUB 1390
640 FOR N = 6 TO 11
650     IF R = A(N) THEN 630
660 NEXT N
670 A(12) = R
680 GOSUB 1390
690 FOR N = 6 TO 12
700     IF R = A(N) THEN 680
710 NEXT N
720 A(13) = R
730 GOSUB 1390
740 FOR N = 6 TO 13
750     IF R = A(N) THEN 730
760 NEXT N
770 A(14) = R
780 GOSUB 1390
790 FOR N = 6 TO 14
800     IF R = A(N) THEN 780
810 NEXT N
820 A(15) = R
830 CLS
840 PRINT "I HAVE ASSIGNED THE TASKS."
850 PRINT:PRINT "I WOULD SUGGEST THAT YOU GET PAPER AND PENCIL."
860 PRINT:GOSUB 1460
870 CLS
880 R = A(1):GOSUB 1300
890 GOSUB 1430
900 R = A(6):GOSUB 1300
910 GOSUB 1480
920 R = A(7):GOSUB 1300
930 GOSUB 1480
940 GOSUB 1460
950 CLS
```

```
960 R = A(2):GOSUB 1300
970 GOSUB 1430
980 R = A(8):GOSUB 1300
990 GOSUB 1480
1000 R = A(9):GOSUB 1300
1010 GOSUB 1480
1020 GOSUB 1460
1030 CLS
1040 R = A(3):GOSUB 1300
1050 GOSUB 1430
1060 R = A(10):GOSUB 1300
1070 GOSUB 1480
1080 R = A(11):GOSUB 1300
1090 GOSUB 1480
1100 GOSUB 1460
1110 CLS
1120 R = A(4):GOSUB 1300
1130 GOSUB 1430
1140 R = A(12):GOSUB 1300
1150 GOSUB 1480
1160 R = A(13):GOSUB 1300
1170 GOSUB 1480
1180 GOSUB 1460
1190 CLS
1200 R = A(5):GOSUB 1300
1210 GOSUB 1430
1220 R = A(14):GOSUB 1300
1230 GOSUB 1480
1240 R = A(15):GOSUB 1300
1250 GOSUB 1480
1260 GOSUB 1460
1270 CLS
1280 INPUT "HIT ENTER TO EFFECT REASSIGNMENT";A
1290 GOTO 10
1300 RESTORE
```

```
1310 FOR N = 1 TO R
1320     READ A$
1330 NEXT N
1340 RETURN
1350 R = RND(5)
1360 R = INT(R)
1370 IF R < 1 THEN 1350
1380 RETURN
1390 R = RND(15)
1400 R = INT(R)
1410 IF R < 6 THEN 1390
1420 RETURN
1430 PRINT "CHORES FOR: ";A$
1440 PRINT
1450 RETURN
1460 PRINT:PRINT:INPUT "PRESS ENTER TO CONTINUE";A
1470 RETURN
1480 PRINT:PRINT TAB(5);A$
1490 RETURN
1500 DATA "KAREN"
1510 DATA "TIMMY"
1520 DATA "MICHAEL"
1530 DATA "MATTHEW"
1540 DATA "KATHLEEN"
1550 DATA "DISHES"
1560 DATA "GARBAGE"
1570 DATA "LAUNDRY"
1580 DATA "VACUUM"
1590 DATA "RUBBISH"
1600 DATA "LAWN"
1610 DATA "WINDOWS"
1620 DATA "BASEMENT"
1630 DATA "GARAGE"
1640 DATA "GROCERIES"
```

YOUR AUTO AND THE TRS-80

Our love for the automobile is well documented. Whether anyone will ever fall in love with microcomputers in general, or the TRS-80 in particular, is still an open question. But using the latter can help you to love the former. What follows is a program to help you to monitor the performance of your automobile and to track the associated expenses. And this one, unlike many of the others, depends heavily upon the use of the cassette tape.

The program which follows will be an invaluable aid in assisting you to keep the mileage (miles per gallon) where it should be. You will be able to track the expenses, which will be valuable at tax time, and it can assist in keeping your expenses as low as possible in this time of rising gasoline prices.

There is a base of data which must be developed and which is subsequently modified to give you the record of your automobile performance.

```
10 CLS
20 FOR Z = 1 TO 7:PRINT:NEXT Z
30 PRINT TAB(10);"A U T O M O B I L E    P E R F O R M A N C E"
40 GOSUB 1950
50 CLS
60 INPUT "FIRST RUN (Y/N)";A$
70 IF A$ = "N" THEN 750
1950 FOR Z = 1 TO 1000:NEXT Z:RETURN
```

As the data is gathered, the assumption has been made that it is accurate. No edits are performed on the data, although some default options are used. The "first run" is to build the base of the data. If you have answered "N", then a zero base is assumed.

```
80 PRINT
90 INPUT "ENTER CURRENT MILEAGE";M
100 PRINT
110 PRINT "ENTER CURRENT MILES PER GALLON, IF KNOWN."
120 INPUT "15 MPG ASSUMED IF NO NUMBERS ARE ENTERED";C
130 IF C < 1 THEN C = 15
140 PRINT
150 INPUT "ENTER MILEAGE AT LAST TUNE-UP";T
160 PRINT
```

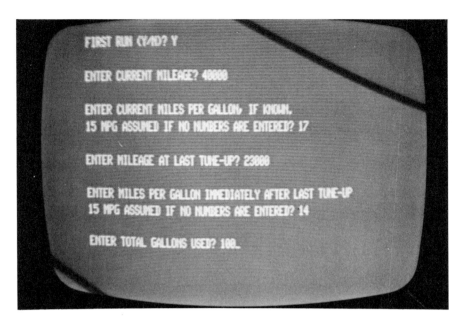

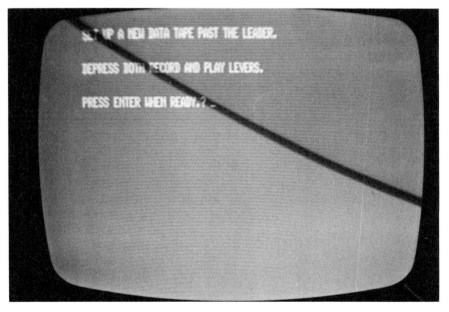

Figure 33.   Auto Maintenance Program

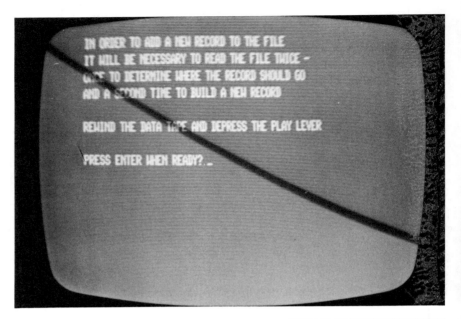

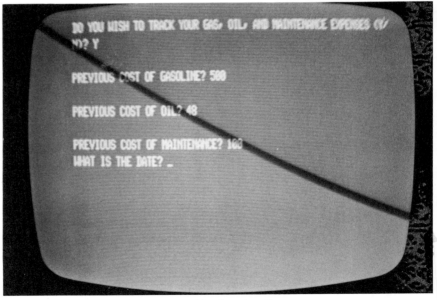

Figure 33. *(continued)*

```
170 PRINT "ENTER MILES PER GALLON IMMEDIATELY AFTER LAST TUNE-UP"
180 INPUT "15 MPG ASSUMED IF NO NUMBERS ARE ENTERED";L
190 IF L < 1 THEN L = 15
200 PRINT:INPUT "ENTER TOTAL GALLONS USED";U
210 CLS
220 INPUT "DO YOU WISH TO TRACK TIRE WEAR (Y/N)";A$
230 IF A$ < > "Y" THEN 270
240 PRINT
250 INPUT "ENTER MILES WHEN TIRES WERE INSTALLED";W
260 PRINT
270 PRINT "AT WHAT MILE PER GALLON RATE DO YOU WISH TO BE ALERTED"
280 INPUT "FOR THE NEED OF A TUNE-UP";N
290 CLS
300 INPUT "DO YOU WISH TO TRACK YOUR GAS, OIL, AND MAINTENANCE
    EXPENSES (Y/N)";A$
310 IF A$ < >"Y" THEN 360
320 PRINT
330 INPUT "PREVIOUS COST OF GASOLINE";G
340 PRINT:INPUT "PREVIOUS COST OF OIL";O
350 PRINT:INPUT "PREVIOUS COST OF MAINTENANCE";R
360 INPUT "WHAT IS THE DATE";B$
370 GOSUB 1500
1500 CLS
1510 PRINT "SET UP A NEW DATA TAPE PAST THE LEADER.":PRINT
1520 PRINT "DEPRESS BOTH RECORD AND PLAY LEVERS.":PRINT
1530 INPUT "PRESS ENTER WHEN READY.";A
1540 RETURN
```

Now the data file can be built:

```
380 REM "WRITE THE TAPE RECORD"
390 S = 0
400 GOSUB 1450
1450 S = S + 1
1460 PRINT #,S;",";C;",";G;",";L;",";M;",";N;",";O;",";R;",";T;",";
    U;",";W;",";B$
1470 RETURN
```

Note that the records receive a sequence number (S). This routine will then be cycled through until the decision is made to terminate the program:

```
410 CLS:PRINT "WHAT NEXT?":PRINT
420 PRINT TAB(5);"1.  MAKE A NEW ENTRY"
430 PRINT
440 PRINT TAB(5);"2.  TERMINATE PROGRAM"
450 PRINT:INPUT "WHICH";A
460 ON A GOTO 750,470:GOTO 410
```

When the decisions is made to terminate, this is how things are closed off:

```
470 X = 9999:GOSUB 1520
480 GOSUB 1910
1910 X = 9999:C = X:G = X:L = X:M = X:N = X
1920 O = X:R = X:T = X:U = X:W = X
1930 GOSUB 1450
1940 RETURN
```

And offer a summary:

```
490 CLS
500 INPUT "DO YOU WISH A SUMMARY (Y/N)";A$
510 IF A$ = "Y" THEN 540
520 CLS:PRINT "END OF AUTOMOBILE PERFORMANCE PROGRAM"
530 GOTO 530
```

Here's the routine to call the data back into memory:

```
540 GOSUB 1550
550 GOSUB 1480
560 IF (C = 9999) * (G = 9999) THEN 580
570 GOSUB 1590:GOTO 550
1550 CLS
1560 PRINT "REWIND THE DATA TAPE AND DEPRESS THE PLAY LEVER"
1570 PRINT:INPUT "PRESS ENTER WHEN READY";A
1580 RETURN
```

```
1480 INPUT #,S,C,G,L,M,N,O,R,T,U,W,B$
1490 RETURN
1590 PRINT "RECORD",S,,"DATE: ";B$
1600 PRINT "MILES: ",M
1610 PRINT "MILES PER GALLON",C
1620 PRINT "MILES LAST TUNE-UP",T
1630 Q = M - T
1640 PRINT "MILES SINCE TUNE-UP",Q
1650 PRINT "M.P.G. LAST TUNE-UP",L
1660 IF L > C PRINT "DECREASE"
1670 IF L < C PRINT "INCREASE"
1680 IF N > = C PRINT "TIME FOR A TUNE-UP"
1690 PRINT "TIRES INSTALLED AT ";W;"MILES"
1700 PRINT "TIRE WEAR ";M - W;"MILES"
1710 PRINT "COSTS THIS CYCLE:"
1720 PRINT TAB(5):"GASOLINE","$";G
1730 PRINT TAB(5);"OIL","$";O
1740 PRINT TAB(5);"MAINTENANCE","$";R
1750 PRINT TAB(5);"TOTAL GALLONS USED",U
1760 A(1) = M:A(101) = A(101) + M
1770 A(2) = C:A(102) = A(202) + C
1780 A(3) = T
1790 IF A(103) < A(3) THEN A(103) = A(3)
1800 A(4) = L
1810 IF A(104) < A(4) THEN A(104) = A(4)
1820 A(5) = W
1830 IF A(105) < A(5) THEN A(105) = A(5)
1840 A(6) = N
1850 IF A(106) < A(6) THEN A(106) = A(6)
1860 A(107) = A(107) + G
1870 A(108) = A(108) + Q
1880 A(109) = A(109) + R
1890 A(110) = A(110) + U
1900 RETURN
```

And then get the total:

```
580 CLS
590 PRINT "TOTAL MILES",A(101)
600 PRINT "TOTAL GALLONS",A(110)
610 Q = A(101) / A(110)
620 PRINT "AVERAGE MILES PER GALLON";Q
630 IF Q < A(106) PRINT "TUNE-UP NEEDED"
640 PRINT "TOTAL COST OF GAS","$";A(107)
650 PRINT "TOTAL COST OF OIL","$";A(108)
660 PRINT "TOTAL COST OF MAINTENANCE","$";A(109)
670 PRINT:PRINT "DO YOU WISH FOR THESE FIGURES TO BE"
680 PRINT "THE NEW BASE (Y/N)?"
690 INPUT A$:IF A$ <> "Y" THEN 520
700 PRINT "SORRY TO HAVE TO ASK YOU AGAIN,"
710 INPUT "BUT WHAT IS TODAY'S DATE";B$
720 S = 0:GOSUB 1450
730 GOSUB 1910
740 GOTO 520
```

If it is desired to build the file:

```
750 CLS
760 PRINT "IN ORDER TO ADD A NEW RECORD TO THE FILE"
770 PRINT "IT WILL BE NECESSARY TO READ THE FILE TWICE -"
780 PRINT "ONCE TO DETERMINE WHERE THE RECORD SHOULD GO"
790 PRINT "AND A SECOND TIME TO BUILD A NEW RECORD"
800 PRINT:GOSUB 1560
810 GOSUB 1480
820 IF (C = 9999) * (G = 9999) THEN 840
830 GOTO 810
840 S = S - 1
850 GOSUB 1550
860 FOR Z = 1 TO S
870     GOSUB 1480
880 NEXT Z
890 CLS
```

```
900 INPUT "ENTER CURRENT MILEAGE";M
910 IF M > A(101) THEN 950
920 PRINT "MILEAGE NOT GREATER THAN LAST RECORDING"
930 GOSUB 1950
940 GOTO 890
```

Note that the file is protected by not allowing an old record (lower mileage) to be entered.

And then select the additions you wish to make to the file.

```
950 C = 0:W = 0:G = 0:O = 0:R = 0:U = 0
960 CLS:PRINT "SELECT THE OPTION YOU WISH:"
970 PRINT:PRINT "1.  GASOLINE PURCHASE"
980 PRINT:PRINT "2.  OIL PURCHASE"
990 PRINT:PRINT "3.  MAINTENANCE EXPENSES"
1000 PRINT:PRINT "4.  NEW TIRES"
1010 PRINT:PRINT "5.  TUNE-UP"
1020 PRINT:PRINT "6.  SUMMARY"
1030 PRINT:PRINT "7.  TERMINATE PROGRAM"
1040 ON A GOTO 1060,1120,1150,1180,1380,1260,1360
1050 GOTO 950
1060 CLS:PRINT "GASOLINE PURCHASE":PRINT
1070 INPUT "HOW MANY GALLONS";U:PRINT
1080 INPUT "HOW MUCH DID YOU PAY? $";G:PRINT
1090 INPUT "MORE OPTIONS (Y/N)";A$
1100 IF A$ = "Y" THEN 960
1110 GOSUB 1450:GOSUB 1910:GOTO 520
1120 CLS:PRINT "OIL PURCHASE":PRINT
1130 INPUT "HOW MUCH DID YOU PAY? $";O
1140 GOTO 1090
1150 CLS:PRINT "MAINTENANCE EXPENSES":PRINT
1160 INPUT "HOW MUCH DID YOU PAY? $";R
1170 GOTO 1090
1180 CLS:PRINT "AT WHAT MILES DID YOU INSTALL NEW TIRES?"
1190 INPUT A
1200 IF A > W THEN 1250
1210 PRINT "MILES ARE ILLOGICAL"
```

```
1220 PRINT "LAST TIRES WERE INSTALLED AT ";W;"MILES"
1230 PRINT "ENTRY REJECTED"
1240 GOSUB 1950:GOTO 960
1250 W = A:GOTO 960
```

Again, note the protections which have been programmed into the routines.

Finally, we come to a discussion of the summary. Note that it flags the tune-up when necessary, and does so quite explosively, by flashing. Instructions 1360-1440 are routines used in the coding, but held here for insertion:

```
1260 CLS:PRINT "YOU HAVE REQUESTED A SUMMARY":PRINT
1270 GOSUB 1520
1280 C = M / U
1290 IF C > N THEN 1350
1300 FOR Z = 1 TO 100
1310     PRINT "TUNE-UP REQUIRED"
1320     FOR B = 1 TO 500:NEXT B
1330     CLS
1340 NEXT Z
1350 GOSUB 1460:GOTO 540
1360 CLS:PRINT "YOU HAVE REQUESTED TERMINATION OF THE PROGRAM"
1370 GOSUB 1950:GOTO 470
1380 CLS:PRINT "AT WHAT MILES DID YOU HAVE A TUNE-UP?"
1390 INPUT A
1400 IF A > T THEN 1440
1410 PRINT "MILES ARE ILLOGICAL"
1420 PRINT "LAST TUNE-UP WAS DONE AT ";T;"MILES"
1430 GOSUB 1950:GOTO 960
1440 T = A:L = C:GOTO 960
```

The entire program follows. You can see the intent of the program, but if you decide to use it, give some serious consideration to a Level II disk system. This program will work for the purpose stated, but the tape cassette is *slow*!

```
10 CLS
20 FOR Z = 1 TO 7:PRINT:NEXT Z
```

```
30 PRINT TAB(10);"A U T O M O B I L E    P E R F O R M A N C E"
40 GOSUB 1950
50 CLS
60 INPUT "FIRST RUN (Y/N)";A$
70 IF A$ = "N" THEN 750
80 PRINT
90 INPUT "ENTER CURRENT MILEAGE";M
100 PRINT
110 PRINT "ENTER CURRENT MILES PER GALLON, IF KNOWN."
120 INPUT "15 MPG ASSUMED IF NO NUMBERS ARE ENTERED";C
130 IF C < 1 THEN C = 15
140 PRINT
150 INPUT "ENTER MILEAGE AT LAST TUNE-UP";T
160 PRINT
170 PRINT "ENTER MILES PER GALLON IMMEDIATELY AFTER LAST TUNE-UP"
180 INPUT "15 MPG ASSUMED IF NO NUMBERS ARE ENTERED";L
190 IF L < 1 THEN L = 15
200 PRINT:INPUT "ENTER TOTAL GALLONS USED";U
210 CLS
220 INPUT "DO YOU WISH TO TRACK TIRE WEAR (Y/N)";A$
230 IF A$ < > "Y" THEN 270
240 PRINT
250 INPUT "ENTER MILES WHEN TIRES WERE INSTALLED";W
260 PRINT
270 PRINT "AT WHAT MILE PER GALLON RATE DO YOU WISH TO BE ALERTED"
280 INPUT "FOR THE NEED OF A TUNE-UP";N
290 CLS
300 INPUT "DO YOU WISH TO TRACK YOUR GAS, OIL, AND MAINTENANCE
    EXPENSES (Y/N)";A$
310 IF A$<>"Y" THEN 360
320 PRINT
330 INPUT "PREVIOUS COST OF GASOLINE";G
340 PRINT:INPUT "PREVIOUS COST OF OIL";O
350 PRINT:INPUT "PREVIOUS COST OF MAINTENANCE";R
360 INPUT "WHAT IS THE DATE";B$
```

```
370 GOSUB 1500
380 REM "WRITE THE TAPE RECORD"
390 S = 0
400 GOSUB 1450
410 CLS:PRINT "WHAT NEXT?":PRINT
420 PRINT TAB(5);"1.  MAKE A NEW ENTRY"
430 PRINT
440 PRINT TAB(5);"2.  TERMINATE PROGRAM"
450 PRINT:INPUT "WHICH";A
460 ON A GOTO 750,470:GOTO 410
470 X = 9999:GOSUB 1520
480 GOSUB 1910
490 CLS
500 INPUT "DO YOU WISH A SUMMARY (Y/N)";A$
510 IF A$ = "Y" THEN 540
520 CLS:PRINT "END OF AUTOMOBILE PERFORMANCE PROGRAM"
530 GOTO 530
540 GOSUB 1550
550 GOSUB 1480
560 IF (C = 9999) * (G = 9999) THEN 580
570 GOSUB 1590:GOTO 550
580 CLS
590 PRINT "TOTAL MILES",A(101)
600 PRINT "TOTAL GALLONS",A(110)
610 Q = A(101) / A(110)
620 PRINT "AVERAGE MILES PER GALLON";Q
630 IF Q < A(106) PRINT "TUNE-UP NEEDED"
640 PRINT "TOTAL COST OF GAS","$";A(107)
650 PRINT "TOTAL COST OF OIL","$";A(108)
660 PRINT "TOTAL COST OF MAINTENANCE","$";A(109)
670 PRINT:PRINT "DO YOU WISH FOR THESE FIGURES TO BE"
680 PRINT "THE NEW BASE (Y/N)?"
690 INPUT A$:IF A$ <> "Y" THEN 520
700 PRINT "SORRY TO HAVE TO ASK YOU AGAIN,"
710 INPUT "BUT WHAT IS TODAY'S DATE";B$
720 S = 0:GOSUB 1450
```

```
730 GOSUB 1910
740 GOTO 520
750 CLS
760 PRINT "IN ORDER TO ADD A NEW RECORD TO THE FILE"
770 PRINT "IT WILL BE NECESSARY TO READ THE FILE TWICE -"
780 PRINT "ONCE TO DETERMINE WHERE THE RECORD SHOULD GO"
790 PRINT "AND A SECOND TIME TO BUILD A NEW RECORD"
800 PRINT:GOSUB 1560
810 GOSUB 1480
820 IF (C = 9999) * (G = 9999) THEN 840
830 GOTO 810
840 S = S - 1
850 GOSUB 1550
860 FOR Z = 1 TO S
870     GOSUB 1480
880 NEXT Z
890 CLS
900 INPUT "ENTER CURRENT MILEAGE";M
910 IF M > A(101) THEN 950
920 PRINT "MILEAGE NOT GREATER THAN LAST RECORDING"
930 GOSUB 1950
940 GOTO 890
950 C = 0:W = 0:G = 0:O = 0:R = 0:U = 0
960 CLS:PRINT "SELECT THE OPTION YOU WISH:"
970 PRINT:PRINT "1.  GASOLINE PURCHASE"
980 PRINT:PRINT "2.  OIL PURCHASE"
990 PRINT:PRINT "3.  MAINTENANCE EXPENSES"
1000 PRINT:PRINT "4.  NEW TIRES"
1010 PRINT:PRINT "5.  TUNE-UP"
1020 PRINT:PRINT "6.  SUMMARY"
1030 PRINT:PRINT "7.  TERMINATE PROGRAM"
1040 ON A GOTO 1060,1120,1150,1180,1380,1260,1360
1050 GOTO 950
1060 CLS:PRINT "GASOLINE PURCHASE":PRINT
1070 INPUT "HOW MANY GALLONS";U:PRINT
1080 INPUT "HOW MUCH DID YOU PAY? $";G:PRINT
```

```
1090 INPUT "MORE OPTIONS (Y/N)";A$
1100 IF A$ = "Y" THEN 960
1110 GOSUB 1450:GOSUB 1910:GOTO 520
1120 CLS:PRINT "OIL PURCHASE":PRINT
1130 INPUT "HOW MUCH DID YOU PAY? $";O
1140 GOTO 1090
1150 CLS:PRINT "MAINTENANCE EXPENSES":PRINT
1160 INPUT "HOW MUCH DID YOU PAY? $";R
1170 GOTO 1090
1180 CLS:PRINT "AT WHAT MILES DID YOU INSTALL NEW TIRES?"
1190 INPUT A
1200 IF A > W THEN 1250
1210 PRINT "MILES ARE ILLOGICAL"
1220 PRINT "LAST TIRES WERE INSTALLED AT ";W;"MILES"
1230 PRINT "ENTRY REJECTED"
1240 GOSUB 1950:GOTO 960
1250 W = A:GOTO 960
1260 CLS:PRINT "YOU HAVE REQUESTED A SUMMARY":PRINT
1270 GOSUB 1520
1280 C = M / U
1290 IF C > N THEN 1350
1300 FOR Z = 1 TO 100
1310     PRINT "TUNE-UP REQUIRED"
1320     FOR B = 1 TO 500:NEXT B
1330     CLS
1340 NEXT Z
1350 GOSUB 1460:GOTO 540
1360 CLS:PRINT "YOU HAVE REQUESTED TERMINATION OF THE PROGRAM"
1370 GOSUB 1950:GOTO 470
1380 CLS:PRINT "AT WHAT MILES DID YOU HAVE A TUNE-UP?"
1390 INPUT A
1400 IF A > T THEN 1440
1410 PRINT "MILES ARE ILLOGICAL"
1420 PRINT "LAST TUNE-UP WAS DONE AT ";T;"MILES"
1430 GOSUB 1950:GOTO 960
1440 T = A:L = C:GOTO 960
```

```
1450 S = S + 1
1460 PRINT #,S;",";C;",";G;",";L;",";M;",",,"N;",";O;",";R;",";R;",";
     U;",";W;",";B$
1470 RETURN
1480 INPUT #,S,C,G,L,M,N,O,R,T,U,W,B$
1490 RETURN
1500 CLS
1510 PRINT "SET UP A NEW DATA TAPE PAST THE LEADER.":PRINT
1520 PRINT "DEPRESS BOTH RECORD AND PLAY LEVERS.":PRINT
1530 INPUT "PRESS ENTER WHEN READY.";A
1540 RETURN
1550 CLS
1560 PRINT "REWIND THE DATA TAPE AND DEPRESS THE PLAY LEVER"
1570 PRINT:INPUT "PRESS ENTER WHEN READY";A
1580 RETURN
1590 PRINT "RECORD",S,,"DATE: ";B$
1600 PRINT "MILES: ",M
1610 PRINT "MILES PER GALLON",C
1620 PRINT "MILES LAST TUNE-UP",T
1630 Q = M - T
1640 PRINT "MILES SINCE TUNE-UP",Q
1650 PRINT "M.P.G. LAST TUNE-UP",L
1660 IF L > C PRINT "DECREASE"
1670 IF L > C PRINT "INCREASE"
1680 IF N > = C PRINT "TIME FOR A TUNE-UP"
1690 PRINT "TIRES INSTALLED AT ";W;"MILES"
1700 PRINT "TIRE WEAR ";M - W;"MILES"
1710 PRINT "COSTS THIS CYCLE:"
1720 PRINT TAB(5):"GASOLINE","$";G
1730 PRINT TAB(5);"OIL","$";O
1740 PRINT TAB(5);"MAINTENANCE","$";R
1750 PRINT TAB(5);"TOTAL GALLONS USED",U
1760 A(1) = M:A(101) = A(101) + M
1770 A(2) = C:A(102) = A(202) + C
1780 A(3) = T
1790 IF A(103) < A(3) THEN A(103) = A(3)
```

```
1800 A(4) = L
1810 IF A(104) < A(4) THEN A(104) = A(4)
1820 A(5) = W
1830 IF A(105) < A(5) THEN A(105) = A(5)
1840 A(6) = N
1850 IF A(106) < A(6) THEN A(106) = A(6)
1860 A(107) = A(107) + G
1870 A(108) = A(108) + Q
1880 A(109) = A(109) + R
1890 A(110) = A(110) + U
1900 RETURN
1910 X = 9999:C = X:G = X:L = X:M = X:N = X
1920 O = X:R = X:T = X:U = X:W = X
1930 GOSUB 1450
1940 RETURN
1950 FOR Z = 1 TO 1000:NEXT Z:RETURN
```

HI, THERE!

The two programs which follow are just for fun. You may gain some enjoyment from them.

The first is a picture, produced by graphics. It happens that this program was the very first graphics program the author wrote after obtaining his TRS-80. As it is written, it makes great use of the SET and RESET commands. If the author were to write this program today, he would make great use of READ X, Y and place coordinates into DATA lines.

So why present it now? Because it works, it draws one of America's best known cartoon characters, and the kids enjoy seeing it. It also serves to demonstrate some of the techniques to which you must resort to compress a program.

Before looking at it, a Level I/Level II capability comparison should be made. Level I has "wrap-around" capability on the screen. That is, you can run a graphics line off the right side of the screen and it will reappear at the left side. The same is true of top and bottom. Thus, under Level I you can execute a SET (X, Y) command with Y having a value of above 47 or below 0 and it will work. This is useful when doing a multiple-line graphics drawing, as is used in the following program. But it won't work in Level II, so to get the program to work it was necessary to add instructions.

Under normal circumstances this would make no difference—except that the last PRINT MEM command showed a balance of only 8 bytes—after all

the compression had been done! Therefore, from the following coding, adjustments will have to be made:
   Statement 40:

Change 48 to 127
Change Z to X

   Remove 100-120
   This program will not be broken up. It is presented in full. Discussion will follow the program:

```
10 GOTO140
20 X=0:Y=127:Z=47
30 PRINT AT 620,"HI, THERE!";
40 FOR N=1TO48:SET(X,0):SET(0,Z)
50 IFZ<=-1GOTO70
60 SET(127,Z)
70 SET(Y,47)
80 X=X+1:Y=Y-1:Z=Z-1
90 NEXT N
100 FOR N = 1 TO 127
110    SET (N,0):SET (N,47)
120 NEXT N
130 GOTO 130
140 CLS:X=20:Y=0:A=98
150 FORZ=1TO10
160 FORN=1TO48:SET(X,Y):SET(A,Y)
170 SET(X+10,Y):SET(A-10,Y)
180 SET(X+20,Y):SET(A-20,Y)
190 SET(X+30,Y):SET(A-30,Y)
200 Y=Y+1:NEXTN
210 X=X+1:Y=0:A=A-1:NEXTZ
220 FORX=20TO98:RESET(X,Y):NEXTX:Y=1
230 FORX=20TO98:RESET(X,Y):NEXTX
240 A=20:B=98:Y=2
250 FORX=ATO30:RESET(X,Y):NEXTX
260 FORX=49TO61:RESET(X,Y):NEXTX
```

```
270 FORX=82TOB:RESET(X,Y):NEXTX:Y=3
280 FORX=ATO29:RESET(X,Y):NEXTX
290 FORX=51TO54:RESET(X,Y):NEXTX
300 FORX=88TOB:RESET(X,Y):NEXTX:Y=4
310 FORX=ATO27:RESET(X,Y):NEXTX
320 FORX=90TOB:RESET(X,Y):NEXTX:Y=5
330 GOSUB1380
340 FORX=90TOB:RESET(X,Y):NEXTX:Y=6
350 GOSUB 1370
360 FORX=93TOB:RESET(X,Y):NEXTX:Y=7
370 GOSUB1370
380 FORX=88TOB:RESET(X,Y):NEXTX:Y=8
390 GOSUB1380
400 FORX=90TOB:RESET(X,Y):NEXTX:RESET(34,Y):Y=9
410 FORX=ATO33:RESET(X,Y):NEXTX:RESET(34,Y)
420 FORX=70TO72:RESET(X,Y):NEXTX
430 FORX=87TOB:RESET(X,Y):NEXTX:Y=10
440 FORX=ATO33:RESET(X,Y):NEXTX:RESET(40,Y)
450 FORX=72TO84:RESET(X,Y):NEXTX:Y=11
460 FORX=ATO33:RESET(X,Y):NEXTX:RESET(40,Y):RESET(93,Y)
470 FORX=72TO84:RESET(X,Y):NEXTX:Y=12
480 FORX=ATO39:RESET(X,Y):NEXTX:RESET(49,Y)
490 FORX=64TO69:RESET(X,Y):NEXTX
500 FORX=76TO80:RESET(X,Y):NEXTX
510 FORX=86TO88:RESET(X,Y):NEXTX
520 FORX=93TOB:RESET(X,Y):NEXTX:Y=13
530 FORX=ATO39:RESET(X,Y):NEXTX
540 FORX=84TOB:RESET(X,Y):NEXTX
550 FORX=43TO46:RESET(X,Y):NEXTX
560 FORX=66TO68:RESET(X,Y):NEXTX
570 FORX=77TO79:RESET(X,Y):NEXTX:Y=14
580 FORX=ATO38:RESET(X,Y):NEXTX
590 FORX=83TO85:RESET(X,Y):NEXTX:RESET(78,Y):RESET(81,Y)
600 FORX=84TOB:RESET(X,Y):NEXTX:Y=15
610 FORX=ATO37:RESET(X,Y):NEXTX:RESET(62,Y):RESET(67,Y)
620 FORX=84TOB:RESET(X,Y):NEXTX:Y=16
```

```
630 FORX=ATO37:RESET(X,Y):NEXTX:RESET(62,Y):RESET(67,Y)
640 FORX=84TOB:RESET(X,Y):NEXTX:Y=17
650 FORX=ATO36:RESET(X,Y):NEXTX:RESET(63,Y)
660 FORX=74TO81:RESET(X,Y)NEXTX
670 FORX=84TOB:RESET(X,Y)NEXTX:Y=18
680 FORX=ATO34:RESET(X,Y):NEXTX
690 FORX=47TO50:RESET(X,Y):NEXTX
700 FORX=89TOB:RESET(X,Y):NEXTX:RESET(69,Y):Y=19
710 FORX=ATO33:RESET(X,Y):NEXTX:RESET(45,Y)
720 FORX=89TOB:RESET(X,Y):NEXTX:Y=20
730 FORX=ATO32:RESET(X,Y):NEXTX:RESET(44,Y)
740 FORX=88TOB:RESET(X,Y):NEXTX:Y=21
750 FORX=ATO31:RESET(X,Y):NEXTX:RESET(44,Y):RESET(49,Y)
760 FORX=87TOB:RESET(X,Y):NEXTX:Y=22
770 FORX=ATO30:RESET(X,Y):NEXTX
780 FORX=86TOB:RESET(X,Y):NEXTX:Y=23
790 FORX=ATO29:RESET(X,Y):NEXTX:RESET(46,Y):RESET(68,Y)
800 FORX=85TOB:RESET(X,Y):NEXTX:Y=24
810 FORX=ATO28:RESET(X,Y):NEXTX:RESET(48,Y):RESET(49,Y)
820 FORX=70TOB:RESET(X,Y):NEXTX:Y=25
830 FORX=ATO28:RESET(X,Y):NEXTX:RESET(71,Y):RESET(72,Y)
840 FORX=80TOB:RESET(X,Y):NEXTX:Y=26
850 FORX=ATO27:RESET(X,Y):NEXTX:RESET(72,Y)
860 FORX=82TOB:RESET(X,Y):NEXTX:Y=27
870 GOSUB1380:RESET(72,Y)
880 FORX+82TOB:RESET(X,Y):NEXTX:Y=28
890 GOSUB1370:RESET(73,Y)
900 FORX=83:TOB:RESET(X,Y):NEXTX:Y=29
910 GOSUB 1370:RESET(74,Y)
920 FORX=84TOB:RESET(X,Y):NEXTX:Y=30
930 GOSUB1370:RESET(75,Y)
940 FORX=85TOB:RESET(X,Y):NEXTX:Y=31
950 FORX=ATO24:RESET(X,Y):NEXTX:RESET(76,Y)
960 FORX=86TOB:RESET(X,Y):NEXTX:Y=32
970 FORX=24TO25:RESET(X,Y):NEXTX
980 FORX=56TO60:RESET(X,Y):NEXTX
```

```
99Ø FORX=87TOB:RESET(X,Y):NEXTX:Y=33:RESET(2Ø,Y)
1ØØØ FORX=64TO77:RESET(X,Y):NEXTX:RESET(58,Y)
1Ø1Ø FORX=88TOB:Y=34
1Ø2Ø FORX=ATO23:RESET(X,Y):NEXTX:RESET(32,Y):RESET(33,Y)
1Ø3Ø RESET(6Ø,Y):RESET(61,Y)
1Ø4Ø FORX=88TO96:RESET(X,Y):NEXTX:Y=35
1Ø5Ø FORX=ATO23:RESET(X,Y):NEXTX:RESET(33,Y):RESET(34,Y)
1Ø6Ø RESET(63,Y):RESET(64,Y)
1Ø7Ø FORX=88TO94:RESET(X,Y):NEXTX:Y=36
1Ø8Ø FORX=96TOB:RESET(X,Y-1):NEXTX
1Ø9Ø GOSUB137Ø
11ØØ FORX=37TO4Ø:RESET(X,Y):NEXTX:RESET(66,Y):RESET(67,Y)
111Ø FORX=95TOB:RESET(X,Y):NEXTX
112Ø FORX=87TO89:RESET(X,Y):NEXTX:Y=37
113Ø FORX=ATO27:RESET(X,Y):NEXTX
114Ø FORX=41TO43:RESET(X,Y):NEXTX
115Ø FORX=68TO69:RESET(X,Y):NEXTX:RESET(86,Y)
116Ø FORX=94TOB:RESET(X,Y):NEXTX:Y=38
117Ø FORX=ATO29:RESET(X,Y):NEXTX
118Ø FORX=45TO47:RESET(X,Y):NEXTX:RESET(85,Y)
119Ø FORX=93TOB:RESET(X,Y):NEXTX:Y=39
12ØØ FORX=ATO31:RESET(X,Y):NEXTX
121Ø FORX=49TO51:RESET(X,Y):NEXTX:RESET(84,Y)
122Ø FORX=92TOB:RESET(X,Y):NEXTX:Y=4Ø
123Ø FORX=ATO33:RESET(X,Y):NEXTX:RESET(83,Y)
124Ø FORX=53TO55:RESET(X,Y):NEXTX
125Ø FORX=91TOB:RESET(X,Y):NEXTX:Y=41
126Ø FORX=ATO35:RESET(X,Y):NEXTX:RESET(82,Y)
127Ø FORX=56TO59:RESET(X,Y):NEXTX
128Ø FORX=9ØTOB:RESET(X,Y):NEXTX:Y=42
129Ø FORX=ATO36:RESET(X,Y):NEXTX
13ØØ FORX=61TO63:RESET(X,Y):NEXTX:RESET(81,Y)
131Ø FORX=89TOB:RESET(X,Y):NEXTX:Y=43
132Ø FORX=ATO98:RESET(X,Y):NEXTX
133Ø Y=Y+3
```

```
1340 IFY>47GOTO1360
1350 GOTO1320
1360 GOTO20
1370 FORX=ATO25:RESET(X,Y):NEXTX:RETURN
1380 FORX=ATO26:RESET(X,Y):NEXTX:RETURN
```

This program throws a curve. It doesn't CLS at 10, it just goes to 140—but it does CLS there. The construction is made in this manner so that it can be easily made to be self-repeating, by removing statement 130.

At 140 the screen is "painted." But this time, it's done a little unusually. Only that portion of the screen which falls between X-Axis positions 20 and 98 is painted—and that is done in eight sections, each increasing in size until they merge. They are painted top-to-bottom for a width of ten. Why only 20 to ninety-eight? That's all that is needed to build the block of light from which the cartoon will be "carved."

From that point on to nearly the end of the program, selective positions are turned off via RESET until the picture is complete. A pattern cannot be explained in text, but it was done with careful planning and with some meticulous video worksheet work, and finally a frame was drawn.

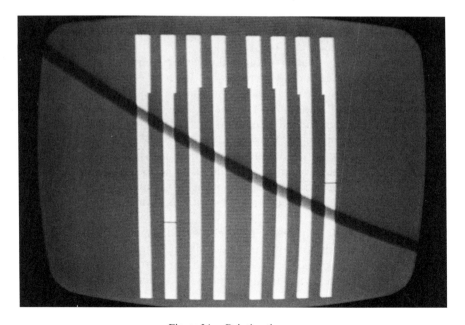

Figure 34.   Painting the screen

As has been previously stated, if the program were written on the basis of lessons learned in this book, it would have been done with DATA statements and X, Y coordinates. But it is a fun program and a good way to demonstrate your TRS-80 to your friends.

The TRS-80 software market has really grown since the release of the device, and many publications about the device have come and gone. Amongst the offerings, you'll find many practical programs, such as have been offered here. You'll also find a considerable number of games. It takes a special kind of person to develop a computerized game—some insight into the process will be shared in the next chapter.

One of these publications is known as CLOAD Magazine. CLOAD Magazine is a monthly tape distribution from that organization, located at Box 1267, Galeta, CA 93017. Clyde, whose picture adorns the cover, is their mascot.

Did you know that you can use your TRS-80 to produce music? There are several music-oriented applications, including some from Radio Shack. The following program, JUKEBOX, appeared in CLOAD Magazine in 1978 and is reprinted here with their permission. The program is presented exactly as written in Level I shorthand.

How does it work? That's easy to answer. *Why* it works is another matter entirely. The program works on the basis that the keyboard generates a radio frequency signal (RF) of sufficient magnitude to be detected by a standard AM radio receiver. It also effects the FM band in places and produces snow on TV Channel 3.

Since RF can be varied to oscillate at differing frequencies, it's a function of determining what codes generate what tones. "A" above "Middle C" oscillates at 44 hertz, for instance. The whole musical scale can be duplicated on a range of about 50 to 5000 hertz. Of course, you can't hear much above 3000 hertz (standard telephone speech audio frequency), but it is capable of producing to 5000 hertz.

In any event, the author learned what codes to use and how to calculate the timing of the musical notes, and the result is a Jukebox with six songs. We won't guarantee that this works, but the program is as we copied it from the screen, after having been treated to a rendition of "Oh My Darling Clementine."

The use of a radio to monitor program loading is not a bad idea anyway. If you've had the opportunity to listen to what the program tape sounds like, then you can appreciate what the radio can do to assist you, particularly if you're trying to load a tape and are having difficulty doing it.

Here's the program:

```
1 U=.6:G.310
10 F.K=1T012*L
11 A=12-12+1
12 N.K:RET.
15 F.K=1T013*L
16 A=A-1+10
17 N.K:RET.
20 F.K=1T014*L
21 A=A-A+123456
22 N.K:RET.
25 F.K=1T015*1
26 A=A-A+12
27 N.K:RET.
30 F.K=1T016*L
31 A=1+1
32 N.K:RET.
40 F.K=1T017*L
41 A=A+111
42 N.K:RET.
45 F.K=1T018*L
46 A=00000000
47 N.K:RET
50 F.K=1T019*L
51 A=A-A
52 N.K:RET.
55 F.K=1T020*L
56 A=111
57 N.K:RET.
60 F.K=1T021*L
61 A=11:N.K:RET
65 F.K=1T022*L:A=1:N.K:RET.
70 F.K=1T023*L
71 A=A
```

```
72 N.K:RET.
110 F.K=1TO24*L:A$="":REM
112 N.K:RET.
115 F.K+1TO26*L
116 A$="COUNTERPOINT"
117 N.K:RET.
120 F.K=1TO28*L
121 A$="CLOAD***MAGAZINE"
122 N.K:RET.
130 F.K=1TO32*L
131 A$=E
132 N.K:RET.
140 F.K=1TO34*L:A$=
141 N.K:RET.
310 V=U+U:W=V+V:X=W+W:Y=X+X:S=U+V:T=V+W:Q=W+X
320 C.:P.AT970;"(PLACE AM-RADIO NEAR SPACE-BAR ON KEYBOARD)";
400 P.AT84;"TRS-80 JUKEBOX"
410 P.:P."1)MICHAEL ROW THE BOAT ASHORE"
420 P."2)MARINES HYMN":P."3)CLEMENTINE":P."4)OH SUSANNAH"
430 P."5)SILENT NIGHT":P."6)THE SOUND OF SILENCE"
490 P.:I."NUMBER";A:P.AT640
495 IF (A < 1)+(A > 6)T.320
500 P.AT160+64*A;"₫₫₫NOW PLAYING";
510 ONAGOS.999,2000,3000,4000,5000,6000:G.320
999 F.R=1TO2
1010 L=W:GOS.10:GOS.30:L=T:GOS.50:L=V:GOS.30:GOS.50:L=T:GOS:60
1020 L=X:GOS.50:L=W:GOS.30:GOS50:L=Y:GOS.60:L=X:GOS.50
1030 L=V:GOS.30:L=T:GOS.50:GOS.50:L=V:GOS.30:GOS.40:L=T:GOS.30
1040 L=X:GOS.20:L=W:GOS.10:GOS.20:L=X:GOS.30:GOS.20:GOS.10:N.R
1050 L=V:GOS.15:L=T:GOS.40:GOS.55:L=V:GOS.40:GOS.55:L=T:GOS.65
1060 L=X:GOS.55:L=W:GOS.115:GOS.110:L=Y:GOS.65:L=X:GOS.55
1100 L=V:GOS.40:L=V+W:GOS.55:GOS.55:L=V:GOS.40:GOS.45
1110 L=T:GOS.40:L=X:GOS.25:L=W:GOS.15:GOS.25
1120 GOS.40:GOS.55:L=V:GOS.65:L=T:GOS.110:L=X:GOS.115:RET.
2000 F.R=1TO4:ONRGOS.2010,2010,2050,2010:N.R:RET.
```

```
2010 L=S.GOS.10:L=U:GOS.30:L=W:F.I=1TO4:GOS.50:N.I
2020 L=T:GOS.50:L=V:GOS.110:L=W:GOS.50
2030 L=S:GOS.30:L=U:GOS.40:L=W:GOS.50:GOS.50:L=V:GOS.40:L=T
2040 GOS.20:L=W+X:GOS.10:RET.
2050 L=S:GOS.110:L=U:GOS.70:L=W:GOS.60:GOS.40:GOS.60:GOS.110
2060 L=T:GOS.50:L=V:GOS.30:L=W:GOS.50
2070 L=S:GOS.110:L=U:GOS.70:L=W:GOS.60:GOS.40
2080 L=V:GOS.60:L=T:GOS.110:L=W+X:GOS.50:RET.
3000 F.R=1TO2:L=S:GOS.40:L=U:GOS.40:L=W:GOS.40:GOS.10:L=S:GOS.60
3020 L=U:GOS.60:L=W:GOS.60:GOS.40:L=S:GOS.40:L=U:GOS.60
3030 L=T:GOS.110:L=V:GOS.110:L=S:GOS.65:L=U:GOS.60:L=X:GOS.50
3040 L=S.GOS.50:L=U:OGS.60:L=W:GOS.65:GOS.65:L=S:GOS.60:L=U
3050 GOS.50:L=W:GOS.60:GOS.40:L=S:GOS.40:L=U:GOS.60:L=T:GOS.50
3060 L=V:GOS.10:L=S:GOS.30:L=U:GOS.50:L=X:GOS.40:N.R:RET.
4000 F.R=1TO7:ONRGOS.4010,4040,4010,4050,4060,4010,4050:N.R:RET.
4010 L=U:GOS.50:GOS.60:L=V:GOS.70:GOS.120
4020 L=S:GOS.120:L=U:GOS.130:L=V:GOS.120:GOS.70
4030 L=S:GOS.50:L=U:GOS.60:L=V:GOS.70:GOS.70
4035 L=(U+V)/2:GOS.60:L=V:RET.
4040 GOS.50:L=T:GOS.60:RET.
4050 GOS.60:L=X:GOS.50:RET.
4060 L=W:GOS.110:GOS.110:L=V:GOS.130:L=W:GOS.130:L=V:F.N=1TO5
4070 ONNGOS.130,120,120,70,50:N.N:L=T:GOS.60:RET.
5000 F.R=1TO2:L=T:GOS.50:L=V:GOS.60:L=W:GOS.50:L=Q:GOS.30:N.R
5020 L=X:GOS.120:L=W:GOS.120:L=Q:GOS.70:L=X:GOS.110:L=W
5030 GOS.110:L=Q:GOS.50:F.R=1TOZ:L=X:GOS.60:L=W:GOS.60:L=T
5040 GOS.110:L=V:GOS.70:L=W:GOS.60:L=T:GOS.50:L=V:GOS.60:L=W
5050 GOS.50:L=Q:GOS.30:N.R:L=X:GOS.120:L=W:GOS.120:L=T:GOS.140
5060 L=V:GOS.120:L=W:GOS.70:L=Q:GOS.110:GOS.130:L=W:GOS.110
5070 GOS.50:GOS.30:L=T:GOS.50:L=V:GOS.40:L=W:GOS.20
5080 L=Q+X:GOS.10:RET.
6000 F.P=1TO2:L=V:F.N=1TO6:ONNGOS.20,20,40,40,60,60:N.N:L=Y:GOS.50
6030 L=V:F.N=1TO8:ONNGOS.10,10,10,30,30,50,50,40,:N.N:L=Y-V
6040 GOS.20:F.R=1TO2:L=V:F.N=1TO7:ONNGOS.40,40,40,60,60,110,110
6050 N.N:L=W:GOS.120:L=V:GOS:120:L=Q:GOS.110:N.R
```

```
6060  L=V:GOS.40:GOS.40:GOS.120:L=T+W:GOS.120:L=V:GOS.120:GOS.130
6070  GOS.140:L=T:GOS.140:L=V:GOS.130:L=T:GOS.120:L=Q:GOS.110
6080  L=V:GOS.120:GOS.110:L=Y:GOS.60:L=V:GOS.40:GOS.40:GOS:40:L=Q
6080  GOS.110:L=V:GOS.30:GOS.40:L=Y:GOS.20:N.P:RET.
```

7
Using the Computer to Play Games

Wherever you see a TRS-80 being demonstrated, it's likely that you'll see a game in progress. Radio Shack, in fact, distributes two games with the device—Blackjack and Backgammon.

By and large, computer games are the product of very intelligent minds which have little productive work to do, at least that is so with TRS-80. That statement is made with tongue in cheek, as it is recognized that the amount of work involved to get a complicated game working on nearly any computer far exceeds the scope of anything which is presented in this book. The building of a game of chess, for instance, is no simple task, and it is the type of intellectual challenge that appeals to a special group of people.

Games are a good demonstration tool for any computer which has a CRT display. They attract young people, they're easy for the salesperson to demonstrate, and they're *fun*. Practical? That's another matter. Games are a worthwhile diversion for the computer owner, but not really sufficient justification alone for the purchase of the computer.

Use of the computer for playing games provides intellectual challenge and diversion. From a variety of sources you can purchase game software—chess, checkers, Othello, Star Trek, Hunt the Wumpus, Dungeon, Troll's Gold, and many, many more.

No attempt will be made to present very complex games here. The interest is to demonstrate an approach to building a game application. In so doing, perhaps your creativity will be stirred and you might wish to attempt to build a game by yourself.

There is a variety of games you can build or buy, although it is not always easy to classify a game because many contain one or more of the elements contained below:

- Games of chance—card games, dice games—any game wherein random selection may be made. This is the type of game which is demonstrated after a fashion by the horse race shown earlier in the book.
- Games of chance and skill—some card games, normally random chance games, also involve some skill. For instance, contrast a game of five-card stud, where you take just the five cards dealt to you, with any other similar game—deuces wild, seven-card draw, etc. In these instances, there is the option to discard, compound bets, etc. These are more complicated to construct.
- Games of strategy—nearly any board game falls into this category. Most certainly chess is such a game, and far beyond the scope of this book. Board games such as checkers and Othello are on the market. There are blind games, or semiblind games, such as Battleship or Hunt the Wumpus.
- Simulation games—these are the "what will happen if . . ." games. Included in these is Hammurabi, wherein you become the ruler of Babylon and are required to manage the land, people, and food resources.
- Games of intellect—these may be considered to be educational in nature. Included in these are spelling bees, mathematics drills, exercises in deductive reasoning.
- Games to kill time—tic-tac-toe can be included here, and one such game will be attempted in this chapter. Included also in this category might be the "combat" games, wherein the player battles spacemen, pirates, or monsters.

SLOT MACHINE

With thanks to Mr. Don Kidd of Caesar's Palace, Las Vegas, Nevada, for his assistance, the first project to be undertaken will be a computerized slot machine.

If you've ever played a slot machine, you know that:

- It costs money to play. Fictitious money will be used here, of course, and this will be a dollar machine.
- There are a variety of symbols on the wheels. According to Mr. Kidd, they include cherries, bells, oranges, plums, dollar signs, bars, sevens, and lemons. For the purpose of the program, an additional two items will be used, pears and clocks. These symbols appear on each of the three "wheels" of the slot machine. Unlike the slot machine itself, however, the items will not be colorful and will not travel from top to bottom. The program is constructed to provide consciousness of movement.

According to Mr. Kidd, payoff methods vary with the type of slot machine, and there is no set formula. Likewise, the items which produce payoffs vary from machine to machine. On some machines, the seven produces the jackpot, while on others the bars produce the jackpot. For the purposes of this illustration, the bars will be used. In this application, there are three types of payoff:

- Jackpot, in which the entire money contents of the slot machine are dumped in your lap. Sorry, but the TRS-80 doesn't have an alarm to let everyone know you've hit it, but then you don't have to pick up all that messy money, either. The jackpot will be stocked with one thousand dollars.
- Three of a kind, or minijackpot payoff on three of a kind will pay ten dollars.
- Two of a kind, in any two positions, will pay five dollars.

In order to "favor the house," the player will not be allowed to hit a second jackpot until the machine has acquired at least $500, and if you have a statistical background, you're aware of the following "odds:"

- Hitting the jackpot—.001 (1 in a thousand)—tests showed that the jackpot frequently hit in the 600 to 800 trial range.
- Hitting three of a kind—same odds as jackpot.
- Hitting two of a kind—.01 (1 in a hundred).

As stated, the machine is stocked with $1000. The player is also provided with $100 with which to play. The game ends when either the player runs out of money or it is decided to just stop playing. If you run out of money, the slot machine will have its $1000 plus your $100. You will then be allowed to "borrow" another $100 to continue to play, but the computer will be aware of the debt and once you have regained the outstanding debt plus $10, the computer will be paid back.

Here's what's on the wheel:

Position	Item
1	Bell
2	Cherry
3	Orange
4	Pear
5	Jackpot (Bar)
6	Plum

7	7's
8	Clock
9	Lemon
10	$'s

These are then placed in DATA lines, as follows:

```
9ØØØ DATA "BELLb̸b̸b̸b̸"
9Ø1Ø DATA "CHERRYb̸b̸"
9Ø2Ø DATA "ORANGEb̸b̸"
9Ø3Ø DATA "PEARb̸b̸b̸b̸"
9Ø4Ø DATA "JACKPOTb̸"
9Ø5Ø DATA "PLUMb̸b̸b̸b̸"
9Ø6Ø DATA "77777777"
9Ø7Ø DATA "CLOCKb̸b̸b̸"
9Ø8Ø DATA "LEMON b̸b̸b̸"
9Ø9Ø DATA "$$$$$$$$"
```

Variable S will be used for the amount of money in the machine:

```
1ØØ S = 1ØØØ
```

Variable P will represent the money given to the player:

```
11Ø P = 1ØØ
```

And the "borrow" account will be established for the player:

```
12Ø B = Ø
```

Variable A will be the utility variable and variable A$ will be used to obtain the descriptor from the DATA statements, when that time comes. Initially, however, the program concentrates upon the selection, matching, and displaying of numbers. Here's where it begins:

```
2ØØ CLS
21Ø FOR N = 1TO8:PRINT:NEXT N
22Ø PRINT TAB(2Ø);"S L O T   M A C H I N E"
23Ø FOR N = 1 TO 3:GOSUB 99ØØ:NEXT N
99ØØ FOR Z = 1 TO 1ØØØ:NEXT Z:RETURN
```

In the routine above, variable N is used for miscellaneous loop control and variable Z is used in a subroutine for time delay. Change the value at 9900 to lengthen or shorten the time, as necessary.

```
240 CLS
250 GOSUB 9910:PRINT
9910 PRINT "THE MACHINE NOW HOLDS $";S
9920 PRINT:PRINT "PLAYER'S ACCOUNT $";P
9930 PRINT:PRINT "BORROW ACCOUNT $";B
9950 RETURN *
```

Again, a subroutine has been used to indicate status. The game can now begin with a "roll:"

```
260 INPUT "PRESS ENTER TO 'PULL'";A:CLS
```

And now the game has begun. The first thing to do is to select three numbers at random:

```
270 J = RND(10)
280 J = INT(J)
290 IF J < 1 THEN 270
300 K = RND(10)
310 K = INT(K)
320 IF K < 1 THEN 300
330 L = RND(10)
340 L = INT(L)
350 IF L < 1 THEN 330
```

Above are three sets of three instructions. The first selects the number; the second ensures we are working with integers; and the third rejects any zeros or negative numbers.

And, by the way, it costs you $1 to play:

```
360 P = P - 1
370 S = S + 1
```

*An instruction will be added later.

Your dollar has been given to the machine. The next step is to show what has arrived on the wheels after the "pull." Before that is done, however, it is desired to create upon the screen the illusion of rolling the wheels. The computer already knows its answer, but the program will review the list on the screen. It won't be a "pure" roll, but will have some of the similarities:

```
380 RESTORE
390 FOR X = 1 TO 10
400     READ A$
410     PRINT AT 493, A$
420     PRINT AT 493, "ØBBBBBBB"
430     PRINT AT 473, A$
440     PRINT AT 473, "BBBBBBBB"
450     PRINT AT 453, A$
460     PRINT AT 453, "ØBBBBBBB"
470 NEXT X
```

Note: Statements 480-550 were found to slow the program down and were removed.

The next step, before proceeding, is to ensure that if a jackpot has been hit there is more than $500 in the machine. The three "wheels" are matched with a series of "and" commands:

```
560 IF (J=5) * (K=5) * (L=5) * (S > 500) THEN 590
570 IF (J=5) * (K=5) * (L=5) THEN 650
580 GOTO 750
590 GOSUB 9800
600 PRINT AT 605, "J A C K P O T"
610 GOSUB 9900
620 P = P + S:S = 0:P = P - B:B = 0
630 GOSUB 9910:GOSUB 9900
640 CLS:GOTO 260
650 GOSUB 9800
660 PRINT AT 605, "JACKPOT HIT - INSUFFICIENT FUNDS"
670 PRINT AT 669, "PAYING AS THREE OF A KIND"
680 P = P + 10:S = S - 10
690 IF P - B > 10 THEN 720
700 GOSUB 9910:GOSUB 9900
710 CLS:GOTO 260
```

```
720 P = P - B:B = 0:GOTO 700
9800 RESTORE:CLS
9810 FOR N = 1 TO L:READ A$
9820      PRINT AT 493, A$:NEXT N:RESTORE
9830 FOR N = 1 TO K:READ A$
9840      PRINT AT 473, A$:NEXT N: RESTORE
9850 FOR N = 1 TO J:READ A$
9860      PRINT AT 453, A$:NEXT N:RESTORE
9870 RETURN
```

At 560, if the jackpot has been hit *and* there is more than $500 in the machine, the computer advises the player (at 600), updates and displays the new totals, and repeats the process. If a jackpot has been hit and there is *not* more than $500, the player has been paid for three-of-a-kind (650 to 680). In both cases, settlement is made for any borrowed monies (720). If neither criteria is met, the evaluation process continues and will pick up again at 750. The subroutine at 9800 selects and displays where the "wheels" came to rest. The subroutine at 9910 displays the totals.

```
750 IF (J=K)*(J=L) THEN 900
760 IF (J=K)+(J=L)THEN 970
770 IF (K=J)+(K=L)THEN 970
780 IF (L=J)+(L=K)THEN 970
790 GOSUB 9800:GOSUB 9900
800 PRINT AT 669, "YOU LOSE"
810 GOSUB 9910:GOSUB 9900
820 IF P=0 THEN 840
830 GOTO 260
840 FOR N=1 TO 5:GOSUB 9900:NEXT N:
    CLS:PRINT "DO YOU WISH TO BORROW (Y/N)?"
850 PRINT:INPUT A$
860 IF A$ = "Y" THEN 890
870 PRINT:PRINT "GAME ENDED"
880 GOTO 880
890 P = P + 10:B = B + 10:GOSUB 9910:GOTO 260
900 GOSUB 9800:GOSUB 9900
910 PRINT AT 669, "THREE OF A KIND"
920 GOSUB 9900
```

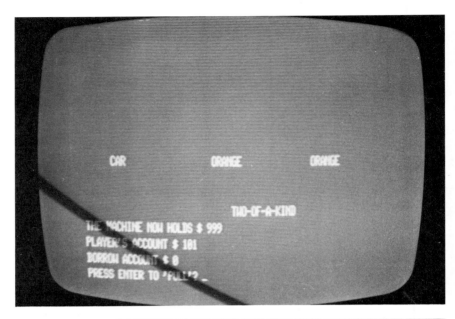

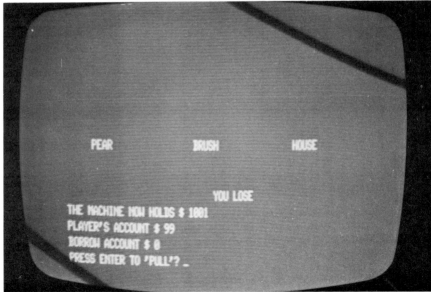

Figures 35 A and B.   Slot Machine Displays

With the jackpot situation handled, other kinds of payoffs can be checked and paid—three-of-a-kind and pairs. Also, if the player is out of money, he is offered the opportunity to borrow. If he accepts the borrowed money, he proceeds, if not, the game is ended:

```
930 S = S - 10:P = P + 10
940 IF P - B > 10 THEN 960
950 GOSUB 9910:GOTO 260
960 P = P - B:B = 0:GOTO 950
970 P = P + 5:S = S - 5
980 GOSUB 9800:GOSUB 9900
990 PRINT AT 669, "TWO OF A KIND"
1000 GOSUB 9910:GOSUB 9900
1010 IF P - B > 10 THEN 1030
1020 GOTO 260
1030 P = P - B:B = 0:GOTO 260
```

All that now remains is the insertion, in the subroutine beginning with 9910, of the end-of-game check:

```
9940 IF P = 0 THEN 840
```

And there you have it, a computerized slot machine with one definite advantage, you get to keep your shirt. The slot machine program is now reorganized and presented in its entirety.

```
100 S = 1000
110 P = 100
120 B = 0
200 CLS
210 FOR N = 1 TO 8:PRINT:NEXT N
220 PRINT TAB(20);"S L O T   M A C H I N E"
230 FOR N = 1 TO 3:GOSUB 9900:NEXT N
240 CLS
250 GOSUB 9910:PRINT
260 INPUT "PRESS ENTER TO 'PULL'";A:CLS
270 J = RND(10)
280 J = INT(J)
```

```
290 IF J < 1 THEN 270
300 K = RND(10)
310 K = INT(K)
320 IF K < 1 THEN 300
330 L = RND(10)
340 L = INT (L)
350 IF L < 1 THEN 330
360 P = P - 1
370 S = S + 1
380 RESTORE
390 FOR X = 1 TO 10
400     READ A$
410     PRINT AT 493,A$
420     PRINT AT 493,"ØØØØØØØØ"
430     PRINT AT 473,A$
440     PRINT AT 473,"ØØØØØØØØ"
450     PRINT AT 453,A$
460     PRINT AT 453,"ØØØØØØØØ"
470 NEXT X
```

Note: Statements 480-550 were found to slow the program down and were removed.

```
560 IF (J = 5) * (K = 5) * (L = 5) * (S > 500) THEN 590
570 IF (J = 5) * (K = 5) * (L = 5) THEN 650
580 GOTO 750
590 GOSUB 9800
600 PRINT AT 605, "J A C K P O T"
610 GOSUB 9900
620 P=P+S:S=0:P=P-B:B=0
630 GOSUB 9910:GOSUB 9900
640 CLS:GOTO 260
650 GOSUB 9800
660 PRINT AT 605, "JACKPOT HIT - INSUFFICIENT FUNDS"
670 PRINT AT 669, "PLAYING AS THREE OF A KIND"
```

```
680 P = P + 10:S = S - 10
690 IF P - B > 10 THEN 720
700 GOSUB 9910:GOSUB 9900
710 CLS:GOTO 260
720 P=P-B:B=0:GOTO 700
750 IF (J = K) * (J = L) THEN 900
760 IF (J = K) + (J = L)THEN 970
770 IF (K = J) + (K = L)THEN 970
780 IF (L = J) + (L = K)THEN 970
790 GOSUB 9800:GOSUB 9900
800 PRINT AT 669, "YOU LOSE"
810 GOSUB 9910:GOSUB 9900
820 IF P = 0 THEN 840
830 GOTO 260
840 FOR N = 1 TO 5:GOSUB 9900:NEXT N:
    CLS:PRINT "DO YOU WISH TO BORROW (Y/N)?"
850 PRINT:INPUT A$
860 IF A$ = "Y" THEN 890
870 PRINT:PRINT "GAME ENDED"
880 GOTO 880
890 P = P + 10:B = B + 10:GOSUB 9910:GOTO 260
900 GOSUB 9800:GOSUB 9900
910 PRINT AT 669, "THREE OF A KIND"
920 GOSUB 9900
930 S = S - 10:P = P + 10
940 IF P - B > 10 THEN 960
950 GOSUB 9910:GOTO 260
960 P = P - B:B = 0:GOTO 950
970 P = P + 5:S = S - 5
980 GOSUB 9800:GOSUB 9900
990 PRINT AT 669, "TWO OF A KIND"
1000 GOSUB 9910:GOSUB 9900
1010 IF P - B > 10 THEN 1030
1020 GOTO 260
```

```
1Ø3Ø P = P - B:B = Ø:GOTO 26Ø
9ØØØ DATA "BELLbbbb"
9Ø1Ø DATA "CHERRYbb"
9Ø2Ø DATA "ORANGEbb"
9Ø3Ø DATA "PEARbbbb"
9Ø4Ø DATA "JACKPOTb"
9Ø5Ø DATA "HOUSEbbb"
9Ø6Ø DATA "EARbbbbb"
9Ø7Ø DATA "BRUSHbbb"
9Ø8Ø DATA "CLOCKbbb"
9Ø9Ø DATA "PENbbbbb"
98ØØ RESTORE:CLS
981Ø FOR N = 1 TO L:READ A$
982Ø     PRINT AT 493, A$:NEXT N:RESTORE
983Ø FOR N = 1 TO K:READ A$
984Ø     PRINT AT 473, A$:NEXT N: RESTORE
985Ø FOR N = 1 TO J:READ A$
986Ø     PRINT AT 453, A$:NEXT N:RESTORE
987Ø RETURN
99ØØ FOR Z=1 TO 1ØØ:NEXT Z:RETURN
991Ø PRINT "THE MACHINE NOW HOLDS $";S
992Ø PRINT:PRINT "PLAYER'S ACCOUNT $";P
993Ø PRINT:PRINT "BORROW ACCOUNT $";B
994Ø IF P = Ø THEN 84Ø
995Ø RETURN
```

Under test more than 600 iterations were required to obtain a JACKPOT, while Two-Of-A-Kind and Three-Of-A-Kind got proportional distribution. Of course, according to the laws of pure probability, the JACKPOT could occur on the first try or the 10,000th try.

If you would like to set up the program to run automatically until you get the JACKPOT, make the following changes:

```
26Ø I = I + 1:CLS
6Ø5 GOTO 6Ø5
8Ø5 T = T + 1
```

```
9Ø5 U = U + 1
985 V = V + 1
9935 PRINT "ITERATION";I;"LOSSES";T:"THREE";U;"TWO";V
```

The only instruction which is completely changed is 26Ø. The rest are new instructions.

That's all there is to it. If you're really ambitious, try modifying the program to display graphic caricatures of each of the 10 items on each wheel.

Ready for the next one? Onward to the very old game of TIC-TAC-TOE!

TIC-TAC-TOE

On the surface, putting together a game of tic-tac-toe would seem to be easy. In fact, what follows is about the most logically complex program presented so far in this book. There are many games of tic-tac-toe on the market, some simpler than this one. The approach taken in this program has been selected for its educational benefit, rather than its efficiency.

While the program is logically more difficult than others presented, the application is presented in small pieces and fully explained. This application should be entered in shorthand on a 4K Level I.

As the program is developed, areas of compression will be identified. The reason the program is not shown in final form is that it would appear to be much too complex if initially presented that way.

The opportunity is also taken to present yet another graphics technique— one method for forming large-size numbers and letters graphically. Anyone can build these letters with a complex series of SET commands. In this application, however, the numbers and letters are placed in DATA statements in a form of the binary numbering system (ones and zeros), and using those DATA statements, a single routine will be used to build the large-size graphics characters.

The tic-tac-toe matrix is a three-by-three matrix, as follows; the positions have been numbered:

1	2	3
4	5	6
7	8	9

Figure 36.   Tic-Tac-Toe Matrix

There are eight ways to win the game of tic-tac-toe. They are:

1. 1 - 2 - 3
2. 4 - 5 - 6
3. 7 - 8 - 9
4. 1 - 4 - 7
5. 2 - 5 - 8
6. 3 - 6 - 9
7. 1 - 5 - 9
8. 7 - 5 - 3

Thus, the program must be able to handle any of those combinations, as well as to check amongst those combinations for strategic responses and to see who, if anyone, has won. Here's how it begins:

```
1Ø CLS
2Ø FOR N = 1 TO 2ØØ A(N) = Ø:NEXT N
3Ø RESTORE:CLS:B = Ø:E = Ø:F = Ø:D = Ø
```

Do not be concerned about the duplication of the CLS in statements 1Ø and 3Ø. Statement 3Ø falls within an internal loop and clears the screen each time through the loop. Statement 1Ø is just the initial clear screen instruction. In the program, 200 places are reserved in the array (2Ø) even though only 18 of those places are used in the program. The reason for this is that within the program the array is divided in half and there are references to the second hundred units of the array. If memory is full, it can be cut to 20, but it will be necessary to make considerable changes to the internal logic of the program, so it's better to leave the reservation at 200—statement 2Ø initializes the array to zeros. It's generally good business to allow yourself considerable array room—a technique which will be absolutely necessary when you get to Level II.

Statement 3Ø does a little housekeeping. Since DATA statements will be used, the RESTORE elevates the pointer to the head of the DATA list. RESTORE will be used in several places in the program as it becomes necessary to search for a specific character. Of the variables, B will be used for a one-time-through switch in the program, E is the ENDing counter (when it gets to 1Ø the program is over, whether or not anybody has won), F is used to develop one of the eight combinations listed above and is used in the "CHECK WIN" routine, and D is the switch which is posted if there is a draw (all places taken and no winner). This program has been purposely not constructed to anticipate a draw, as it was felt that it should not be made more complex than it already is. All positions must be played, unless a winner is found beforehand. There will be other switches throughout the program, mostly of the on/off variety.

Drawing the matrix:

```
40 Y = 10:P = 20:Q = 100:GOSUB 940
50 Y = 20:GOSUB 940
60 X = 45:P = 0:Q = 30:GOSUB 980
70 X = 75:GOSUB 980
```

In developing the matrix, three things must be considered: the X or Y coordinate upon which the line will be drawn; the beginning point of the line; and the ending point of the line. The latter two, of course, constitute the length of the line. In statement 40, the Y-Axis line has been established at 10 and its length will be from X-Axis position 20 to X-Axis position 100. These factors are supplied to variables P and Q, which are used in the subroutine at 940, presented below. Statement 50 merely changes the Y-Axis line for the second horizontal line. The X-Axis positions will be the same, so they need not be changed. This would be valid only if there were no intervening instructions which would affect the variables. Here's the routine for drawing the horizontal lines:

```
940 FOR X - P TO Q
950    SET (X,Y)
960 NEXT X
970 RETURN
```

And here's the routine for drawing the vertical lines:

```
980 FOR Y = P TO Q
990    SET (X,Y):SET (X + 1,Y)
1000 NEXT Y
1010 RETURN
```

Before progressing, the approach taken in developing the graphics display should be discussed. Please examine the following:

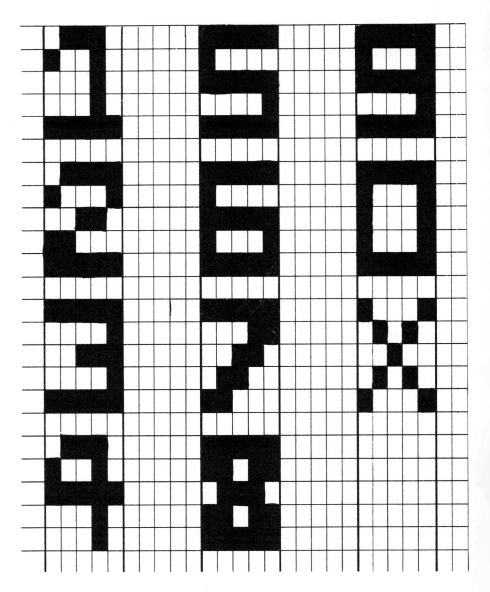

Figure 37.   Matrix Numerical Display

If each character were dissected, coding a "1" for each solid space and a Ø for each empty space, a DATA line which represents the character in graphics form could be constructed like this:

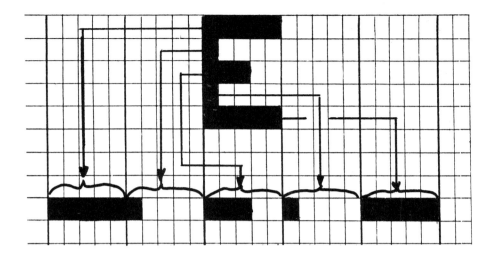

Figure 38.   Binary Graphical Data Representation

If the entire character set (from Figure 37) were constructed in the same manner, these are the DATA lines which would result:

```
830 DATA 0,1,1,1,0,1,0,0,1,0,0,0,0,1,0,0,0,0,1,0,1,1,1,1,1        #1
840 DATA 0,1,1,1,1,1,0,0,0,1,0,0,1,1,0,1,1,0,0,0,1,1,1,1,1        #2
850 DATA 1,1,1,1,1,0,0,0,0,1,0,0,1,1,1,0,0,0,0,1,1,1,1,1,1        #3
860 DATA 0,1,1,1,0,1,0,0,1,0,1,1,1,1,1,0,0,0,1,0,0,0,0,1,0       #4
870 DATA 1,1,1,1,1,1,0,0,0,0,1,1,1,1,1,0,0,0,0,1,1,1,1,1,1        #5
880 DATA 1,1,1,1,1,1,0,0,0,0,1,1,1,1,1,1,0,0,0,1,1,1,1,1,1        #6
890 DATA 1,1,1,1,1,0,0,0,1,1,0,0,1,1,0,0,1,1,0,0,1,1,0,0,0        #7
900 DATA 1,1,1,1,1,1,1,0,1,1,0,1,1,1,0,1,1,0,1,1,1,1,1,1,1        #8
910 DATA 1,1,1,1,1,1,0,0,0,1,1,1,1,1,1,0,0,0,0,1,1,1,1,1,1        #9
920 DATA 1,1,1,1,1,1,0,0,0,1,1,0,0,0,1,1,0,0,0,1,1,1,1,1,1       LTR 0
930 DATA 1,0,0,0,1,0,1,0,1,0,0,0,1,0,0,0,1,0,1,0,1,0,0,0,1       LTR X
```

Now to the instructions which will obtain those DATA lines and draw the graphics characters. There will be common READing mechanisms at 1020 and 1200 and a standard drawing mechanism at 1070. Both are presented further into the chapter:

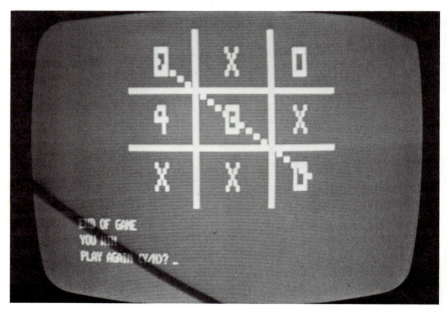

Figure 39 A and B.   Tic-Tac-Toe Matrix and a winning game

```
80 REM "GO AFTER #1"
90 GOSUB 1020
100 Q = 1:X = 30:Y = 3:GOSUB 1070
110 REM "GO AFTER #2"
120 GOSUB 1020
130 Q = 1:X = 58:Y = 3:GOSUB 1070
140 REM "GO AFTER #3"
150 GOSUB 1020
160 Q = 1:X = 85:Y = 3:GOSUB 1070
170 REM "GO AFTER #4"
180 GOSUB 1020
190 Q = 1:X = 30:Y = 13:GOSUB 1070
200 REM "GO AFTER #5"
210 GOSUB 1020
220 Q = 1:X = 58:Y = 13:GOSUB 1070
230 REM "GO AFTER #6"
240 GOSUB 1020
250 Q = 1:X = 85:Y = 13:GOSUB 1070
260 REM "GO AFTER #7"
270 GOSUB 1020
280 Q = 1:X = 30:Y = 23:GOSUB 1070
290 REM "GO AFTER #8"
300 GOSUB 1020
310 Q = 1:X = 58:Y = 23:GOSUB 1070
320 REM "GO AFTER #9"
330 GOSUB 1020
340 Q = 1:X = 85:Y = 23:GOSUB 1070
```

And, of course, the subroutines:

```
1070 FOR Z = 1 TO 5
1080    FOR N = Q TO Q + 4
1090       IF A(N) = 0 THEN RESET (X,Y)
1100       IF A(N) = 1 THEN SET (X,Y)
1110       X = X + 1
1120    NEXT N
```

```
1130     Y = Y + 1:X = X - 5:Q = Q + 5
1140 NEXT Z
1150 RETURN
```

The characters are drawn from the upper left-hand corner, in the coordinates as given:

TTT Number	X-Axis	Y-Axis
1	30	3
2	58	3
3	85	3
4	30	13
5	58	13
6	85	13
7	30	23
8	58	23
9	85	23

Figure 40.   Coordinates of Tic-Tac-Toe Entries

As in the example, each character has been divided into five groups of five elements (ones or zeroes) each. The scanning of each five is a function of the variable Q and the scanning is done from Q to Q + 4. Variable Z controls the number of groups, and variables X and Y are incremented individually—X within the loop and Y outside the loop. Note that X is reset and Q is incremented at the completion of each group.

The program begins:

```
350 E = 0
360 PRINT AT 704, "DO YOU WISH TO GO FIRST (Y/N)":INPUT A$
370 S = 1
380 IF A$ = "N" THEN 400
390 T = 1:GOTO 610
400 E = E + 1:GOSUB 1160
410 IF S = 1 THEN 430
```

```
420 Q = 200:RESTORE:GOSUB 1200:GOTO 450
430 Q = 225:RESTORE
440 GOSUB 1200
```

The program offers you the option of beginning or of letting the computer do so. It's a logical option, of course, but there is a considerable amount of programming which supports it. Variable S (switch) determines whether it is the "X" or the "O" which is placed. The "X" is the first player (either you or the computer). Variable T is used to determine whether it's your turn or the computer's turn. T has a value of 1 when it's your turn and 0 when it's the computer's turn. The "Y" answer at 360 will ultimately take you to 610 , where that option will be treated. But first follow the "N" answer.

After incrementing the counter which will signal that the game is completed (E), a choice must be made as to whether it is the "X" or "O" which is wanted. That, of course, is determined with variable S. The DATA lines are RESTOREd, and a counter is established for the READ routine, located at 1200. The letter "O" is the 10th DATA line and the letter "X" is the 11th. But it should be remembered that each letter or number in the DATA lines is comprised of five groups of five units (1's and 0's). The count stored at Q is that count which is necessary to position immediately before the specific letter required to build (X at 225 and O at 200). The subroutine at 1200 will, in turn, select the proper DATA line by an individual character READ in the subroutine at 1020. The second read precedes the first in the coding for no special reason. Where a 1 is located in the DATA line, a graphics character is turned on. Where a 0 is located, the character is not lit.

The routine at 1160 is just a routine for clearing the bottom part of the display. As mentioned before, the graphics must be kept separate from the printing. In this instance, the printing or displaying of the words need not precede the graphics, as they are printed beneath the graphics display. It does, however, require that you identify the specific print position. The routine to clear out that area is as follows:

```
1160 PRINT AT 704,"                         ";
1170 PRINT AT 768,"                        ";
1180 PRINT AT 832,"                        ";
1190 RETURN
```

And now the READing mechanisms:

```
1200 FOR N = 1 TO Q
1210    READ A
1220 NEXT N
1230 GOSUB 1020
1240 RETURN
```

And also:

```
1020 FOR N = 1 TO 25
1030    READ A
1040     A(N) = A
1050 NEXT N
1060 RETURN
```

When the computer gets to go first, the offensive and defensive strategy included in the program is of no value on the first move. The first move of the computer is determined by a random number. Some Tic-Tac-Toe programs merely select position five. This program gives the player an opportunity to win. When the number has been generated, variable B (a unistable switch) is set to bypass the random number generation for second and subsequent moves by the computer. Also, Q is reset for its next usage and a check on E is performed:

```
450 Q = 1:IF B = 1 THEN 470
460 P = RND(9):P = INT(P):GOTO 490
470 IF E = 10 THEN 710
```

Recall that variable F is used to record winning information. It is cleared initially. Variables J and K are preset, K is set to zero and J is set to 2—the numbers 2 and 0 are arbitrary values, used to distinguish them from the 1's and 0's used in the letter formation. Since it's impossible to store alphabetic data in the array, numbers are stored there instead. If X scores the position in the matrix, the array position which corresponds to the matrix position receives a 0. If O scores, the array gets a two.

The following Tic-Tac-Toe matrix shows the various array positions which correspond to the matrix positions. It also shows two of the methods of reference to the array:

1Ø1	1Ø2	1Ø3
P + 1ØØ	P + 1ØØ	P + 1ØØ
N	N + 1	N + 2
1Ø4	1Ø5	1Ø6
P + 1ØØ	P + 1ØØ	P + 1ØØ
N + 3	N + 4	N + 5
1Ø7	1Ø8	1Ø9
P + 1ØØ	P + 1ØØ	P + 1ØØ
N + 6	N + 7	N + 8

Figure 41.   Array and Reference Data

The top number in each position refers to the array position which is being used to manage the display. The P + references refers to that portion of the array where control of the character placed on the screen (X or O) is kept. There is also a variable N reference included in the coding.

Variable P is developed in the routine, as a result of those positions taken. The variable J and K are used alternatively to select defense strategy. Thus, if in any sequence of three matrix positions (horizontal, vertical, or diagonal), Ø22, 2Ø2, or 22Ø are detected, the computer knows that it must plug the position represented by the Ø to block. The same is true of Ø11, 1Ø1, and 11Ø. Only if the Ø is not accounted for by the opposite player will the computer place its move there.

It should be mentioned that the routine is constructed to find the *first* occurrence of such a situation. Therefore, the computer may respond with a *correct* logical choice, but not necessarily the *best* logical choice. This will give the player the opportunity to win. Here is the coding for the computer to determine its defense and make its move. Variables W and T are used identically, to identify the player, but W is kept separate due to its use in the array:

```
48Ø F = Ø:K = Ø:J = 2:GOSUB 135Ø
49Ø IF A(P + 1ØØ) < > Ø THEN 46Ø
5ØØ PRINT AT 7Ø4, "HERE'S MY MOVE - ";P;
51Ø W = 1:T = 1:B = 1
52Ø FOR N = 1 TO 5ØØ:NEXT N
```

And this is the subroutine. Note that it is comprised of logical ANDs, the values of J and K having been supplied at 48Ø. Examine statement 136Ø: it states that if positon 1Ø1 of the array is equal to J (2, from statement 48Ø) *and* if position 102 is *also* a 2, *and* if position 103 is a zero, then proceed to 1620. At 1620 P is set equal to 3, F is identified as the 1-2-3 line (of the matrix), etc. This logic is the same for each of the eight combinations whereby a person might win. The value of F is not used at this time, but will be used later in the program. Here is the complete strategy logic routine:

```
1350 FOR Z = 1 TO 100:PRINT AT 768,"DEFENSE":NEXT Z
1360 IF (A(101)=J) * (A(102)=J) * (A(103)=K) THEN 1620
1370 IF (A(101)=K) * (A(102)=J) * (A(103)=J) THEN 1630
1380 IF (A(101)=J) * (A(102)=K) * (A(103)=J) THEN 1640
1390 IF (A(104)=J) * (A(105)=J) * (A(106)=K) THEN 1650
1400 IF (A(104)=K) * (A(105)=J) * (A(106)=J) THEN 1660
1410 IF (A(104)=J) * (A(105)=K) * (A(106)=J) THEN 1670
1420 IF (A(107)=J) * (A(108)=J) * (A(109)=K) THEN 1680
1430 IF (A(107)=K) * (A(108)=J) * (A(100)=J) THEN 1690
1440 IF (A(107)=J) * (A(108)=K) * (A(109)=J) THEN 1700
1450 IF (A(101)=J) * (A(104)=J) * (A(107)=K) THEN 1710
1460 IF (A(101)=K) * (A(104)=J) * (A(107)=J) THEN 1720
1470 IF (A(101)=J) * (A(104)=K) * (A(107)=J) THEN 1730
1480 IF (A(102)=J) * (A(105)=J) * (A(108)=K) THEN 1740
1490 IF (A(102)=K) * (A(105)=J) * (A(108)=J) THEN 1750
1500 IF (A(102)=J) * (A(105)=K) * (A(108)=J) THEN 1760
1510 IF (A(103)=J) * (A(106)=J) * (A(109)=K) THEN 1770
1520 IF (A(103)=K) * (A(106)=J) * (A(109)=J) THEN 1780
1530 IF (A(103)=J) * (A(106)=K) * (A(109)=J) THEN 1790
1540 IF (A(101)=J) * (A(105)=J) * (A(109)=K) THEN 1800
1550 IF (A(101)=K) * (A(105)=J) * (A(109)=J) THEN 1810
1560 IF (A(101)=J) * (A(105)=K) * (A(109)=J) THEN 1820
1570 IF (A(103)=J) * (A(105)=J) * (A(107)=K) THEN 1830
1580 IF (A(103)=K) * (A(105)=J) * (A(107)=J) THEN 1840
1590 IF (A(103)=J) * (A(105)=K) * (A(107)=J) THEN 1850
1600 F = 0
1610 RETURN
1620 P = 3:F = 123:GOTO 1610
1630 P = 1:F = 123:GOTO 1610
1640 P = 2:F = 123:GOTO 1610
1650 P = 6:F = 456:GOTO 1610
```

```
1660 P = 4:F = 456:GOTO 1610
1670 P = 5:F = 456:GOTO 1610
1680 P = 9:F = 789:GOTO 1610
1690 P = 7:F = 789:GOTO 1610
1700 P = 8:F = 789:GOTO 1610
1710 P = 7:F = 147:GOTO 1610
1720 P = 1:F = 147:GOTO 1610
1730 P = 4:F = 147:GOTO 1610
1740 P = 8:F = 258:GOTO 1610
1750 P = 2:F - 258:GOTO 1610
1760 P = 5:F = 258:GOTO 1610
1770 P = 9:F = 369:GOTO 1610
1780 P = 3:F = 369:GOTO 1610
1790 P = 6:F = 369:GOTO 1610
1800 P = 9:F = 159:GOTO 1610
1810 P = 1:F = 159:GOTO 1610
1820 P = 5:F = 159:GOTO 1610
1830 P = 7:F = 357:GOTO 1610
1840 P = 3:F = 357:GOTO 1610
1850 P = 5:F = 357:GOTO 1610
```

Now that there is a value for P, the value of W (who took the square) can now be placed into the array position P + 100. That is done in the sequence of instructions which follows. After that is done, the program can now check for the win, and the value of F can be used:

```
530 ON F GOSUB 1250,1260,1270,1280,1300,1310,1320,1330
1250 A(P+100)=W:X=30:Y=3:GOSUB 1020:GOSUB 1070:GOTO 1340
1260 A(P+100)=W:X=58:Y=3:GOSUB 1020:GOSUB 1070:GOTO 1340
1270 A(P+100)=W:X=85:Y=3:GOSUB 1020:GOSUB 1070:GOTO 1340
1280 A(P+100)=W:X=30:Y=13:GOSUB 1020:GOSUB 1070:GOTO 1340
1290 A(P+100)=W:X=58:Y=13:GOSUB 1020:GOSUB 1070:GOTO 1340
1300 A(P+100)=W:X=85:Y=13:GOSUB 1020:GOSUB 1070:GOTO 1340
1310 A(P+100)=W:X=30:Y=23:GOSUB 1020:GOSUB 1070:GOTO 1340
1320 A(P+100)=W:X=58:Y=23:GOSUB 1020:GOSUB 1070:GOTO 1340
1330 A(P+100)=W:X=85:Y=23:GOSUB 1020:GOSUB 1070
1340 RETURN
```

This routine can be condensed for more efficient memory usage by inserting: 1335 GOSUB 1020:GOSUB 1070 and changing instructions 1270 through 1330 to remove the same and to change the GOTOs in 1270 through 1320 to GOTO 1335.

```
540 P = 0:GOSUB 1860:GOSUB 2230
1860 K = 1:J = 1:GOSUB 1350
1870 IF F > 0 THEN 1910
1880 K = 2:J = 2:GOSUB 1350
1890 IF F > 0 THEN 1910
1900 RETURN
1910 IF F = 123 THEN 2010
1920 IF F = 456 THEN 2020
1930 IF F = 789 THEN 2030
1940 IF F = 147 THEN 2040
1950 IF F = 258 THEN 2050
1960 IF F = 369 THEN 2060
1970 IF F = 159 THEN 2070
1980 IF F = 357 THEN 2080
1990 IF E = 10 THEN 740
2000 GOTO 1900
```

If the value of F has been developed, then it will carry through to the win logic (all the THEN conditions on statements 1910 through 1980). Theoretically, the instructions at 1990 and 2000 will never get executed, but you learn very quickly that Murphy's Law (If Anything Can Go Wrong It Will) aplies very much to programming.

At 2010, and the instructions which immediately follow it, the determination is made as to where the "win line" is to be drawn. There are four subroutines for that: one to draw vertical lines, one to draw horizontal lines, and two to draw diagonal lines:

```
2010 Y = 5:GOTO 2170
2020 Y = 15:GOTO 2170
2030 Y = 25:GOTO 2170
2040 X = 32:goto 2200
2050 X = 60:GOTO 2200
2060 X = 87:GOTO 2200
```

```
2070 Y = 5
2080 FOR X = 30 TO 90 STEP 3
2090    SET (X,Y):SET (X + 1,Y)
2100    Y = Y + 1:D = 1
2110 NEXT X:GOSUB 1160:GOTO 720
2120 Y = 25
2130 FOR X = 30 TO 90 STEP 3
2140    SET (X,Y):SET (X + 1,Y)
2150    Y = Y - 1:D = 1
2160 NEXT X:GOSUB 1160:GOTO 720
2170 FOR X = 20 TO 100
2180    SET (X,Y):D = 1
2190 NEXT X:GOSUB 1160:GOTO 720
2200 FOR Y = 0 TO 30
2210    SET (X,Y):D = 1
2220 NEXT Y:GOSUB 1160:GOTO 720
```

If there happens not to be a winner at this point, the process continues, first with a check to see if all the moves have been made. If not, variable S, which tells whether X or O is moving, is flipped, the bottom part of the display is cleared, update the move counter, and return to the appropriate player.

```
550 IF E = 10 THEN 710
560 IF S = 1 THEN 580
570 S = 1:GOTO 590
580 S = 0
590 GOSUB 1160
600 IF T = 0 THEN 400
610 E = E + 1
620 IF E = 0 THEN 710
630 GOSUB 1160:PRINT AT 704, "YOUR MOVE";
```

The player has now made a selection. It is given to the program in INTeger form, checked for validity (between 1 and 9) and the process continues. If it is not valid, it's rejected and another opportunity is given. Again the turns are switched, the X/O combination is changed, the DATA lines are RESTOREd. While the READ logic is duplicated, the ON P GOTO logic at 530 is used again. When all spaces on the tac-tac-toe matrix have been exhausted and if there is no winner, a draw is declared. If there is a winner, that is declared, complete with a line drawn through the winning frames. The program comes to an end with the option to repeat it:

```
640 INPUT P:P = INT(P):W = 2
650 IF (P < 1) + (P > 9) THEN 670
660 IF A(P + 100) = 0 THEN 680
670 PRINT AT 704,"INVALID - SELECT ANOTHER":GOTO 640
680 T = 0:IF S = 1 THEN 700
690 Q = 200:RESTORE:GOSUB 1200:Q = 1:GOTO 530
700 Q = 225:RESTORE:SUBUB 1200:Q = 1:GOTO 530
710 GOSUB 1160:F = 0:GOSUB 1860
720 IF D = 0 THEN 740
730 GOTO 750
740 PRINT AT 704,"GAME IS A DRAW":GOTO 780
750 PRINT AT 704,"END OF GAME"
760 IF T = 1 PRINT "I WIN"
770 IF T = 0 PRINT "YOU WIN"
780 INPUT "PLAY AGAIN (Y/N)";A$
790 IF A$ = "Y" THEN 20
800 GOSUB 1160
810 PRINT AT 704, "GOODBYE"
820 GOTO 820
```

That's the end of the program's execution, but it isn't the end of the coding. Back at statement 540 there was a subroutine call for 2230. The subroutine at 2230 is one "offense" subroutine. Theoretically it is used to select the move to be made if no defensive move is necessary. The program does go after the defensive move before it tries to win, to give the player the opportunity to beat it. It would be otherwise impossible. This routine differs, however, in that it is dependent upon the player (person or computer) in power at the time it is invoked, the factors selected (022, 202, 220 or 011, 101,110) and placed in the common variables G, H, and I. The factors are "scaled," that is, the first is multiplied by 100, the second is multiplied by 10, and all three are added together. The concept and reasons for the scaling will be fully explained in another chapter, but for the time

being, it's being done to implement the strategy of offense. The balance of
the coding of this program should be pretty much self-explanatory:

```
2230 IF E = 10 THEN 710
2240 IF T = 0 THEN 2260
2250 G = 22:H = 202:I = 220:GOTO 2270
2260 G = 11:H = 101:I = 110
2270 PRINT AT 768,"OFFENSE"
2280 N = 101:GOSUB 2940
2290 IF L = G THEN 2330
2300 IF L = H THEN 2340
2310 IF L = I THEN 2350
2320 GOTO 2360
2330 P = 1:GOTO 2930
2340 P = 2:GOTO 2930
2350 P = 3:GOTO 2930
2360 N = 104:GOSUB 2940
2370 IF L = G THEN 2410
2380 IF L = H THEN 2420
2390 IF L = I THEN 2430
2400 GOTO 2440
2410 P = 4:GOTO 2930
2420 P = 5:GOTO 2930
2430 P = 6:GOTO 2930
2440 N = 107:GOSUB 2940
2450 IF L = G THEN 2490
2460 IF L = H THEN 2500
2470 IF L = I THEN 2510
2480 GOTO 2520
2490 P = 7:GOTO 2930
2500 P = 8:GOTO 2930
2510 P = 9:GOTO 2930
2520 N = 101:GOSUB 2960
2530 IF L = G THEN 2570
2540 IF L = H THEN 2580
2550 IF L = I THEN 2590
```

```
2560 GOTO 2600
2570 P = 1:GOTO 2930
2580 P = 4:GOTO 2930
2590 P = 7:GOTO 2930
2600 N = 102:GOSUB 2960
2610 IF L = G THEN 2650
2620 IF L = H THEN 2660
2630 IF L = I THEN 2670
2640 GOTO 2680
2650 P = 2:GOTO 2930
2660 P = 5:GOTO 2930
2670 P = 8:GOTO 2930
2680 N = 103:GOSUB 2960
2690 IF L = G THEN 2730
2700 IF L = H THEN 2740
2710 IF L = I THEN 2750
2720 GOTO 2760
2730 P = 3:GOTO 2930
2740 P = 6:GOTO 2930
2750 P = 9:GOTO 2930
2760 L = (A(101) * 100) + (A(105) * 10) + A(109)
2770 IF L = G THEN 2810
2780 IF L = H THEN 2820
2790 IF L = I THEN 2830
2800 GOTO 2840
2810 P = 1:GOTO 2930
2820 P = 5:GOTO 2930
2830 P = 9:GOTO 2930
2840 L = (A(107) * 100) + (A(105) * 10) + A(103)
2850 IF L = G THEN 2890
2860 IF L = H THEN 2900
2870 IF L = I THEN 2910
2880 GOTO 2920
2890 P = 7:GOTO 2930
2900 P = 5:GOTO 2930
2910 P = 3:GOTO 2930
```

```
2920 RETURN
2930 GOTO 550
2940 L = (A(N) * 100) + (A(N + 1) * 10) + A(N + 2)
2950 RETURN
2960 L = (A(N) * 100) + (A(N + 3) * 10) + A(N + 6)
2970 RETURN
```

And there it is, Tic-Tac-Toe. Again, use shorthand and compress wherever possible. One other place where you might pick up considerable space is in the routine from 1620 to 1860. Move the F factor to the front of the instruction and group the occurrences of P (P = 3 is at 1620, 1780, and 1840, for instance). This is possible as they all branch to 1610. The entire program, in its proper sequence, follows:

```
10 CLS
20 FOR N = 1 TO 200 A(N) = 0:NEXT N
30 RESTORE:CLS:B = 0:E = 0:F = 0:D = 0
40 Y = 10:P = 20:Q = 100:GOSUB 940
50 Y = 20:GOSUB 940
60 X = 45:P = 0:Q = 30:GOSUB 980
70 X = 75:GOSUB 980
80 REM "GO AFTER #1"
90 GOSUB 1020
100 Q = 1:X = 30:Y = 3:GOSUB 1070
110 REM "GO AFTER #2"
120 GOSUB 1020
130 Q = 1:X = 58:Y = 3:GOSUB 1070
140 REM "GO AFTER #3"
150 GOSUB 1020
160 Q = 1:X = 85:Y = 3:GOSUB 1070
170 REM "GO AFTER #4"
180 GOSUB 1020
190 Q = 1:X = 30:Y = 13:GOSUB 1070
200 REM "GO AFTER #5"
210 GOSUB 1020
220 Q = 1:X = 58:Y = 13:GOSUB 1070
230 REM "GO AFTER #5"
```

```
240 GOSUB 1020
250 Q = 1:X = 85:Y = 13:GOSUB 1070
260 REM "GO AFTER #7"
270 GOSUB 1020
280 Q = 1:X = 30:Y = 23:GOSUB 1070
290 REM "GO AFTER #8"
300 GOSUB 1020
310 Q = 1:X = 58:Y = 23:GOSUB 1070
320 REM "GO AFTER #9"
330 GOSUB 1020
340 Q = 1:X = 85:Y = 23:GOSUB 1070
350 E = 0
360 PRINT AT 704, "DO YOU WISH TO GO FIRST (Y/N)":INPUT A$
370 S = 1
380 IF A$ = "N" THEN 400
390 T = 1:GOTO 610
400 E = E + 1:GOSUB 1160
410 IF S = 1 THEN 430
420 Q = 200:RESTORE:GOSUB 1200:GOTO 450
430 Q = 225:RESTORE
440 GOSUB 1200
450 Q = 1:IF B = 1 THEN 470
460 P = RND(9):P = INT(P):GOTO 490
470 IF E = 10 THEN 710
480 F = 0:K = 0:J = 2:GOSUB 1350
490 IF A(P + 100) < > 0 THEN 460
500 PRINT AT 704, "HERE'S MY MOVE - ";P;
510 W = 1:T = 1:B = 1
520 FOR N = 1 TO 500:NEXT N
530 ON P GOSUB 1250,1260,1270,1280,1290,1300,1310,1320,1330
540 F = 0:GOSUB 1860:GOSUB 2230
550 IF E = 10 THEN 710
560 IF S = 1 THEN 580
570 S = 1:GOTO 590
580 S = 0
```

```
590 GOSUB 1160
600 IF T = 0 THEN 400
610 E = E + 1
620 IF E = 0 THEN 710
630 GOSUB 1160:PRINT AT 704, "YOUR MOVE";
640 INPUT P:P = INT(P):W = 2
650 IF (P < 1) + (P > 9) THEN 670
660 IF A(P + 100) = 0 THEN 680
670 PRINT AT 704,"INVALID - SELECT ANOTHER":GOTO 640
680 T = 0:IF S = 1 THEN 700
690 Q = 200:RESTORE:GOSUB 1200:Q = 1:GOTO 530
700 Q = 225:RESTORE:SUBUB 1200:Q = 1:GOTO 530
710 GOSUB 1160:F = 0:GOSUB 1860
720 IF D = 0 THEN 740
730 GOTO 750
740 PRINT AT 704,"GAME IS A DRAW":GOTO 780
750 PRINT AT 704,"END OF GAME"
760 IF T = 1 PRINT "I WIN"
770 IF T = 0 PRINT "YOU WIN"
780 INPUT "PLAY AGAIN (Y/N)";A$
790 IF A$ = "Y" THEN 20
800 GOSUB 1160
810 PRINT AT 704, "GOODBYE"
820 GOTO 820
830 DATA 0,1,1,1,0,1,0,0,1,0,0,0,0,1,0,0,0,0,1,0,1,1,1,1,1
840 DATA 0,1,1,1,1,1,0,0,0,1,0,0,1,1,0,1,1,0,0,0,0,1,1,1,1,1
850 DATA 1,1,1,1,1,0,0,0,0,1,0,0,1,1,1,0,0,0,0,0,1,1,1,1,1,1
860 DATA 0,1,1,1,0,1,0,0,1,0,1,1,1,1,1,0,0,0,1,0,0,0,0,1,0
870 DATA 1,1,1,1,1,1,0,0,0,0,1,1,1,1,1,0,0,0,0,1,1,1,1,1,1
880 DATA 1,1,1,1,1,1,0,0,0,0,1,1,1,1,1,1,0,0,0,1,1,1,1,1,1
890 DATA 1,1,1,1,1,0,0,0,1,1,0,0,1,1,0,0,1,1,0,0,1,1,0,0,0
900 DATA 1,1,1,1,1,1,1,0,1,1,0,1,1,1,0,1,1,0,1,1,1,1,1,1,1
910 DATA 1,1,1,1,1,1,0,0,0,1,1,1,1,1,1,0,0,0,0,1,1,1,1,1,1
920 DATA 1,1,1,1,1,1,0,0,0,1,1,0,0,0,1,1,0,0,0,1,1,1,1,1,1
930 DATA 1,0,0,0,1,0,1,0,1,0,0,0,1,0,0,0,1,0,1,0,1,0,0,0,1
```

```
940 FOR X - P TO Q
950    SET (X,Y)
960 NEXT X
970 RETURN
980 FOR Y = P TO Q
990    SET (X,Y):SET (X + 1,Y)
1000 NEXT Y
1010 RETURN
1020 FOR N = 1 TO 25
1030    READ A
1040    A(N) = A
1050 NEXT N
1060 RETURN
1070 FOR Z = 1 TO 5
1080    FOR N = Q TO Q + 4
1090    IF A(N) = 0 THEN RESET (X,Y)
1100    IF A(N) = 1 THEN SET (X,Y)
1110    X = X + 1
1120    NEXT N
1130    Y = Y + 1:X = X - 5:Q = Q + 5
1140 NEXT Z
1150 RETURN
1160 PRINT AT 704," bbbbbbbbbbbbbbbbbbbb";
1170 PRINT AT 768,"bbbbbbbbbbbbbbbbbbbb";
1180 PRINT AT 832,"bbbbbbbbbbbbbbbbbbbb";
1190 RETURN
1200 FOR N = 1 TO Q
1210    READ A
1220 NEXT N
1230 GOSUB 1020
1240 RETURN
1250 A(P+100)=W:X=30:Y=3:GOSUB 1020:GOSUB 1070:GOTO 1340
1260 A(P+100)=W:X=58:Y=3:GOSUB 1020:GOSUB 1070:GOTO 1340
1270 A(P+100)=W:X=85:Y=3:GOSUB 1020:GOSUB 1070:GOTO 1340
1280 A(P+100)=W:X=30:Y=13:GOSUB 1020:GOSUB 1070:GOTO 1340
```

```
1290 A(P+100)=W:X=58:Y=13:GOSUB 1020:GOSUB 1070:GOTO 1340
1300 A(P+100)=W:X=85:Y=13:GOSUB 1020:GOSUB 1070:GOTO 1340
1310 A(P+100)=W:X=30:Y=23:GOSUB 1020:GOSUB 1070:GOTO 1340
1320 A(P+100)=W:X=58:Y=23:GOSUB 1020:GOSUB 1070:GOTO 1340
1330 A(P+100)=W:X=85:Y=23:GOSUB 1020:GOSUB 1070
1340 RETURN
1350 FOR Z = 1 TO 100:PRINT AT 768,"DEFENSE":NEXT Z
1360 IF (A(101)=J) * (A(102)=J) * (A(103)=K) THEN 1620
1370 IF (A(101)=K) * (A(102)=J) * (A(103)=J) THEN 1630
1380 IF (A(101)=J) * (A(102)=K) * (A(103)=J) THEN 1640
1390 IF (A(104)=J) * (A(105)=J) * (A(106)=K) THEN 1650
1400 IF (A(104)=K) * (A(105)=J) * (A(106)=J) THEN 1660
1410 IF (A(104)=J) * (A(105)=K) * (A(106)=J) THEN 1670
1420 IF (A(107)=J) * (A(108)=J) * (A(109)=K) THEN 1680
1430 IF (A(107)=K) * (A(108)=J) * (A(109)=J) THEN 1690
1440 IF (A(107)=J) * (A(108)=K) * (A(109)=J) THEN 1700
1450 IF (A(101)=J) * (A(104)=J) * (A(107)=K) THEN 1710
1460 IF (A(101)=K) * (A(104)=J) * (A(107)=J) THEN 1720
1470 IF (A(101)=J) * (A(104)=K) * (A(107)=J) THEN 1730
1480 IF (A(102)=J) * (A(105)=J) * (A(108)=K) THEN 1740
1490 IF (A(102)=K) * (A(105)=J) * (A(108)=J) THEN 1750
1500 IF (A(102)=J) * (A(105)=K) * (A(108)=J) THEN 1760
1510 IF (A(103)=J) * (A(106)=J) * (A(109)=K) THEN 1770
1520 IF (A(103)=K) * (A(106)=J) * (A(109)=J) THEN 1780
1530 IF (A(103)=J) * (A(106)=K) * (A(109)=J) THEN 1790
1540 IF (A(101)=J) * (A(105)=J) * (A(109)=K) THEN 1800
1550 IF (A(101)=K) * (A(105)=J) * (A(109)=J) THEN 1810
1560 IF (A(101)=J) * (A(105)=K) * (A(109)=J) THEN 1820
1570 IF (A(103)=J) * (A(105)=J) * (A(107)=K) THEN 1830
1580 IF (A(103)=K) * (A(105)=J) * (A(107)=J) THEN 1840
1590 IF (A(103)=J) * (A(105)=K) * (A(107)=J) THEN 1850
1600 F = 0
1610 RETURN
1620 P = 3:F = 123:GOTO 1610
1630 P = 1:F = 123:GOTO 1610
```

```
1640 P = 2:F = 123:GOTO 1610
1650 P = 6:F = 456:GOTO 1610
1660 P = 4:F = 456:GOTO 1610
1670 P = 5:F = 456:GOTO 1610
1680 P = 9:F = 789:GOTO 1610
1690 P = 7:F = 789:GOTO 1610
1700 P = 8:F = 789:GOTO 1610
1710 P = 7:F = 147:GOTO 1610
1720 P = 1:F = 147:GOTO 1610
1730 P = 4:F = 147:GOTO 1610
1740 P = 8:F = 258:GOTO 1610
1750 P = 2:F - 258:GOTO 1610
1760 P = 5:F = 258:GOTO 1610
1770 P = 9:F = 369:GOTO 1610
1780 P = 3:F = 369:GOTO 1610
1790 P = 6:F = 369:GOTO 1610
1800 P = 9:F = 159:GOTO 1610
1810 P = 1:F = 159:GOTO 1610
1820 P = 5:F = 159:GOTO 1610
1830 P = 7:F = 357:GOTO 1610
1840 P = 3:F = 357:GOTO 1610
1850 P = 5:F = 357:GOTO 1610
1860 K = 1:J = 1:GOSUB 1350
1870 IF F > 0 THEN 1910
1880 K = 2:J = 2:GOSUB 1350
1890 IF F > 0 THEN 1910
1900 RETURN
1910 IF F = 123 THEN 2010
1920 IF F = 456 THEN 2020
1930 IF F = 789 THEN 2030
1940 IF F = 147 THEN 2040
1950 IF F = 258 THEN 2050
1960 IF F = 369 THEN 2060
1970 IF F = 159 THEN 2070
1980 IF F = 357 THEN 2080
```

```
1990 IF E = 10 THEN 740
2000 GOTO 1900
2010 Y = 5:GOTO 2170
2020 Y = 15:GOTO 2170
2030 Y = 25:GOTO 2170
2040 X = 32:GOTO 2200
2050 X = 60:GOTO 2200
2060 X = 87:GOTO 2200
2070 Y = 5
2080 FOR X = 30 TO 90 STEP 3
2090     SET (X,Y):SET (X + 1,Y)
2100     Y = Y + 1:D = 1
2110 NEXT X:GOSUB 1160:GOTO 720
2120 Y = 25
2130 FOR X = 30 TO 90 STEP 3
2140     SET (X,Y):SET (X + 1,Y)
2150     Y = Y - 1:D = 1
2160 NEXT X:GOSUB 1160:GOTO 720
2170 FOR X = 20 TO 100
2180     SET (X,Y):D = 1
2190 NEXT X:GOSUB 1160:GOTO 720
2200 FOR Y = 0 TO 30
2210     SET (X,Y):D = 1
2220 NEXT Y:GOSUB 1160:GOTO 720
2230 IF E = 10 THEN 710
2240 IF T = 0 THEN 2260
2250 G = 22:H = 202:I = 220:GOTO 2270
2260 G = 11:H = 101:I = 110
2270 PRINT AT 768,"OFFENSE"
2280 N = 101:GOSUB 2940
2290 IF L = G THEN 2330
2300 IF L = H THEN 2340
2310 IF L = I THEN 2350
2320 GOTO 2360
2330 P = 1:GOTO 2930
```

```
2340 P = 2:GOTO 2930
2350 P = 3:GOTO 2930
2360 N = 104:GOSUB 2940
2370 IF L = G THEN 2410
2380 IF L = H THEN 2420
2390 IF L = I THEN 2430
2400 GOTO 2440
2410 P = 4:GOTO 2930
2420 P = 5:GOTO 2930
2430 P = 6:GOTO 2930
2440 N = 107:GOSUB 2940
2450 IF L = G THEN 2490
2460 IF L = H THEN 2500
2470 IF L = I THEN 2510
2480 GOTO 2520
2490 P = 7:GOTO 2930
2500 P = 8:GOTO 2930
2510 P = 9:GOTO 2930
2520 N = 101:GOSUB 2960
2530 IF L = G THEN 2570
2540 IF L = H THEN 2580
2550 IF L = I THEN 2590
2560 GOTO 2600
2570 P = 1:GOTO 2930
2580 P = 4:GOTO 2930
2590 P = 7:GOTO 2930
2600 N = 102:GOSUB 2960
2610 IF L = G THEN 2650
2620 IF L = H THEN 2660
2630 IF L = I THEN 2670
2640 GOTO 2680
2650 P = 2:GOTO 2930
2660 P = 5:GOTO 2930
2670 P = 8:GOTO 2930
2680 N = 103:GOSUB 2960
2690 IF L = G THEN 2730
```

```
2700 IF L = H THEN 2740
2710 IF L = I THEN 2750
2720 GOTO 2760
2730 P = 3:GOTO 2930
2740 P = 6:GOTO 2930
2750 P = 9:GOTO 2930
2760 L = (A(101) * 100) + (A(105) * 10) + A(109)
2770 IF L = G THEN 2810
2780 IF L = H THEN 2820
2790 IF L = I THEN 2830
2800 GOTO 2840
2810 P = 1:GOTO 2930
2820 P = 5:GOTO 2930
2830 P = 9:GOTO 2930
2840 L = (A(107) * 100) + (A(105) * 10) + A(103)
2850 IF L = G THEN 2890
2860 IF L = H THEN 2900
2870 IF L = I THEN 2910
2880 GOTO 2920
2890 P = 7:GOTO 2930
2900 P = 5:GOTO 2930
2910 P = 3:GOTO 2930
2920 RETURN
2930 GOTO 550
2940 L = (A(N) * 100) + (A(N + 1) * 10) + A(N + 2)
2950 RETURN
2960 L = (A(N) * 100) + (A(N + 3) * 10) + A(N + 6)
2970 RETURN
```

BOWLING ALLEY

For the final selection in ths chapter, the approach is changing, and the reader will be asked to do some of the programming. A commonplace item, the bowling alley, is the scene. This bowling program is a little different from those commercially available, in that the ball is smaller in this program and the ability to put a little "English" on the ball is included in the strategy.

The ability to shoot and destroy a target, be it space ship or bowling pins, is reserved for Level II and the INKEY$ function. The INKEY$ is a function which queries the keyboard in to allow the modification of the program dynamically. In Level I the only responce which is allowed in the INPUT function, which, of course, requires the program to stop and places a question mark on the screen. This does not mean, however, that the player is powerless to affect what goes on. All that it does mean is that some conditions must be preset in the program. In the case of a bowling game, such things as the speed of the ball, the position of the bowler, and tendencies for curves on the ball can be preset, or at least randomly determined.

The program which follows is a complete bowling game. The ball is "rolled" and it knocks down the pins, which are then reset. It keeps score, by frame and by total. It has the mechanisms for determining strikes and spares, but does not include the mechanisms for scoring the additional pins for either, that's up to you. "Curve" is placed upon the ball via a system of random numbers, but you have the option to modify that "curve" based upon the input you would like to add to the program. Speed of the ball is variable, according to another random number function, and you have the option to modify that, if you'll work your input into the program. Finally, while the "ball" knocks down the "pins," no pin action has been pro-

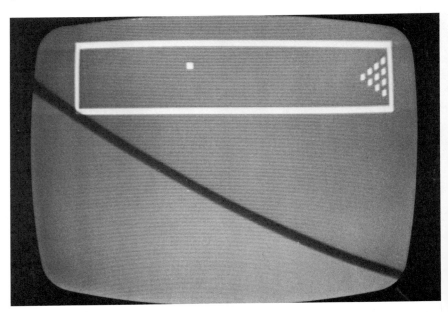

Figure 42.   The Alley

grammed into the routine, the ball merely knocks down pins which are directly in its path.

The program is presented as it has been written, pointing out what happens and where you can add programming to have the routine do what you, the reader, wish it to do.

Standard beginning:

```
1Ø CLS
```

Now, a little discussion as to how the array will be used. There are three sets of 10 items to track. First is the current frame, the pins which are knocked down in the frame in which the player is bowling. The 10 positions in A(1) through A(1Ø) of the array are used to store whichever ball (1 or 2) knocked down the pins. The determination as to which ball is in use is stored in variable W. In the following, variable G is the gutter switch (indicates that the ball has traveled into the gutter), R is the first ball count of pins knocked down, S is the count of pins knocked down by the second ball, T is the frame total, and Q will be used later to keep a running count.

The second 10 positions of the array, A(11) through A(2Ø), are used to store the current frame pin count (variable T). That count is developed and kept, but since no doubling up for strikes and spares is included, you must add that. The current value of Q, the total pin accumulator, is stored in the third 10 positions of the array, A(21) through A(3Ø). Variables D and E will be used in later coding to "step through" each sequence of frames in the arrays. In statement 3Ø the second and third sections of the array are cleared. Clearing of the first section is at statement 6Ø, and placed within a loop, as it will be cleared after every frame:

```
2Ø D = 11:E = 21:Q = Ø
3Ø FOR N = 21 TO 3Ø:A(N) = Ø:NEXT N
4Ø G = Ø:R = Ø:S = Ø:T = Ø:W = 1
5Ø PRINT AT 128 " ";TAB(18);"B O W L I N G   A L L E Y"
6Ø FOR N = 1 TO 1Ø:A(N) = Ø:NEXT N
```

Throughout the program there is a considerable amount of manipulation of graphics via the SET and RESET commands. Some of them have been set into common subroutines, others are affected as they are needed.

The first step is to build an alley. It has been established as a subroutine, and is redrawn within the program. This recognizes the occasional time that the ball jumps the alley:

```
7Ø GOSUB 212Ø
212Ø FOR Y = 1 TO 13 STEP 12
213Ø    FOR X = Ø TO 127
214Ø        SET (X,Y)
215Ø    NEXT X
216Ø NEXT Y
```

Now to set the pins. The pin-setting is also established as a subroutine:

```
8Ø GOSUB 18Ø
18Ø FOR X = 115 TO 124 STEP 3
19Ø    FOR Y = 2 TO 11
2ØØ    RESET (X,Y)
21Ø    NEXT Y
22Ø NEXT X
23Ø FOR X = 13 TO 63
24Ø    FOR Y = 2 TO 11
25Ø        RESET (X,Y):RESET (X + 5Ø,Y)
26Ø    NEXT Y
27Ø NEXT X
28Ø X = 115:Y = 7:SET (X,Y)
29Ø X = 118:Y = 6:SET (X,Y):SET (X,Y + 2)
3ØØ X = 121:Y = 5:SET (X,Y):SET (X,Y + 2):SET (X,Y + 4)
31Ø X = 124:Y = 4:SET (X,Y):SET (X,Y + 2):SET (X,Y + 4):
    SET (X,Y + 6)
32Ø RETURN
```

To allow some "curve" to be placed on the ball, variable V is used to determine where that curve will occur, beginning at position 14 (X-Axis) on the display. The very long FOR . . . NEXT loop handles the rolling of the ball. It's presented in small pieces:

```
9Ø GOSUB 33Ø
33Ø Y = 7:V = 14
34Ø FOR X = 2 TO 125
35Ø    SET (X + 1,Y):RESET (X - 1,Y):SET (X,Y)
36Ø    B = RND(2):IF B < 1 THEN 36Ø
```

```
370    ON B GOTO 380,490
380    IF (X=114)*(Y=8)*(C=0)*(W=1) THEN 440
390    IF (X=114)*(Y=6)*(C=0)*(W=1) THEN 440
400    B = RND(10):B = INT(B)
410    IF (X=114)*(Y=8)*(B=5)*(W=2) THEN 480
420    IF (X=114)*(Y=6)*(B=5)*(W=2) THEN 480
430    GOTO 490
440    PRINT AT 704, "S T R I K E !":
       H = 10:W = 2:S = H:T = H:GOSUB 1650
450    FOR N = 1 TO 500:NEXT N
460    GOSUB 2570:GOSUB 1530:GOTO 2220
470    PRINT AT 704,"S P A R E !":I = 10:W = 2:
       S = H:T = H:GOSUB 1650
480    GOTO 450
```

The roll begins in the middle of the alley. You may modify the starting position by changing the value of Y in statement 330. The "ball" is a two-position graphics element which moves forward and erases behind itself (that is in statement 350). Statement 360 is a two-position random number generator which allows changing from "fast" to "slow" roll, by changing the amount of logic through which the program passes. You may change the speed of the ball at this point.

Statements 380 through 480 identify the conditions under which a strike or a spare is identified. Essentially there are two positions of the ball at X-Axis 114 which will permit a strike or a spare. The ball must be in "standard" position, just to the right of the head-pin, or in the "Brooklyn" position, just to the left of the head-pin—Y-Axis positions 8 and 6 respectively. Further, it is only allowed 10% of the time—variable C cycles through 10 positions, and even that 10% of the time is based on obtaining a "1" in the random number generator at 360. You'll note that W is "1" in one instance (strike) and "2" in the other instance (spare). Finding a strike or a spare is easy, the difficult challenge for you is to combine it with the score. The pin count is located now at H (strike) and I (spare) and the ball count and frame count have been "flooded" with the value of 10. You must now "back-load" the previous frame with the proper value, recognizing that on spares, only the next ball (first of the next frame) counts, while on a strike, the next two balls count. Also, while you're planning your changes, no consideration has been given to a strike or spare in the 10th frame. You'll have to add the logic to run an 11th frame, combining it with the total contained in the 10th frame.

The next bit of coding is that which interrupts the travel of the ball at somewhat random places along the alley, to obtain the "curve" action. Unfortunately, since TRS-80 can't give us true curves via graphics, the ball does tend to jump on the display, but the net effect is the same. First, the travel (we start out with 14 as the first place of change) position 14 on the X-Axis, that is. We then generate a random number in the range of 1 to 5 at statement 510, and based upon whatever we obtain we add 12, 24, 36, 48, or 150 to the variable. The 150 is merely an option to obtain a straight line travel, and could have been any value above 113. Occasionally the span of travel changes right in the middle of the pins. At that time, the ball takes out more pins than appear in its line of travel.

```
490     IF X = V THEN 510
500     GOTO 1260
510     B = RND(5):B = INT(B)
520     ON B GOTO 530,540,550,560,570
530     V = V + 12:GOTO 580
540     V = V + 24:GOTO 580
550     V = V + 36:GOTO 580
560     V = V + 48:GOTO 580
570     V = V + 150
580     B = RND(5):B = INT(B)
590     IF B = 1 THEN 620
600     IF B = 5 THEN 620
610     GOTO 640
620     C = C + 1:IF C < > 10 THEN 580
630     C = 0
640     G = 0
650     ON B GOTO 800,660,1260,730,820
660     GOSUB 1500:IF G = 1 THEN 900
```

In statements 580 to 600, the numbers 1 and 5 generate a gutter ball if the ball is on that side of the alley—that is, if the ball is on the left and a 1 is generated or if it is on the right and a 5 is generated. This action is inhibited until the 10th occurrence of variable C. In other words, only on the 10th occurrence of a 1 or 5, and then only if the ball is the appropriate position.

From this point on, the travels of the ball under varying sets of circumstances are handled. If it's a gutter ball, variable G is set to 1, if not, G is set to zero. If the ball is moving to the left of the alley, the value of Y is decreased (up on the screen); if to the right, the value of Y is increased (down on the screen). There is no formula for clearing out the trail left by the ball when it changes direction. The area around the ball is cleared, no matter where it is. This will result in breaks in the alley walls, but, as stated before, the walls are regenerated. Here is that coding:

```
670     SET (X,Y - 1)
680     RESET (X,Y)
690     RESET (X + 1,Y)
700     GOSUB 1290
710     Y = Y - 1
720     GOTO 1260
730     GOSUB 1570:IF G = 1 THEN 840
740     SET (X,Y + 1)
750     RESET (X,Y)
760     RESET (X + 1,Y)
770     GOSUB 1290
780     Y = Y + 1
790     GOTO 1260
800     GOSUB 1500:IF G = 1 THEN 900
810     GOTO 960
820     GOSUB 1570:IF G = 1 THEN 840
830     GOTO 1110
840     RESET (X,Y):RESET (X,Y + 1):RESET (X,Y + 2):RESET (X,Y + 3)
850     RESET (X - 1,Y):RESET (X - 1,Y + 1):RESET (X-1,Y+2):
        RESET (X - 1,Y + 3)
860     RESET (X + 1,Y):RESET (X + 1,Y + 1):RESET (X + 1,Y + 2):
        RESET (X + 1,Y + 3)
870     GOSUB 1290
880     Y = 11:V = 150
890     GOTO 1260
900     RESET (X,Y):RESET (X,Y - 1):RESET (X,Y - 2)
910     RESET (X - 1,Y):RESET (X - 1,Y - 1):RESET (X - 1,Y - 2)
920     RESET (X + 1,Y):RESET (X + 1,Y - 1):RESET (X + 1,Y - 2)
930     GOSUB 1290
940     Y = 2:V = 150
```

```
950       GOTO 1260
960       SET (X,Y - 1)
970       GOSUB 1640
980       SET (X + 1,Y - 2)
990       GOSUB 1640
1000      SET (X + 2,Y - 3)
1010      GOSUB 1640
1020      GOSUB 1290
1030      RESET (X,Y - 1)
1040      GOSUB 1640
1050      RESET (X + 1,Y - 2)
1060      GOSUB 1640
1070      RESET (X + 2, Y - 3)
1080      GOSUB 1640
1090      GOSUB 1290
1100      X = X + 2:Y = Y - 3:GOTO 1260
1110      SET (X,Y + 1)
1120      GOSUB 1640                          530
1130      SET (X + 1,Y + 2)                   540
1140      GOSUB 1640                          550
1150      SET (X + 2),Y + 3)                  560
1160      GOSUB 1640                          570
1170      GOSUB 1290                          580
1180      RESET (X,Y + 1)                     590
1190      GOSUB 1640                          600
1200      RESET (X + 1,Y + 2)                 610
1210      GOSUB 1640                          620
1220      RESET (X + 2,Y + 3)                 630
1230      GOSUB 1640                          640
1240      GOSUB 1290                          650
1250      X = X + 2,Y = Y + 3)                660
1260 NEXT X
1270 RESET (X - 1,Y):RESET (X,Y)
1280 RETURN
```

That concludes the main subroutine. From this point on, the subroutines are largely subordinate subroutines:

```
1290 RESET (X,Y):RESET(X - 1,Y)
1300 RESET (X + 1,Y):RESET (X + 1,Y - 1):RESET (X + 1,Y + 1)
1310 RESET (X - 1,Y):RESET (X - 1,Y - 1):RESET (X - 1,Y + 1)
1320 IF Y > 7 THEN 1440
1330 IF Y < 5 THEN 1370
1340 RESET (X,Y + 1):RESET (X + 1,Y + 2):RESET (X + 2,Y + 3)
1350 RESET (X,Y - 1):RESET (X + 1,Y - 2):RESET (X + 2,Y - 3)
1360 GOTO 1430
1370 IF Y - 1 < 2 THEN 1430
1380 RESET (X,Y - 1)
1390 IF Y - 2 < 2 THEN 1430
1400 REST (X + 1,Y - 2)
1410 IF Y - 3 < 2 THEN 1430
1420 RESET (X + 2,Y - 3)
1430 RETURN
1440 IF Y + 1 > 11 THEN 1430
1450 RESET (X,Y + 1)
1460 IF Y + 2 > 11 THEN 1430
1470 RESET (X,Y + 2)
1480 IF Y + 3 > 11 THEN 1430
1490 RESET (X,Y + 3):GOTO 1430
1500 IF (Y < 3) + (Y - 1 < 3) + (Y - 2 < 3) + (Y - 3 < 3)
     THEN G = 1
1510 IF (G = 1) * (C = 0) THEN PRINT AT 640,"GUTTER BALL"
1520 IF G < > 1 THEN 1560
1530 RESET (X,Y):RESET (X - 1):RESET (X - 2,Y)
1540 RESET (X,Y + 1):RESET (X - 1,Y + 1):RESET (X - 2,Y + 1)
1550 IF G = 1 THEN Y = 2
1560 RETURN
1570 IF (Y > 11) + (Y + 1 > 11) + (Y + 2 > 11) + (Y + 3 > 11)
     THEN G = 1
1580 IF G < > 1 THEN 1620
```

```
1590 IF (G = 1) * (C = Ø) THEN PRINT AT 64Ø,"GUTTER BALL"
1600 RESET (X,Y):RESET (X - 1,Y):RESET (X - 2,Y)
1610 RESET (X,Y - 1):RESET (X - 1,Y - 1):RESET (X - 2,Y - 1)
1620 IF G = 1 THEN Y = 11
1630 RETURN
```

And now for the pin-counting subroutine. It's easy enough to scan the pins using the POINT instruction, but distinguishing the first roll's pins from the second roll's pins is more difficult. A scan is made at the end of each roll and the value of W is placed in the proper place within the array to denote which roll got the pins. This is done by testing the array position against the value of Ø and completing the value if a Ø is found:

```
1640 FOR N = 1 TO 10:NEXT N:RETURN
1650 REM "PIN COUNT SUBROUTINE"
1660 IF POINT (115,7) = 1 THEN 1690
1670 IF A(1) < > Ø THEN 1690
1680 A(1) = W
```

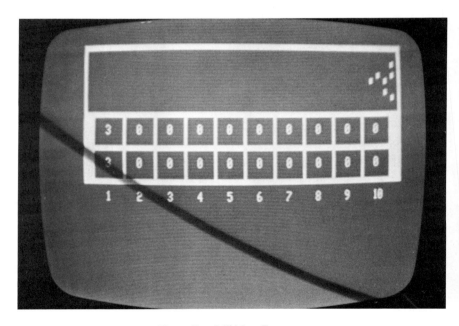

Figure 43.   Still More Frames

```
1690 IF POINT (118,6) = 1 THEN 1720
1700 IF A(2) < > 0 THEN 1720
1710 A(2) = W
1720 IF POINT (118,8) = 1 THEN 1750
1730 IF A(3) < > 0 THEN 1750
1740 A(3) = W
1750 IF POINT (121,5) = 1 THEN 1780
1760 IF A(4) < > 0 THEN 1780
1770 A(4) = W
1780 IF POINT (121,7) = 1 THEN 1810
1790 IF A(5) < > 0 THEN 1810
1800 A(5) = W
1810 IF POINT (121,9) = 1 THEN 1840
1820 IF A(6) < > 0 THEN 1840
1830 A(6) = W
1840 IF POINT (124,4) = 1 THEN 1870
1850 IF A(7) < > 0 THEN 1870
1860 A(7) = W
1870 IF POINT (124,6) = 1 THEN 1900
1880 IF A(8) < > 0 THEN 1900
1890 A(8) = W
1900 IF POINT (124,8) = 1 THEN 1930
1910 IF A(9) < > 0 THEN 1930
1920 A(9) = W
1930 IF POINT (124,10) = 1 THEN 1970
1940 IF A(10) < > 0 THEN 1970
1950 A(10) = W
```

At this point variable W is used as a switch, bypassing the initialization of the total counters when it is a two. The first 10 positions of the array are then scanned for the count, placing the appropriate messages onto the screen. On the first time through (W = 1), the PINS THIS ROLL message contains the first roll count, as does the PINS THIS FRAME message. During the second time through, however, (W = 2), the PINS THIS ROLL depicts the pin count for the second roll, but the PINS THIS FRAME message will have the total count.

```
1960 IF W = 2 THEN 1980
1970 R = Ø:S = Ø:T = Ø
1980 FOR N = 1 TO 10
1990     IF A(N) = 1 THEN 2040
2000     IF A(N) = 2 THEN 2050
2010 NEXT N
2020 IF W = 2 THEN T = R + S
2030 GOTO 2060
2040 R = R + 1:GOTO 2010
2050 S = S + 1:GOTO 2010
2060 IF W = 2 THEN 2090
2070 PRINT "PINS THIS ROLL";R:T = R
2080 GOTO 2100
2090 PRINT "PINS THIS ROLL";S
2100 PRINT "PINS THIS FRAME";T:W = W + 1
2110 RETURN
```

Next the subroutine for redrawing the alley:

```
2120 FOR Y = 1 TO 13 STEP 12
2130     FOR X = Ø TO 127
2140     SET (X,Y)
2150     NEXT X
2160 NEXT Y
2170 FOR Y = 1 TO 13
2180     SET (Ø,Y)
2190     SET (127,Y)
2200 NEXT Y
2210 RETURN
```

The next routine is the end-of-frame routine. In it the box score is developed (which is not present until some pins have been knocked down). The printing destroys the graphics, which are restored at 2260 and 2270.

```
2220 PRINT "FRAME COMPLETE"
2230 Q = Q + T
2240 A(D) = T:D = D + 1
```

```
2250 A(E) = Q:E = E + 1
2260 GOSUB 2350
2270 GOSUB 2510
2280 PRINT AT 580,"1";TAB(10);"2";TAB(16);"3";TAB(22);
     "4";TAB(28);"5";TAB(34);"6";TAB(40);"7";TAB(46);
     "8";TAB(52);"9";TAB(58);"10"
2290 PRINT AT 323,A(11);TAB(9);A(12);TAB(15);A(13);TAB(21);
     A(14);TAB(27);A(15);TAB(33);A(16);TAB(39);A(17);TAB(45);
     A(18);TAB(51);A(19);TAB(57);A(20)
2300 PRINT AT 451,A(21);TAB(9);A(22);TAB(15);A(23);TAB(21);
     A(24);TAB(27);A(25);TAB(33);A(26);TAB(39);A(27);TAB(45);
     A(28);TAB(51);A(19);TAB(57);A(30)
2310 GOSUB 2350:GOSUB 2430
2320 IF E = 31 THEN 2490
2330 PRINT AT 832, "6"
2340 INPUT "ROLL";A:GOSUB 180:GOSUB 2510:GOTO 40
```

Note that the return to the beginning is with a simple GOTO. Note also that the end of the program is determined by checking to see if the size of the array has been exceeded. When you add the strikes and spares logic, modify statement 2320.

Here are the subroutines for drawing the scorebox:

```
2350 FOR X = 0 TO 127
2360     SET (X,25):SET (X,19)
2370 NEXT X
2380 FOR X = 0 TO 3
2390     FOR Y = 14 TO 24
2400         SET (X,Y):SET (X + 124,Y)
2410     NEXT Y
2420 NEXT X
2430 FOR X = 3 TO 124 STEP 12
2440     FOR Y = 14 TO 24
2450         SET (X,Y)
2460     NEXT Y
2470 NEXT X
2480 RETURN
```

Now to return to the logic which opened this segment. Note that there are two places where the "roll" instruction is given to the player, one for each ball to be rolled. Note that the routine at 2220, the FRAME COMPLETE routine, is determined when the ball counter has risen to three. The printing of one blank at 576 (statement 100) positions the cursor under the graphics.

```
100 PRINT AT 576, "b"
110 GOSUB 1660
120 IF W = 3 THEN 2220
130 GOSUB 2120:INPUT "ROLL";A
140 GOSUB 2510
150 R = R + 1
160 GOSUB 330
170 GOTO 100
```

OK, the game has displayed its messages, how are they cleared?

```
2510 Z = 640
2520 FOR N = 1 TO 5
2530     PRINT AT Z, "bbbbbbbbbbbbbbbbbbbbbbbb"
2540     Z = Z + 64
2550 NEXT N
2560 RETURN
```

And here is the routine to clear the alley (you'll note that the message BOWLING ALLEY disappears one letter at a time). This is an unusually slow process of clearing the alley, but made necessary by the random variation of the "ball." Without it, the ball occasionally leaves a trail. If you want to speed the process up and are not concerned with the trail, remove the subroutine. And if you can figure a way to clear the trail 100% of the time without the routine, write to the author. So far he hasn't been able to figure it out.

```
2570 FOR X = 115 TO 124 STEP 3
2580     FOR Y = 2 TO 11
2590         RESET (X,Y)
2600     NEXT Y
2610 NEXT X
2620 RETURN
```

Time to tie the wraps on it. Simply:

```
2490 PRINT AT 704, "GAME OVER"
2500 GOTO 2500
```

That's it as far as it has been programmed. You may now add the sophistication to the process.

On the pages following is a complete listing of the program, in the proper sequence. Key this much into the machine and get it working before adding your enhancements:

```
10 CLS
20 D = 11:E = 21:Q = 0
30 FOR N = 21 TO 30:A(N) = 0:NEXT N
40 G = 0:R = 0:S = 0:T = 0:W = 1
50 PRINT AT 128 " ";TAB(18);"B O W L I N G   A L L E Y"
60 FOR N = 1 TO 10:A(N) = 0:NEXT N
70 GOSUB 2120
80 GOSUB 180
90 GOSUB 330
100 PRINT AT 576, "ƀ"
110 GOSUB 1660
120 IF W = 3 THEN 2220
130 GOSUB 2120:INPUT "ROLL";A
140 GOSUB 2510
150 R = R + 1
160 GOSUB 330
170 GOTO 100
180 FOR X = 115 TO 124 STEP 3
190     FOR Y = 2 TO 11
200         RESET (X,Y)
210     NEXT Y
220 NEXT X
230 FOR X = 13 TO 63
240     FOR Y = 2 TO 11
250         RESET (X,Y):RESET (X + 50,Y)
260     NEXT Y
```

```
270 NEXT X
280 X = 115:Y = 7:SET (X,Y)
290 X = 118:Y = 6:SET (X,Y):SET (X,Y + 2)
300 X = 121:Y = 5:SET (X,Y):SET (X,Y + 2):SET (X,Y + 4)
310 X = 124:Y = 4:SET (X,Y):SET (X,Y + 2):SET (X,Y + 4):
    SET (X,Y + 6)
320 RETURN
330 Y = 7:V = 14
340 FOR X = 2 TO 125
350     SET (X + 1,Y):RESET (X - 1,Y):SET (X,Y)
360     B = RND(2):IF B < 1 THEN 360
370     ON B GOTO 380,490
380     IF (X=114)*(Y=8)*(C=0)*(W=1) THEN 440
390     IF (X=114)*(Y=6)*(C=0)*(W=1) THEN 440
400     B = RND(10):B = INT(B)
410     IF (X=114)*(Y=8)*(B=5)*(W=2) THEN 480
420     IF (X=114)*(Y=6)*(B=5)*(W=2) THEN 480
430     GOTO 490
440     PRINT AT 704, "S T R I K E !":
        H = 10:W = 2:S = H:T = H:GOSUB 1650
450     FOR N = 1 TO 500:NEXT N
460     GOSUB 2570:GOSUB 1530:GOTO 2220
470     PRINT AT 704,"S P A R E !":I = 10:W = 2:
        S = H:T = H:GOSUB 1650
480     GOTO 450
490     IF X = V THEN 510
500     GOTO 1260
510     B = RND(5):B = INT(B)
520     ON B GOTO 530,540,550,560,570
530     V = V + 12:GOTO 580
540     V = V + 24:GOTO 580
550     V = V + 36:GOTO 580
560     V = V + 48:GOTO 580
570     V = V + 150
580     B = RND(5):B = INT(B)
```

```
590    IF B = 1 THEN 620
600    IF B = 5 THEN 620
610    GOTO 640
620    C = C + 1:IF C < > 10 THEN 580
630    C = 0
640    G = 0
650    ON B GOTO 800,660,1260,730,820
660    GOSUB 1500:IF G = 1 THEN 900
670    SET (X,Y - 1)
680    RESET (X,Y)
690    RESET (X + 1,Y)
700    GOSUB 1290
710    Y = Y - 1
720    GOTO 1260
730    GOSUB 1570:IF G = 1 THEN 840
740    SET (X,Y + 1)
750    RESET (X,Y)
760    RESET (X + 1,Y)
770    GOSUB 1290
780    Y = Y + 1
790    GOTO 1260
800    GOSUB 1500:IF G = 1 THEN 900
810    GOTO 960
820    GOSUB 1570:IF G = 1 THEN 840
830    GOTO 1110
840    RESET (X,Y):RESET (X,Y + 1):RESET (X,Y + 2):RESET (X,Y + 3)
850    RESET (X - 1,Y):RESET (X - 1,Y + 1):RESET (X-1,Y+2):
       RESET (X - 1,Y + 3)
860    RESET (X + 1,Y):RESET (X + 1,Y + 1):RESET (X + 1,Y + 2):
       RESET (X + 1,Y + 3)
870    GOSUB 1290
880    Y = 11:V = 150
890    GOTO 1260
900    RESET (X,Y):RESET (X,Y - 1):RESET (X,Y - 2)
910    RESET (X - 1,Y):RESET (X - 1,Y - 1):RESET (X - 1,Y - 2)
```

```
920    RESET (X + 1,Y):RESET (X + 1,Y - 1):RESET (X + 1,Y - 2)
930    GOSUB 1290
940    Y = 2:V = 150
950    GOTO 1260
960    SET (X,Y - 1)
970    GOSUB 1640
980    SET (X + 1,Y - 2)
990    GOSUB 1640
1000    SET (X + 2,Y - 3)
1010    GOSUB 1640
1020    GOSUB 1290
1030    RESET (X,Y - 1)
1040    GOSUB 1640
1050    RESET (X + 1,Y - 2)
1060    GOSUB 1640
1070    RESET (X + 2, Y - 3)
1080    GOSUB 1640
1090    GOSUB 1290
1110    SET (X,Y + 1)
1100    X = X + 2:Y = Y - 3:GOTO 1260
1120    GOSUB 1640
1130    SET (X + 1,Y + 2)
1140    GOSUB 1640
1150    SET (X + 2),Y + 3)
1160    GOSUB 1640
1170    GOSUB 1290
1180    RESET (X,Y + 1)
1190    GOSUB 1640
1200    RESET (X + 1,Y + 2)
1210    GOSUB 1640
1220    RESET (X + 2,Y + 3)
1230    GOSUB 1640
1240    GOSUB 1290
1250    X = X + 2,Y = Y + 3)
1260 NEXT X
1270 RESET (X - 1,Y):RESET (X,Y)
```

```
1280 RETURN
1290 RESET (X,Y):RESET(X - 1,Y)
1300 RESET (X + 1,Y):RESET (X + 1,Y - 1):RESET (X + 1,Y + 1)
1310 RESET (X - 1,Y):RESET (X - 1,Y - 1):RESET (X - 1,Y + 1)
1320 IF Y > 7 THEN 1440
1330 IF Y < 5 THEN 1370
1340 RESET (X,Y + 1):RESET (X + 1,Y + 2):RESET (X + 2,Y + 3)
1350 RESET (X,Y - 1):RESET (X + 1,Y - 2):RESET (X + 2,Y - 3)
1360 GOTO 1430
1370 IF Y - 1 < 2 THEN 1430
1380 RESET (X,Y - 1)
1390 IF Y - 2 < 2 THEN 1430
1400 REST (X + 1,Y - 2)
1410 IF Y - 3 < 2 THEN 1430
1420 RESET (X + 2,Y - 3)
1430 RETURN
1440 IF Y + 1 > 11 THEN 1430
1450 RESET (X,Y + 1)
1460 IF Y + 2 > 11 THEN 1430
1470 RESET (X,Y + 2)
1480 IF Y + 3 > 11 THEN 1430
1490 RESET (X,Y + 3):GOTO 1430
1500 IF (Y < 3) + (Y - 1 < 3) + (Y - 2 < 3) + (Y - 3 < 3)
     THEN G = 1
1510 IF (G = 1) * (C = 0) THEN PRINT AT 640,"GUTTER BALL"
1520 IF G < >1 THEN 1560
1530 RESET (X,Y):RESET (X - 1):RESET (X - 2,Y)
1540 RESET (X,Y + 1):RESET (X - 1,Y + 1):RESET (X - 2,Y + 1)
1550 IF G = 1 THEN Y = 2
1560 RETURN
1570 IF (Y > 11) + (Y + 1 > 11) + (Y + 2 > 11) + (Y + 3 > 11)
     THEN G = 1
1580 IF G < >1 THEN 1620
1590 IF (G = 1) * (C = 0) THEN PRINT AT 640,"GUTTER BALL"
1600 RESET (X,Y):RESET (X - 1,Y):RESET (X - 2,Y)
```

```
1610 RESET (X,Y - 1):RESET (X - 1,Y - 1):RESET (X - 2,Y - 1)
1620 IF G = 1 THEN Y = 11
1630 RETURN
1640 FOR N = 1 TO 10:NEXT N:RETURN
1650 REM "PIN COUNT SUBROUTINE"
1660 IF POINT (115,7) = 1 THEN 1690
1670 IF A(1) < > 0 THEN 1690
1680 A(1) = W
1690 IF POINT (118,6) = 1 THEN 1720
1700 IF A(2) < > 0 THEN 1720
1710 A(2) = W
1720 IF POINT (118,8) = 1 THEN 1750
1730 IF A(3) < > 0 THEN 1750
1740 A(3) = W
1750 IF POINT (121,5) = 1 THEN 1780
1760 IF A(4) < > 0 THEN 1780
1770 A(4) = W
1780 IF POINT (121,7) = 1 THEN 1810
1790 IF A(5) < > 0 THEN 1810
1800 A(5) = W
1810 IF POINT (121,9) = 1 THEN 1840
1820 IF A(6) < > 0 THEN 1840
1830 A(6) = W
1840 IF POINT (124,4) = 1 THEN 1870
1850 IF A(7) < > 0 THEN 1870
1860 A(7) = W
1870 IF POINT (124,6) = 1 THEN 1900
1880 IF A(8) < > 0 THEN 1900
1890 A(8) = W
1900 IF POINT (124,8) = 1 THEN 1930
1910 IF A(9) < > 0 THEN 1930
1920 A(9) = W
1930 IF POINT (124,10) = 1 THEN 1970
1940 IF A(10) < > 0 THEN 1970
1950 A(10) = W
1960 IF W = 2 THEN 1980
```

```
1970 R = Ø:S = Ø:T = Ø
1980 FOR N = 1 TO 1Ø
1990     IF A(N) = 1 THEN 2Ø4Ø
2ØØØ     IF A(N) = 2 THEN 2Ø5Ø
2Ø1Ø NEXT N
2Ø2Ø IF W = 2 THEN T = R + S
2Ø3Ø GOTO 2Ø6Ø
2Ø4Ø R = R + 1:GOTO 2Ø1Ø
2Ø5Ø S = S + 1:GOTO 2Ø1Ø
2Ø6Ø IF W = 2 THEN 2Ø9Ø
2Ø7Ø PRINT "PINS THIS ROLL";R:T = R
2Ø8Ø GOTO 21ØØ
2Ø9Ø PRINT "PINS THIS ROLL";S
21ØØ PRINT "PINS THIS FRAME";T:W = W + 1
211Ø RETURN
212Ø FOR Y = 1 TO 13 STEP 12
213Ø     FOR X = Ø TO 127
214Ø         SET (X,Y)
215Ø     NEXT X
216Ø NEXT Y
217Ø FOR Y = 1 TO 13
218Ø     SET (Ø,Y)
219Ø     SET (127,Y)
22ØØ NEXT Y
221Ø RETURN
222Ø PRINT "FRAME COMPLETE"
223Ø Q = Q + T
224Ø A(D) = T:D = D + 1
225Ø A(E) = Q:E = E + 1
226Ø GOSUB 235Ø
227Ø GOSUB 251Ø
228Ø PRINT AT 58Ø,"1";TAB(1Ø);"2";TAB(16);"3";TAB(22);
     "4";TAB(28);"5";TAB(34);"6";TAB(4Ø);"7";TAB(46);
     "8";TAB(52);"9";TAB(58);"1Ø"
229Ø PRINT AT 323,A(11);TAB(9);A(12);TAB(15);A(13);TAB(21);
     A(14);TAB(27);A(15);TAB(33);A(16);TAB(39);A(17);TAB(45);
```

```
          A(18);TAB(51);A(19);TAB(57);A(20)
2300 PRINT AT 451,A(21);TAB(9);A(22);TAB(15);A(23);TAB(21);
          A(24);TAB(27);A(25);TAB(33);A(26);TAB(39);A(27);TAB(45);
          A(28);TAB(51);A(19);TAB(57);A(30)
2310 GOSUB 2350:GOSUB 2430
2320 IF E = 31 THEN 2490
2330 PRINT AT 832, "▮"
2340 INPUT "ROLL";A:GOSUB 180:GOSUB 2510:GOTO 40
2350 FOR X = 0 TO 127
2360     SET (X,25):SET (X,19)
2370 NEXT X
2380 FOR X = 0 TO 3
2390     FOR Y = 14 TO 24
2400         SET (X,Y):SET (X + 124,Y)
2410     NEXT Y
2420 NEXT X
2430 FOR X = 3 TO 124 STEP 12
2440     FOR Y = 14 TO 24
2450         SET (X,Y)
2460     NEXT Y
2470 NEXT X
2480 RETURN
2490 PRINT AT 704, "GAME OVER"
2500 GOTO 2500
2510 Z = 640
2520 FOR N = 1 TO 5
2530     PRINT AT Z, "▮▮▮▮▮▮▮▮▮▮▮▮▮▮▮▮▮▮▮▮"
2540     Z = Z + 64
2550 NEXT N
2560 RETURN
2570 FOR X = 115 TO 124 STEP 3
2580     FOR Y = 2 TO 11
2590         RESET (X,Y)
2600     NEXT Y
2610 NEXT X
2620 RETURN
```

That concludes the chapter on using TRS-80 for games. Our objective was not so much to give you games to play as to demonstrate how games are constructed and to give you some insight into the process and thinking which goes into them. You can purchase games in tape form from numerous sources advertising in such magazines as *Kilobaud, Creative Computing, Personal Computing, 80 Microcomputing*, etc. They may or may not be directly suitable for your machine—but they'll be in BASIC. If all you want is to have some games to play, then for the right money you can obtain them. The most expensive game seen at this point costs about twenty dollars. But if you really want a challenge and have a lot of time on your hands to prove the game in every possible combination, you now have the approach to do so.

8
A Personal Accounts Payable System

Up to this point in the book, the approach has been to develop a program to perform a specific function. The program was a self-contained entity which performed a narrowly defined set of functions. So long as it could be made to fit into the available memory, that was sufficient. When memory became full, then it was necessary to find ways to either compress the program or reduce the features it was designed to perform.

In this chapter we will discuss the concept of a computer *system,* or more accurately, an *applications* system. The application is known to business as *Accounts Payable.* To us common folk, the process is known as "paying bills."

The concept of an applications system is that there are several programs, each designed to fulfill a specific function and each communicating some piece of information to a successive phase. As in the previous chapters, this application will be built in pieces, each built upon the previous one. The Accounts Payable System will be comprised of three programs, all large ones. They have been developed on a 32K TRS-80 system, to remove the otherwise necessary duplication, which would contribute little to the discussion. Where duplication is necessary to fit the system to a 4K system, instructions are contained in their proper place to assist you to do that. And now to the application itself.

At least once each month, each of us performs a ritual known as "paying bills." The word *ritual* is the key to this discussion, as the *process* is essentially the same for every bill: (1) The bill is received, and thereby "entered" to the process; (2) a check of available funds is made; (3) consideration is given to the due date of the bill; (4) records are kept for history and tax purposes; and (5) a demand certificate (check) is prepared and sent.

As in any manual system used for paying bills, an automated system must have places where decisions may be made. Will this bill be paid, will that one be deferred, what is the discount period and rate? This personal accounts payable system provides that flexibility.

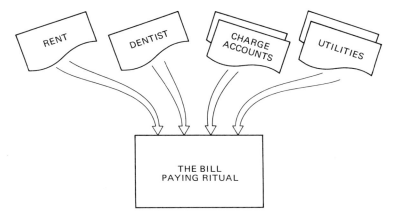

Figure 44.   Bill Payment Flow

It starts, of course, with the receipt and accumulation of invoices or with the recognition that an amount is due. In computer terms, this is the *input* to the system.

The bills which will be used as examples in this exercise may not be all of the bills you might consider for payment, but they are a representation of the types of bills most of us must pay. The first step, either manually or through the computer, is a review of the bills which someone wishes to have paid. For explanation, let's assume that your invoice stack consists of:

- One rent invoice
- One invoice from the dentist
- Two charge account invoices
- Two utilities invoices

There is one additional input, the amount of money available to pay these bills, perhaps the contents (or some portion of the contents) of your checking account.

The next step which is usually taken is to add up the bills to be paid and take a total, which is then checked against the available cash to determine if the supply of cash is sufficient to pay them all. For illustration, let's assume that your checkbook shows a balance of $205.17. Each document, in turn, is read; the "amount due" is read; and you record it on a piece of "scratch paper."

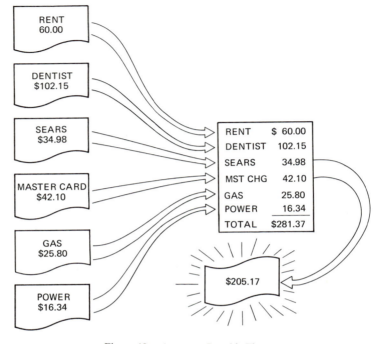

Figure 45.   Accounts Payable Flow

But there is a problem, there isn't enough money to cover the bills. While that is a "normal" situation, the process whereby that determination is made is significant. As can be seen from the preceding illustration, each invoice is "read" *individually*. The same approach is taken on the computer, except that a running total is kept on the scratchpad, rather than waiting until all items are listed and then taking the total.

In computer terms, each invoice, being examined one at a time, is in the loop. The recording on the scratchpad might take many forms. Included in these may be keeping track, in memory, of the total; writing it onto cassette tape; or printing it on paper. The loop ends when there is no more data to be considered. In the system which will be built here, the user of the system will provide the input one data item at a time, the computer does its operation upon that data, and then displays the resulting information or action. This, in fact, is the process whereby the microcomputer is said to be *interactive*. In flowchart form, that process looks like this:

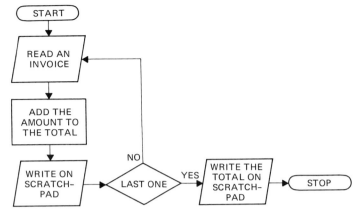

Figure 46.   Scratchpad process

The computer, of course, cannot manufacture money. It cannot produce money you do not have to pay your existing bills. It can, however, record that you have paid the debt, even though you may not have paid it, as it must assume that the data you provide is accurate. Every bill in the business world has what is known in the trade as a "drop dead" date, the date beyond which there will be some dire consequences. If you've ever gone too long on a utility bill and were threatened with disconnection, you will be familiar with the concept. The computer is a management tool. All the computer can be expected to do is advise you of what actions are recommended.

All of the transactions are now entered to the computer and are stored in memory. Alternatively, they could be stored on cassette tape and read into the computer. The program which will be presented following the discussion will assume keyboard input, but will identify where cassette tape routines could be appended.

The next phase of the system will be the edit phase where numbers can be examined to determine that they are indeed numbers and not letters; invoices can be displayed for visual verification; programmed checks can be incorporated to reject or at least identify for action a charge which could be considered to be "unreasonable." An unreasonable charge might just be an entry error. With enhanced equipment, such as disk storage, vendor files could be checked. Since the book assumes you do not have disk storage, that discussion will be treated only conceptually.

As the data about the referenced invoices have been entered, technically, a table which looks like this has been constructed:

PAYEE	INVOICE DATE	INVOICE AMOUNT	PAYMENT DATE	DIS-COUNT	DISCOUNT DATE	STATUS CODE	D.D. DATE
RENT	09/23/78	$ 60.00	09/30/78	.00	00/00/00	N	10/10/78
DENTIST	07/11/78	$102.15	03/03/78	.10	09/03/78	C	10/11/78
SEARS	08/03/78	$ 34.98	09/15/78	.06	10/14/78	B	11/03/78
MASTER CARD	09/15/78	$ 42.10	10/01/78	.00	00/00/00	A	11/15/78
GAS COMPANY	09/30/78	$ 25.80	10/27/78	.10	10/10/78	A	12/30/78
POWER COMPANY	09/30/78	$ 16.34	10/20/78	.10	10/10/78	A	12/30/78

Figure 47. Payables Table

Of course, in the computer's memory, the data isn't so nicely formatted, with headings, tabulations, and punctuation. It looks like this:

```
RENT∅9237860.∅∅∅93∅78.∅∅∅∅∅∅∅∅N1∅1∅78
```

And so on throughout the table. The status code will be discussed later. But there *is* one very important consideration: in order to work upon any data contained within the computer, it's necessary to define the size of the data. Since it is not known, at the beginning, how lengthy the table will be, it becomes necessary to provide a sentinel, as was done previously. The sentinel will go at the end of the table, and the table, will become DATA lines. (As previously stated, alphabetic data cannot be stored in an array, but with a combination of array usage and DATA line usage, the table can be constructed.) The ending of the table would look like this:

```
POWER COMPANY∅93∅7816.341∅2∅78.1∅1∅1∅78A123∅78
99999999
```

The sentinel will be constructed to provide 9s for every field in the table. The termination of the table will be the first step in Phase II (edit). It could have been included in Phase I (input) had that been desired. Either way, it must be done before any processing is done in Phase II. The table will be in the array, except for the alphabetic data, which will be stored in the DATA lines, however, the array *will* hold a reference to the appropiate DATA line.

Not everything the reader might need for an effective accounts payable system will be found in this application. Logical extensions of what is presented here might include the printing of checks and the preparation of printed registers. To do so, however, would require additional equipment. This application has been developed to be implementable on the Level I. If you have a 4K machine, it will be necessary to remove REMarks statements and subdivide the application as directed throughout the application. If you have a 16K system, removal of the REMarks should be sufficient. The system will fit nicely in 32K. If you do use a larger (Level II) system, however, include the following in your program:

```
5 DIM A(8∅∅)
```

The controlling mechanism of this Accounts Payable System is, as might be suspected, the number of people to be paid. In this system, the vendor number and name of the person or firm who is customarily paid is stored in DATA lines, like this:

```
1410 DATA 1, "RENT"
1420 DATA 2, "DENTIST"
1430 DATA 3, "SEARS"
1440 DATA 4, "MASTER CHARGE"
1450 DATA 5, "GAS COMPANY"
1460 DATA 6, "POWER COMPANY"
1470 DATA 9999, "9999"
```

Note that there is a sentinel line at the end of the DATA lines. That sentinel line is tremendously important, and is used at several places throughout the system for determination as to when things come to a halt: in this case, the scan of the DATA lines. If it is desired to add vendors to the list, they must be added between statements 1460 and 1470, because of the sequence number, at the first parameter of the DATA line. The list can be spotted at the end of Phase I, where additions may be made with relative ease. When you have advanced to Level II, resequencing programs are available which will allow expansion of the statement sequence numbers.

Phase I

Phase I is the data gathering phase. In this phase will be entered all the pertinent dates, amounts, and other data which will be used by the system. Phase I is a stand-alone data entry module; that is, no provision has been made for combining other invoices which have been previously stored on tape or other media. The logical place for this combination is, however, Phase II, and the interface point will be identified in the discussion of Phase II.

The first step is to clear out the array. The array will be 20 positions for each invoice, but since the total number of invoices is unknown, an amount equal to 20 times the number of vendors is cleared. That assumes one invoice per vendor, which may not be enough. In Level II, if the DIMension statement mentioned is used, there is space enough for 40 invoices. In Level I, however, there is a practical restriction of about 45 invoices, owing to the size of the available array. Also, the assumption has been made that the complete list of vendors will fit on one screen. If the number exceeds 10, then coding will have to be added to display them one group of 10 at a time. In any event, the array is cleared to permit the storage of data in this manner:

```
10 CLS:RESTORE
20 PRINT "CLEARING THE ARRAY"
30 FOR N = 1 TO 99
```

```
40      READ B,B$
50       IF B = 9999 THEN 70
60 NEXT N
70 Z = N
80 FOR N = 1 TO Z * 20
90      A(N) = 0
100 NEXT N
110 CLS:RESTORE:Z = 0
```

The next routine is not essential to the running of the system, so readers with limited memory configurations could consider its deletion. It allows the computer to be used as a hand calculator to allow you to determine the amounts of the bills in hand:

```
120 B = 0:A = 0
130 INPUT "DO YOU WISH TO DO A QUICK CALCULATION (Y/N)";A$
140 IF A$ < >"Y" THEN CLS:GOTO 210
150 INPUT "ENTER AMOUNT OF BILL";A
160 B = B + A
170 INPUT "IS THAT THE LAST NUMBER TO BE ENTERED (Y/N)";A$
180 IF A$ = "N" THEN CLS:GOTO 150
190 PRINT "TOTAL OF ALL BILLS IS: $";B
200 GOSUB 1390:GOSUB 1390:CLS
```

Statement 1390 is the timer subroutine, set at 500.

The actual opening to Phase I follows:

```
210 PRINT TAB(15);"SAM'S BILL PAYING RITUAL":PRINT
220 PRINT "ENTER ALL DOLLAR AMOUNTS IN DECIMAL FORMAT ONLY'
230 PRINT "DO NOT ENTER DOLLAR SIGNS OR COMMAS TO DOLLAR
    AMOUNTS":PRINT
240 PRINT "ENTER DATES IN MONTH, DAY, AND YEAR FORMAT"
250 PRINT "DO NOT ENTER WITH SLASHES"
260 PRINT "ENTER EACH SEPARATELY, HITTING THE ENTER KEY WITH
    EACH";PRINT
270 INPUT "PRESS ENTER KEY TO PROCEED";A
```

Substitute your name for SAM.

The process of data collection now begins, beginning with the collection of the current date. For the purposes of this illustration, the date is collected once. If the system is broken up, this coding should be duplicated in each seperate piece, as the current date is used in both Phase II and Phase III.

```
280 CLS
290 INPUT "ENTER MONTH OF CURRENT DATE";J
300 IF (J < 1) + (J > 12) THEN GOSUB 1400:GOTO 290
310 INPUT "ENTER DAY OF CURRENT DATE";K
320 IF (K < 1) + (K > 31)THEN GOSUB 1400:GOTO 310
330 INPUT "ENTER YEAR OF CURRENT DATE";L
340 IF (L < 79) + (L > 81) THEN GOSUB 1400:GOTO 330
350 M = L * 10000:M = M + (J * 100):M = M + K
```

Examine the instruction at 350. The instruction is constructed to "scale" the date. Beginning with the year, which has been INPUT to variable L, it is multiplied by 10,000—moving it to the left side of a six-digit number. If 79 had been entered as the year, it would now look like 790000. In similar fashion, the month is scaled by 100, to fit it into the middle positions of the six-digit number. If 12 were the month, the number would look like 791200. Then the day is simply added to the right-hand positions of the six-digit number. If the day of the month were 14, the number would be 791214. The reason for placing the date into this format is to structure it for comparison to other dates. In this manner, January 1, 1980, is larger *numerically* (800101) than January 1, 1979 (790101) or than December 31, 1979 (791231). If this were not done and the original format were retained, 123179 (12/31/79) would be numerically larger than 010180 (01/01/80). Note that with each item of data gathered, a range check is performed. The month is range-checked between 1 and 12, and the day of the month is range-checked between 1 and 31. While it is reconized that some months have fewer than 31 days, that logic would have to be added, if deemed to be important.

The next step is to list the people who are commonly paid, and who are located in the DATA lines. As mentioned, if there are more than 10, there should be added those instructions to cause the names to be listed on the screen 10 at a time. This is accomplished by a subroutine. Note that the printed line in the subroutine is displaced by one zone (statement 560) by the presence of the leading comma. Variable T will be used shortly to load the vendor number to the array.

```
360 CLS
370 T = 1
380 GOSUB 540

530 REM ****************************************************
540 RESTORE
550 PRINT "THESE ARE THE PAYEES WHOM YOU CUSTOMARILY PAY:":PRINT
560 PRINT, "PAYEE NUMBER","PAYEE NAME":PRINT
570 FOR N = 1 TO 99
580     READ B,B$
590     IF (B = 9999) + (B$ = "9999") THEN 620
600     PRINT ,B,B$
610 NEXT N
620 PRINT
630 RETURN
640 REM ****************************************************
```

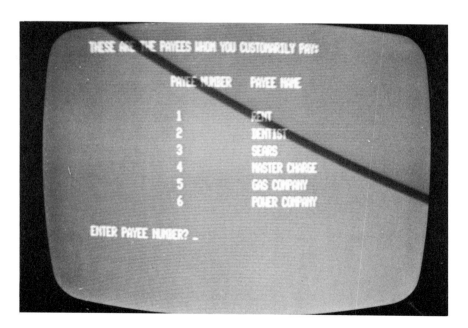

Figure 48. Payables Menu

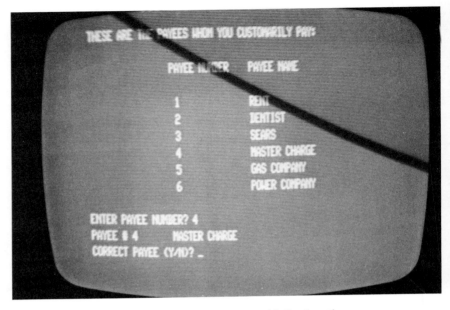

Figure 49.   Payables Menu with Confirmation

Once the vendor list has been displayed, the option to select the individual vendor is given. After a vendor is selected, confirmation is required before proceeding.

```
390 RESTORE
400 INPUT "ENTER PAYEE NUMBER";A
410 FOR N = 1 TO A
420     READ B.B$
430     IF (B = 9999) * (B$ = "9999") THEN 510
440 NEXT N
450 PRINT "PAYEE #":B,B$
460 INPUT "CORRECT PAYEE (Y/N)";A$
470 IF A$ = "Y" THEN 650
```

If the correct one has not been selected, the list is displayed again and the selection is offered a second time. If a vendor which is *not* displayed on the screen is selected, the message "PAYEE NOT IN DATA LINES" is displayed:

```
480 CLS
490 GOSUB 540
500 GOTO 390
510 CLS:PRINT "PAYEE NOT IN DATA LINES"
520 GOSUB 540:GOTO 390
```

It would be wise, at this point in the program, to relate how data is to be stored and manipulated in the program. In essence, there is a table of 20 entries for each vendor. All entries are numeric in the table, but they need not be numeric in nature:

1. Payee (numeric locator of vendor number from DATA lines)
2. Date of invoice month
3. Date of invoice day
4. Date of invoice year
5. Amount of invoice
6. Payment date month
7. Payment date day
8. Payment date year
9. Discount percent
10. Discount date month
11. Discount date day
12. Discount date year
13. Status code—numeric in table but refers to alphabetic code.
14. Drop dead date month
15. Drop dead date day
16. Drop dead date year
17. Table flag—will contain reconciliation codes.
18. Check number
19. Check amount
20. Check date

The first 16 are completed in Phase I, the remaining four are completed in either Phase II or Phase III.

The following are four one-line subroutines used with the Phase I coding. Statement 1370 stores the data element into the array (for 16 consecutive elements) while statement 1380 completes the remaining four elements (loaded with zero), making up the twenty. In this instance a FOR . . . NEXT loop is not used, as it is easy to account for all 20 positions.

```
1370 A(T) = A:T = T + 1:RETURN
1380 FOR N = 1 TO 4:A(T) = 0:T = T + 1:NEXT N:GOTO 990
1390 FOR N = 1 TO 500:NEXT N:RETURN
1400 PRINT "OUT OF RANGE":RETURN
```

Statement 1390 is a timer routine, used in several phases. Statement 1400 is an OUT OF RANGE message used wherever there is a range check made on dates in the following coding:

```
650 A(T) = A
660 T = T + 1
670 CLS
680 INPUT "ENTER INVOICE DATE - MONTH";A
690 IF (A < 1) + (A > 12) THEN GOSUB 1400:GOTO 680
700 GOSUB 1370
710 INPUT "ENTER INVOICE DATE - DAY";A
720 IF (A < 1) + (A > 31) THEN GOSUB 1400:GOTO 710
730 GOSUB 1370
740 INPUT "ENTER INVOICE DATE - YEAR";A
750 IF (A < 79) + (A > 81) THEN GOSUB 1400:GOTO 740
760 GOSUB 1370
770 INPUT "ENTER INVOICE AMOUNT $";A:Z = Z + A:GOSUB 1370:CLS
780 INPUT "ENTER PAYMENT DATE - MONTH";A
790 IF (A < 1) + (A > 12) THEN GOSUB 1400:GOTO 780
800 GOSUB 1370
810 INPUT "ENTER PAYMENT DATE - DAY";A
820 IF (A < 1) + (A > 31) THEN GOSUB 1400:GOTO 810
830 GOSUB 1370
840 INPUT "ENTER PAYMENT DATE - YEAR";A
850 IF (A < 79) + (A > 81) THEN GOSUB 1400:GOTO 840
860 GOSUB 1370:CLS
```

In succession, the following has occurred: the invoice date is requested and range-checked. Also requested is the invoice amount and the payment date, which is also range-checked. Note that the range is 1979 to 1981; although that can be easily modified, if necessary.

The discount information and the drop dead date information which will follow later in the coding are included with an eye to future expansion of the system. As the program is constructed, there is no comparison against the discount date nor any discount calculation done. Likewise, there is no review of those invoices which have passed the drop dead date. The former would come in Phase III, while the latter would belong to Phase II. But the proper place to load them is here. In the coding which follows, an alphabetic status code is also used, but that alphabetic status code must be converted to numeric for storage in the array. The process must be reversed when removing the code from the array.

```
870 INPUT "WILL THERE BE A DISCOUNT? (Y/N)";A$:PRINT
880 IF A$ = "N" THEN CLS:GOTO 1380
890 INPUT "ENTER DISCOUNT PERCENT (WITH DECIMAL)";A:GOSUB 1370
900 INPUT "ENTER DISCOUNT DATE - MONTH";A
910 IF (A < 1) + (A > 12) THEN GOSUB 1400:GOTO 900
920 GOSUB 1370
930 INPUT "ENTER DISCOUNT DATE - DAY";A
940 IF (A < 1) + (A > 31) THEN GOSUB 1400:GOTO 930
950 GOSUB 1370
960 INPUT "ENTER DISCOUNT DATE - YEAR";A
970 IF (A < 79) + (A > 81) THEN GOSUB 1400:GOTO 960
980 GOSUB 1370:CLS
990 PRINT "ENTER STATUS CODE":PRINT
1000 PRINT "A = CURRENT":PRINT
1010 PRINT "B = ONE MONTH IN ARREARS":PRINT
1020 PRINT "C = TWO MONTHS IN ARREARS":PRINT
1030 PRINT "N = NOT APPLICABLE":PRINT
1040 INPUT "WHICH";A$
1050 IF A$ = "A" THEN A(T) = 1:GOTO 1090
1060 IF A$ = "B" THEN A(T) = 2:GOTO 1090
1070 IF A$ = "C" THEN A(T) = 3:GOTO 1090
1080 A(T) = 0
1090 T = T + 1
1100 CLS
1110 INPUT "ENTER 'DROP DEAD' DATE - MONTH";A
```

```
1120 IF (A < 1) + (A > 12) THEN GOSUB 1400:GOTO 1110
1130 GOSUB 1370
1140 INPUT "ENTER 'DROP DEAD' DATE - DAY";A
1150 IF (A < 1) + (A > 31) THEN GOSUB 1400:GOTO 1140
1160 GOSUB 1370
1170 INPUT "ENTER 'DROP DEAD' DATE - YEAR";A
1180 IF (A < 79) + (A > 81) THEN GOSUB 1400:GOTO 1170
1190 GOSUB 1370
1200 FOR N = 1 TO 4:A(T) = 0:T = T + 1:NEXT N
```

Once that is done, the program askes if there is any more data to be entered. If there is, the process is repeated, if there is not, then a trial balance is struck. Once the trial balance is struck, statement 1250 places a sentinel line in the array. The array is then displayed to ensure that the loading has indeed taken place. If memory limitations are important, statements 1260 through 1350 may be removed with no noticeable damage. This is the trial balance routine, and should be used to balance against the calculated total you had before the process was begun:

```
1210 CLS:INPUT "LAST ENTRY TO BE MADE (Y/N)";A$
1220 IF A$ = "N" THEN GOSUB 540:GOTO 390
1230 CLS:PRINT "TRIAL BALANCE IS ";Z
1240 GOSUB 1390
1250 FOR N = 1 TO 20:A(T) = 9999:T = T + 1:NEXT N
1260 V = 1
1270 FOR N = 1 TO 99
1280    IF A(V) = 9999 THEN 1350
1290    FOR H = V TO V + 19
1300       PRINT A(H);
1310    NEXT H
1320    V = V + 20
1330    PRINT
1340 NEXT N
1350 GOSUB 1390:GOSUB 1390
1360 GOTO 1500
```

And that, with the exception of the one instruction and the documentation which follows, concludes Phase I:

```
1480 REM ***********************************************
1490 REM *
1500 GOTO 1940
1510 REM *
1520 REM ***********************************************
1530 REM *                                             *
1540 REM * THIS IS THE INTERFACE POINT - IF YOU WISH TO *
1550 REM * CONSTRUCT THIS AS A SEPARATE PROGRAM, YOU    *
1560 REM * SHOULD AT THIS POINT WRITE BOTH THE CURRENT  *
1570 REM * DATE (VARIABLE M) AND THE ENTIRE DATA ARRAY  *
1580 REM * TO CASSETTE TAPE.  IT WILL BE NECESSARY TO   *
1590 REM * CONSTRUCT A FOR...NEXT LOOP WHICH WILL DO    *
1600 REM * THE WRITING (PRINT #).  IMBEDDED IN THE LOOP *
1610 REM * SHOULD BE THE TEST FOR THE SENTINELS (9999). *
1620 REM *                                             *
1630 REM ***********************************************
1640 REM *
```

Statements 1480, 1490, and 1510 through 1640 may be removed if so desired.

PHASE II

Phase II is the "do everything" phase—it provides a variety of services, as the following documentation will attest:

```
1650 REM ***********************************************
1660 REM *                                             *
1670 REM * THIS IS THE BEGINNING OF PHASE II.  IF YOU  *
1680 REM * DESIRE TO HAVE THIS AS A SEPARATE PROGRAM,  *
1690 REM * YOU SHOULD HAVE INSERTED THE ROUTINES IN    *
1700 REM * PHASE I TO STORE THE CURRENT DATE (VARIABLE *
1710 REM * M) AND THE TABLE THAT WAS BUILT ON THE      *
1720 REM * CASSETTE TAPE.  ALSO, IF YOU SEPARATE       *
1730 REM * THIS PHASE, IT WILL BE NECESSARY TO DUPLI-  *
1740 REM * CATE THE DATA LINES, AS THEY HAVE NOT BEEN  *
1750 REM * STORED ON THE TAPE.  ALTERNATIVELY, YOU     *
1760 REM * COULD HAVE STORED THEM IN PHASE I AND       *
```

```
1770 REM * RETRIEVED THEM HERE.  FOR OUR PURPOSES, WE    *
1780 REM * WILL CONTINUE WITH THE PROGRAM, EVEN THOUGH   *
1790 REM * WE KNOW WE WILL EXCEED THE LEVEL I 4K         *
1800 REM * MEMORY.  IN VIEW OF THIS, THIS PHASE WILL     *
1810 REM * OFFER SIX OPTIONS:                            *
1820 REM *    1.  THE ABILITY TO TAKE A CURRENCY         *
1830 REM *        STATUS CHECK.                          *
1840 REM *    2.  THE ABILITY TO TAKE AN AGING REPORT.   *
1850 REM *    3.  THE ABILITY TO TAKE A FORECAST.        *
1860 REM *    4.  THE ABILITY TO LIST THE ARRAY IN AN    *
1870 REM *        INTELLIGIBLE FORMAT.                   *
1880 REM *    5.  A UTILITY SUBROUTINE WHICH ALLOWS      *
1890 REM *        SELECTION OPTIONS ON THE ARRAY.        *
1900 REM *    6.  A BY-PASS OPTION TO PASS DIRECTLY      *
1910 REM *        TO PHASE III FOR CHECKWRITING          *
1920 REM *                                               *
1930 REM ************************************************
```

Again, it should be stated that REMarks may be omitted from the program when memory limitations are a concern.

The menu options to provide Phase II services look like this:

```
1940 CLS:RESTORE
1950 PRINT "THIS IS PHASE II.  SELECT THE OPTION YOU DESIRE"
1960 PRINT:PRINT TAB(5);"1.  STATUS CHECK (SUBROUTINE A)"
1970 PRINT:PRINT TAB(5);"2.  AGING REPORT (SUBROUTINE B)"
1980 PRINT:PRINT TAB(5);"3.  FORECAST REPORT (SUBROUTINE C)"
1990 PRINT:PRINT TAB(5);"4.  COMPLETE A/P LIST (SUBROUTINE D)"
2000 PRINT:PRINT TAB(5);"5.  UTILITY SUBROUTINE (SUBROUTINE E)"
2010 PRINT:PRINT TAB(5);"6.  PHASE III (CHECKWRITER)"
2020 A = 0:PRINT:INPUT "WHICH";A
2030 ON A GOTO 2090,2300,2620,2940,3200,4920:GOTO 1940
```

Every program or system has one load-bearing routine, and the routine which follows is that routine for this program/system. It shoulders much of the display load, at least that which is devoted to the display of the record. As such, it is used in several places in both Phase II and Phase III. If the

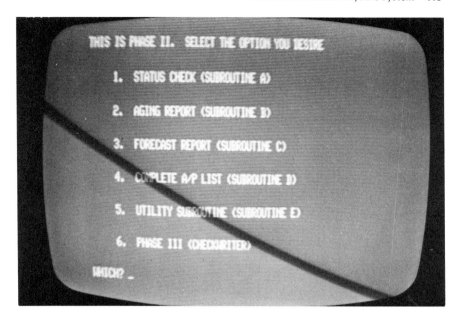

Figure 50.   Phase II Menu

phases are to be separated, this routine, plus the DATA lines, should be duplicated.

```
3020 PRINT AT 128,"PAYEE","DATE OF INV","AMT OF INV","PMT DATE"
3030 FOR F = 1 TO A(V):READ B,B$:NEXT F:RESTORE
3040 PRINT B$,A(V+1);A(V+2);A(V+3),"$";A(V+4),A(V+5),A(V+6);A(V+7):
     PRINT
3050 PRINT "DISC PCT","DISC DATE","STATUS","DROP DEAD DATE"
3060 IF A(V+12) = 0 THEN A$ = "N":GOTO 3100
3070 IF A(V+12) = 1 THEN A$ = "A":GOTO 3100
3080 IF A(V+12) = 2 THEN A$ = "B":GOTO 3100
3090 IF A(V+12) = 3 THEN A$ = "C"
3100 PRINT A(V+8),A(V+9),A(V+10),A(V+11),"%";A$,A(V+13);
     A(V+14);A(V+15)
3110 PRINT:PRINT "TABLE FLAG","CHECK NR","AMT OF CK","DT OF CHECK"
3120 PRINT A(V+16),A(V+17),"$";A(V+18),A(V+19):PRINT
3130 INPUT "PRESS ENTER TO CONTINUE";A
3140 RETURN
```

The first menu of the phase offers the ability to extract the records which fit one of the status codes. Status codes include A (current), B (in arrears 1 month), C (in arrears 2 months), and N (not applicable). As part of your contemplated expansion of the system, consider reviewing the data to determine which records would change from one code to another (e.g., from A to B) at the appropriate time. This routine selects those which meet the criteria provided to the program at the time of operation:

```
2040 REM ***************************************************
2050 REM * THIS ROUTINE IS NEARLY SELF-CONTAINED AND CAN BE  *
2060 REM * SEPARATED.  IT DOES REQUIRE ALL PRECONDITIONS FOR *
2070 REM * PHASE II PLUS ONE COPY OF SUBROUTINE AT 3020.     *
2080 REM ***************************************************
2090 CLS:PRINT "STATUS CHECK ROUTINE":PRINT
2100 PRINT "WHICH RECORDS DO YOU WISH TO EXAMINE:":PRINT
2110 PRINT TAB(5);"1.   STATUS A - CURRENT":PRINT
2120 PRINT TAB(5);"2.   STATUS B - ONE MONTH IN ARREARS":PRINT
2130 PRINT TAB(5);"3.   STATUS C - TWO MONTHS IN ARREARS":PRINT
2140 PRINT TAB(5);"4.   STATUS N - NOT APPLICABLE":PRINT
2150 INPUT "WHICH";A:CLS
2160 ON A GOTO 2180,2180,2180,2170:GOTO 2090
2170 A = 0
2180 V = 1
2190 FOR N = 1 TO 99
2200     IF A(V) = 9999 THEN 1940
2210     IF A(V + 12) = A THEN GOSUB 3020
2220     V = V + 20
2230 NEXT N
2240 GOTO 1940
```

The next two menu options (routines) are similar. The first allows you to pick a date in the past and to present on the screen all the records whose payment date falls between the past date and the current date entered to the system in Phase I. The second allows you to select a date in the future and identify all records whose payment date falls between the current date and the future date. Note that the year parameters have been moved back to 77 and foward to 82, respectively:

```
2250 REM ****************************************************
2260 REM * THIS ROUTINE IS NEARLY SELF-CONTAINED AND CAN BE  *
2270 REM * SEPARATED.  IT DOES REQUIRE ALL PRECONDITIONS FOR *
2280 REM * PHASE II PLUS ONE COPY OF SUBROUTINE AT 3020.    *
2290 REM ****************************************************
2300 CLS:PRINT "ACCOUNTS RECEIVABLE AGING REPORT":PRINT
2310 PRINT "THE CURRENT DATE IS :":PRINT
2320 L = M
2330 J = L / 10000:J = INT(J):L = L - (J * 10000)
2340 K = L / 100:K = INT(K):L = L - (K * 100)
2350 PRINT "DAY","MONTH","YEAR"
2360 PRINT L,K,J
2370 PRINT:PRINT "THE REPORT IS STRUCTURED TO PROVIDE ALL DATA"
2380 PRINT "FROM THE DATE YOU WILL ENTER TO THE CURRENT DATE."
2390 PRINT:INPUT "ENTER YEAR OF INCLUSIVE DATE";J
2400 IF J < 77 PRINT "OUT OF RANGE - RE-ENTER":GOTO 2390
2410 IF J > INT(M / 10000) PRINT "INVALID ENTRY":GOTO 2390
2420 PRINT:INPUT "ENTER MONTH OF INCLUSIVE DATE";K
2430 IF (K < 1) + (K > 12) PRINT "OUT OF RANGE":GOTO 2420
2440 PRINT:INPUT "ENTER DAY OF INCLUSIVE DATE":L
2450 IF (L < 1) + (L > 31) PRINT "OUT OF RANGE":GOTO 2440
2460 V = 1:CLS
2470 P = (J * 10000) + (K * 100) + L
2480 Q = (A(V + 7) * 10000) + (A(V + 6) * 100) + A(V + 5)
2490 FOR N = 1 TO 99
2500     IF A(V) = 9999 THEN 1940
2510     IF (Q > = P) * (Q < = M) THEN 2530
2520     GOTO 2550
2530     GOSUB 3020
2540     V = V + 20
2550 NEXT N
2560 GOTO 1940
2570 REM ****************************************************
2580 REM * THIS ROUTINE IS NEARLY SELF-CONTAINED AND CAN BE  *
2590 REM * SEPARATED.  IT DOES REQUIRE ALL PRECONDITIONS FOR *
```

```
2600 REM * PHASE II PLUS ONE COPY OF SUBROUTINE AT 3020.      *
2610 REM ****************************************************
2620 CLS:PRINT "ACCOUNTS RECEIVABLE FORECAST REPORT"
2630 PRINT "THE CURRENT DATE IS: ":PRINT
2640 L = M
2650 J = L / 10000:J = INT(J):L = L - (J * 10000)
2660 K = L / 100:K = INT(K):L = L - (K * 100)
2670 PRINT "DAY","MONTH","YEAR"
2680 PRINT L,K,J
2690 PRINT:PRINT "THE REPORT IS STRUCTURED TO PROVIDE ALL DATA"
2700 PRINT "FROM THE CURRENT DATE TO THE DATE YOU WILL ENTER."
2710 PRINT:INPUT "ENTER YEAR OF INCLUSIVE DATE";J
2720 IF J > 82 PRINT "OUT OF RANGE - RE-ENTER":GOTO 2710
2730 IF J < INT(M / 10000) PRINT "INVALID ENTRY":GOTO 2710
2740 PRINT:INPUT "ENTER MONTH OF INCLUSIVE DATE";K
2750 IF (K < 1) + (K > 12) PRINT "OUT OF RANGE":GOTO 2740
2760 PRINT:INPUT "ENTER DAY OF INCLUSIVE DATE";L
2770 IF (L < 1) + (L > 31) PRINT "OUT OF RANGE":GOTO 2760
2780 V = 1:CLS
2790 P = (J * 10000) + (K * 100) + L
2800 Q = (A(V + 7) * 10000) + (A(V + 6) * 100) + A(V + 5)
2810 FOR N = 1 TO 99
2820     IF A(V) = 9999 THEN 1940
2830     IF (Q < = P) * (Q > = M) THEN 2850
2840     GOTO 2870
2850     GOSUB 3020
2860     V = V + 20
2870 NEXT N
2880 GOTO 1940
```

The fourth menu option is simply the ability to display all the accounts payable records:

```
2890 REM ****************************************************
2900 REM * THIS ROUTINE IS NEARLY SELF-CONTAINED AND CAN BE  *
2910 REM * SEPARATED.  IT DOES REQUIRE ALL PRECONDITIONS FOR *
2920 REM * PHASE II PLUS ONE COPY OF SUBROUTINE AT 3020.      *
```

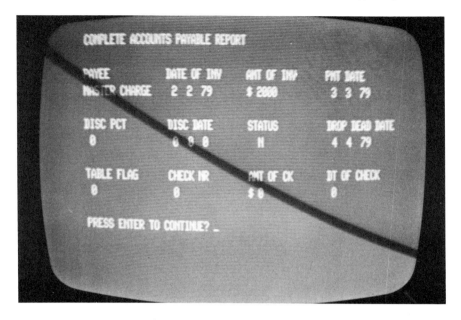

Figure 51.   Complete Accounts Payable Report

```
2930 REM ***************************************************
2940 CLS:PRINT "COMPLETE ACCOUNTS PAYABLE REPORT"
2950 V = 1
2960 FOR N = 1 TO 99
2970     IF A(V) = 9999 THEN 1940
2980     GOSUB 3020
2990     V = V + 20
3000 NEXT N
3010 GOTO 1940
```

The next routine, the maintenance routine, permits you to modify any portion of the record without controls. In this manner, assuming you know what you are doing, you can modify records beyond the parameters detailed in Phase I. It begins with a caution:

```
3150 REM ***************************************************
3160 REM * THIS ROUTINE IS NEARLY SELF-CONTAINED AND CAN BE  *
3170 REM * SEPARATED.  IT DOES REQUIRE ALL PRECONDITIONS FOR *
3180 REM * PHASE II PLUS ONE COPY OF SUBROUTINE AT 3020.     *
```

```
3190 REM ***********************************************************
3200 CLS:PRINT "THIS ROUTINE GIVES YOU THE ABILITY TO MODIFY"
3210 PRINT "ANY PORTION OF THE RECORD UNDER EXAMINATION."
3220 PRINT:PRINT "IT DOES SO WITHOUT REGARD TO EDIT RULES,"
3230 PRINT "SO IF YOU CHANGE IT, YOU DO SO AT YOUR OWN PERIL."
3240 PRINT:INPUT "PRESS ENTER TO BEGIN";A
3250 CLS:PRINT "THE RECORD WILL BE DISPLAYED FIRST AND YOU"
3260 PRINT "WILL BE GIVEN TIME TO EXAMINE IT.  YOU MUST THEN"
3270 PRINT "PRESS ENTER TO RECEIVE THE OPTIONS."
3280 PRINT:INPUT "PRESS ENTER TO CONTINUE";A
```

And then, the menu:

```
3290 V = 1:CLS
3300 FOR N = 1 TO 999
3310     IF A(V) = 9999 THEN 1940
3320     GOSUB 3020
3330     INPUT "PRESS ENTER TO RECEIVE OPTIONS";A
3340     CLS
3350     PRINT "MODIFICATION OF PAYEE NOT PERMITTED":PRINT
3360     PRINT TAB(5);"1.  MODIFY DATE OF INVOICE"
3370     PRINT TAB(5);"2.  MODIFY AMOUNT OF INVOICE"
3380     PRINT TAB(5);"3.  MODIFY PAYMENT DATE"
3390     PRINT TAB(5);"4.  MODIFY DISCOUNT PERCENT"
3400     PRINT TAB(5);"5.  MODIFY DISCOUNT DATE"
3410     PRINT TAB(5);"6.  MODIFY STATUS CODE"
3420     PRINT TAB(5);"7.  MODIFY DROP DEAD DATE"
3430     PRINT TAB(5);"8.  MODIFY TABLE FLAG"
3440     PRINT TAB(5);"9.  MODIFY CHECK NUMBER"
3450     PRINT:INPUT "SELECT";A
3460     ON A GOTO 3470,3580,3660,3770,3850,3960,4170,
         4280,4410:GOTO 1940
```

Note that the menu (and the whole routine, for that matter) is located inside a FOR . . . NEXT loop that is sufficiently large so it should not be exhausted. Note also that only 9 of the 20 items in the table can be modified. This can be expanded at will, using the same principles that are followed in the 9 routines which may be selected.

The routines which follow correspond to the menu options. They are designed to modify the array directly without benefit of editing. They do, however, make use of two additional subroutines, as follows:

```
4630 CLS:PRINT "EXAMINE FOR ACCURACY":PRINT:RETURN
4640 PRINT:INPUT "CORRECT (Y/N)";A$:RETURN
```

And now the menu routines, in succession:

```
3470    CLS:PRINT "YOU HAVE CHOSEN TO CHANGE THE INVOICE
        DATE":PRINT
3480    GOSUB 4520
3490    PRINT A(V + 1),A(V + 2),A(V + 3):PRINT
3500    PRINT:INPUT "ENTER CORRECTED YEAR";A(V + 3)
3510    PRINT:INPUT "ENTER CORRECTED MONTH";A(V + 2)
3520    PRINT:INPUT "ENTER CORRECTED DAY";A(V + 1)
3530    GOSUB 4630
3540    GOSUB 3020
3550    GOSUB 4640
3560    IF A$ <> "Y" THEN 3470
3570    GOTO 4560
3580    CLS:PRINT "YOU HAVE CHOSEN TO CHANGE THE AMOUNT OF THE
        INVOICE"
3590    PRINT:PRINT "CURRENT INVOICE AMOUNT IS $";A(V + 4)
3600    PRINT:INPUT "ENTER THE CORRECTED AMOUNT $";A(V + 4)
3610    GOSUB 4630
3620    GOSUB 3020
3630    GOSUB 4640
3640    IF A$ <> "Y" THEN 3580
3650    GOTO 4560
3660    CLS:PRINT "YOU HAVE CHOSEN TO CHANGE THE PAYMENT
        DATE":PRINT
3670    GOSUB 4520
3680    PRINT A(V + 5),A(V + 6),A(V + 7):PRINT
3690    INPUT "ENTER CORRECTED YEAR";A(V + 7)
3700    INPUT "ENTER CORRECTED MONTH";A(V + 6)
3710    INPUT "ENTER CORRECTED DAY";A(V + 5)
```

```
3720        GOSUB 4630
3730        GOSUB 3020
3740        GOSUB 4640
3750        IF A$ <> "Y" THEN 3660
3760        GOTO 4560
3770        CLS:PRINT "YOU HAVE CHOSEN TO CHANGE THE DISCOUNT
            PERCENT":PRINT
3780        PRINT:PRINT "CURRENT DISCOUNT PERCENT IS ";A(V + 8):PRINT
3790        INPUT "WHAT WOULD YOU LIKE IT TO BE";A(V + 8):PRINT
3800        GOSUB 4630
3810        GOSUB 3020
3820        GOSUB 4640
3830        IF A$ <> "Y" THEN 3770
3840        GOTO 4560
3850        CLS:PRINT "YOU HAVE CHOSEN TO CHANGE THE DISCOUNT
            DATE":PRINT
3860        GOSUB 4520
3870        PRINT A(V + 9),A(V + 10),A(V + 11):PRINT
3880        PRINT:INPUT "ENTER CORRECTED YEAR";A(V + 11)
3890        PRINT:INPUT "ENTER CORRECTED MONTH";A(V + 10)
3900        PRINT:INPUT "ENTER CORRECTED DAY";A(V + 9)
3910        GOSUB 4630
3920        GOSUB 3020
3930        GOSUB 4640
3940        IF A$ <> "Y" THEN 3850
390        GOTO 4560
3960        CLS:PRINT "YOU HAVE CHOSEN TO MODIFY THE STATUS CODE":PRIN
3970        IF A(V + 12) = 1 THEN B$ = "A":GOTO 4010
3980        IF A(V + 12) = 2 THEN B$ = "B":GOTO 4010
3990        IF A(V + 12) = 3 THEN B$ = "C":GOTO 4010
4000        B$ = "N"
4010        PRINT "CURRENT STATUS CODE IS ";B$:PRINT
4020        PRINT "AVAILABLE STATUS CODES ARE:":PRINT
4030        PRINT TAB(5);"A - CURRENT"
4040        PRINT TAB(5);"B - ONE MONTH IN ARREARS"
4050        PRINT TAB(5);"C - TWO MONTHS IN ARREARS"
```

```
4060        PRINT TAB(5);"N - NOT APPLICABLE":PRINT
4070        INPUT "SELECT WHICH CODE APPLIES";A$
4080        IF A$ = "A" THEN A(V + 12) = 1:GOTO 4120
4090        IF A$ = "B" THEN A(V + 12) = 2:GOTO 4120
4100        IF A$ = "C" THEN A(V + 12) = 3:GOTO 4120
4110        A(V + 12) = 0
4120        GOSUB 4630
4130        GOSUB 3020
4140        GOSUB 4640
4150        IF A$ < > "Y" THEN 3960
4160        GOTO 4560
4170        CLS:PRINT "YOU HAVE CHOSEN TO MODIFY THE
            DROP-DEAD-DATE":PRINT
4180        GOSUB 4520
4190        PRINT A(V + 13),A(V + 14),A(V + 15):PRINT
4200        INPUT "ENTER CORRECTED YEAR";A(V + 15):PRINT
4210        INPUT "ENTER CORRECTED MONTH";A(V + 14):PRINT
4220        INPUT "ENTER CORRECTED DAY";A(V + 13):PRINT
4230        GOSUB 4630
4240        GOSUB 3020
4250        GOSUB 4640
4260        IF A$ < > "Y" THEN 4170
4270        GOTO 4560
4280        CLS:PRINT "YOU HAVE CHOSEN TO MODIFY THE TABLE FLAG":PRINT
4290        PRINT "ACCEPTABLE CODES ARE:":PRINT
4300        PRINT TAB(5);"1.  CHECK VOIDED":PRINT
4310        PRINT TAB(5);"2.  PARTIAL PAYMENT":PRINT
4320        PRINT TAB(5);"3.  NON-TAX ITEM":PRINT
4330        INPUT "WHICH";A
4340        IF (A < 1) + (A > 3) THEN 4280
4350        A(V + 16) = A
4360        GOSUB 4630
4370        GOSUB 3020
4380        GOSUB 4640
4390        IF A$ < > "Y" THEN 4280
4400        GOTO 4560
```

```
4410    CLS:PRINT "YOU HAVE CHOSEN TO CHANGE THE CHECK
        NUMBER":PRINT
4420    PRINT "CURRENT CHECK NUMBER IS ";A(V + 17):PRINT
4430    INPUT "ENTER THE CORRECTED NUMBER";A(V + 17):PRINT
4440    GOSUB 4630
4450    GOSUB 3020
4460    GOSUB 4640
4470    IF A$ <> "Y" THEN 4410
4480    GOTO 4560
4490    V = V + 20
4500 NEXT N
4510 GOTO 1940
4520 PRINT:PRINT "MANDATORY TO COMPLETE ALL ENTRIES"
4530 PRINT:PRINT "DATE ON RECORD IS:"
4540 PRINT "DAY","MONTH","YEAR":PRINT
4550 RETURN
4560 CLS:PRINT "ENDING OPTIONS:":PRINT
4570 PRINT "1.  MAKE MORE CHANGES TO THE RECORD":PRINT
4580 PRINT "2.  OBTAIN THE NEXT RECORD":PRINT
4590 PRINT "3.  RETURN TO THE MAINTENANCE MENU":PRINT
4600 PRINT "4.  RETURN TO THE PHASE II MENU":PRINT
4610 INPUT "WHICH";A:CLS
4620 ON A GOTO 4500,4490,3200,1940:GOTO 4560
4650 REM *************************************************
4660 REM * THIS IS THE INTERFACE POINT BETWEEN PHASE II  *
4670 REM * PHASE III.  IN ORDER TO SUCCESSFULLY USE PHASE *
4680 REM * III AT THIS POINT, IT IS AGAIN NECESSARY TO    *
4690 REM * EITHER CONTINUE FROM THE POINT OR TO STORE THE *
4700 REM * ARRAY ONTO A TAPE FOR SUBSEQUENT ENTRY TO THE  *
4710 REM * PHASE.  IT WILL NOT BE NECESSARY TO STORE THE  *
4720 REM * CURRENT DATE (VARIABLE M), BUT THERE WOULD BE  *
4730 REM * NO REASON TO CHANGE THE ROUTINE YOU DEVELOP    *
4740 REM * FOR USE BETWEEN PHASE I AND II.  JUST BE SURE  *
4750 REM * TO RECOGNIZE THAT YOU HAVE IT ON TAPE.  SINCE  *
4760 REM * PHASE II IS THE EDIT PHASE, IT SHOULD BE VERY  *
4770 REM * OBVIOUS THAT YOU CAN PROGRESS FROM PHASE I TO  *
```

```
4780 REM * PHASE III DIRECTLY, BUT TO DO SO NEGATES THE   *
4790 REM * VALUE OF THE EDITS PERFORMED.                  *
4800 REM ************************************************
```

That does it for Phase II

PHASE III

Phase III is the checkwriter program. In it you can write either the full amount or a partial payment. You are also given the option to bypass the record. It begins by determining how much you have in your checkbook and what the next check number is:

```
4800 REM ************************************************
4810 REM *                                              *
4820 REM * THIS IS PHASE III.  YOU GET HERE EITHER BY   *
4830 REM * TAKING OPTION 6 FROM THE PHASE II MENU OR BY *
4840 REM * ENTRY TO THIS PROGRAM DIRECT.                *
4850 REM *                                              *
4860 REM * LIKE THE OTHER ROUTINES, PHASE III ALSO MAKES *
4870 REM * USE OF THE SUBROUTINE AT 3020, SO IF YOU ARE *
4880 REM * TO MAKE THIS A STAND-ALONE ROUTINE, IT WILL  *
4890 REM * ALSO BE NECESSARY TO DUPLICATE THAT ROUTINE  *
4900 REM * HERE.  THE SAME IS TRUE FOR THE DATE LINES.  *
4910 REM ************************************************
4920 CLS:PRINT "THIS IS THE CHECK-WRITING PHASE OF THE ACCOUNTS"
4930 PRINT "PAYABLE SYSTEM.  IT DOES NOT WRITE CHECKS, PER SE,"
4940 PRINT "BUT IT DOES PERMIT YOU TO VIEW EACH RECORD, MAKE A"
4950 PRINT "DETERMINATION AS TO WHAT YOU WISH TO PAY, WHETHER"
4960 PRINT "YOU WISH TO MAKE FULL OR PARTIAL PAYMENTS, ASSIGNS"
4970 PRINT "CHECK NUMBERS, KEEPS YOUR CHECKBOOK BALANCE, AND"
4980 PRINT "PREPARES A LEDGER ENTRY.":PRINT
4990 INPUT "PRESS ENTER TO CONTINUE";A
5000 CLS:PRINT "ENTER THE BALANCE IN YOUR CHECKBOOK AFTER ALL"
5010 INPUT "DEPOSITS HAVE BEEN CREDITED AND ALL CHARGES DEBITED.";H
5020 PRINT:PRINT "YOUR CHECKBOOK BALANCE IS $";H
5030 INPUT "IS THAT CORRECT (Y/N)";A$
5040 IF A$ <> "Y" THEN 5000
```

```
5050 CLS:INPUT "ENTER THE NEXT CHECK NUMBER";C
5060 PRINT:PRINT "YOU SAID THE NEXT CHECK NUMBER IS #";C
5070 INPUT "IS THAT CORRECT (Y/N)";A$
5080 IF A$ <>"Y" THEN 5050
5090 K = C
5100 CLS:PRINT "ONCE YOU HAVE MADE THE ENTRY, YOU WILL HAVE"
5110 PRINT "TO ENTER PHASE II MAINTENANCE TO REVERSE AN ENTRY."
5120 PRINT:INPUT "PRESS ENTER TO BEGIN";A
```

In addition, there is the ability to view the invoice again and also the ability to terminate the checkwriting process if you suddenly discover that you're out of money.

```
5130 V = 1:CLS
5140 FOR N = 1 TO 999
5150     IF A(V) = 9999 THEN 5720
5160     GOSUB 3020
5170     INPUT "PRESS ENTER TO REVIEW OPTIONS";A
5180     CLS:PRINT "THE OPTIONS ARE:":PRINT
5190     PRINT "1.  WRITE THE CHECK FOR THE FULL AMOUNT":PRINT
5200     PRINT "2.  WRITE THE CHECK FOR A PARTIAL AMOUNT":PRINT
5210     PRINT "3.  BYPASS THE INVOICE":PRINT
5220     PRINT "4.  VIEW THE INVOICE AGAIN":PRINT
5230     PRINT "5.  TERMINATE THE CHECKWRITING PROCESS":PRINT
5240     PRINT:INPUT "SELECT";A
5250     ON A GOTO 5290,5520,5700,5150,5720:GOTO 5180
```

The full payment routine begins by checking the amount of the invoice against what you have in your account. If there are not sufficient funds to cover it, you are so advised and you may go back to the menu and determine if you wish to make a partial payment. If you make a full payment, the amount of the invoice is reduced to zero, and your balance reduced by the amount of the invoice. The check number is posted, the amount of the check, and the date in the 6-digit format:

```
5260 REM ***********************************************
5270 REM *            PAYMENT IN FULL ROUTINE          *
5280 REM ***********************************************
```

```
5290     CLS:PRINT "YOU HAVE CHOSEN TO PAY THE INVOICE IN FULL"
5300 PRINT
5310     IF H >= A(V + 4) THEN 5370
5320     PRINT "THERE ARE INSUFFICIENT FUNDS TO COVER THIS INVOICE"
5330     PRINT "THE BILL IS FOR $";A(V + 4)
5340     PRINT:PRINT "YOUR BALANCE IS $";H
5350     PRINT:INPUT "PRESS ENTER TO RETURN TO MENU";A:CLS
5360     GOTO 5180
5370     CLS:PRINT "PAYMENT MADE":PRINT
5380     H = H = A(V + 4)
5390     PRINT "CHECKBOOK BALANCE NOW $";H:PRINT
5400     A(V + 17) = C:C = C + 1
5410     A(V + 18) = A(V + 4)
5420     A(V + 4) = 0
5430     A(V + 19) = M
5440     INPUT "IS THIS A TAX-EXEMPT PURCHASE (Y/N)";A$
5450     IF A$ = "Y" THEN A(V + 16) = 3
5460     PRINT:INPUT "PRESS ENTER TO VIEW RECORD";A:CLS
5470     GOSUB 3020
5480     GOTO 5700
```

Also, you are asked if the purchase is tax-exempt for tax purposes.

The partial payment routine presents the amount of the invoice and then questions how much you wish to pay. Again, if there are not sufficient funds in your account, you are so advised. If the edits pass, then the amount of your partial payment is deducted from the invoice amount, and the appropriate table flag for partial payment is made, the check assigned, and the date.

```
5490 REM ***********************************************
5500 REM *          PARTIAL PAYMENT ROUTINE           *
5510 REM ***********************************************
5520     CLS:PRINT "YOU HAVE CHOSEN TO PARTIALLY PAY THE INVOICE"
5530     PRINT:PRINT "THE AMOUNT OF THE INVOICE IS $";A(V + 4)
5540     PRINT:INPUT "HOW MUCH DO YOU WISH TO PAY - $";A
5550     IF A <= H THEN 5600
5560     PRINT "INSUFFICIENT FUNDS"
```

```
5570      PRINT "THE INVOICE IS FOR $";A(V + 4)
5580      PRINT "YOUR BALANCE IS $";H
5590      GOTO 5540
5600      CLS:PRINT "PARTIAL PAYMENT ACCEPTED":PRINT
5610      H = H - A:A(V + 4) = A(V + 4) - A
5620      PRINT:PRINT "CHECKBOOK BALANCE NOW $";H
5630      PRINT:PRINT "BALANCE OF ACCOUNT NOW $";A(V + 4)
5640      A(V + 17) = C:C = C + 1
5650      A(V + 18) = A
5660      A(V + 19) = M
5670      A(V + 16) = 2
5680      PRINT:INPUT "PRESS ENTER TO VIEW RECORD";A:CLS
5690      GOSUB 3020
5700      V = V + 20
5710 NEXT N
```

Finally, the paid invoices are displayed for you to post to your manual check ledger. And, as the REMarks point out, it is here that you may add some additional features to the system:

```
5720 CLS:PRINT "CHECKWRITING PROCESS TERMINATED":PRINT
5730 PRINT:PRINT "THE INVOICES UPON WHICH PAYMENT HAS BEEN MADE"
5740 PRINT "WILL NOW BE PRESENTED, ONE AT A TIME.  YOU WILL HAVE"
5750 PRINT "TIME TO RECORD THEM IN YOUR CHECKBOOK LEDGER."
5760 PRINT:INPUT "PRESS ENTER WHEN YOU ARE READY.";A
5770 REM ***********************************************
5780 REM * AT THIS POINT YOU SHOULD INSTALL THE ROUTINE TO    *
5790 REM * COPY THE SCREEN ENTRIES ONTO A TAPE.  THIS TAPE    *
5800 REM * WILL BE YOUR AUTOMATED LEDGER, WHICH WILL PERMIT   *
5810 REM * YOU TO RECONCILE YOUR CHECKS WHEN THEY ARE         *
5820 REM * RETURNED.  ALSO, YOU SHOULD DEVELOP A UTILITY TO   *
5830 REM * COMBINE ALL SUCH TAPES BEFORE BUILDING THE CHECK   *
5840 REM * RECONCILIATION ROUTINE.                            *
5850 REM *                                                    *
5860 REM * AT THE COMPLETION OF THIS TAPE YOU SHOULD ALSO     *
5870 REM * DRAW A TAPE OF ALL REMAINING INVOICE BALANCES.     *
```

```
5880 REM * THE ROUTINE TO READ THIS TAPE SHOULD BE ADDED TO   *
5890 REM * PHASE II TO BE COMBINED WITH INVOICES WHICH ARE     *
5900 REM * DERIVED FROM PHASE I.                               *
5910 REM ******************************************************
5920 V = 1 CLS
5930 FOR N = 1 TO 99
5940     IF A(V) = 9999 THEN 6030
5950     IF A(V + 17) = K THEN 6000
5960     IF A(V + 17) = C - 1 THEN 6040
5970     V = V + 20
5980 NEXT N
5990 GOTO 6040
6000 GOSUB 3020
6010 K = K + 1
6020 GOTO 5920
6030 IF K  <>  C - 1 PRINT "NO MATCH FOR CHECK #ʊ";K:GOTO 6010
```

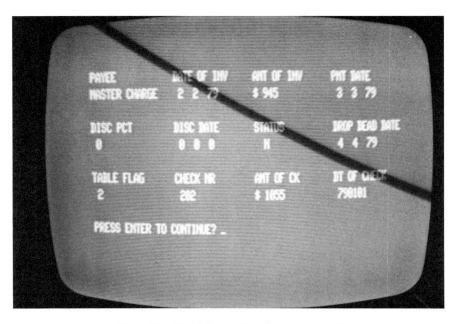

Figure 52.   Check Recap (Note the overpayment)

From Figure 52, it would appear that the invoice has been overpaid. Actually, this screen was the result of a partial payment of $1055. The invoice balance of $975 is the outstanding amount.

And then all that remains is to close the program and the system with the following:

```
6040 CLS
6050 FOR N = 1 TO 7:PRINT:NEXT N
6060 PRINT TAB(15);"E N D   O F   A C C O U N T S"
6070 PRINT TAB(15); "P A Y A B L E   S Y S T E M"
6080 GOTO 6080
```

As has been pointed out, this is really not the end of the system. Depending upon how much memory you have and what level you are using, it may be necessary to add other modules—tape writes and loads between the phases, utilities to combine data tapes by reading each into memory and writing them out as a whole. These are perhaps beyond the scope of this book, but you have the necessary knowledge at this point to accomplish that. You should also consider adding the features to calculate the discounts by percent and by date comparison to the current date. Finally, you should include, as part of the projection module, the ability to do your projection survey on the drop-dead dates. Also, you might consider adding that consideration to the complete accounts payable report and to the payment routines . .

Here is the system in its entirety, in sequence. Remember to remove the REMarks lines if memory is limited. And if you have only 4K, break it up as indicated.

```
10 CLS:RESTORE
20 PRINT "CLEARING THE ARRAY"
30 FOR N = 1 TO 99
40     READ B,B$
50     IF B = 9999 THEN 70
60 NEXT N
70 Z = N
80 FOR N = 1 TO Z * 20
90     A(N) = 0
100 NEXT N
110 CLS:RESTORE:Z = 0
120 B = 0:A = 0
```

```
130 INPUT "DO YOU WISH TO DO A QUICK CALCULATION (Y/N)";A$
140 IF A$ < > "Y" THEN CLS:GOTO 210
150 INPUT "ENTER AMOUNT OF BILL";A
160 B = B + A
170 INPUT "IS THAT THE LAST NUMBER TO BE ENTERED (Y/N)";A$
180 IF A$ = "N" THEN CLS:GOTO 150
190 PRINT "TOTAL OF ALL BILLS IS: $";B
200 GOSUB 1390:GOSUB 1390:CLS
210 PRINT TAB(15);"SAM'S BILL PAYING RITUAL":PRINT
220 PRINT "ENTER ALL DOLLAR AMOUNTS IN DECIMAL FORMAT ONLY"
230 PRINT "DO NOT ENTER DOLLAR SIGNS OR COMMAS TO DOLLAR
    AMOUNTS":PRINT
240 PRINT "ENTER DATES IN MONTH, DAY, AND YEAR FORMAT"
250 PRINT "DO NOT ENTER WITH SLASHES"
260 PRINT "ENTER EACH SEPARATELY, HITTING THE ENTER KEY WITH
    EACH";PRINT
270 INPUT "PRESS ENTER KEY TO PROCEED";A
280 CLS
290 INPUT "ENTER MONTH OF CURRENT DATE";J
300 IF (J < 1) + (J > 12) THEN GOSUB 1400:GOTO 290
310 INPUT "ENTER DAY OF CURRENT DATE";K
320 IF (K < 1) + (K > 31)THEN GOSUB 1400:GOTO 310
330 INPUT "ENTER YEAR OF CURRENT DATE";L
340 IF (L < 79) + (L > 81) THEN GOSUB 1400:GOTO 330
350 M = L * 10000:M = M + (J * 100):M = M + K
360 CLS
370 T = 1
380 GOSUB 540
390 RESTORE
400 INPUT "ENTER PAYEE NUMBER";A
410 FOR N = 1 TO A
420     READ B,B$
430     IF (B = 9999) * (B$ = "9999") THEN 510
440 NEXT N
450 PRINT "PAYEE #";B,B$
460 INPUT "CORRECT PAYEE (Y/N)";A$
```

```
470 IF A$ = "Y" THEN 650
480 CLS
490 GOSUB 540
500 GOTO 390
510 CLS:PRINT "PAYEE NOT IN DATA LINES"
520 GOSUB 540:GOTO 390
530 REM ******************************************************
540 RESTORE
550 PRINT "THESE ARE THE PAYEES WHOM YOU CUSTOMARILY PAY:":PRINT
560 PRINT, "PAYEE NUMBER","PAYEE NAME":PRINT
570 FOR N = 1 TO 99
580     READ B,B$
590     IF (B = 9999) + (B$ = "9999") THEN 620
600     PRINT ,B,B$
610 NEXT N
620 PRINT
630 RETURN
640 REM ******************************************************
650 A(T) = A
660 T = T + 1
670 CLS
680 INPUT "ENTER INVOICE DATE - MONTH";A
690 IF (A < 1) + (A > 12) THEN GOSUB 1400:GOTO 680
700 GOSUB 1370
710 INPUT "ENTER INVOICE DATE - DAY";A
720 IF (A < 1) + (A > 31) THEN GOSUB 1400:GOTO 710
730 GOSUB 1370
740 INPUT "ENTER INVOICE DATE - YEAR";A
750 IF (A < 79) + (A > 81) THEN GOSUB 1400:GOTO 740
760 GOSUB 1370
770 INPUT "ENTER INVOICE AMOUNT $";A:Z = Z + A:GOSUB 1370:CLS
780 INPUT "ENTER PAYMENT DATE - MONTH";A
790 IF (A < 1) + (A > 12) THEN GOSUB 1400:GOTO 780
800 GOSUB 1370
810 INPUT "ENTER PAYMENT DATE - DAY";A
820 IF (A < 1) + (A > 31) THEN GOSUB 1400:GOTO 810
```

```
830 GOSUB 1370
840 INPUT "ENTER PAYMENT DATE - YEAR";A
850 IF (A < 79) + (A > 81) THEN GOSUB 1400:GOTO 840
860 GOSUB 1370:CLS
870 INPUT "WILL THERE BE A DISCOUNT? (Y/N)";A$:PRINT
880 IF A$ = "N" THEN CLS:GOTO 1380
890 INPUT "ENTER DISCOUNT PERCENT (WITH DECIMAL)";A:GOSUB 1370
900 INPUT "ENTER DISCOUNT DATE - MONTH";A
910 IF (A < 1) + (A > 12) THEN GOSUB 1400:GOTO 900
920 GOSUB 1370
930 INPUT "ENTER DISCOUNT DATE - DAY";A
940 IF (A < 1) + (A > 31) THEN GOSUB 1400:GOTO 930
950 GOSUB 1370
960 INPUT "ENTER DISCOUNT DATE - YEAR";A
970 IF (A < 79) + (A > 81) THEN GOSUB 1400:GOTO 960
980 GOSUB 1370:CLS
990 PRINT "ENTER STATUS CODE":PRINT
1000 PRINT "A = CURRENT":PRINT
1010 PRINT "B = ONE MONTH IN ARREARS":PRINT
1020 PRINT "C = TWO MONTHS IN ARREARS":PRINT
1030 PRINT "N = NOT APPLICABLE":PRINT
1040 INPUT "WHICH";A$
1050 IF A$ = "A" THEN A(T) = 1:GOTO 1090
1060 IF A$ = "B" THEN A(T) = 2:GOTO 1090
1070 IF A$ = "C" THEN A(T) = 3:GOTO 1090
1080 A(T) = 0
1090 T = T + 1
1100 CLS
1110 INPUT "ENTER 'DROP DEAD' DATE - MONTH";A
1120 IF (A < 1) + (A > 12) THEN GOSUB 1400:GOTO 1110
1130 GOSUB 1370
1140 INPUT "ENTER 'DROP DEAD' DATE - DAY";A
1150 IF (A < 1) + (A > 31) THEN GOSUB 1400:GOTO 1140
1160 GOSUB 1370
1170 INPUT "ENTER 'DROP DEAD' DATE - YEAR";A
1180 IF (A < 79) + (A > 81) THEN GOSUB 1400:GOTO 1170
```

```
1190 GOSUB 1370
1200 FOR N = 1 TO 4:A(T) = 0:T = T + 1:NEXT N
1210 CLS:INPUT "LAST ENTRY TO BE MADE (Y/N)";A$
1220 IF A$ = "N" THEN GOSUB 540:GOTO 390
1230 CLS:PRINT "TRIAL BALANCE IS ";Z
1240 GOSUB 1390
1250 FOR N = 1 TO 20:A(T) = 9999:T = T + 1:NEXT N
1260 V = 1
1270 FOR N = 1 TO 99
1280    IF A(V) = 9999 THEN 1350
1290    FOR H = V TO V + 19
1300        PRINT A(H);
1310    NEXT H
1320    V = V + 20
1330    PRINT
1340 NEXT N
1350 GOSUB 1390:GOSUB 1390
1360 GOTO 1500
1370 A(T) = A:T = T + 1:RETURN
1380 FOR N = 1 TO 4:A(T) = 0:T = T + 1:NEXT N:GOTO 990
1390 FOR N = 1 TO 500:NEXT N:RETURN
1400 PRINT "OUT OF RANGE":RETURN
1410 DATA 1, "RENT"
1420 DATA 2, "DENTIST"
1430 DATA 3, "SEARS"
1440 DATA 4, "MASTER CHARGE"
1450 DATA 5, "GAS COMPANY"
1460 DATA 6, "POWER COMPANY"
1470 DATA 9999,"9999"
1480 REM ********************************************
1490 REM *
1500 GOTO 1940
1510 REM *
1520 REM ********************************************
1530 REM *                                         *
1540 REM * THIS IS THE INTERFACE POINT - IF YOU WISH TO *
```

```
1550 REM * CONSTRUCT THIS AS A SEPARATE PROGRAM, YOU    *
1560 REM * SHOULD AT THIS POINT WRITE BOTH THE CURRENT  *
1570 REM * DATE (VARIABLE M) AND THE ENTIRE DATA ARRAY  *
1580 REM * TO CASSETTE TAPE.  IT WILL BE NECESSARY TO   *
1590 REM * CONSTRUCT A FOR...NEXT LOOP WHICH WILL DO    *
1600 REM * THE WRITING (PRINT #).  IMBEDDED IN THE LOOP *
1610 REM * SHOULD BE THE TEST FOR THE SENTINELS (9999). *
1620 REM *                                              *
1630 REM ************************************************
1640 REM *
1650 REM ************************************************
1660 REM *                                              *
1670 REM * THIS IS THE BEGINNING OF PHASE II.  IF YOU   *
1680 REM * DESIRE TO HAVE THIS AS A SEPARATE PROGRAM,   *
1690 REM * YOU SHOULD HAVE INSERTED THE ROUTINES IN     *
1700 REM * PHASE I TO STORE THE CURRENT DATE (VARIABLE  *
1710 REM * M) AND THE TABLE THAT WAS BUILT ON THE       *
1720 REM * CASSETTE TAPE.  ALSO, IF YOU SEPARATE        *
1730 REM * THIS PHASE, IT WILL BE NECESSARY TO DUPLI-   *
1740 REM * CATE THE DATA LINES, AS THEY HAVE NOT BEEN   *
1750 REM * STORED ON THE TAPE.  ALTERNATIVELY, YOU      *
1760 REM * COULD HAVE STORED THEM IN PHASE I AND        *
1770 REM * RETRIEVED THEM HERE.  FOR OUR PURPOSES, WE   *
1780 REM * WILL CONTINUE WITH THE PROGRAM, EVEN THOUGH  *
1790 REM * WE KNOW WE WILL EXCEED THE LEVEL I 4K        *
1800 REM * MEMORY.  IN VIEW OF THIS, THIS PHASE WILL    *
1810 REM * OFFER SIX OPTIONS:                           *
1820 REM *    1.  THE ABILITY TO TAKE A CURRENCY        *
1830 REM *        STATUS CHECK.                         *
1840 REM *    2.  THE ABILITY TO TAKE AN AGING REPORT.  *
1850 REM *    3.  THE ABILITY TO TAKE A FORECAST.       *
1860 REM *    4.  THE ABILITY TO LIST THE ARRAY IN AN   *
1870 REM *        INTELLIGIBLE FORMAT.                  *
1880 REM *    5.  A UTILITY SUBROUTINE WHICH ALLOWS     *
1890 REM *        SELECTION OPTIONS ON THE ARRAY.       *
1900 REM *    6.  A BY-PASS OPTION TO PASS DIRECTLY     *
```

```
1910 REM *          TO PHASE III FOR CHECKWRITING          *
1920 REM *                                                 *
1930 REM ***************************************************
1940 CLS:RESTORE
1950 PRINT "THIS IS PHASE II.  SELECT THE OPTION YOU DESIRE"
1960 PRINT:PRINT TAB(5);"1.  STATUS CHECK (SUBROUTINE A)"
1970 PRINT:PRINT TAB(5);"2.  AGING REPORT (SUBROUTINE B)"
1980 PRINT:PRINT TAB(5);"3.  FORECAST REPORT (SUBROUTINE C)"
1990 PRINT:PRINT TAB(5);"4.  COMPLETE A/P LIST (SUBROUTINE D)"
2000 PRINT:PRINT TAB(5);"5.  UTILITY SUBROUTINE (SUBROUTINE E)"
2010 PRINT:PRINT TAB(5);"6.  PHASE III (CHECKWRITER)"
2020 A = 0:PRINT:INPUT "WHICH";A
2030 ON A GOTO 2090,2300,2620,2940,3200,4920:GOTO 1940
2040 REM ********************************************************
2050 REM * THIS ROUTINE IS NEARLY SELF-CONTAINED AND CAN BE  *
2060 REM * SEPARATED.  IT DOES REQUIRE ALL PRECONDITIONS FOR *
2070 REM * PHASE II PLUS ONE COPY OF SUBROUTINE AT 3020.     *
2080 REM ********************************************************
2090 CLS:PRINT "STATUS CHECK ROUTINE":PRINT
2100 PRINT "WHICH RECORDS DO YOU WISH TO EXAMINE:":PRINT
2110 PRINT TAB(5);"1.  STATUS A - CURRENT":PRINT
2120 PRINT TAB(5);"2.  STATUS B - ONE MONTH IN ARREARS":PRINT
2130 PRINT TAB(5);"3.  STATUS C - TWO MONTHS IN ARREARS":PRINT
2140 PRINT TAB(5);"4.  STATUS N - NOT APPLICABLE":PRINT
2150 INPUT "WHICH";A:CLS
2160 ON A GOTO 2180,2180,2180,2170:GOTO 2090
2170 A = 0
2180 V = 1
2190 FOR N = 1 TO 99
2200     IF A(V) = 9999 THEN 1940
2210     IF A(V + 12) = A THEN GOSUB 3020
2220     V = V + 20
2230 NEXT N
2240 GOTO 1940
2250 REM ********************************************************
2260 REM * THIS ROUTINE IS NEARLY SELF-CONTAINED AND CAN BE  *
```

```
2270 REM * SEPARATED.  IT DOES REQUIRE ALL PRECONDITIONS FOR *
2280 REM * PHASE II PLUS ONE COPY OF SUBROUTINE AT 3020.     *
2290 REM ********************************************************
2300 CLS:PRINT "ACCOUNTS RECEIVABLE AGING REPORT":PRINT
2310 PRINT "THE CURRENT DATE IS :":PRINT
2320 L = M
2330 J = L / 10000:J = INT(J):L = L - (J * 10000)
2340 K = L / 100:K = INT(K):L = L - (K * 100)
2350 PRINT "DAY","MONTH","YEAR"
2360 PRINT L,K,J
2370 PRINT:PRINT "THE REPORT IS STRUCTURED TO PROVIDE ALL DATA"
2380 PRINT "FROM THE DATE YOU WILL ENTER TO THE CURRENT DATE."
2390 PRINT:INPUT "ENTER YEAR OF INCLUSIVE DATE";J
2400 IF J < 77 PRINT "OUT OF RANGE - RE-ENTER":GOTO 2390
2410 IF J > INT(M / 10000) PRINT "INVALID ENTRY":GOTO 2390
2420 PRINT:INPUT "ENTER MONTH OF INCLUSIVE DATE";K
2430 IF (K < 1) + (K > 12) PRINT "OUT OF RANGE":GOTO 2420
2440 PRINT:INPUT "ENTER DAY OF INCLUSIVE DATE";L
2450 IF (L < 1) + (L > 31) PRINT "OUT OF RANGE":GOTO 2440
2460 V = 1:CLS
2470 P = (J * 10000) + (K * 100) + L
2480 Q = (A(V + 7) * 10000) + (A(V + 6) * 100) + A(V + 5)
2490 FOR N = 1 TO 99
2500     IF A(V) = 9999 THEN 1940
2510     IF (Q > = P) * (Q < = M) THEN 2530
2520     GOTO 2550
2530     GOSUB 3020
2540     V = V + 20
2550 NEXT N
2560 GOTO 1940
2570 REM ********************************************************
2580 REM * THIS ROUTINE IS NEARLY SELF-CONTAINED AND CAN BE  *
2590 REM * SEPARATED.  IT DOES REQUIRE ALL PRECONDITIONS FOR *
2600 REM * PHASE II PLUS ONE COPY OF SUBROUTINE AT 3020.     *
2610 REM ********************************************************
2620 CLS:PRINT "ACCOUNTS RECEIVABLE FORECAST REPORT"
```

```
2630 PRINT "THE CURRENT DATE IS: ":PRINT
2640 L = M
2650 J = L / 10000:J = INT(J):L = L - (J * 10000)
2660 K = L / 100:K = INT(K):L = L - (K * 100)
2670 PRINT "DAY","MONTH","YEAR"
2680 PRINT L,K,J
2690 PRINT:PRINT "THE REPORT IS STRUCTURED TO PROVIDE ALL DATA"
2700 PRINT "FROM THE CURRENT DATE TO THE DATE YOU WILL ENTER."
2710 PRINT:INPUT "ENTER YEAR OF INCLUSIVE DATE";J
2720 IF J > 82 PRINT "OUT OF RANGE - RE-ENTER":GOTO 2710
2730 IF J < INT(M / 10000) PRINT "INVALID ENTRY":GOTO 2710
2740 PRINT:INPUT "ENTER MONTH OF INCLUSIVE DATE";K
2750 IF (K < 1) + (K > 12) PRINT "OUT OF RANGE":GOTO 2740
2760 PRINT:INPUT "ENTER DAY OF INCLUSIVE DATE";L
2770 IF (L < 1) + (L > 31) PRINT "OUT OF RANGE":GOTO 2760
2780 V = 1:CLS
2790 P = (J * 10000) + (K * 100) + L
2800 Q = (A(V + 7) * 10000) + (A(V + 6) * 100) + A(V + 5)
2810 FOR N = 1 TO 99
2820     IF A(V) = 9999 THEN 1940
2830     IF (Q < = P) * (Q > = M) THEN 2850
2840     GOTO 2870
2850     GOSUB 3020
2860     V = V + 20
2870 NEXT N
2880 GOTO 1940
2890 REM ****************************************************
2900 REM * THIS ROUTINE IS NEARLY SELF-CONTAINED AND CAN BE  *
2910 REM * SEPARATED.  IT DOES REQUIRE ALL PRECONDITIONS FOR *
2920 REM * PHASE II PLUS ONE COPY OF SUBROUTINE AT 3020.     *
2930 REM ****************************************************
2940 CLS:PRINT "COMPLETE ACCOUNTS PAYABLE REPORT"
2950 V = 1
2960 FOR N = 1 TO 99
2970     IF A(V) = 9999 THEN 1940
2980     GOSUB 3020
```

```
2990    V = V + 20
3000 NEXT N
3010 GOTO 1940
3020 PRINT AT 128,"PAYEE","DATE OF INV","AMT OF INV","PMT DATE"
3030 FOR F = 1 TO A(V):READ B,B$:NEXT F:RESTORE
3040 PRINT B$,A(V+1);A(V+2);A(V+3),"$";A(V+4),A(V+5),A(V+6);A(V+7):
     PRINT
3050 PRINT "DISC PCT","DISC DATE","STATUS","DROP DEAD DATE"
3060 IF A(V+12) = 0 THEN A$ = "N":GOTO 3100
3070 IF A(V+12) = 1 THEN A$ = "A":GOTO 3100
3080 IF A(V+12) = 2 THEN A$ = "B":GOTO 3100
3090 IF A(V+12) = 3 THEN A$ = "C"
3100 PRINT (AV+8),A(V+9),A(V+10),A(V+11)," ";A$,A(V+13);
     A(V+14);A(V+15)
3110 PRINT:PRINT "TABLE FLAG","CHECK NR","AMT OF CK","DT OF CHECK"
3120 PRINT A(V+16),A(V+17),"$";A(V+18),A(V+19):PRINT
3130 INPUT "PRESS ENTER TO CONTINUE";A
3140 RETURN
3150 REM ****************************************************
3160 REM * THIS ROUTINE IS NEARLY SELF-CONTAINED AND CAN BE  *
3170 REM * SEPARATED.  IT DOES REQUIRE ALL PRECONDITIONS FOR *
3180 REM * PHASE II PLUS ONE COPY OF SUBROUTINE AT 3020.     *
3190 REM ****************************************************
3200 CLS:PRINT "THIS ROUTINE GIVES YOU THE ABILITY TO MODIFY"
3210 PRINT "ANY PORTION OF THE RECORD UNDER EXAMINATION."
3220 PRINT:PRINT "IT DOES SO WITHOUT REGARD TO EDIT RULES,"
3230 PRINT "SO IF YOU CHANGE IT, YOU DO SO AT YOUR OWN PERIL."
3240 PRINT:INPUT "PRESS ENTER TO BEGIN";A
3250 CLS:PRINT "THE RECORD WILL BE DISPLAYED FIRST AND YOU"
3260 PRINT "WILL BE GIVEN TIME TO EXAMINE IT.  YOU MUST THEN"
3270 PRINT "PRESS ENTER TO RECEIVE THE OPTIONS."
3280 PRINT:INPUT "PRESS ENTER TO CONTINUE";A
3290 V = 1:CLS
3300 FOR N = 1 TO 999
3310     IF A(V) = 9999 THEN 1940
3320     GOSUB 3020
```

```
3330    INPUT "PRESS ENTER TO RECEIVE OPTIONS";A
3340    CLS
3350    PRINT "MODIFICATION OF PAYEE NOT PERMITTED":PRINT
3360    PRINT TAB(5);"1.  MODIFY DATE OF INVOICE"
3370    PRINT TAB(5);"2.  MODIFY AMOUNT OF INVOICE"
3380    PRINT TAB(5);"3.  MODIFY PAYMENT DATE"
3390    PRINT TAB(5);"4.  MODIFY DISCOUNT PERCENT"
3400    PRINT TAB(5);"5.  MODIFY DISCOUNT DATE"
3410    PRINT TAB(5);"6.  MODIFY STATUS CODE"
3420    PRINT TAB(5);"7.  MODIFY DROP DEAD DATE"
3430    PRINT TAB(5);"8.  MODIFY TABLE FLAG"
3440    PRINT TAB(5);"9.  MODIFY CHECK NUMBER"
3450    PRINT:INPUT "SELECT";A
3460    ON A GOTO 3470,3580,3660,3770,3850,3960,4170,
        4280,4410:GOTO 1940
3470    CLS:PRINT "YOU HAVE CHOSEN TO CHANGE THE INVOICE
        DATE":PRINT
3480    GOSUB 4520
3490    PRINT A(V + 1),A(V + 2),A(V + 3):PRINT
3500    PRINT:INPUT "ENTER CORRECTED YEAR";A(V + 3)
3510    PRINT:INPUT "ENTER CORRECTED MONTH";A(V + 2)
3520    PRINT:INPUT "ENTER CORRECTED DAY";A(V + 1)
3530    GOSUB 4630
3540    GOSUB 3020
3550    GOSUB 4640
3560    IF A$ < > "Y" THEN 3470
3570    GOTO 4560
3580    CLS:PRINT "YOU HAVE CHOSEN TO CHANGE THE AMOUNT OF THE
        INVOICE"
3590    PRINT:PRINT "CURRENT INVOICE AMOUNT IS $";A(V + 4)
3600    PRINT:INPUT "ENTER THE CORRECTED AMOUNT $";A(V + 4)
3610    GOSUB 4630
3620    GOSUB 3020
3630    GOSUB 4640
3640    IF A$ < > "Y" THEN 3580
3650    GOTO 4560
```

```
3660    CLS:PRINT "YOU HAVE CHOSEN TO CHANGE THE PAYMENT
        DATE":PRINT
3670    GOSUB 4520
3680    PRINT A(V + 5),A(V + 6),A(V + 7):PRINT
3690    INPUT "ENTER CORRECTED YEAR";A(V + 7)
3700    INPUT "ENTER CORRECTED MONTH";A(V + 6)
3710    INPUT "ENTER CORRECTED DAY";A(V + 5)
3720    GOSUB 4630
3730    GOSUB 3020
3740    GOSUB 4640
3750    IF A$ < > "Y" THEN 3660
3760    GOTO 4550
3770    CLS:PRINT "YOU HAVE CHOSEN TO CHANGE THE DISCOUNT
        PERCENT":PRINT
3780    PRINT:PRINT "CURRENT DISCOUNT PERCENT IS ";A(V + 8):PRINT
3790    INPUT "WHAT WOULD YOU LIKE IT TO BE";A(V + 8):PRINT
3800    GOSUB 4630
3810    GOSUB 3020
3820    GOSUB 4540
3830    IF A$ < > "Y" THEN 3770
3840    GOTO 4560
3850    CLS:PRINT "YOU HAVE CHOSEN TO CHANGE THE DISCOUNT
        DATE":PRINT
3860    GOSUB 4520
3870    PRINT A(V + 9),A(V + 10),A(V + 11):PRINT
3880    PRINT:INPUT "ENTER CORRECTED YEAR";A(V + 11)
3890    PRINT:INPUT "ENTER CORRECTED MONTH";A(V + 10)
3900    PRINT:INPUT "ENTER CORRECTED DAY";A(V + 9)
3910    GOSUB 4630
3920    GOSUB 3020
3930    GOSUB 4640
3940    IF A$ < > "Y" THEN 3850
3950    GOTO 4560
3960    CLS:PRINT "YOU HAVE CHOSEN TO MODIFY THE STATUS CODE":PRINT
3970    IF A(V + 12) = 1 THEN B$ = "A":GOTO 4010
3980    IF A(V + 12) = 2 THEN B$ = "B":GOTO 4010
```

```
3990      IF A(V + 12) = 3 THEN B$ = "C":GOTO 4010
4000      B$ = "N"
4010      PRINT "CURRENT STATUS CODE IS ";B$:PRINT
4020      PRINT "AVAILABLE STATUS CODES ARE:":PRINT
4030      PRINT TAB(5);"A - CURRENT"
4040      PRINT TAB(5);"B - ONE MONTH IN ARREARS"
4050      PRINT TAB(5);"C - TWO MONTHS IN ARREARS"
4060      PRINT TAB(5);"N - NOT APPLICABLE":PRINT
4070      INPUT "SELECT WHICH CODE APPLIES";A$
4080      IF A$ = "A" THEN A(V + 12) = 1:GOTO 4120
4090      IF A$ = "B" THEN A(V + 12) = 2:GOTO 4120
4100      IF A$ = "C" THEN A(V + 12) = 3:GOTO 4120
4110      A(V + 12) = 0
4120      GOSUB 4630
4130      GOSUB 3020
4140      GOSUB 4640
4150      IF A$ <> "Y" THEN 3960
4160      GOTO 4560
4170      CLS:PRINT "YOU HAVE CHOSEN TO MODIFY THE
          DROP-DEAD-DATE":PRINT
4180      GOSUB 4520
4190      PRINT A(V + 13),A(V + 14),A(V + 15):PRINT
4200      INPUT "ENTER CORRECTED YEAR";A(V + 15):PRINT
4210      INPUT "ENTER CORRECTED MONTH";A(V + 14):PRINT
4220      INPUT "ENTER CORRECTED DAY";A(V + 13):PRINT
4230      GOSUB 4630
4240      GOSUB 3020
4250      GOSUB 4640
4260      IF A$ <> "Y" THEN 4170
4270      GOTO 4560
4280      CLS:PRINT "YOU HAVE CHOSEN TO MODIFY THE TABLE FLAG":PRIN
4290      PRINT "ACCEPTABLE CODES ARE:":PRINT
4300      PRINT TAB(5);"1.  CHECK VOIDED":PRINT
4310      PRINT TAB(5);"2.  PARTIAL PAYMENT":PRINT
4320      PRINT TAB(5);"3.  NON-TAX ITEM":PRINT
4330      INPUT "WHICH";A
```

```
4340    IF (A < 1) + (A  >3) THEN 4280
4350    A(V + 16) = A
4360    GOSUB 4630
4370    GOSUB 3020
4380    GOSUB 4640
4390    IF A$  <> "Y" THEN 4280
4400    GOTO 4560
4410    CLS:PRINT "YOU HAVE CHOSEN TO CHANGE THE CHECK
        NUMBER":PRINT
4420    PRINT "CURRENT CHECK NUMBER IS ";A(V + 17):PRINT
4430    INPUT "ENTER THE CORRECTED NUMBER";A(V + 17):PRINT
4440    GOSUB 4630
4450    GOSUB 3020
4460    GOSUB 4640
4470    IF A$ <> "Y" THEN 4410
4480    GOTO 4560
4490    V = V + 20
4500 NEXT N
4510 GOTO 1940
4520 PRINT:PRINT "MANDATORY TO COMPLETE ALL ENTRIES"
4530 PRINT:PRINT "DATE ON RECORD IS:"
4540 PRINT "DAY","MONTH","YEAR":PRINT
4550 RETURN
4560 CLS:PRINT "ENDING OPTIONS:":PRINT
4570 PRINT "1.  MAKE MORE CHANGES TO THE RECORD":PRINT
4580 PRINT "2.  OBTAIN THE NEXT RECORD":PRINT
4590 PRINT "3.  RETURN TO THE MAINTENANCE MENU":PRINT
4600 PRINT "4.  RETURN TO THE PHASE II MENU":PRINT
4610 INPUT "WHICH";A:CLS
4620 ON A GOTO 4500,4490,3200,1940:GOTO 4560
4650 REM ************************************************
4660 REM * THIS IS THE INTERFACE POINT BETWEEN PHASE II  *
4670 REM * PHASE III.  IN ORDER TO SUCCESSFULLY USE PHASE *
4680 REM * III AT THIS POINT, IT IS AGAIN NECESSARY TO    *
4690 REM * EITHER CONTINUE FROM THE POINT OR TO STORE THE *
4700 REM * ARRAY ONTO A TAPE FOR SUBSEQUENT ENTRY TO THE  *
```

```
4710 REM * PHASE.  IT WILL NOT BE NECESSARY TO STORE THE   *
4720 REM * CURRENT DATE (VARIABLE M), BUT THERE WOULD BE   *
4730 REM * NO REASON TO CHANGE THE ROUTINE YOU DEVELOP     *
4740 REM * FOR USE BETWEEN PHASE I AND II.  JUST BE SURE   *
4750 REM * TO RECOGNIZE THAT YOU HAVE IT ON TAPE.  SINCE   *
4760 REM * PHASE II IS THE EDIT PHASE, IT SHOULD BE VERY   *
4770 REM * OBVIOUS THAT YOU CAN PROGRESS FROM PHASE I TO   *
4780 REM * PHASE III DIRECTLY, BUT TO DO SO NEGATES THE    *
4790 REM * VALUE OF THE EDITS PERFORMED.                   *
4800 REM ************************************************
4810 REM *                                                 *
4820 REM * THIS IS PHASE III.  YOU GET HERE EITHER BY      *
4830 REM * TAKING OPTION 6 FROM THE PHASE II MENU OR BY    *
4840 REM * ENTRY TO THIS PROGRAM DIRECT.                   *
4850 REM *                                                 *
4860 REM * LIKE THE OTHER ROUTINES, PHASE III ALSO MAKES   *
4870 REM * USE OF THE SUBROUTINE AT 3020, SO IF YOU ARE    *
4880 REM * TO MAKE THIS A STAND-ALONE ROUTINE, IT WILL     *
4890 REM * ALSO BE NECESSARY TO DUPLICATE THAT ROUTINE     *
4900 REM * HERE.  THE SAME IS TRUE FOR THE DATE LINES.     *
4910 REM ************************************************
4920 CLS:PRINT "THIS IS THE CHECK-WRITING PHASE OF THE ACCOUNTS"
4930 PRINT "PAYABLE SYSTEM.  IT DOES NOT WRITE CHECKS, PER SE,"
4940 PRINT "BUT IT DOES PERMIT YOU TO VIEW EACH RECORD, MAKE A
4950 PRINT "DETERMINATION AS TO WHAT YOU WISH TO PAY, WHETHER"
4960 PRINT "YOU WISH TO MAKE FULL OR PARTIAL PAYMENTS, ASSIGNS"
4970 PRINT "CHECK NUMBERS, KEEPS YOUR CHECKBOOK BALANCE, AND"
4980 PRINT "PREPARES A LEDGER ENTRY.":PRINT
4990 INPUT "PRESS ENTER TO CONTINUE";A
5000 CLS:PRINT "ENTER THE BALANCE IN YOUR CHECKBOOK AFTER ALL"
5010 INPUT "DEPOSITS HAVE BEEN CREDITED AND ALL CHARGES DEBITED.";
5020 PRINT:PRINT "YOUR CHECKBOOK BALANCE IS $";H
5030 INPUT "IS THAT CORRECT (Y/N)";A$
5040 IF A$ < > "Y" THEN 5000
5050 CLS:INPUT "ENTER THE NEXT CHECK NUMBER";C
5060 PRINT:PRINT "YOU SAID THE NEXT CHECK NUMBER IS #";C
```

```
5070 INPUT "IS THAT CORRECT (Y/N)";A$
5080 IF A$ < > "Y" THEN 5050
5090 K = C
5100 CLS:PRINT "ONCE YOU HAVE MADE THE ENTRY, YOU WILL HAVE"
5110 PRINT "TO ENTER PHASE II MAINTENANCE TO REVERSE AN ENTRY."
5120 PRINT:INPUT "PRESS ENTER TO BEGIN";A
5130 V = 1:CLS
5140 FOR N = 1 TO 999
5150     IF A(V) = 9999 THEN 5720
5160     GOSUB 3020
5170     INPUT "PRESS ENTER TO REVIEW OPTIONS";A
5180     CLS:PRINT "THE OPTIONS ARE:":PRINT
5190     PRINT "1.  WRITE THE CHECK FOR THE FULL AMOUNT":PRINT
5200     PRINT "2.  WRITE THE CHECK FOR A PARTIAL AMOUNT":PRINT
5210     PRINT "3.  BYPASS THE INVOICE":PRINT
5220     PRINT "4.  VIEW THE INVOICE AGAIN":PRINT
5230     PRINT "5.  TERMINATE THE CHECKWRITING PROCESS":PRINT
5240     PRINT:INPUT "SELECT";A
5250     ON A GOTO 5290,5520,5700,5160,5720:GOTO 5180
5260 REM ****************************************************
5270 REM *              PAYMENT IN FULL ROUTINE            *
5280 REM ****************************************************
5290     CLS:PRINT "YOU HAVE CHOSEN TO PAY THE INVOICE IN FULL"
5300 PRINT
5310     IF H > = A(V + 4) THEN 5370
5320     PRINT "THERE ARE INSUFFICIENT FUNDS TO COVER THIS INVOICE"
5330     PRINT "THE BILL IS FOR $";A(V + 4)
5340     PRINT:PRINT "YOUR BALANCE IS $";H
5350     PRINT:INPUT "PRESS ENTER TO RETURN TO MENU";A:CLS
5360     GOTO 5180
5370     CLS:PRINT "PAYMENT MADE":PRINT
5380     H = H = A(V + 4)
5390     PRINT "CHECKBOOK BALANCE NOW $";H:PRINT
5400     A(V + 17) = C:C = C + 1
5410     A(V + 18) = A(V + 4)
5420     A(V + 4) = 0
```

```
5430      A(V + 19) = M
5440      INPUT "IS THIS A TAX-EXEMPT PURCHASE (Y/N)";A$
5450      IF A$ = "Y" THEN A(V + 16) = 3
5460      PRINT:INPUT "PRESS ENTER TO VIEW RECORD";A:CLS
5470      GOSUB 3020
5480      GOTO 5700
5490 REM ****************************************************
5500 REM *          PARTIAL PAYMENT ROUTINE             *
5510 REM ****************************************************
5520      CLS:PRINT "YOU HAVE CHOSEN TO PARTIALLY PAY THE INVOICE"
5530      PRINT:PRINT "THE AMOUNT OF THE INVOICE IS $";A(V + 4)
5540      PRINT:INPUT "HOW MUCH DO YOU WISH TO PAY - $";A
5550      IF A < = H THEN 5600
5560      PRINT "INSUFFICIENT FUNDS"
5570      PRINT "THE INVOICE IS FOR $";A(V + 4)
5580      PRINT "YOUR BALANCE IS $";H
5590      GOTO 5540
5600      CLS:PRINT "PARTIAL PAYMENT ACCEPTED":PRINT
5610      H = H - A:A(V + 4) = A(V + 4) - A
5620      PRINT:PRINT "CHECKBOOK BALANCE NOW $";H
5630      PRINT:PRINT "BALANCE OF ACCOUNT NOW $";A(V + 4)
5640      A(V + 17) = C:C = C + 1
5650      A(V + 18) = A
5660      A(V + 19) = M
5670      A(V + 15) = 2
5680      PRINT:INPUT "PRESS ENTER TO VIEW RECORD";A:CLS
5690      GOSUB 3020
5700      V = V + 20
5710 NEXT N
5720 CLS:PRINT "CHECKWRITING PROCESS TERMINATED":PRINT
5730 PRINT:PRINT "THE INVOICES UPON WHICH PAYMENT HAS BEEN MADE"
5740 PRINT "WILL NOW BE PRESENTED, ONE AT A TIME.  YOU WILL HAVE"
5750 PRINT "TIME TO RECORD THEM IN YOUR CHECKBOOK LEDGER."
5760 PRINT:INPUT "PRESS ENTER WHEN YOU ARE READY.";A
5770 REM ******************************************************
5780 REM * AT THIS POINT YOU SHOULD INSTALL THE ROUTINE TO    *
5790 REM * COPY THE SCREEN ENTRIES ONTO A TAPE.  THIS TAPE    *
5800 REM * WILL BE YOUR AUTOMATED LEDGER, WHICH WILL PERMIT   *
```

```
5810 REM * YOU TO RECONCILE YOUR CHECKS WHEN THEY ARE          *
5820 REM * RETURNED.  ALSO, YOU SHOULD DEVELOP A UTILITY TO     *
5830 REM * COMBINE ALL SUCH TAPES BEFORE BUILDING THE CHECK     *
5840 REM * RECONCILIATION ROUTINE.                              *
5850 REM *                                                      *
5860 REM * AT THE COMPLETION OF THIS TAPE YOU SHOULD ALSO       *
5870 REM * DRAW A TAPE OF ALL REMAINING INVOICE BALANCES.       *
5880 REM * THE ROUTINE TO READ THIS TAPE SHOULD BE ADDED TO     *
5890 REM * PHASE II TO BE COMBINED WITH INVOICES WHICH ARE      *
5900 REM * DERIVED FROM PHASE I.                                *
5910 REM ***********************************************************
5920 V = 1 CLS
5930 FOR N = 1 TO 99
5940     IF A(V) = 9999 THEN 6030
5950     IF A(V + 17) = K THEN 6000
5960     IF A(V + 17) = C - 1 THEN 6040
5970     V = V + 20
5980 NEXT N
5990 GOTO 6040
6000 GOSUB 3020
6010 K = K + 1
6020 GOTO 5920
6030 IF K < > C - 1 PRINT "NO MATCH FOR CHECK #b";K:GOTO 6010
6040 CLS
6050 FOR N = 1 TO 7:PRINT:NEXT N
6060 PRINT TAB(15);"E N D   O F   A C C O U N T S"
6070 PRINT TAB(15); "P A Y A B L E   S Y S T E M"
6080 GOTO 6080
```

EPILOG

I've written longer books and shorter books, but writing this book has to rank as the most exhausting writing I've ever undertaken. It has been a demanding mistress.

Part of the reason for the amount of time spent was strictly my insistance that those programs which were presented were useful, educational, and most importantly that they worked. And the worst part of it, in retrospect, is that throughout the revisions (and there have been several), reproductions, multiple proofreadings, and typesetting, a single missing comma or omitted semi-colon could negate much of the effort.

Like you, I started with the TRS-80 and an instruction manual. I had written BASIC for several computers before, so that was not strange. Microcomputers, on the other hand were both new and strange; and even today, I still have much to learn. The microcomputer—the home computer—is a new device which in time will change the way we think and live. In this book I have dealt with applications, more than with the computer itself.

I'm not the world's best programmer. There are programmers who will take issue with how I have programmed these applications. I will be faulted for form and substance, but not for one simple fact—the programs work. Writing a program is only half of the battle. It is also important to be able to explain what the program does in sufficient detail to impart the kind of knowledge needed to apply solutions to similar problems. Our only limitation is our collective lack of imagination.

When Robb Ware first advanced the idea, it seemed like the thing to do. My own microcomputer! But then the bug hit, and in short order, Level II was installed, followed, in succession, by 16K, 32K, and then the business system, illustrated by this picture courtesy of Radio Shack:

With each augmentation there was, and is, much to learn. I couldn't justify it as a toy, but as a cost-saver or revenue producer, it was a different matter.

You, too, may be bitten by the bug. The move to 16K, Level II is a wise move, and the costs of the system are coming down. The increased capabilities will permit much more flexibility and the types of applications which can be constructed will permit the investment to be paid back many times over. It's the only way to escape some of the Level I limitations.

The Radio Shack people are, and have been, very important to this ef-

Figure 53.   32k Business System

fort, and they will be for you, as well. In addition to the help you can get at more than 5000 company stores, computer centers, and franchises, they also maintain a help hotline:

1-800-433-1679 (1-800-772-5914 in Texas)

Or you can write to them at 900 Two Tandy Center, Fort Worth, TX 76102.

Once you obtain the TRS-80, you'll be besieged with literature describing software, hardware, and publications. You should be selective about those publications to which you subscribe and the hardware and software you buy. Even now, after the device has been out a number of years, there are still charlatans trying to make a fast buck, so be selective.

Find other TRS-80 owners in your area. There are many good ideas floating around. Try new languages, new techniques, and if you have a good idea for a program, do it and then try to sell it—we've only begun to scratch the surface.

In the three years since this book was begun, Radio Shack has brought to the marketplace additional TRS-80 models—in color, in size, in capability. No doubt by the time this book finally "hits the streets," the early TRS-80's will no longer be available as new products. Nearly a quarter million of them were produced, however, and will always be available. The applications and concepts presented in this book will apply to any TRS-80 computer.

As for me, I have only one more thing to say and then I'm done:

```
10 CLS:RESTORE
20 FOR N = 1 TO 16
30 PRINT TAB(5);"A  M E S S A G E   F R O M   T H E   A U T H O R"
40 NEXT N
50 FOR Y = 0 TO 47
60      FOR X = 0 TO 127
70           SET(X,Y)
80      NEXT X
90 NEXT Y
100 FOR N = 1 TO 299
110      READ X,Y
120      RESET (X,Y)
130 NEXT N
140 GOTO 140
150 DATA 26,6,27,6,28,6,29,6,30,6,31,6,32,6,33,6,40,6,41,6,46,6
160 DATA 47,6,55,6,56,6,57,6,58,6,60,6,59,6,68,6,69,6,70,6,71,6,72,6
```

```
170 DATA 73,6,74,6,75,6,84,6,85,6,95,6,96,6,97,6,98,6,99,6,100,6
180 DATA 32,41,33,41,34,41,35,41,46,41,47,41,52,41,53,41,60,41
190 DATA 61,41,74,41,75,41,76,41,77,41,78,41,91,41,90,41
200 DATA 46,25,47,25,48,25,49,25,50,25,51,25
210 DATA 52,25,53,25,60,25,61,25,74,25,75,25
220 DATA 29,10,30,10,40,10,41,10,46,10,47,10,54,10,55,10,56,10
230 DATA 57,10,58,10,59,10,60,10,61,10,71,10,72,10,94,10,101,10,
           100,10
240 DATA 47,21,48,21,49,21,50,21,51,21,52,21,60,21,61,21,74,21,75,21
250 DATA 32,44,33,44,47,44,48,44,49,44,50,44,51,44,52,44,60,44
260 DATA 61,44,62,44,63,44,64,44,65,44,66,44,67,44,74,44,75,44
270 DATA 79,44,80,44,89,44,90,44,91,44,92,44,93,44,94,44,95,44
280 DATA 29,8,30,8,40,8,41,8,42,8,43,8,44,8,45,8
290 DATA 46,8,47,8,54,8,55,8,60,8,61,8,71,8,72,8,97,8,96,8
300 DATA 32,39,33,39,34,39,35,39,36,39,37,39,38,39,39,39
310 DATA 47,39,48,39,49,39,50,39,51,39,52,39,60,39,61,39
320 DATA 74,39,75,39,79,39,80,39,89,39,90,39,91,39,93,39,94,39
330 DATA 46,23,47,23,52,23,53,23,60,23,61,23,74,23,75,23
340 DATA 29,9,30,9,40,9,41,9,46,9,47,9,54,9,55,9
350 DATA 60,9,61,9,71,9,72,9,99,9,98,9
360 DATA 32,42,33,42,46,42,47,42,52,42,53,42
370 DATA 60,42,61,42,74,42,75,42,78,42,79,42,93,42,94,42
380 DATA 46,22,47,22,52,22,53,22,60,22,61,22,74,22,75,22
390 DATA 29,11,30,11,40,11,41,11,46,11,47,11,54,11
400 DATA 55,11,60,11,61,11,71,11,72,11,95,11,96,11,97,11,98,11
410 DATA 99,11,100,11,101,11
420 DATA 32,40,33,40,46,40,47,40,52,40,53,40
430 DATA 60,40,61,40,74,40,44,75,40,78,40,79,40,88,40,89,40,95,40
440 DATA 46,26,47,26,52,26,53,26,60,26,61,26,62,26,63,26,64,26
450 DATA 65,26,66,26,67,26,74,26,75,26,76,26,77,26,78,26,79,26
460 DATA 88,26,81,26
470 DATA 32,43,33,43,46,43,47,43,52,43,53,43,60,43
480 DATA 61,43,74,43,75,43,78,43,79,43,88,43,94,43,95,43
490 DATA 29,7,30,7,40,7,41,7,46,7,47,7,54,7,55,7
500 DATA 60,7,61,7,71,7,72,7,85,7,94,7,95,7,101,7
510 DATA 46,24,47,24,52,24,53,24,60,24,61,24,74,24,75,24,75,24
```

And an afterthought—here are two displays which were not shown in the text:

Figure 54

Figure 55

Index